THE BIBLE TELLS ME SO

READING THE BIBLE AS SCRIPTURE

Richard P. Thompson and Thomas Jay Oord, Editors

SacraSage

The Bible Tells Me So
Reading the Bible as Scripture

Cover Design: Jay Akkerman
Cover Photograph: Thomas Jay Oord

SacraSage Press
Nampa, Idaho

ISBN: 978-0-578-09363-5

PRINTED IN THE UNITED STATES OF AMERICA

Table of Contents

New Testament Chapters

Introduction

For millennia, the Bible has played a key role for helping Christians understand something about God and the world in which they live. The writing of the original manuscripts, their collection into what we call the "Bible," diverse translations and publications, and the various ways in which Scripture has been interpreted all solidify the Bible as central to Christian faith.

Christians believe God inspires this process—from authorship to canonization to translating and printing to interpretation. But Christians do not always agree about how best to understand this inspiration and various parts of this process. Diversity reigns within the Christian tradition.

The Bible plays an especially important role in the Wesleyan tradition of Christianity. John Wesley believed "the Scriptures are a complete rule of faith and practice," and "they are clear in all necessary points." To this affirmation, Wesley immediately adds, "and yet their clearness does not prove that they need not be explained."[1]

Christians in the Wesleyan tradition affirm the high place of Scripture, while stressing its importance for revealing what is necessary to salvation. These Christians also believe understanding the Bible well is an ongoing task.

The book you are holding emerged as a companion to a conference at Northwest Nazarene University held in February, 2011. The conference shares the title with this book, "The Bible Tells Me So." More than 40 scholars, more than 100 pastors, and hundreds of students and laity met to explore Wesleyan approaches to Scripture. Topics of exploration included themes in various books of the Bible, biblical inspiration, the trustworthiness of Scripture, inerrancy, interpretation, the influence of postmodernism, and a host of other topics.

Many of the scholars present at "The Bible Tells Me So" conference contributed the essays of this book. As editors, we have divided the material they produced in two halves in this book. The first half contains essays addressing general concerns and issues pertaining to the Bible. This collection should help readers reflect on a variety of issues important for reading and understanding the Bible. They serve as introductions for how Wesleyans understand Scripture.

The second half of this book offers essays on themes found in various books of the Bible. We asked biblical scholars to offer advice to preachers about the books these scholars know well. In many cases, scholars list topics or ideas they think helpful for preaching or should be avoided when preaching. Many of these essayists have published full-scale Beacon Hill commentaries on the books they address. These essays highlight some of the best in their commentary work.

In his letter to Christians living in ancient Rome, the Apostle Paul wrote the following: "Whatever was written in former days was written for our instruction, so that by steadfastness and by the encouragement of the scriptures we might have hope" (Rom 15:4). Although Paul had in mind books that now comprise what Christians call the Old Testament, the principle of his statement applies to the New Testament as well. What was written in the past instructs us today.

We hope this book will help you, the reader, find instruction, encouragement, and hope as you read the Bible. We offer this collection of essays as a gift. We invite you to explore, ponder, and develop the ideas you discover here. We believe God can use the material in this book, *The Bible Tells Me So*, in the work of salvation God has already begun.

Thomas Jay Oord and Richard P. Thompson

---

1. John Wesley, "Letter to Conyers Middleton," §5 *Works* (Jackson) 10:14.

Topic Chapters

I

Archaeological Contributions to the Study of the Bible

A. Wendell Bowes

I have noticed that whenever I am asked to speak about archaeology and the Bible, people are fascinated by this topic. Why is this so? Part of it is probably due to modern books and movies that portray the life of an archaeologist as one of adventure and mystery. Some of it may be related to a few spectacular finds that occurred in the twentieth century, such as King Tut's tomb in Egypt, the Dead Sea Scrolls in Israel, and the Bronze Age man in the Alps of Europe.

Most of this fascination, however, is probably connected to the curiosity we all have about the past and the people who lived before us. Just the thought of finding an arrowhead, a piece of pottery, or an item of jewelry someone used 3000 years ago is exciting. It makes a connection between an ancient culture and us. Sometimes there is even a fingerprint on the pottery. We find ourselves asking, Who made this piece of pottery? What language did they speak? What did they look like? What kind of clothes did they wear? What did they eat? What did they think about? We are all curious about the past, are we not? We want to know from where we have come.

When archaeology is applied to the countries of the Near East, it is even more exciting. We can actually dig up cities and artifacts that existed in Jesus' day, in Moses' day, and in Abraham's day.

Using these artifacts, we can attempt to understand what it was like to live when these biblical characters lived.

One hundred years ago, most of the information we had about ancient cultures such as the Israelites, Moabites, and Philistines was found in the Bible. *Today* we have a wealth of additional information about these ancient civilizations *because of archaeology*. And we will continue to gain more information each year as archaeology continues to uncover the past. Archaeology will never answer all of our questions about biblical events and people, but it is one of the few means available to discover more about the past. Today, it is impossible to have a good understanding of the Bible without some knowledge of archaeology and the archaeological discoveries of the past one hundred years.

Let's start with a definition. Archaeology may be described as the study of ancient cultures using the artifactual evidence they left behind. By artifactual evidence, we mean objects such as tools, bones, pottery, jewelry, buildings, and writings. In short, archaeology looks for anything indicating that human beings once lived there. Using these artifacts, archaeology attempts to understand an ancient culture.

Archaeologists primarily dig up the ruins of ancient cities, which are called "tells." In ancient times when people built a new city, they typically looked for four things: (1) water, (2) good farmland, (3) transportation routes nearby so they could trade with neighboring cities, and (4) a low hill so they could defend themselves if attacked. If their city was destroyed, the most logical place to rebuild was in the same place. The location typically still had water, farmland, transportation routes, and a low hill. People would simply level off the old site and build another city on top.

Over centuries and through many destructions and rebuildings, these city building sites or tells grew higher and higher. Some are nearly a hundred feet high today and have remains of more than twenty different cities in them stretching all the way from the

Neolithic period (8500–4300 BC) up to the Roman period (63 BC – AD 324). The average tell is relatively small, about 7–20 acres in size. The largest are over 200 acres, and the smallest are less than an acre. Regardless of their size, a vertical slice out of one of these tells would look much like a layer cake; each layer can be dated using the pottery and other artifacts within it. There are thousands of these tells all over the Near East: in Israel, Jordan, Lebanon, Egypt, Syria, Turkey, Iraq, and Iran. However, archaeologists have excavated only a small fraction. This is why there is such promise for future discovery by archaeological research.

When archaeologists first started digging in the Near East, they were primarily interested in artifacts to display in museums. But some people also wanted to "prove" the events in the Bible. It was easy to raise funds for a project claiming it would prove the walls of Jericho really did fall down, or Abraham really did come from the city of Ur, or King Herod really did build a beautiful temple in Jerusalem.

We now know, however, that archaeology is not very good at "proving" events in the Bible. It is much better at providing the cultural background for a story and supporting the possibility of an event's occurrence. Archaeology can prove that a city existed in a certain century or that it was destroyed in a certain century. But it usually cannot tell us who was responsible for that destruction. For that, we need written records from the site.

Consider the story of the conquest in the book of Joshua. Archaeologists have shown that a handful, but not all, of the Canaanite cities mentioned in the book of Joshua were actually destroyed in the 13th century BC. They have also shown that hundreds of small villages began appearing in the hill country of Palestine around 1200–1000 BC. In other words, archaeology provides some evidence for the destruction of a few key cities and the infiltration of a new ethnic group into Canaan in the time period between 1300–1000 BC. However, archaeology has been unable to "prove" that a man named Joshua was responsible for all of this. Unfortunately, Joshua never left any calling cards or inscriptions at the places he attacked. We know that a city in Palestine could have been destroyed for any number of reasons: an earthquake, an attack by Egypt, an attack by another Palestinian city, an attack by Bedouin tribes, a revolt within the city, or maybe a fire that started when some cow kicked over a lamp and ended up burning down the city. Without some kind of written record, we are usually at a loss to explain the cause of a city's destruction, or sometimes even its name. Therefore, archaeologists always work with incomplete evidence. Some of this evidence may be connected with a biblical story, but most of it would not be considered "proof."

On the other hand, archaeology is very good at painting a broad picture of ancient cultures that enables us to understand the biblical stories much better. This is like an artist who paints a broad background on the canvas first and finishes the painting by adding people in the foreground. The Bible gives us many people and events in the foreground. Archaeology makes the painting more enjoyable and understandable by filling in the background. Archaeology usually cannot name the people, but it can describe for us their food and water systems, defensive projects and weapons of war, religious buildings and objects, pottery and utensils, crafts and industries, houses and streets, clothing and jewelry, and even their games and entertainment. Thus, archaeology opens a window into the past and provides us with a wealth of new knowledge that we cannot gain from any other source.

There are at least five main areas where archaeology has contributed to our understanding of the Bible. The Bible is silent in some of these areas, and archaeology helps to fill in the blanks. Others are areas where archaeology confirms the name of an individual or the possibility of events taking place like the Bible describes.

I. Archaeology has provided an accurate chronology of ancient times.

Prior to the 1900's, our main sources for ancient chronology were the Bible and a few classical writings from the Hellenistic and Roman cultures. It was impossible to determine when most Old Testament stories occurred, because the Bible does not connect them with our calendar and only rarely with known events in other ancient countries. Today we know a great deal more about the progression of ancient history. Archaeologists have put together a timeline for the Near East that looks something like this:

Neolithic period	8500–4300 BC
Chalcolithic period	4300–3300 BC
Early Bronze period	3300–2000 BC
Middle Bronze period	2000–1550 BC
Late Bronze period	1550–1200 BC
Iron period	1200–587 BC
Persian period	587–332 BC
Hellenistic period	332–63 BC
Roman period	63 BC – AD 324

This chronological chart did not exist 120 years ago when archaeology first became a science. Then, people simply added up the life spans of names mentioned in the Bible and came up with a chronology beginning in 4004 BC. Today, scholars may still argue over exactly when one age ended and another began, but the overall picture of the division of ancient times into the Neolithic, Chalcolithic, Bronze, and Iron periods is universally accepted. We can place most biblical characters beginning with Abraham into these periods. Can you identify in which period these people lived: Abraham, Moses, David, Hezekiah, Nehemiah, and Paul?

Archaeologists determine these dates in a number of ways. One is by analyzing pottery. Pottery is an excellent dating tool, because it will last for thousands of years in the ground with no observable changes. In ancient times, potters changed their styles from time to time, like we change our styles of automobiles, clothing, music, etc. They varied such things as thickness, color, decoration, and shape. If a person knows what changes happened when, he or she can easily date each layer of a tell using the pottery fragments found within it. That is pretty amazing! The only difference between ancient and modern times is that our styles change much more frequently. Ancient people might have kept a certain style of pottery for 100–200 years. Pottery was invented in the Near East about 6000 BC, so most archaeological sites can be easily dated after that time.

Because the Bible gives us few specific dates, we have to estimate them using the evidence from pottery, as well as from radiocarbon dating, astronomical observations, and correlations with other civilizations. For example, in the book of Exodus, two Egyptian pharaohs are mentioned in the time of Moses. One of them enslaved the Israelites, and the second one eventually released the people under the leadership of Moses. If we knew their names, we could figure out when the exodus took place. However, the Bible does not mention the names of these pharaohs. Archaeology now supports the identification of these two as king Seti I (1305–1290 BC) and king Rameses II (1290–1224 BC).

Using these available tools, archaeology has been able to provide a chronology that enables us to make some good estimates about when various biblical characters lived. The next time you look at a timeline in the back of your Bible, remember that archaeology provided the means to make that timeline possible.

2. Archaeology has given us some reasonable population estimates of ancient Israel.

The Old Testament has a number of conflicting statements about the population of the Israelites after the exodus. Was it several million, as the census in Numbers seems to indicate? Or was it in the thousands, as the books of Deuteronomy and Joshua imply? How do we estimate the size of ancient populations? This has been a subject of investigation in the last thirty years.

Archaeologists tackle this problem by conducting ground surveys throughout Palestine. They begin by surveying a small region, noting every town where ancient people lived. They determine the number of acres and estimate their population density. Then they survey the countryside, noting the remains of farmhouses, caves, cemeteries, olive presses, etc. and estimating the population in rural areas. By surveying all areas of Palestine using these methods, archaeologists have been able to offer rough estimates of the population of the Israelite people.[1] The actual number was probably no more than about 400,000 people in the Iron II period (the time of the Israelite monarchy). Earlier populations would have been much smaller. The total Canaanite population in the period before Israel invaded Palestine was probably around 200,000. The size of the capital city of Israel (Samaria) could have been as much as 15,000 at its maximum, and the capital of Judah (Jerusalem) could have been around 7,500. In terms of modern calculations, we would label these sites as towns rather than cities, but in ancient times a population of 15,000 was a very large city. Most Israelite towns were only a few hundred people in size. A handful of the larger ones could have numbered several thousand people at most.

Survey work has also confirmed what the Bible tells us about the locations of Israelite towns. Most of the population lived in the hill country of Galilee, Samaria, and Judah. Few Israelites ever lived along the Mediterranean coast in the Old Testament period, and there were large areas of wilderness along the shore of the Dead

Sea and the Jordan River where no one lived. The actual inhabited area of Palestine attributed to the Israelites was much smaller than most biblical maps indicate.

3. Archaeology has offered fantastic insights into the daily lives of the Israelite people.

Many people read the stories in the Bible and assume that the ancient world was quite primitive. For example, they read the story of Abraham and note that he never lived in a house; he just wandered around living in tents. So they associate Abraham with the Stone Age. But in reality most people in Abraham's time lived in houses. One needs to keep in mind that the Old Testament only describes certain individuals who are important to the story of Israel. Most of the history and culture remains unmentioned. Archaeology provides us a much broader picture of how the majority of people actually lived in ancient times.

We now know that people were making significant cultural advances for thousands of years before the time of Moses. By the time of the exodus (13th century BC), cities such as Jericho had existed for at least 7000 years. Pottery had been in use for 5000 years. Writing had been invented 2000 years earlier. People knew how to grow crops, raise animals, build elaborate temples and palaces with painted frescoes on the walls, harness large rivers such as the Nile and the Euphrates for irrigation, build boats and sail for thousands of miles, tell time and calculate dates, and write beautiful poetry and other literary works. Both Moses and Abraham lived in a very cultured world. Archaeology can tell us a great deal about this ancient world and the lives of average Israelite people.

Many Israelites lived in what archaeologists call "four-room houses."[2] Hundreds of them have been found in Palestine. These houses consisted of three parallel, long, narrow rooms and one broad room across the back. A few houses of wealthier families also had a second story where the family ate, slept, and entertained.

The walls were made of large boulders of various sizes. Small chink stones and mortar were placed in the gaps for stability. The entire wall was often plastered to create a flat surface. The floor was made of beaten earth composed of fine layers of ash and clay. The roof was constructed of large wooden beams about the diameter of a telephone pole. These were laid horizontally on top of the walls and supported in the middle with vertical beams about 7–8 feet high. Smaller branches and twigs were placed at right angles to the first ones. The final layer consisted of clay and mud mixed with sand, charcoal, and ash. The entire roof was rolled flat with a roller. This 15-inch thick roof needed to be repaired and rolled flat again after every rainy season. Israelite houses were no turnkey projects built by contractors for the buyer to enjoy. Each family built their own house. It was a major project requiring the help of all the men in an extended family over several months. As they built, these men also kept their farms running.

One room in each house was used as a pantry to store food products. This room would have contained 3-foot tall storage jars whose contents included such products as wheat, barley, broad beans, chickpeas, grapes, lentils, and green beans. Each jar could hold several bushels. Other jars were used to store olive oil and water. The family probably secured these products by growing some on farmland they owned outside the city and trading for other products. They also may have collected wild berries in the summer and hunted wild animals for food. It is estimated that a family would have needed 8–10 of these storage jars for the annual food needs of each person in the household.

Some of the other typical household items found in Israelite houses included various types of pottery jars, bowls, lamps, and cooking pots. They often had large millstones for grinding grain, small mortars and pestles for crushing nuts, herbs, and spices, spindle whorls for spinning wool into thread, loom weights used for weaving cloth, jewelry such as rings, earrings, necklaces, and bracelets, axes and sledgehammers, spear and javelin points, sling stones, figurines, and seals for impressing one's mark in a piece of clay. Because spoons and forks are entirely missing, archaeologists conclude that people ate with their hands. Although none of the bedding survived, families probably slept on mats on the floor and covered themselves with blankets.

Working with textiles was a major part of every woman's life. The average woman spent 2–3 hours per day making the clothing her family needed. Clothing was made primarily from wool. First, sheep had to be raised and sheared. The wool was washed, cleaned, and spun into thread. It was dyed into various colors and later woven into cloth, either on a vertical or horizontal ground loom. After weaving, the cloth was washed and preshrunk. Then it was cut and sewn. Most garments were fairly straight line in construction in order not to waste the precious fabric. Because clothing production was such a time consuming project, most people probably had very few clothes: a main set and an extra set to wear on wash day.

Every family also needed a set of knives for cutting, scraping, and butchering. Knives were made from flint nodules, which are found extensively in Palestine. A hammer stone was used to flake off different types of blades. Probably every family made most of their own knives. Ancient men may have preferred to let their beards grow, rather than try to shave with these knives.

Other industries that existed in ancient times included pottery making and flint knapping. Every home needed a minimum of several dozen pieces of pottery to store and prepare food products. Bowls, platters, goblets, cooking pots, jugs, and pitchers were all a part of every kitchen. However, pottery making was not easy. It took skill with the wheel and knowledge about the types of clay available in the area. And it required access to a kiln. Because of this, pottery making was probably centralized among a few families in every town.

When we study the artifacts found in an average Israelite

home, we start to recognize the tremendous amount of effort and physical labor needed to survive in ancient times. A person's food, clothing, health, and house—just the basic needs of life—took countless hours of time each day to maintain. Like many farming families today, the lives of the ancient Israelites depended on their resourcefulness, ingenuity, and hard labor. Life was not easy, and the average age at death was only 35–40 years. Yet none of these aspects of Israelite culture is described in the Bible. No one knew even what Israelite houses looked like until archaeologists started digging them up. So through the window that archaeology provides us, we have a fantastic view into ancient Israel's past

4. Archaeology has provided a "flavor of probability" for many biblical stories.

Although archaeology cannot "prove" many events in the Bible, it can provide a meaningful background against which we can view biblical stories more realistically. In many cases, archaeology has shown that biblical events "could have happened" much like they are described.

John Bright uses the phrase "a flavor of probability" to characterize the support that archaeology provides for biblical studies. By this, he means that archaeology has shown that people with the names of Abraham, Moses, Samuel, and David could actually have lived and done the things attributed to them in the Bible. But archeology, says Bright "has not proved the stories true in detail, and cannot do so."[3]

Such an admission may not be popular with those who insist on using archaeology to "prove" the accuracy of every historical detail in the Bible. But we need to be honest in evaluating the contribution archaeology can make to biblical studies. Archaeology's main contributions have been and will continue to be primarily in enlarging our understanding of the cultural background of the ancient world and providing a "flavor of probability" for biblical stories.

Because so much more evidence still in the ground needs to be dug up, archaeology will continue to play a substantial role in biblical studies for many decades to come.

Of course, archaeology sometimes creates more questions. This is typical of most scientific investigations. If archaeology is going to be taken seriously as a tool of biblical studies, we must be willing to live with the new evidence and new understandings it uncovers. For example, the evidence from archaeology now supports a 13th-century BC rather than a 15th-century BC dating of the exodus. See also the information on "population estimates" above.

5. Archaeology has actually confirmed the names and dates of a few biblical characters.

In a few cases, archaeologists have uncovered written documents outside the Bible that mention the names of some biblical characters. The stele (stone monument) of king Merneptah in Egypt mentions the word "Israel" for the first time in a historical source (about 1220 BC). At least five Assyrian kings from the ninth through the seventh centuries BC record the names of Israelite and Judean kings, such as Ahab, Jehu, Jehoahaz, Menahem, Pekah, Hoshea, Hezekiah, and Manasseh. A picture of king Jehu even appears on a stele of Shalmaneser III (858-824 BC). The Babylonian king Nebuchadnezzar mentions king Jehoiachin of Judah and describes the fall of Jerusalem. The Mesha stele from Moab mentions king Omri and describes the war between Moab and Israel mentioned in 2 Kings 3:5. Within Israel itself, archaeologists have uncovered over 1200 seals and bullae (seal impressions) that have Israelite names; some contain the name of an Israelite or Judean king.[4] In 1993, an Aramaean stele that mentions the "House of David" was uncovered in the city of Dan. In addition to these finds, a number of ostraca (letters written in Hebrew on broken pieces of pottery) have appeared.

Unfortunately, the sources above are the only written sources that relate to the Bible, and all except one are later than 900 BC. But they are better than nothing, which is where we were 100 years ago. Who knows what additional evidence will come out of the ground in the next 100 years?

In summary, archaeology has contributed an enormous amount of information that has significantly affected our understanding of the people and events of the Bible. We now have:

1. A chronology of ancient times,
2. Some reasonable population estimates,
3. Some insights into the daily lives of the Israelite people,
4. A flavor of probability that many biblical events could have happened much like they are described in the Bible, and
5. Some actual confirmed names and dates of a few biblical characters.

As long as archaeologists are permitted to dig in the Near East, this knowledge base will grow. Archaeologists rightfully deserve our utmost respect for the contributions they make to our study of the Bible.

---

1. Magen Broshi and Israel Finkelstein, "The Population of Palestine in Iron Age II," *Bulletin of the American Schools of Oriental Research* 287 (Aug. 1992): 47-60.
2. For a description of a typical four-room Israelite house, see Larry G. Herr and Douglas R. Clark, "Excavating the Tribe of Reuben," *Biblical Archaeology Review* 27.2 (Mar.–Apr., 2001): 36-47, 64-65.
3. John Bright, *A History of Israel* (Philadelphia: Westminster, 1959), 75.
4. A few of these seals with kings' names on them have been shown to be forgeries, so one has to rely on the evaluations made by experts with regard to the legitimacy of each one.

What the Dead Sea Scrolls Can Tell Us About Contemporary Biblical Issues

W. Randolph Bynum

A few years ago, I entered the fascinating world of the Dead Sea Scrolls. With other contemporary scholars, I began to explore some of what happened during the formation of biblical texts during the last three centuries BC through the first century AD. I studied how these texts might inform our understanding of the Bible we have today. This essay sets out to disclose some of those discoveries and to explore what they can tell us about our own contemporary interactions with Scripture. In particular, I consider how features of the Dead Sea Scrolls, also referred to as Judean Desert Discoveries, may help us address issues facing the church such as inerrancy, inspiration, biblical authority, and interpretation.

Dead Sea Scrolls: A Brief Overview

The designation "Dead Sea Scrolls" represents a series of manuscript discoveries beginning in 1947. They were discovered in various places in the wilderness of Judea, including Qumran, Nahal Hever, Wadi Murabba'at, Masada, and other locations. Some of the most important discoveries occurred at Qumran. Over 900 manuscripts were found at Qumran alone, including over 200 biblical manuscripts. Archaeologists have dated these documents from approximately 250 BC to AD 100.

The Dead Sea Scrolls include all Old Testament books except Esther. This may be due either to historical accident or because the Qumran community simply did not celebrate Purim and had no copy of the book.[1] Discoveries include tiny fragments, individual pages, and complete scrolls such as the Isaiah and Psalms Scrolls.

Although the Dead Sea Scrolls include biblical and communal documents, the biblical scrolls in particular share a number of basic, general characteristics:

- They are written in three languages: predominantly Hebrew, plus Aramaic and Greek;
- Those written in Hebrew, like all other Hebrew texts of that time, have only consonants (there is no full vowel pointing for more precise pronunciation in the Hebrew Bible until the sixth century AD);
- They represent parallel textual traditions that cannot be reconciled to one original text;
- They generally exhibit the following basic textual traditions: (a) Qumran texts that the Qumran scribes copied and edited, (b) texts resembling the later Hebrew standard Masoretic Text but not identical to it, (c) texts that represent the Hebrew text behind the Septuagint Greek translation of the Old Testament, and (e) "non-aligned" texts that cannot be identified with any known textual tradition;
- Each book or passage may reflect a unique textual history, and so it must be studied on its own;
- Parallel texts hold essential authoritative status as sacred texts without any demand for precise conformity; and
- There is no evidence for a preferred textual tradition.

A Specific Section of Scripture: The Book of the Twelve

Since the Dead Sea Scrolls are a large body of material for study, I will focus attention on a particular section of Scripture, the Minor Prophets, also known in the Hebrew Bible as the Book of the Twelve. I will look at three different manuscript discoveries regarding that section of Scripture, which are representative of the issues involved with the scrolls at large.

1. 4QXII (=4Q76-82)

From the fourth cave (4) of Qumran (Q), these fragments of the Twelve (XII) contain portions of Hosea, Joel, Amos, Jonah, Micah, Nahum, Zephaniah, Haggai, Zechariah, and Malachi. They date from 150–25 BC (i.e., before an official canon of the Old Testament). There are seven fragments: two align with the Hebrew text (technically called the "proto-Masoretic Text") that later became the standard Old Testament text. Two align with the Hebrew text behind the Septuagint. Two are not identified with any known textual tradition ("non-aligned"). And one cannot be identified.

2. 8HevXIIgr

From the eighth cave (8) of Nahal Hever (Hev), these fragments of the Twelve (XII) are written in Greek (gr) and contain parts of Jonah, Micah, Nahum, Habakkuk, Zephaniah, and Zechariah. They date between 50 BC and AD 50, which includes the era of Christ's ministry and the first two decades of the early church. They are based on a Hebrew text that is similar to, but not identical with, the Masoretic Text. Because of the similarities and differences with other Hebrew and Greek texts, these fragments represent a movement within Judaism to correct the Greek Septuagint toward a prominent Hebrew text of the day.

3. MurXII

From Wadi Murabba'at (Mur), these fragments of the Twelve

(XII) contain parts of Joel, Amos, Obadiah, Jonah, Micah, Nahum, Habakkuk, Zephaniah, Haggai, and Zechariah. They date from the latter part of the first century AD, notably the era of virtually all the New Testament writings. They are textually quite close to the proto-Masoretic Text. However, they vary from that text at some points, mostly minor ones. These fragments represent the move toward a standardized Hebrew text during the era of AD 70–135, following the cataclysmic events of AD 70 and the destruction of Jerusalem.

What Does This Say to Contemporary Biblical Issues?

The Dead Sea Scrolls provide us valuable information about the development of biblical texts in the era of 250 BC to AD 100. It is not always obvious, however, what that information means or how it may apply to contemporary times. Our understanding of the biblical writing process, our view of Scripture, and our thoughts about its inspiration will all significantly affect how we interpret Scripture. After a careful examination of some of the features of the Dead Sea Scrolls, several observations about their use of biblical texts may instruct us as we read and interpret Scripture in the contemporary church.[2]

1. The Dead Sea Scrolls demonstrate multiple types of texts that we cannot overlook.

In the oldest texts available, multiple manuscripts vary from one another. We cannot reconcile these various texts back to a single original document.[3] We not only find variant readings from one text to the other and minor spelling differences. We also find "multiple literary editions" of biblical books and passages.[4] For the Old Testament in general and for the Book of the Twelve in particular, the history of the biblical text from these manuscripts demonstrates the unmistakable presence of multiple textual traditions from 150 BC through AD 100. There is little or no indication that one type of text was preferred over another. This did not seem a problem for the Qumran community or Judaism in general in the pre-canonical era. These issues continue to affect the biblical text, both in early church times (i.e., the era of the writing of texts that would later comprise the New Testament) and into the era of a standard text and a recognized canon.

2. The canon of Scripture that we now have took several centuries to emerge.

We too often impose more simplistic modern views of book writing onto the ancient texts. In previous eras, writing was not a short and simple process. It did not move from a single author to editor to formal publication, with author's name, date, and publisher included.

There was no Bible as we think of it today in the era of the Dead Sea Scrolls. Believers certainly had collections of sacred writings to which they granted respect and authority. However, they did not have an official "Bible" in a single large bound book as we now hold in our hands. They did not have an official canon as we know it today, because there were no strictly defined limits on what books to include. Even the order of books was not clear.[5]

The writers of texts that would later comprise the New Testament had at their disposal neither an authoritative canon nor biblical manuscripts with a single text-type. No single, official, biblical text existed in the context of the early church. This explains why we find different quotations of the same Old Testament verse or passage within the New Testament. Certainly, early believers agreed that the main books that later became canonical were authoritative. They also insisted on sound doctrinal teaching. But they seemed little concerned about strict limits or "fences" around the outer edges, e.g., deuterocanonical writings.[6] Even into the eras of canonization and textual standardization (approximately AD 70–135 for the Old Testament and AD 100–400 for the New Testament), there existed manuscripts with some degree of variant readings.

3. The transmission of the Scriptures was a complex process.

It is quite evident that the Scriptures are the result of long periods of literary development. We must take into account the work of creative scribes who did not merely copy ancient texts but who *themselves* were creative agents, editors, interpreters, and translators as well. Scribes updated the texts and made them understandable to a new era. They felt these texts must continue to be relevant, because it is difficult for any ancient text to speak directly to a different day. They did not perceive their updating and editing work as playing "fast and loose" with the sacred texts. Rather, the Qumran community in particular and Judaism in general took these texts seriously and felt compelled to make them relevant to their era.

The well-known orchestral and choral work of Mozart's *Requiem* provides a good example to illustrate the ancient writing process. Mozart began the work, but his untimely death left his work unfinished. Mozart's student, Franz Süssmayr, finished what needed to be completed. The version of this popular work we hear today is usually Süssmayr's version. What part Mozart wrote and what Süssmayr added is not certain.[7] We might ask ourselves, where does Mozart's own work end and the other begin? And if someone could clearly separate the two, would Mozart's original work be more inspired than the finished work? Further, to which would it be more inspiring to listen?

Here is another example. When my father passed away, he left behind notebooks full of sermon outlines with notes. Let's say that I decide to edit those into a manuscript for publication. I take my father's notes and add what I remember from hearing him preach. However, after editing them, my sister reads my edited version and treasures the collection. But perhaps she decides to add a few details here and there from her own memory of those same sermons (some preached on more than one occasion and so may have had slightly different forms). Then my brother takes a copy of my edited version, rearranges some of the material and inserts some details in the margins as he recalls them. This process would produce three similar versions that share the same essential content. But they also have variations as they are copied and passed along.

Now let's add to our example our grandchildren. Suppose they take these copies and update some of the material. For example, one sermon illustration mentions "Baker, Oregon." In their updating, they may wonder whether to update it to reflect the current name of the city. Should they update it to read "Baker City, Oregon," or should they leave it?

These two examples illustrate the complex process by which others hand down texts. We know that manuscripts, even sacred biblical writings, can undergo change for various reasons. Though such changes need not diminish our view of divine inspiration, they should lead us to rethink our assumptions about the writing of the Bible.

4. The Dead Sea Scrolls show us that most views of verbal inspiration are difficult to sustain.

Our perspective about the inspiration of Scripture (i.e., the divine-human interaction in the production of scripture) is critical. We may review the classical theories of biblical inspiration and come to our own conclusions.[8] At the same time, we must be true to the realities of the biblical texts as we have them. The presence of variant manuscripts and multiple literary editions makes it difficult to hold to a verbal or dictation theory of inspiration. One's view of inspiration needs to be perceptive and broad enough to account for the full history of the text as we have it.

5. The search for the original text of Old Testament books is increasingly difficult.

We do not have any original copies of the biblical books. Nor do we have a copy of any Old Testament text originating anytime close to the era of its original writers. Therefore, we cannot know precisely what the original text contained. It is simply beyond our reach to know what the text looked like as it left the hand of its original writers.

We must account for this fact in our perspective and use of Scripture. Although it may stretch our understanding, we need to appreciate what we *do* have in Scripture. That means being honest about its "diachronic complexity" and textual plurality. It means dealing with its complex history of compilation, editing, and revising.

6. The job of Bible translators has not become easier.

The preceding should help us take a more helpful and productive view of contemporary modern translations. Translations may take on a life and authority of their own. Yet we must recognize that they are all approximations, including the KJV, the NIV, the NRSV, and others. If they are not, they why is there the need for the NKJV, the TNIV, and the like? Because contemporary translations move from ancient languages to the present, they must include elements of interpretation. In fact, they even include instances of rewriting the biblical text to respond to contemporary issues.

In the light of the Dead Sea Scroll discoveries, should Bible translators take into account a better reading found among those discoveries? The NRSV, for one, has incorporated several readings based on these biblical manuscripts. For example, a reading in 1 Sam 10–11 from 4QSama has an explanatory paragraph not found in the standard Hebrew text. Although the question is not a simple one to answer, the textual variations in the biblical manuscripts found in the Dead Sea Scrolls have implications for the ongoing task of translation and transmission.

Suggestions for Contemporary Readers of Scripture

I want to ask us to look at the evidence with open minds and hearts. We need to learn all we can about the Bible and the history of the text. We can allow it to speak to us and challenge us without overlaying our contemporary assumptions or taking a defensive position about ideas that are no longer sustainable. Narrow and brittle views of the biblical text that ignore the historical reality of the text's development need to be infused with new life and new insight from the truth of the biblical textual history. Therefore, I offer the following four suggestions:

1. The best solution to discrepancies between biblical books (or even within a book) is not found in trying to reconcile all differences and difficulties. The best solutions accept the polyphonic or "multiple voice" character of the books of the Bible.[9]

The great themes and truths of Scripture are in harmony throughout the biblical canon. The Dead Sea Scroll discoveries do not call these central themes and truths into question. Yet some details in Scripture are not reconcilable and not understandable, even to the best scholars in our day with a more stable text and a recognized canon. Therefore, it is not helpful to theorize that we might solve all these difficulties if we had more information or if we could have access to the original writings. Perhaps we could. Perhaps we could not. Perhaps we need not. In fact, the plurality of text-types may be positive for giving us a broader and richer perspective on the biblical narrative.

2. We need to see divine inspiration as encompassing more than just the writing of the biblical text but also the broader process that includes the editing, transmission, and canonization of these texts.

Several questions and issues come to mind: Since these discoveries come from an era before the finalization of the canon, is the Bible more inspired before it became canon or after? Which version is more inspired? If we hold to the canonical Scriptures as inspired, we must ask: Isn't the canonical process as inspired as the original author's work? Is the rough draft more inspired than the final product?

An original sketch or rough collection may be more "original," but it is not necessarily more authoritative or inspiring for the community of faith. Perhaps we should see the hand of God throughout the entire process, instead of resorting to some hypothesis of perfect originals that not only do not exist but about whose form we do not have good understanding. My conviction is that the Scriptures are the product of a community process under divine inspiration in the total trajectory of their formation.

3. We can affirm that the heart of God's self-revelation has been preserved intact through the ages. This has not occurred by a static or mechanical process of word or document preservation. Rather, it has occurred by a dynamic process of transmission through the ages of faithful people in relationship with God, who have taken the biblical texts seriously, who have listened carefully to their messages, and who have responded appropriately.

The Bible is a collection of texts that engages us. It is by nature interrelational. It is not first a textbook, an intellectual construct, or a set of propositions that one can simply analyze from an objective viewpoint. It does not glow with unequivocal divine authority simply because it exists. These texts, as we interact with them, begin to draw us into relationship with God and with the community of faith.

For instance, 2 Samuel 22:31 begins with descriptions of God's way being perfect and the Lord's word being flawless. However, the last line speaks of relation: "He shields all who take refuge in him" (TNIV). Or take Jesus' familiar words: "I am the way, and the truth, and the life" (John 14:6 TNIV). Of course, Jesus is the truth from

God. But Jesus is not truth in the form of a text alone, but truth-in-relationship: "no one comes to the Father except through me."

Compare also Jesus' words in John 5:39-40: "You search the Scriptures because in them you think you have eternal life, but they are the ones that testify about me, yet you don't want to come to me in order to have life" (author's translation). The Scriptures, however perfectly written and transmitted, are insufficient to give full knowledge of God. They have no absolute authority if relationship with the Living Word is absent.

Relationship with God in a community of faith that takes the Scriptures seriously should draw us toward the center of God's heart and the depth of what God has in mind when God says, "I will be their God, and they will be my people." This is why the Wesleyan tradition has consistently affirmed the Bible's absolute reliability in matters related to salvation or to faith and practice. This contrasts with claims in some Christian circles of the Bible's total inerrancy in everything that it contains. However, if the community of faith is drawn constantly and consistently toward the center-flow of God's self-revelation, the deep, abiding themes from the flow of the biblical narrative become the Bible's authentication of truth. A questionable historical reference or an inaccurate citing of a place or name, whether responsibility for such a difficulty lies with the author of the text or someone who copied that text at some point in its transmission, does not affect these themes. If we are always drawn toward the center, we can relax about the "outer edges."

4. When interpreting Scripture, we should have a realistic view of Scripture in mind that adequately takes into account the nature of the biblical texts and how they have come to us.

We do not have the originals of any biblical writings. If we did, those written in Hebrew would only have consonants without vowel pointing, so we would have to decipher what they said. If we correctly deciphered them, we would still face the task of interpretation and application for today.

If possession of the original copies from the respective authors or the "autographs" was of utmost importance, certainly God could have seen to it that these were preserved and passed along. Further, from our limited perspective so many centuries later, would we even recognize them if they were discovered? Or would we suddenly realize that what we have now is better than an original "rough draft"?

The realities of the biblical textual history, as seen in the Dead Sea Scrolls themselves, invalidate views about the Bible that depend upon hypothetically perfect and pristine original texts. Instead, it is much more productive to deal with the biblical texts as we have actually received them. Taking into account *that* reality gives us a more realistic perspective of how God has worked to inspire and transmit the Scriptures. We must recognize God's hand at work *all along the way*, not just at the supposed beginning point of scriptural writing.

---

1. The phraseology of Esther is, however, apparent in some of the sectarian or non-biblical compositions. See George J. Brooke, "The Dead Sea Scrolls for Christians Today," (unpublished lectures, Manchester, U.K., 2010).
2. I am indebted for the essence of these general conclusions to Brooke, "The Dead Sea Scrolls for Christians Today," while the discussion and development are my own.
3. Four prominent theories explain the variety of textual readings from this era: (1) manuscripts are grouped by families from different regions (Albright and Cross); (2) manuscripts are varied from the social groups that preserved them (Talmon); 3) each manuscript has an individual character, and some are independent and unclassifiable (Tov); and (4) each book has its own history of transmission, and many books have multiple literary editions (Ulrich). Perhaps these theories are not mutually exclusive; each has some insight to add to the discussion.
4. Eugene Ulrich, *The Dead Sea Scrolls and the Origins of the Bible* (Grand Rapids: Eerdmans, 1999), 23.
5. See Ulrich, *The Dead Sea Scrolls and the Origins of the Bible*, 20–22.
6. It would be instructive for us to be aware of our own tendency to be selective about our favorite scriptural passages and books, which become our "functional canon."
7. For more on the story of Mozart's *Requiem*, see http://www.bbc.co.uk/dna/h2g2/alabaster/A59598616.
8. See H. Orton Wiley, *Christian Theology* (3 vols.; Kansas City, MO: Beacon Hill Press of Kansas City, 1940), 1:167–84.
9. Brooke, "The Dead Sea Scrolls for Christians Today."

3

Four Thoughts on Preaching and Teaching the Bible— Mostly the Old Testament

Brent A. Strawn

Trueto its title, this essay offers four thoughts on preaching and teaching the Bible—mostly the Old Testament. While I originally formulated these thoughts for teaching future pastors about the specific task of preaching from the Old Testament, I believe they also apply to teaching as well as preaching and to the New Testament as well as the Old.

Before getting to these four thoughts, both a disclaimer and a caveat are in order. First, the disclaimer: I am an Old Testament professor and teach Old Testament studies exclusively. One job hazard is that I must frequently justify this vocational focus. For example, I sometimes find it necessary to point out to my students that I am an Old Testament professor both by training and by choice. It is not because I failed the New Testament exam! A more significant and worrisome job hazard is that I often must justify the Old Testament itself. I will return to this last point momentarily.

Second is the caveat: I have intentionally left the title of this essay—particularly the last part—open to more than one interpretation. On the one hand, I offer these four thoughts mostly *about* preaching the Old Testament, because that is how I originally formulated them. However, I believe they also apply to the New Testament and thus the whole of the Christian Bible. On the other hand, the second meaning of "Mostly the Old Testament" is that, if I had my druthers, Christian preaching and teaching from Scripture would be mostly preaching *from* the Old Testament! I do not have space or time to argue this point extensively or explicitly, but I do believe such a position is justifiable. It must suffice here to observe that the sheer size and mass of the Old Testament alone indicate that one should preach from it far more often than from the New Testament. The Old Testament comprises approximately 77 percent of the Christian Bible, so one could easily imagine, statistically speaking alone, preaching from it three times as often as the New Testament! One might also appeal to the great German theologian-turned-martyr Dietrich Bonhoeffer, who wrote the following: "In my opinion it is not Christian to want to take our thoughts and feelings too quickly and too directly from the New Testament."[1] Bonhoeffer's statement is stunning—all the more so when we remember that one of his most famous books, *Psalms: The Prayer Book of the Bible*, is a thoroughly Christological reading of the book of Psalms.[2] I believe what enabled Bonhoeffer to make his statement is precisely the first point I wish to make on preaching and teaching the Old Testament. It concerns *address*.

Address

I agree completely with Ellen F. Davis who, in her excellent book *Wondrous Depth: Preaching the Old Testament*, states that the fundamental starting point for all good preaching of the Old Testament treats the Old Testament as *an urgent speaking presence that exercises salutary pressure on our lives.*[3]

Most Christians, I suspect, believe that about the New Testament or at least *think* they believe that about the New Testament. But many Christians are disturbingly open about the fact that they do *not* feel that way about the Old Testament. That is a very serious problem that good preaching and teaching can and must correct.[4] *Why* this is a very serious problem goes back to the heresy of Marcion, who already in the second century AD wanted to dismiss the Old Testament and "the Old Testament God" as fundamentally different from Jesus and the writings that would eventually become the New Testament. However, the Christian church decreed Marcion a heretic. By doing so, the church reasserted its belief in the inseparable and fundamental unity of the Old and New Testaments and their conjoined witness to the one God.[5]

How good preaching and teaching of the Bible will correct this very serious problem is precisely by treating the Old Testament and New, whether taught or preached, as an urgent speaking presence exercising salutary pressure on our lives. This is what I mean by "address," and I believe that the best preaching and teaching, from either Testament or from both, proceeds from this fundamental starting point: that Scripture demands our attention and obedience. And Scripture especially makes *these* demands because it is not just talking *at* us or *past* us, but is rather bearing in *on* us, bearing in *upon* us, and exercising pressure on us. But that pressure is ultimately of the best, most benevolent, and salvific kind.

Again, I believe most Christians, preachers, and teachers of Scripture believe this about the Bible (at least the New Testament) or *think* they believe this about the Bible (at least the New Testament). But I think they may be wrong, because in actual practice the use and function (or *non*-use and *non*-function) of the Old Testament in many churches bears little similarity to the demands of attention and obedience. This is why "address" is so important, and this is why I mention it here as the first of my four thoughts.

Sola Scriptura

The import of Scripture's address leads directly to the second thought: *sola Scriptura* or "Scripture alone." This was, of course, one of the clarion calls of the Reformation.[6] By invoking it in this context, I mean that the Bible is sufficiently deep and significant that good preaching and teaching rarely, if ever, needs to move beyond it.

Stated more pointedly with reference to preaching, *sola Scriptura* means the preacher need not worry about finding just the right illustration, movie clip, or image from the internet to "make" the sermon. The biblical text, *rightly preached*, is more than enough; the rest is often only a distraction. That is, the perfect illustration, image, or story *is* the biblical text itself or perhaps other related biblical texts. Again, I quote Davis, who makes this point nicely with particular reference to the biblical psalms:

> What I am suggesting is that the psalms have nearly inexhaustible potential for making connections with the larger biblical story. This relieves the preacher of the anxiety that has become a modern trademark of the profession, namely, the perceived need to "find an illustration," on which the success of the sermon is often supposed to depend. That is a pernicious idea, for very often the illustration proves to be the tail that wags the dog of the sermon (and I use that last phrase advisedly).[7]

Elsewhere, Davis states, "The plain fact is that no preacher can ever be astonishing (in a positive sense!) unless she has first been astonished. And the only regular and fully reliable source of astonishment for the Christian preacher is Scripture itself."[8] To put this in language borrowed from Walter Brueggemann, we might say that the task of the preacher or teacher is to create and nurture a reality alternative to the dominant one around us. Thus, Scripture is the primary way we encounter that reality, live it, and live into it.[9] But all such lofty goals are forfeited if, instead of *sola Scriptura*, Scripture is just one item on the menu and maybe the least important and appetizing one at that (but the movie clip is amazing!).

Among other things, *sola Scriptura* underscores that the locus of authority for teachers and preachers of Scripture is *not* the teachers or preachers themselves, *nor* their charisma, *nor* their wisdom, *nor* even their really interesting stories from camp. Instead, the locus of authority is *Scripture*—*its* authority, *its* wisdom, *its* stories and hymns, *its* prayers and poems, *its* prophecies and the like. Here, too, I think we believe this, at least in theory, but I fear we act otherwise. I fear we often preach and teach otherwise.

To be sure, the best preachers and teachers know they must "translate" and (re)present Scripture for and to the contemporary scene. That is never an easy task or a simplistic proposition. Nevertheless, a *sola Scriptura* kind of disposition as defined here remains completely essential. And it is felt (or not felt), I think, even in *how* Scripture is read and *how much* of it is read in church on any given Sunday morning.

Honesty

The third thought, *honesty*, notes that Scripture, especially the Old Testament, is characterized by a remarkable and at times even unbearable honesty about a number of different topics. Although the Old Testament is brutally candid about many things, at the very least two subjects must be mentioned as especially obvious: its honesty about *sin*, and its honesty about *suffering*.

The New Testament, too, is honest, but I think we tend to read it in flat ways so its honesty is often lost on us.[10] But it is very hard indeed to miss the brutal honesty of the Old Testament and the stories of God's people contained there.

It seems to me that the Old Testament sets us an example at precisely this point. Instead of beating up on the Old Testament on account of these moments of extreme candor, we ought to emulate its brutal honesty. Stated differently, the old preaching strategy that repeatedly belittles Israel for "yet again" failing or "yet again" sinning needs to die a quick and painful death. In its place, sensitive preachers and teachers will recognize we only know of Israel's sins and failings because Israel was honest enough to tell us about all that. We ought to take a clue from this and model similarly honest—even brutally honest—dispositions toward and in our life with God.[11] That would mean, at very least, that we become more honest about our own sin and suffering.[12]

Philip Yancey, in his book on the Old Testament, *The Bible Jesus Read*, captures something of this third point about honesty:

> From initial resistance, I moved to a reluctant sense that I *ought* to read the neglected three-quarters of the Bible. As I worked past some of the barriers (much like learning to read Shakespeare), I came to feel a *need* to read, because of what it was teaching me. Eventually I found myself *wanting* to read those thirty-nine books, which were satisfying in me some hunger that nothing else had—not even, I must say, the New Testament. They taught me about Life with God: not how it is supposed to work, but how it actually does work.[13]

> Another example that underscores the power and function of the trenchant honesty found in the Old Testament is the well-known passage from a letter that Franz Kafka wrote to his friend Oskar Pollak, dated January 27, 1904, when Kafka was only twenty years old:

> If the book we are reading does not wake us, as with a fist hammering on our skull, why then do we read it? So that it shall make us happy? Good God, we would also be happy if we had no books, and such books as make us happy we could, if need be, write ourselves. But what we must have are those books which come upon us like ill-fortune, and distress us deeply, like the death of one we love better than ourselves, like suicide. A book must be an ice-axe to break

the sea frozen inside us.[14]

> Kafka is speaking of reading *any* kind of literature, *any* sort
> of book. Yet surely his insight holds true for Scripture as well.
> Surely we also need it to break the sea frozen inside us. That
> kind of work is not accomplished by cover up and denial but
> only by the honest, hard, and often gruesome work of the
> ice-axe, which turns out, in the end, to be a scalpel.

Poetry

In my judgment, honesty is one of the signal contributions the
Old Testament makes to Christian Scripture. Another is poetry,
since fully one-third of the Old Testament is poetic, whereas the
New Testament itself has very little poetry. In several ways, the first
three thoughts on preaching and teaching the Bible come together
in this fourth and final one:

Samuel Taylor Coleridge (1772–1834) famously described poetry as "the best words in their best order." Among other things,
the superiority of poetry allows it to be re-uttered, and therefore
re-appropriated. In this way, for example, the psalms become *our*
prayers, not just David's or Asaph's, and therefore poetry involves
address (the first thought).

The best poetry is also heavily imagistic and metaphorical. Thus,
those images and metaphors can potentially stay with us forever,
changing our ways of thinking and living. Someone might think, for
example, of a life-decision in terms of Robert Frost's two roads that
diverge in a yellow wood and then decide to take the road less traveled. Or, more biblically, someone might think of the righteous as
a tree planted by streams of water, bringing forth its fruit in season, with no withering leaves of which to speak, succeeding in all
endeavors, and so decide to crack open the Lord's law and start
meditating on it day and night (Ps 1). All this is a way of saying that

poetry can be all encompassing literature, and so Scripture in poetic mode is *sola Scriptura* (the second thought).

Poetry is also *honest* literature, often heart-wrenchingly so (the third thought). That point is as old as the prophets and the psalms, of course, and supported philosophically from Aristotle forward. Much more recently, Garrison Keillor has stated that good poems matter because "they offer a truer account than what we're used to getting."[15]

These considerations, especially the last one, provide motivation to read the poetry of Scripture—to get a truer account than we're used to getting. They also motivate one to preach and teach in similar ways—to *give* a truer account than what we or our people are used to getting.

Now thinking about teaching and preaching Scripture as a poetic act is one thing; thinking about Scripture *itself* as poetry is another but equally important thing. In my judgment, the categories of story or narrative, while important, are not fully adequate descriptions of Scripture, in part because so much of the Bible is not a unified narrative and so much of it is poetic.[16]

Not all of Scripture is poetry, of course, but thinking of Scripture in poetic ways and as poetry creates interesting opportunities and has significant benefits. For one thing, it suggests that it is going to take time and energy, hard work and discipline to understand Scripture.[17] I fear that we often treat Scripture otherwise, implying that it is straightforwardly transparent or easily understood and applied. *But Scripture is more like a poem than a newspaper.* Like poetry, it requires slow and careful reading and reflection. And also like poetry, it will probably require rereading, and will benefit from that practice.

Expert testimony supports this point. The great poet and agrarian Wendell Berry has written that a "good poem...cannot be written or read in distraction."[18] Gerhard von Rad said something quite similar about the Old Testament specifically:

> To be sure, the Bible *never was easy reading*; and the finest interpretation cannot and should not make it so. Whatever one wrote in ancient Israel, it was *not for speed-reading*.... *Reading the Bible has always demanded that one be prepared for contemplation.*[19]

With reference to pastoral ministry proper, M. Craig Barnes has recently put forth the image of the poet as a particularly apt metaphor for the minister. According to Barnes, the minister is one of those

> who have been blessed with a vision that allows them to explore, and express, the truth behind the reality. Poets see the despair and heartache as well as the beauty and miracle that lie just beneath the thin veneer of the ordinary, and they describe this in ways that are recognized not only in the mind, but more profoundly in the soul.[20]

The poetry of Scripture helps with these crucial ministerial roles, tasks, arts—especially those concerning contemplative reading and careful interpretation. Indeed, I believe that the Bible itself is the very best schoolhouse for the very best poetic preachers and teachers of Scripture, which is nothing less than the poetry of God.

---

1. Dietrich Bonhoeffer, *Letters and Papers from Prison* (Enlarged ed.; ed. E. Bethge; New York: Collier, 1972), 157.
2. See Dietrich Bonhoeffer, *Psalms: The Prayer Book of the Bible* (Minneapolis: Augsburg Fortress, 1970).
3. See Ellen F. Davis, *Wondrous Depth: Preaching the Old Testament* (Louisville: Westminster John Knox, 2005), xiv: The Old Testament is "an urgent and speaking presence"; and p. 2: the Old Testament is "an immediate presence that exercising shaping force in Christian lives—indeed that serves as a source of salutary pressure on our lives."
4. I agree with Gerhard von Rad, who wrote not only that we *can* preach the Old Testament but that we *must* (see his *Biblical Interpretations in Preaching* [trans. J. E. Steely; Nashville: Abingdon, 1977], 11: "The biblical texts *must* be preached—under all circumstances and at any cost. The people for whom we each have a responsibility need them for living [and for dying].... The biblical texts *can* be preached. This is a battleground, and there is much

that must be clarified here"). *Can* and *must* went together in powerful and dangerous ways for von Rad, who was a member of the Confessing Church movement amidst the terrible circumstances of Nazi Germany during World War II. They also go together in the situation we face today which attests to widespread devaluation and denigration of the Old Testament in much Christian experience and practice. Stated differently, I think very highly of the sacred task of preaching and its capacity to set theological and biblical matters "right" in the local church among contemporary believers.

5. The classic statement remains the five books against Marcion written by the early church writer Tertullian (ca. AD 160–220).

6. The others were *sola gratia* ("grace alone"), *sola fide* ("faith alone"), *solus Christus* "Christ alone"), *soli Deo gloria* ("glory to God alone"). The existence of no less than five "solas," indicates that there are always more than one "sola" operative at any given point in time.

7. Davis, *Wondrous Depth*, 28.

8. Ibid., 2. M. Craig Barnes's wonderful book, *The Pastor as Minor Poet: Texts and Subtexts in the Ministerial Life* (Grand Rapids: Eerdmans, 2009), esp. 24–27, makes similar points.

9. Walter Brueggemann, *The Prophetic Imagination* (2nd ed.; Minneapolis: Fortress, 2001), 3: "The task of prophetic ministry is to nurture, nourish, and evoke a consciousness and perception alternative to the consciousness and perception of the dominant culture around us."

10. Cf., e.g., Paul's not infrequent mentions of his own suffering, esp. in 2 Cor (e.g., 1:4–6, 8–10; 2:1–5; 11:23–29; 12:7–10; cf. Gal 4:19). In my experience, however, one hears less of these matters from the pulpit and far more about "Rejoice always, pray without ceasing, give thanks in all circumstances" (1 Thess 5:16–18a; cf. Phil 4:4).

11. For the benefits of such disclosure, see, among others, James W. Pennebaker, *Opening Up: The Healing Power of Confiding in Others* (New York: William Morrow, 1990).

12. The dynamics of, e.g., Isa 6:5–7 and the Psalms, respectively, show the stunning results of such honesty.

13. Philip Yancey, *The Bible Jesus Read* (Grand Rapids: Zondervan, 1999), 20–21 (his emphasis).

14. George Steiner, *Language and Silence: Essays on Language, Literature, and the Inhuman* (New Haven, CN: Yale University Press, 1998), 67. Apparently this is Steiner's own translation of the letter and other, slightly different versions can be found (see, e.g., http://www.languagehat.com/archives/001062.php [accessed 3/23/2011]). The German original reads "My God" (*Mein Gott*), which Steiner translates as "Good God." Although this phrase may be nothing more than an interjection, the presence of the divine name in this passage is nevertheless important, suggesting that Kafka thought God somehow figures into the need to read difficult literature. Steiner's version goes further, suggesting that God's very *goodness* plays a role—that God's goodness might even be what difficult literature (and reading it) is about. In any event, after citing this passage at the end of an essay on how literature impacts humanity and civility, Steiner comments: "Students of English literature, of any literature, must ask those who teach them, as they must ask themselves, whether they know, and not in their minds alone, what Kafka meant."

15. Garrison Keillor, *Good Poems* (New York: Penguin, 2002), xxv.

16. I have explored these points and what follows more fully in Brent A. Strawn, "Lyric Poetry," in *Dictionary of the Old Testament: Wisdom, Poetry and Writings* (ed. T. Longman III and P. Enns; Downers Grove: IVP Academic, 2008), 437–46.

17. One should note that the metaphors and parables in the Bible are rarely explained, so situations like Isa 5:1–7 or Matt 13:1–9, 18–23 are exceptions, not the rule. Indeed, according to Matt 13:10–17 the reason Jesus speaks in parables is precisely so people do *not* understand (cf. Isa 6:9–10)! A statement from David Shapiro, "Gold and Cardboard," *Poetry* 196/5 (Sept. 2010): 423 is evocative at this point: "Even the literal is a metaphor."

18. Wendell Berry, "The Responsibility of the Poet," in idem, *What Are People For? Essays* (Berkeley: Counterpoint, 2010), 90.

19. Gerhard von Rad, "How to Read the Old Testament," in idem, *God at Work in Israel* (trans. J. H. Marks; Nashville: Abingdon, 1980), 10, 18 (emphasis added).

20. Barnes, *The Pastor as Minor Poet*, 17.

4

Authority Is What Authority Does: Rethinking the Role of the Bible as Scripture

Richard P. Thompson

Authority and the Bible

It is quite natural for contemporary discussions in the church to draw in one way or another upon matters related to the authority of the Bible. In Protestant circles, such tendencies are not surprising, given the *sola scriptura* battle cry that has characterized us since the earliest days of the Reformation. Even in Wesleyan traditions, we expect John Wesley's theological family to follow his footsteps as a people of "one book."[1] Although Wesleyan scholars continue to debate how the four aspects of the so-called "Wesleyan Quadrilateral" (i.e., Scripture, tradition, reason and experience) work together in theological reflection, one thing is abundantly clear: for Wesley and Wesleyans, the Bible serves as the primary authority for matters regarding Christian theology and ethics ... faith and practice. In various ways, the authority of the Bible continues to be affirmed, not only in Wesleyan circles but also generally throughout the Christian church.

We have seen and heard things that suggest declarations regarding the authority of the Bible are not as widespread in the church. For instance, the sign of one church simply declares: "A

Bible-Believing Church" (a description that begs the question about what church would actually describe itself as a "church that does *not* believe the Bible"). Another church posted this on its message board: "We believe in the Bible's authority" (which implies that other churches do *not* believe this!). Of course, such sayings are not limited to church signs and bumper stickers. In the midst of a theological argument, someone makes the comment, "Well, *I* believe what the Bible says" (which implies "and *you* don't").

While the term "authority" frequently appears in such discussions, it is typically associated with different (albeit not unrelated) views regarding the nature of the Bible.[2] Evaluations of someone's understanding of biblical authority are often linked to what others perceive of that person's view of the nature of the Bible itself (e.g., "Does that person have a 'high' view of Scripture or a 'low' view?" "Does that person believe the Bible to be inspired by God?"). In recent times, this may be partly a response to "Da Vinci Code" like questions that challenge the Bible's authority by raising questions about politics and human ambition that may have contaminated the canonical process. As a result, important questions on the authority of the Bible in the twenty-first century become intertwined with issues such as inspiration, inerrancy, and doctrine.

Two basic things happen when other questions fog our vision about the Bible and its authority. First, we give little attention to defining what it means for the Bible to be authoritative. Second, we do not take the time to consider how the theological themes of the Wesleyan tradition may address and shape our conversations about these questions. It seems as though we have too often placed the issue of biblical authority in the context of particular notions *about* the Bible, rather than in the actual function of the Bible in the church.

This raises a basic but largely unanswered question: What might lie behind the continual debate in Christian circles regarding the authority of the Bible? Unfortunately, the current argumentative context may be shaped more by the cultural phenomena of talk radio and "shout out" sections on websites where persons can hide. Without a public identity, these people submit whatever offensive comment or slur about anyone or anything they wish … uncivil discourse, if you will.

Getting into shouting matches over who is and is not correct with regard to the Bible and its authority helps few if any persons. N. T. Wright suggests that shorthand expressions, such as affirmations regarding one believing the Bible or affirming the authority of the Bible, are useful in ways similar to suitcases. Suitcases, states Wright,

> enable us to pick up lots of complicated things and carry them around all together. But we should never forget that the point of doing so, like the point of carrying belongings in a suitcase, is that what has been packed away can then be unpacked and put to use in the new location. Too much debate about scriptural authority has had the form of people hitting one another with locked suitcases. It is time to unpack our shorthand doctrines, to lay them out and inspect them. Long years in a suitcase may have made some of the contents go moldy. They will benefit from fresh air, and perhaps a hot iron.[3]

If we take Wright's advice seriously, perhaps we need to unpack and rethink the concept of biblical authority. Perhaps one needs to find a different or more constructive way of approaching the topic.

This essay reconsiders the authority of the Bible by focusing on that authority in *functional* rather than only *conceptual* terms. My contention is that we have gotten the proverbial cart before the horse when associate the authority of the Bible with concepts of inspiration *limited to the composition of the original biblical texts*. Such tendencies misplace the Bible's ultimate authority. They settle

instead for an incomplete understanding that, for all practical purposes, *minimizes* that authority for the contemporary church.

My suggestion is that we look again at the classic Christian understanding of inspiration. This view considers inspiration not only
as God's activity in the composition of the biblical texts. Rather,
inspiration also occurs *in the church's ongoing reading and engagement of the biblical texts*. This expanded view of inspiration
provides a fuller, more complete context for understanding the authority of the Bible.

Conceptual or Qualitative Authority

The common approach to the question regarding the authority
of the Bible is what is described here as "conceptual" or "qualitative" authority. I use the adjective "conceptual," because this
approach begins with particular affirmations about the Bible before ever reading the biblical texts. In many respects, these notions
about the Bible provide rationale for why we turn to the Bible and
not some other text(s). The common focus of such conversations
typically identifies specific qualities of the biblical texts that deem
these and not other texts as suitable, reliable, or trustworthy for
theological reflection. Attention to such qualitative issues about
the nature of the biblical texts usually directs these discussions to
various ways these texts reflect God's involvement in their writing.
In other words, the idea here is that something qualitatively different must make *these* texts (and not others) authoritative for the
church.

The conceptual approach to the Bible considers the canonical
texts the products of divine inspiration. Most people in the church
would not deny some sort of human involvement in the writing
of these sacred texts. But the focusing claim is that the inspiring
activity of God in that process somehow initiates, sanctifies, and
validates *these* texts over others. God's involvement makes these
texts reliable and trustworthy.

Although there may be some general agreement about issues such as inspiration, substantive differences spark ongoing, heated debates over who does and does not accept the Bible as authoritative. This may be due to concerns that skeptics have accentuated the human side of the Bible and downplayed God's role. The pendulum often swings to the other extreme, however, emphasizing the divine role to such an extent that it leads to downplaying if not eliminating the human contributions to the compositional processes of the Bible.

In these debates over inspiration, affirmations about inerrancy can be welcomed by some as correctives to perceived harmful arguments. Often overlooked are assumptions about the nature of God and humanity that may not reflect basic theological affirmations within the Wesleyan tradition. For some, setting aside Wesleyan theological beliefs is acceptable if it means affirming the trustworthiness of the Bible.[4] Such declarations about the inerrancy of the Bible falter, however, when faced with both the evidence of differing perspectives and details within the biblical texts themselves.[5] The reality is that affirmations about the error-free quality of the original autographs have no pragmatic value, because no autographs are known to exist. And none was used when translating our copies of the Bible.[6] Still, such concepts about the Bible and its qualities remain foundational for many when they assert something like scriptural authority.

The broader, more general perception of biblical inspiration focuses *primarily* on God's involvement in the composition of the biblical texts as the basis for biblical authority. It typically accepts a similar (though not identical) view of the Bible: it has inherent qualities because of God's role in the compositional process. God's role in the writing of the Bible often becomes the starting point for defining the authoritative role of the Bible in the Church.

Most Wesleyan theologians and biblical scholars recognize the problems associated with positions stressing biblical inerrancy with regard to biblical authority.[7] However, affirming divine inspiration of biblical writers as the *primary* means of defining biblical authority offers *neither* the necessary corrective *nor* an adequate alternative to the argument. The reason is rather simple. Although this move avoids issues that conflict with the biblical evidence, it still embraces *in principle* the idea that the Bible has inherent qualities that other texts or sources of authority do not. Thus, battles over the Bible and its authority focus attention and energy on competing concepts about what these biblical qualities may or may not be. These particular concepts about the Bible and its inherent qualities often become more authoritative than the Bible itself.[8]

I do not offer this brief assessment as a refutation of biblical authority or concepts of biblical interpretation. Rather, my observation is that arguments over biblical authority that depend *primarily* on particular notions that deal only with the writing of the respective biblical texts end up too often in unnecessary disputes. We observe the results in rifts within the church and in actions that do not show love for one's neighbor.

However, understanding biblical authority in conceptual or qualitative terms has some theological inadequacies. First, this approach does not address basic questions about authority, such as: "For whom are these texts authoritative?" and "For what are these texts authoritative?" Second, this approach to inspiration does not require commitments from those making such declarations to the witness of the Bible. It is one thing to believe such matters about the Bible or demonstrate detailed knowledge about the biblical materials themselves. It is a different thing to respond faithfully to what the Bible depicts, offers, says, and/or promotes. Third, this approach to inspiration has no correlation with faithful interpretation of the Bible. That is, no statement about the validity of the Bible guarantees the validity of one's interpretation of a biblical text.

The conceptual mode of biblical interpretation typically reduces the Bible to a depository of information. This mode neither acknowledges nor accounts for the important role of ongoing interpretive activities that both shape such activities and are shaped by them.[9] On the one hand, the conceptual approach restricts the text's meaning to the information carried in the text. It does not consider other affective matters typically associated with ancient texts. On the other hand, the text's meaning is restricted to historical categories associated with original historical contexts and authorial intention.[10] The point is not to minimize the importance of historical-critical work. But the notion of Christian canon suggests that other factors in addition to ones associated with the original historical context potentially (and probably should!) contribute to the church's reading and interpretation of the canonical texts.[11]

Overreliance on a conceptual or qualitative view of biblical authority provides an inadequate understanding of the role of the Bible for the church. These approaches have *misplaced* biblical authority by mistakenly associating it with inadequate or less-than-helpful views about the Bible's inherent qualities. Such approaches place their authoritative marbles in a basket with enough holes to render it ineffective.

Functional Authority

A brief look at the first centuries of the Christian church offers an alternative view of biblical authority. Long before the decision of the Council of Carthage (397) regarding the Christian canon, early Christian Fathers such as Irenaeus tell us that Christian texts (most notably the four Gospels and many of Paul's letters) were already functioning in authoritative ways within the church. Although the common belief is that this council's decision established the Christian canon and its authority within the church, the evidence suggests that both Jewish texts (i.e., the Septuagint) and a collection of Christian texts were already functioning authoritatively because of their formative role within the fledgling church.[12]

Such a functional understanding of the authority of the Bible mirrors what one finds with Jewish Scriptures.[13] Similar to the Jewish tradition, early Christians turned to these Jewish sacred texts composed originally for Israel as holding unique status within the church. These texts provided various witnesses to God's self-revelation and saving activity that redeemed and created a people belonging to God. Christians understood these texts were written and preserved for others. But they also read them in continuity with their understanding of the Christ-event. Such appropriation of the Jewish Scriptures granted these texts authoritative status, because they provided lenses through which to see, understand, and respond to God's actions within the Christ-event. The earliest Christians engaged through the Jewish Scriptures in what we may describe as an "integrative act of the imagination."[14] That is, they reflected theologically on God and themselves as God's "called ones" (ekklēsia) through their active and imaginative participation within the world of the biblical texts.

John Wesley and his theological descendants seem to have shared this functional understanding of the authority of the Bible. Wesleyans have consistently maintained the orthodox view of the Bible as authoritative regarding matters of salvation or Christian faith and practice.[15] Wesley's simple declaration about reading the Bible "to find the way to heaven"[16] reminds us that we should ultimately understand the authoritative nature of the Bible in the various ways that the Bible functions within the church to transform and shape her collective life.[17]

This soteriological function among those identified as God's people is what potentially distinguishes the *Bible* from the church's *Scriptures*.[18] The Bible functions authoritatively when the church engages the biblical texts as Scripture. The church not only writes or speaks about what these texts may say, but she also responds in potentially faithful ways to this God ... about whom these texts speak ... and who speaks to the church through these texts.[19]

Wesleyans cannot adequately speak about the Bible as authoritative without considering the church's mission and practices that provoke holy living among her people. This understanding of the authority of the Bible as the church's Scriptures focuses on the functional, (trans)formational role of these sacred texts within the life and practices of the church as the people of God.[20]

Two aspects of functional biblical authority provide helpful glimpses into understanding biblical authority. The first aspect has to do with the inspiration of the church in reading and interpreting the Bible as Scripture. Wesley's statement regarding 2 Timothy 3:16 in his *Explanatory Notes upon the New Testament* points us in helpful directions. "The Spirit of God not only once inspired those who wrote it, but continually inspires, supernaturally assists, *those that read it with earnest prayer*" (emphasis added).[21] In another context, Wesley reiterated that readers "need the same Spirit to understand the Scripture which enabled the holy men of old to write it."[22] Thus, Wesley insisted that the Spirit's inspiring activity complements or enlightens one's mind, so that the reader with the Spirit's inspiring assistance may explore and understand in some measure "the deep things of God."[23] As Randy Maddox states, "[T]he definitive revelation of God may come to us through Scripture but still be immediate because the Spirit who originally addressed the spiritual senses of the writers will also open our spiritual senses to perceive and attest to the truth they expressed."[24] In other words, only the Spirit's activity through the inspiration of biblical readers can transform the words of the Bible into *Scripture*.

Traditional approaches to biblical study over the last few centuries have typically left little or no room for the Spirit's work of inspiration in the interpretive process. I contend, however, that the words of the biblical texts remain dead and ineffective—no matter how much we affirm particular inherent qualities in the biblical texts or the inspiration of the biblical authors—without the Spirit's work within readers in the church who engage those texts.[25]

Literary theorists provide helpful insights into this process, not so much regarding the role of the Spirit but regarding the role of readers in the convergence with a text and the creation of meaning through that encounter. The reader's consistent and persistent evaluation and reevaluation of textual features in both conscious and sub-conscious ways provide the means by which any text comes to life.[26] However, there is no need to separate this work of the faithful, careful reader of the Bible from the work of the Spirit as that reader engages the biblical text as Scripture. These co-operative partners contribute to that sense of "inspired imagination," which enables those readers to envisage or discover potential meaning(s) about God and God's ongoing salvific activities through reading Scripture.[27]

In general ways, *this* is what the canonical process in those earliest centuries confirmed about these canonical texts (and not others): that God somehow spoke in formative ways through these particular texts, which was indicative of the Spirit's work of inspiration within the church. It is likely that early conversations about the inspiration of biblical writers only arose *after* the church's recognition of the effectiveness of these texts as indicative of the Spirit's work and involvement in her midst. In other words, the Church did not appropriate these texts as authoritative Scripture due to their perception of the biblical texts as having particular divine qualities. Rather, the Church appropriated these texts as authoritative Scripture because she "heard" God speak to her as God's people through them. The same rationale continues to describe the role of Scripture as the primary authority for the church's ongoing theological reflection and her identity as the people of God.

The second aspect of functional authority has to do with what constitutes the interpretation of Scripture. If the church is the context within which to read the Bible faithfully in cooperation with the inspiration of the Spirit, the evidence of its authoritative role as Scripture is the living out or the performance of the church's engagement with these sacred texts. That is, any evaluation of scriptural authority must include the reception of and response to the biblical texts as Scripture in the ongoing life of faithful Christian communities of faith. Granted, the validity of biblical interpretation has typically been discerned through a *new* set of words that seek to explain what the *old* set of words in a biblical passage might mean. However, the canonical process and the church's ongoing engagement of these texts as sacred Scripture suggest that these texts were collected together not merely because of what they stated but because of how they *functioned*. That is, behind the collection was what they *did* within the context of the Christian Church. "Getting it" or understanding the text has been and is evident not merely in another set of words. "Getting it" emerges from the church's faithful engagement with these texts as Scripture in terms of worship, practice, and response to others.[28] How respective Christian communities of faith live out, embody, or perform their encounters with the biblical texts reveals how these have functioned formatively as Scripture. Such outcomes disclose the actual importance and authority of these sacred texts for the church's life and practice.

If we consider this suggestion acceptable, subjects such as biblical interpretation and biblical authority no longer belong exclusively to the domains of pious conversations, intellectual debates of the academy, or arguments among talk radio enthusiasts. Rather, human life itself is now fair game. For if the church really does listen with the Spirit's assistance to the biblical texts as Scripture, both the *vocal* message of the church and her active, emergent life will disclose the authoritative role of the Scriptures. Statements about biblical authority and interpretation alone are no longer sufficient. The church's embodiment and performance of those interpretations are open for critical assessment as evidence of the Bible's authority within her as Scripture. Since the primary authoritative sense of the Christian canon is found in the ways that these texts function formatively, faithful living before God is an indispensable standard for the evaluation of biblical interpretation. Because the church's corporate activities will disclose the imaginative and improvisational dimensions of this kind of interpretation, the results will undoubtedly vary, especially among various theological traditions and local congregations.[29] However, a primary criterion for evaluation is the plausibility of these various interpretive performances as authentic, faithful responses to the biblical texts as Scripture. Without such "responsive" reading, talk about the authority of the Bible has limited or no value.[30]

The Bible as Scripture

When we unpack slogans about biblical authority and "believing the Bible" from suitcases of Christian apologists, we find concepts that may have been beneficial in other settings but now have different effects. There is much to affirm about inherent qualities of the biblical texts to which the church returns repeatedly. The hope is that our fresh readings of Scripture will somehow speak to and shape our Christian faith communities in meaningful ways. However, Wesleyans do not gather around these scriptural texts because they exude some sort of inherent divine qualities. Rather, Wesleyans gather to listen to these texts as Scripture, because they hope that, through the Spirit's assistance, they will continue to speak of a God who redeems and forms a people called to be God's very own. Wesleyans turn to these texts as Scripture, because these texts speak about God's salvific activities and cause them to think about and imagine what it might look like to "work out their own salvation" in contemporary settings.

This is the reason why the Bible continues to be the church's primary authority. To base claims of biblical authority upon ideas about inherent qualities of these texts not only *misplaces* that authority. It also *marginalizes* biblical authority from the ongoing life and practice of the contemporary church. In the end, such claims create unnecessary background noise that subtly squelches the biblical voices and distracts from carefully listening and faithfully responding to the Bible as Scripture.

I suggest we return scriptural authority to its rightful place by focusing on the formative role of the Bible as Scripture. The Bible is authoritative as it shapes and guides the church as faithful readers who seek to embody and perform the salvation, grace and compassion of the One who calls them and to whom these texts point.

---

1. "Preface to *Sermons on Several Occasions*, in *Works* (Bicentennial ed.), 1:105.

2. See the essay by Dennis Bratcher in this collection, which deals with this issue.

3. N. T. Wright, *The Last Word: Beyond the Bible Wars to a New Understanding of the Authority of Scripture* (San Francisco: Harper San Francisco, 2005), 24–25.

4. Cf. Craig D. Allert, *A High View of Scripture? The Authority of the Bible and the Formation of the New Testament Canon* (Evangelical Ressourcement; Grand Rapids: Baker Academic, 2007), 147–72, who helpfully works through significant issues regarding inerrancy, including the inconsistent use of the concept by its advocates.

5. E.g., note the differences between the perspectives of the Deuteronomist and the Chronicler, the details and perspectives of the four New Testament Gospels, the recounting of Abraham's call in Genesis (Gen 11:31–12:5) and in Acts (Acts 7:2–4), and the characterization of Paul in Acts and in Paul's letters (see Thomas E. Phillips's recent work, *Paul, His Letters, and Acts* [Grand Rapids: Baker Academic, 2010]).

6. Contemporary translations of the Bible are not based on any original autographs but on critical compilations of the biblical texts. Thus, arguments about the qualities of these autographs contribute little if anything to discussions about the translated Bible texts that the church typically reads.

7. See the essays by Dennis Bratcher, C. S. Cowles, and Michael Lodahl in this collection.

8. Cf. Allert, *A High View of Scripture*, 171–72.

9. Cf. Joel B. Green, *Seized by Truth: Reading the Bible as Scripture* (Nashville: Abingdon, 2007), 146–50. See also Stephen E. Fowl, *Engaging Scripture: A Model for Theological Interpretation* (Malden, MA: Blackwell, 1998), 32–61, who helpfully assesses typical approaches to biblical interpretation and argues for a theory of "underdetermined interpretation" that best suits Christian purposes for reading the Bible.

10. See Max Turner, "Historical Criticism and Theological Hermeneutics of the New Testament," in *Between Two Horizons: Spanning New Testament Studies and Systematic Theology* (ed. J. B. Green and M. Turner; Grand Rapids: Eerdmans, 2000), 44–70, who stresses the necessity of historical-critical work for theological interpretation.

11. See my "Scripture, Christian Canon, and Community: Rethinking Theological Interpretation Canonically," *Journal of Theological Interpretation* 4.2 (2010): 253–72. Cf. A. K. M. Adam, *Faithful Interpretation: Reading the Bible in a Postmodern World* (Minneapolis: Fortress, 2006); and Dale B. Martin, *Pedagogy of the Bible: An Analysis and Proposal* (Louisville: Westminster John Knox, 2008), who both deal with the problems associated with the overdependence of traditional biblical scholarship on historical-critical approaches to studying the Bible.

12. See the important work of William J. Abraham, *Canon and Criterion in Christian Theology* (Oxford: Oxford University Press, 1998), esp. 1–56.

13. See Eugene Ulrich, *The Dead Sea Scrolls and the Origins of the Bible* (Grand Rapids: Eerdmans, 1999), 75. Thanks to my colleague, Dr. W. Randy Bynum, for bringing this resource to my attention.

14. Richard B. Hays, *The Moral Vision of the New Testament: Community, Cross, New Creation; A Contemporary Introduction to New Testament Ethics* (San Francisco: HarperSanFrancisco, 1996), 6, See also A. K. M. Adam, "Poaching on Zion: Biblical Theology as Signifying Practice," in *Reading Scripture with the Church: Toward a Hermeneutic for Theological Interpretation* (Grand Rapids: Baker Academic, 2006), 31.

15. See, e.g., Scott J. Jones, *John Wesley's Conception and Use of Scripture* (Nashville: Kingswood, 1995), 222–23; Randy L. Maddox, *Responsible Grace: John Wesley's Practical Theology* (Nashville: Kingswood, 1994), 36–40; Donald A. D. Thorsen, *The Wesleyan Quadrilateral: Scripture, Tradition, Reason and Experience as a Model of Evangelical Theology* (Grand Rapids: Zondervan, 1990; reprint, Indianapolis: Light and Life, 1997), 135–39; Robert W. Wall, "Toward a Wesleyan Hermeneutic of Scripture," in *Reading the Bible in Wesleyan Ways: Some Constructive Proposals* (ed. B. L. Callen and R. P. Thompson; Kansas City, MO: Beacon Hill Press of Kansas City, 2004), 51–52; and Joel B. Green, "Is There a Contemporary Wesleyan Hermeneutic?" in *Reading the Bible in Wesleyan Ways*, 130–32.

16. "Preface" to *Sermons on Several Occasions*, in *Works* (Bicentennial ed.), 1:105.

17. See Wall, "Toward a Wesleyan Hermeneutic of Scripture," 39–55.

18. Cf. Stephen E. Fowl and L. Gregory Jones, *Reading in Communion: Scripture and Ethics in Christian Life* (Grand Rapids: Eerdmans, 1991), 20.

19. See the important work of Rob Wall, including "Facilitating Scripture's Future Role Among Wesleyans," in *Reading the Bible in Wesleyan Ways*, 112–15; and "The Significance of a Canonical Perspective of the Church's Scriptures," in *The Canon Debate* (ed. L. M. McDonald and J. A. Sanders; Peabody, MA: Hendrickson, 2002), 529–31.

20. See A. K. M. Adam, Stephen E. Fowl, Kevin J. Vanhoozer, and Francis Watson, *Reading Scripture with the Church: Toward a Hermeneutic for Theological Interpretation* (Grand Rapids: Baker Academic, 2006), who identify the church as the context for the reading and interpretation of the Bible as Scripture.

21. John Wesley, *Explanatory Notes upon the New Testament* (London: Epworth Press, 1958), 794.

22. Wesley, "A Letter to the Right Reverend the Lord Bishop of Gloucester," in *Works*, 11:509. See also *Explanatory Notes upon the Old Testament*, 1:ix.

23. Wesley, "An Earnest Appeal to Men of Reason and Religion," in *Works*, 11:57. See also Wesley, "The Case of Reason Impartially Considered," in *Works*, 2:592.

24. Maddox, *Responsible Grace*, 31.

25. See my "Inspired Imagination: John Wesley's Concept of Biblical Inspiration and Literary-Critical Studies," in *Reading the Bible in Wesleyan Ways*, 57–79.

26. See Thompson, "Inspired Imagination," 66–73.

27. See Thompson, "Inspired Imagination," 73–79.

28. Cf. A. K. M. Adam, "Poaching on Zion: Biblical Theology as Signifying Practice," 28; Fowl and Jones, *Reading in Communion*, 20.

29. See Adam, *Faithful Interpretation*, 98–99, who suggests that one should not be surprised that the same biblical texts may be interpreted differently among the variety of ecclesial contexts, with not only their different theological lenses but also their different practices. See also Fowl, *Engaging Scripture*, 75–83, where he considers the importance of "vigilant communities" to safeguard churches from erroneous interpretations of the Bible.

30. Cf. Hays, *The Moral Vision of the New Testament*, 7.

5

Thinking about the Bible Theologically: Inerrancy, Inspiration, and Revelation[1]

Dennis R. Bratcher

Credibility and Inerrancy

If the purpose of theology is to communicate what we understand about God, we should communicate clearly. That is as much a function of language in a culture as it is about truth. If the meaning of a theological term has shifted so that it is no longer clear, we should find a term that communicates better.

This is the situation with the term "inerrant" or "inerrancy" applied to Scripture. People have used that term in the past as a faith confession to affirm the Bible as a reliable guide for the church's faith and practice. But it has now come to signify ideological agendas that often divide and judge other Christians. This creates *more* controversy and debate. And it rarely communicates anything positive about the Christian faith or Scripture.

In the larger social scene, the concept of the inerrancy of Scripture may have the opposite effect than its proponents intend. Advocates intend to affirm Scripture's authority and value as the sole guide to the Christian faith, the source of inspired instruction for meeting the spiritual and ethical challenges of our world. In many cases, however, it has weakened the credibility of Scripture and created pain within the church.

We could better maintain the Bible's credibility before skeptics and provide a more positive witness to God's transforming grace by discarding the concept of inerrancy many advocate today. It creates more problems than it solves. Wesleyans can affirm the truth, authority, and reliability of Scripture far better on other grounds.

Roots of the Modern Inerrancy Debate

a. Response against skeptics

Beyond the problem of communication, a problem with the argument for scriptural inerrancy is that it is based on a very modern and quite rationalistic premise. The modern debate arose early in the twentieth century. It developed in the 1970's as a defense against skeptics who launched some scathing attacks against Scripture's authority from the perspective of historical positivism and scientific naturalism. In their zeal to defend Scripture, however, many Christians tried to defend the Bible on alien rationalistic turf. They fought the "battle for the Bible" largely in areas far removed from Scripture itself.

The scientific premise that forms the basis for modern historiography affirms that only empirically verifiable events can be accepted as true. Skeptics say that because records or empirical data could not verify many biblical events, they must not have occurred. The accounts were not true and were in error.

Of course, defenders assumed the Bible to be true. But the defense took shape as a logical syllogism. *Because* the Bible is true (an assumption), and *because* only verifiable historical events can be true (the rationalists' premise), *then* the Bible must contain only actual, verifiable historical events. In this, we have the birth of inerrancy as a rationalistic response to the rationalists.

A similar line of reasoning developed against those who assumed historical positivism as the only way to explain human history. Historical positivism rejects any metaphysical aspect of reality.

It assumes a closed world in which one can explain historical events in a cause-and-effect relationship with other historical events.

To counter this, defenders adopted a near total metaphysical explanation of history in which God was the prime cause of all human history. God was "in control" of all human events, so there was no need for any other explanation for human history. Scripture recorded what happened, both past and future. It was inerrant because it simply told what God caused to unfold. From that perspective, prophecy is "prewritten history."

The logic here rests on accepting the premises of the rationalists, then defining Scripture in a way that answers them on those grounds. However, many never asked whether the Bible was ever intended to be provable by the standards of scientific empiricism.

b. Role of Reformed thought

Another factor came into play in the development of the inerrancy debate. Most defenders in the early stages were from the Reformed (or Calvinist) tradition, especially those with fundamentalist leanings. This cast the debate from the beginning in terms of specific theological concerns. Two closely related theological ideas from that tradition steered that debate: the emphasis on the total sovereignty of God and the total depravity of humanity.

Wesleyans accept the basic theological idea of depravity as a way to affirm the need for God's grace. They deny that humans are inherently good and can choose good on their own. In the Reformed tradition, however, evil will always dominate humanity. God can forgive humans for their sinfulness, pardon them, and count them as righteous. But they will always exist in this world as imperfect, flawed, and sinful creatures. Some would say they couldn't even choose God, so God in God's sovereignty must choose for them (predestination).

Because of the total depravity of humanity, the emphasis on the complete and absolute sovereignty of God comes to the foreground. From the Reformed perspective, God's sovereignty is understood as the absolute of everything, described in terms of "omni-" (all), infinity, perfection, and similar superlatives. God's sovereignty in this absolute sense extends even to human decision and the flow of human history. Nothing occurs in God's creation without God specifically willing that it should occur. Human freedom is subsumed within God's sovereignty or denied altogether.

Many applied the ideas of God's total control to Scripture. This naturally leads to believing that *God* must have written Scripture. God could *never* trust sinful, flawed, and imperfect humans with Scripture, because they would introduce errors and destroy its reliability. God is the sole author of Scripture. From this conclusion came the idea of inerrancy that emphasizes God's control of Scripture's production and preservation, with the attendant theories of inspiration that would support such a view (dictation and some forms of verbal inspiration).

Another logical syllogism came into play. *Because* God wrote Scripture, and *because* God is perfect and without error, and *because* God knows exactly what happened, *then* the Bible must be absolutely accurate and inerrant in everything it says. The Bible is even accurate in the things that it does not say that we now know to be fact (the earth is round, the solar system is heliocentric, matter consists of atoms, etc.).

This view of scriptural inerrancy developed in a context containing the pressures of culture as well as some very specific theological agendas. I think those who adopt this view read the Bible through the lens developed totally outside Scripture itself. They do so without taking seriously the evidence *within* Scripture. Inerrantists made the Bible serve the doctrine of inerrancy. This move runs counter to a primary tenet of the Reformation: that Scripture is the primary authority for the church's faith and practice.

The entire issue of inerrancy is alien to the Wesleyan tradition for several theological and historical reasons. The modern concept of inerrancy arises out of Reformed fundamentalism that blends a basic position in predeterminism (predestination) with a narrow rationalism to defend Scripture against the excesses of scientific positivism and naturalism.

The motive may have been valid in the face of atheistic naturalism and rationalistic modes of thought. However, there developed a serious overreaction. Defenders of Scripture asserted things about Scripture that neither the Bible itself nor some theological positions outside of a narrowly interpreted Calvinism can possibly sustain.

Inerrant Autographs

These observations usually lead to another topic that enters the conversation: the affirmation of the inerrancy of the Bible's original autographs. An "autograph" is the original manuscript from the hand of its original author.

Those who work with Scripture in the original languages know that our biblical text has errors in spelling, grammar, and syntax. There are hundreds of differences in wording among different ancient manuscripts of the biblical text. We sometimes forget that the Bible was not written on a computer. There is no "master text" of the Bible. We only have it in hundreds, even thousands, of manuscripts that contain differences of greater or lesser degree. Our modern translations are based on the analysis and comparison of these manuscripts.

A careful examination of parallel biblical accounts, where the same story or account occurs in more than one place, reveals many differences. For example, in the Gospels there are many places where the accounts of Jesus' activity and sayings are recorded in versions that vary from each other.

There are places where the events are ordered differently (e.g., the cleansing of the temple or the day and time of the crucifixion in the synoptic Gospels and John). The same sayings of Jesus are often set in different contexts (e.g., Sermon on the Mount, Matt 5–7; Sermon on the Plain, Luke 6). Sometimes, different sayings accompany the same event (e.g., the confession of Peter in Matthew and Mark). Different Greek words are often attributed to Jesus: some are closely synonymous, some give a different nuance to the saying (e.g., Matt 5:3, 6; Luke 6:20–21).

If we approach the biblical text without the presuppositions of inerrancy, we also find historical difficulties. Some biblical accounts do not correspond to what we know of the events. Some events are recounted in different places within Scripture in considerably different scenarios. There are also discrepancies in the use of numbers, genealogies, scriptural citations, and other matters.

For many, these factors present no serious hindrances to accepting the Bible as authoritative Scripture. They understand and interpret the message as it is presented with these factors in mind. However, these are potentially fatal observations to the inerrantist position. One can allow none of these to stand in an absolutist position that many inerrantists take. Although one can explain some issues, difficulties with the biblical text present problems for inerrant views. Inaccuracies exist within the text.

For some innerantists, the solution to this problem is to affirm that only the *original* writings were inerrant. They suppose the original versions were without any inaccuracies when they left the author's hand. They allege that the process of transmission, copying, and translation over the years corrupted our copies. This position of "inerrant autographs" maintains inerrancy in the face of contrary textual evidence.

The practice is unhelpful. It offers nothing helpful in the actual study and use of Scripture in the church beyond making affirmations *about* its original condition. After all, the text we have now *does* have inaccuracies in some details. This practice allows someone to maintain the concept of inerrancy by moving it back to a context where the assertion's validity cannot be tested (since we have no autographs).

It is problematic to assert something about Scripture in a way that we cannot confirm in the light of very different evidence that we *can* confirm. This is more about rationalizing a flawed idea – biblical inerrancy – than about good theology or good biblical study.

Theological problems also arise. If God supervised Scripture's writing so that people produced inerrant writings, why could God not, or why *didn't* God, oversee the text's transmission throughout history so the Bible remained inerrant as people copied it? What is the purpose of having inerrant originals if God did not maintain their inerrancy?

If we allow this, how do we know we can trust the Bibles we have today? After all, these are admittedly inaccurate in some details. If the trustworthiness of the text depends on its inerrancy, how do we affirm its reliability when the Bible we use is not inerrant?

Still another set of problems clusters around the idea of autographs. This assumes that there was at one time a single master copy of Scripture or at least of individual books. But this assumes a certain mode of inspiration and production of Scripture that is not totally supported by the evidence or most ways of understanding how Scripture came to be.

"Autographs" as an idea assumes that a single person wrote individual books of Scripture, at a single time. But this idea eliminates most views of inspiration that allow a role for the community of faith over a period of time to produce Scripture as God worked within the community.

Related to this is the idea of "sources" used for the Gospels or the Pentateuch. Most biblical scholars acknowledge that the Gospels were written from earlier sources that preserved Jesus' teachings in the nearly 40–60 years between his life and the writings of the first Gospels. If the Gospel writers used sources, were those sources also inerrant? If so, on what basis do we affirm that the *sources* were inerrant, because they were not Scripture? What theory of inspiration do we invoke to argue that non-inerrant sources can become inerrant by being placed within a different context?

In sum, pushing inerrancy back to the original manuscripts actually creates more problems than it solves. The problem here is in asserting something *about* the Bible that has very little to do with Scripture as we actually have it.

Revelation and Inspiration: The Foundation in Scripture

Part of the difficulty in the inerrancy debate is understanding Scripture in terms of (a) God's self-revelation in history and (b) inspiration. These are complicated topics, but let me raise the issues in relation to the inerrancy debate. What follows is not definitive or exhaustive. It is one way to address the nature of Scripture and move beyond inerrancy debates.

a. Revelation

The concept of revelation lies at the heart of the Christian faith. We Christians believe God uniquely revealed Godself in human history. Christians do not believe that we first seek and find God. We believe that God chose to reveal Godself to us. Both Judaism and Christianity are responses to God's self-disclosure.

The *content* of revelation is not primarily information or data (propositions). It is *God*.[2] It is self-revelation or self-disclosure, not primarily revelation about things or ideas. Much of the early church, following Augustine, understood all knowledge as revealed by God. This was in contrast to Aristotle, who held that the senses can apprehend some knowledge, as we do now in scientific research.[3]

The idea that all knowledge about everything comes by revelation from God made its way into modern thinking, particularly through the Calvinistic tradition that uses God's sovereignty as a primary theological category. This has relevance in our present discussion of Scripture, because many people view Scripture as God's direct revelation of all knowledge and data. Such a view sees

Scripture in absolute categories. This perspective most often uses the terms "inerrant" and "infallible" to describe the Bible.

However, I do not view Scripture in such terms. I do not understand the Bible to be *direct* revelation. And I do not consider it revelation about *everything*. Scripture is the witness that the community of faith has given about revelation. God is the content of the revelation, and Scripture tells us about that revelation and points toward it. For example, the Gospel writers bear witness of the things they have seen and heard (Luke 1:1–4; cf. 7:22; John 21:24–25; cf. 3:32).

Scripture is revelatory only in the secondary sense that it witnesses and responds to God's revelation. The Bible contains reports about specific revelatory events like the exodus and incarnation. It contains how the communities of faith worked out implications of their encounters with God in doctrinal, social, ethical, and cultural ways (*didache*, "teaching").

For example, we can see the Gospels as the proclamation of God's revelation in Jesus Christ. We can also see Paul's writings as teaching the implications of that revelation and guiding the community in proper response (e.g., "live your life in a manner worthy of the Gospel of Christ"; Phil 2:27 NRSV). We can use the same analogy in seeing the Old Testament connection between the exodus (proclamation) and the giving of the *Torah* at Sinai.[4]

God is revealed to us today through *interpreted* events. God revealed Godself in history (events), and the community of faith interpreted those events in what we now have as Scripture. We have no direct access to those events. We only have mediated access through the witness of the community.

This does not eliminate an objective ground to God's revelation. In fact, it affirms the objective basis in history of God's self-disclosure. But the testimony to God's self-disclosure is not objective in the same sense as the event. This is because part of that testimony is also the interpreted "significance" or "meaning" of that event in relation to *past events*, *present experience*, and *future implications*. That is, that testimony is theological (talking about God) in nature. It is also historical, not because it merely reports data, but because it tells us the ongoing significance of events.

The Scriptures reflect the dynamic of the "story of God" as it was woven into the life of the community of faith through the centuries. When we read, preach, or interpret that story, we add other historical dimensions. We bring ourselves into interaction with the text and apprehend significance and meaning from the text.

This suggests that the "story of God" was told in ways that were influenced by the people who told the story. And it suggests the story will be influenced by people who hear it. While the testimony is true, the characteristics of these people who passed on the testimony through the centuries and grappled with it shaped that testimony. We find their contributions in the vehicle of that testimony: their culture, language, knowledge (or lack of it), historical experience, personality, ethos, etc. Therefore, Scripture as we have it has a dual nature. It is the story of divine revelation (word of God …) told in the vehicle of culturally conditioned literature (. . . in human words).

We hear the story in culturally conditioned ways. We bring our own culture, language, knowledge (or lack of it), historical experience, personality, ethos, and the like to the biblical text when we read it. And we grapple with its implications in living out being the people of God. If we take this dual nature of Scripture seriously, we need theories of biblical inspiration that will also take seriously the word of God in human words.

b. Inspiration

This brings us to the issue of *how* the community bore witness to God, *how* it understood God to be at work in these events, and *how* we know that their testimony is true. It also raises in a secondary way the issue of how we can come to terms with Scripture if it is to be our story as well. How we understand revelation greatly influences how we talk about the inspiration of Scripture.

There are various theories of inspiration of Scripture. The basic issue in dealing with inspiration is the balance between the dual nature of Scripture: *divine* and *human*. Usually inspiration has to do with the work of God in the process. In Christian tradition, this is usually associated with the work of the Holy Spirit as the agent of truth. One can conceive inspiration, in a way, as "in-Spirited" (cf. 2 Tim 3:16–17; 2 Pet 1:20–21). But this does not resolve the question of balance.

On one side are the dictation and verbal theories. They affirm almost exclusively the *divine* role in the writing of Scripture. These theories are heavily influenced by an absolute sovereignty of God model that allows little human input. After all, those who affirm these theories typically also think sin totally contaminates humans. Such contaminated humans cannot be trusted. In these views, Scripture is equated with the mind of God. The physical text is perceived as the locus of inspiration and revelation of absolute truth.

On the other side are elevation theories. They affirm almost exclusively the *human* role in the writing of Scripture. These are heavily influenced either by rationalistic, naturalistic, or deistic models that do not see God active in the world. Or they are shaped by atheistic or agnostic thinking that do not acknowledge anything other than humanity. In these views, Scripture is a book reflecting the same kind of elevated human insight that one might find in Shakespeare, Tolkien, or *Harry Potter*. Here, the writers themselves are the only sources of the writing.

Between these two are various blends. The mediating position is usually called "dynamic inspiration," which tries to balance the roles of God and humans.

In many of these dynamic perspectives, the text is not inspired *per se*. Instead, *the writers* or *the message* is considered inspired. What the writers understand and write is not solely a product of their own thinking. Rather, the Scriptures are the project of what the activity of God enabled through the biblical writers.

Any adequate theory of inspiration must take into consideration three crucial factors. First, it must take seriously the faith confession that (a) God is active in the world, (b) God reveals Godself to humanity, and (c) there is a dimension to God that human reason or experience alone cannot access.

Second, it must deal honestly with the phenomena of Scripture itself. This means dealing with the text of the Bible as we now have it. An adequate theory of inspiration cannot appeal to versions of the biblical text that no longer exist.

Third, an adequate theory must be consistent or compatible with the larger Wesleyan theological understanding of human beings that arises from Scripture. This is especially the case in terms of prevenient grace. This Wesleyan doctrine says God "goes before" and enables creaturely responses, which impacts discussion of human moral freedom.

The best dynamic theories of inspiration balance divine and human involvement in Scripture. I see the locus of inspiration neither in the physical text nor in single writers, but in the message of Scripture: what it tells us about God, ourselves, and how we relate to God. It is not just inspiration as a collection of facts. It is inspiration operative in the message as a witness to the transforming power of God's grace in people's lives!

c. Revelation, inspiration, and the production of Scripture

Without delving too deeply into various possible modes of inspiration within a dynamic understanding, let me explain how the process works in the production of Scripture. It all begins with God revealing God's own self. This revelation may occur to the entire community in historical events like the exodus or incarnation. Those events may be more specific, like the return from exile, Jesus' death, or the resurrection. The revelation may also be to individuals within that community, such as Abraham at Mount Moriah, Moses at the burning bush, or Paul on the Damascus road.

With any divine revelation, however, there must be a response from the community or the person. They must understand the event and communicate its meaning to those who did not directly experience it. They must also translate that revelation into practical living.

God helps people understand revelation through inspiration. Inspiration begins at the point of God enabling people—"in-spiriting" them— to understand God's self-revelatory actions for human living. However, exactly *how* people respond to that revelation, talk about it, tell it, theologize about it, pass it on in tradition, incorporate it into ethical and doctrinal systems, etc., are all influenced by human factors.

People do not pass on eternal, absolute truths devoid of any context. They tell the story of God, which God revealed and helped them understand. But they tell it in their own way. They translate God's revelation into the language, metaphors, symbols, liturgy, and literature. They speak it so other people can hear and understand the testimony.

Inspiration is not the one-time action of God only related to the original revelatory event or the "original" author. Inspiration is the ongoing work of God, whereby God continues to help people understand the message. Inspiration is not static and located at a specific point in time, any more than God is static.

Inspiration is God's work as the witnesses tell the story, enabling them to bear faithful testimony to God. God also enables people who hear the story to understand and respond to the witness to God. In this sense, there is some connection between the idea of inspiration and the Wesleyan doctrine of prevenient grace.

The work of God enabling people to understand extends to the entire community of faith. God is at work in that community as God helps them to understand and to respond to that testimony. As the community does its lawmaking, developing ethical standards,

constructing theology, etc., God helps the entire community understand the things of God. It is a faith community, not just because it
believes a certain set of doctrines or ideas. It is a faith community
also because God is within the community and its individuals, guiding them as the people of God.

So inspiration is an ongoing, dynamic process. We find it in
Moses seeing the burning bush and understanding that this was
God, telling Zipporah when he got home that night, telling the
Israelites what God revealed to him, and later telling Pharaoh. But
it extends far beyond that. God was still at work helping people
understand as this story was told centuries later to Israelites gathered around a family Passover table in David's kingdom, as children
heard the story about God's deliverance and recalled God's great
acts of the past.

We find inspiration as scribes centuries later incorporated that
faith confession into a compilation of writings telling the marvelous
story of God's deliverance and creation of a people. To that story
were added priestly, liturgical instructions for proper observance
of Passover and the importance of proper response to the God
who heard the cries of oppressed slaves. Still later, God helped the
community understand as they further incorporated an analysis of
their own failure as God's people. Exilic and post-exilic prophets
and scribes told the story again, but in the context of catastrophic
failure that ended in exile. The story took on new significance a
century later as exiles returned home. They interpreted the return
from exile as a second exodus as they learned new depths of God's
grace and forgiveness.

As they collected these stories, God helped them understand
their history. They used certain writings within the faith community, because God helped them understand that this way of seeing
their history was a faithful interpretation of how God worked with
them in centuries past.

We could track this process even further into the development of the canon. Even today, as we sit in a twenty-first century living room and read the stories again, the work of Holy Spirit helps us understand the message. We are able to hear again the testimony to the revelation of God. When a preacher or teacher studies the passage and then proclaims it on Sunday morning or leads a class, we find inspiration as God helps her understand something about God and helps the people who hear it respond!

That is why any reading or study of Scripture should begin with the prayer, "Lord, help us understand." It is an acknowledgment of that dynamic quality of inspiration and a confession that finally, after we do all we can to understand, God brings the testimony alive. God makes it a living and active word!

But the vehicle of that message is dependent on the people. There are cultural oddities, of course. There are personal idiosyncrasies. There are discrepancies of fact, science, grammar, spelling, and data. There are different perspectives from different people from different cultures on different continents over a span of 1,800 years. There are inconsistencies in historical data, the use of symbols, and views about future events. Sometimes, leaders went far beyond the old law codes and invented new responses to ethical challenges (Nehemiah). Sometimes, new understandings challenged old orthodoxies (Job, Jonah). Sometimes, in one historical situation, one view was valid. In another historical situation, the opposite view was valid (Deuteronomy, Jeremiah). Sometimes, writers emphasized one aspect and sometimes another, and sometimes those are not directly reconcilable (Proverbs, Leviticus). As Walter Brueggemann put it, there are voices and counter voices, as very human people living in a very real world try to live and apply what they have come to understand about God in radically different and constantly changing contexts.[5]

Throughout all of it, we find God's story! Or perhaps better, it is a story of God! Affirming a dynamic view of inspiration allows the truth about God revealed to us to be faithfully and accurately preserved by the faith community. This takes seriously the faith confession that God is active in the world, God reveals Godself to humanity, and there is a dimension to God that human reason or experience cannot access. In this sense, the Bible is God's word.

A dynamic view of inspiration is very close to the Wesleyan perspective of the balance between God's grace and God-granted human freedom. Contrary to some Christian faith traditions, Wesleyans affirm that God's prevenient grace enables people to respond freely to God and that God's ongoing grace genuinely transforms people. Wesleyans do not believe that human beings are so perverted and corrupted by sin that they can never be righteous or understand the things of God. We believe that God can enable people by God's grace to be righteous rather than simply considered as righteous.

If we believe that, we should believe that God could entrust people with the testimony to God's grace as God continually works with them individually and communally. If God could entrust the Savior of the world to a young Jewish girl from Galilee, surely God can trust the testimony to that event to Jesus' disciples and to the community of faith.

Just as our lives reflect the working together of God's grace and our response, Scripture as the testimony of God's people also demonstrates that same working together. In some sense, there is an incarnational dimension to Scripture: it is truth about God incarnated into the words of human beings. Just as we were called to recognize and respond to the incarnated Word of God in Jesus, we are called to recognize and respond to the incarnated word of God in Scripture. Only then, in the recognition and response, Scripture becomes the living and active word of God (Heb 4:12).

---

1. This essay is an adapted version of the article "The Modern Inerrancy Debate" that is available on the website of CRI/Voice, Institute (http://www.crivoice.org), which has been developed by the author.

2. Or, in philosophical categories, knowledge about God. However, I would prefer to leave God as the *subject* of revelation rather than its *object*, or to leave it in relational categories rather than ontological ones.

3. Interestingly enough, this was a view shared to some degree by the Israelites in the Old Testament wisdom traditions (e.g., Proverbs).

4. I say "by analogy" here because they are both now Scripture for us, which makes it more difficult for us to divide the categories up so neatly.

5. This idea was first presented in *The Prophetic Imagination* (Philadelphia: Fortress, 1978) as the biblical tension between the voices of stability and the voices of change, Since then, the idea has become a central feature of Brueggemann's understanding of Old Testament theology. See Walter Brueggemann, *Old Testament Theology: Essays on Structure, Theme, and Text* (Minneapolis: Fortress, 1992).

6

"Behold, I Show You a More Excellent Way"
Scripture, Salvation, and Inerrancy
C. S. Cowles

W hy does the Church of the Nazarene in its Article of Faith on Holy Scripture limit inerrancy to "all things necessary to salvation?" If there are errors in any part of the Scriptures, how can we trust them to tell us the truth about salvation?

Scriptural inerrancy has been a hotly debated and deeply divisive issue in many churches for over a hundred years. Whole denominations have split over it, as have seminaries, colleges, and local congregations.

It was in the hope of escaping these divisive disputes that the Church of the Nazarene avoided its use. It was only under pressure from a vocal minority at the height of the early twentieth-century Fundamentalist-Modernist controversies that the General Assembly inserted the adverb "inerrantly" into the Manual. In doing so, however, they limited questions about inerrancy *specifically* to the revelation of God's will regarding "all things necessary for salvation." They were rightly concerned as has been the church since apostolic times that focusing undue attention upon what Paul calls "the letter of the law" (Rom 2:27 NASB) would detract from the living Word of God, Jesus of Nazareth, "in whom all fullness of the Deity lives in bodily form" (Col 2:9 NIV). This concern is more relevant today than ever.

If there are errors in any part of the Scriptures, wonder many people, how can we trust these sacred texts to tell us the truth about salvation? We can trust them according to the same standard we apply to virtually all other forms of human communication verbal and written. That is, we do not ask that they are free from incidental errors. We ask if they tell the *essential* truth about that which is being said. If this were not the case, I would have to stop conversing with family and friends, question everything I hear, and cease reading all newspapers, magazines, books, and letters from my grandchildren.

My highway map, for instance, has a notation in the bottom right hand corner that a mile equals $1/10^{th}$ of an inch when it is actually 5,280 feet long—quite a striking discrepancy. Further, every map has a certain amount of distortion embedded in it, because it is impossible for cartographers to render with complete accuracy a curved earth on a flat sheet of paper. Nevertheless, we do not ask that a map be free from inaccuracies and a certain amount of distortion. We ask expect it to guide us unerringly to our destination.

In like manner, we do not ask that the Bible be free from human errors such as when Isaiah speaks of "the four corners of the earth" (Isa 11:12) or when Joshua commands the "sun to stand still" (Josh 10:13), reflective of a pre-Copernican cosmology. However, we do believe that when read through the lens of God's full and final self-revelation in Christ and with the illuminating aid of the Holy Spirit, the Scriptures can be trusted to lead us unerringly into "all things necessary for our salvation" and to guide us in living a holy life (2 Tim 3:14–17). Millions of believers across many centuries can attest to the fact that "the gospel . . . is the power of God that brings salvation to everyone who believes" (Rom 1:16 NIV).

Most Wesleyan denominations, like the great family of churches from the first century until 1881,[1] have avoided ascribing inerrancy to the Scriptures on those matters that *do not* pertain to the essential core of scriptural truth. They have done so for a number of good reasons. I will mention only a few.

1. The Bible is a vast, diverse, and richly textured book.

The Bible resists our squeezing it into one descriptive word, no matter how succinct. This is especially true of a non-biblical word like the adjective "inerrant." Unfortunately, American fundamentalists loaded up an inherently benign word with claims that the Bible does not make about itself, that the Church Fathers and Reformers never made, and that do not accord with the Bible's contents or purposes. Nearly three hundred Calvinistic evangelical scholars gathered in Chicago in 1978 to establish the International Council on Biblical Inerrancy. Out of it came the "Chicago Statement" that built upon these fundamental propositions:

> The Bible, being wholly and *verbally* God given, is without error or fault in all of its teaching in not only its witness to God's saving grace in individual lives, but *in all matters of that which it speaks,* not only in the whole but in *every part.* . . . The Holy Spirit [is] Scripture's divine author. . . . We affirm the unity and internal consistency of Scripture. . . . *We affirm that what Scripture says, God says* (emphasis added).

Inerrancy's logic is deceptively simple. God verbally dictated the Bible. God does not lie. Therefore, every word in the Bible is true.

That "God verbally dictated the Bible," however, has no scriptural support. The phrase derives from John Calvin's (1509–1564) theology of divine determinism. Calvin taught that all events are predetermined and governed by God's secret plan in such a way that nothing happens except what God knowingly and willingly decrees. Fundamentalists in the Calvinist tradition apply this view of God to the Scriptures. Because God is righteous and perfect, every word in the Bible must of necessity be righteous and perfect as well. Inerrancy's seductive appeal lies in that it offers believers something physical and tangible: a secure 'rock,' upon which to build their faith in a turbulent and scary world.

Catholic Christians claim to have an infallible Pope. Muslims say that have an infallible Qur'an. Christian inerrantists believe they have an infallible Bible.

The claim of an absolutely inerrant Bible works until we begin to read the Bible itself. We quickly discover that the contents of the Bible do not fit into that simple and reductionist box. While the Scriptures faithfully record the witness of "men [who] spoke from God" (2 Pet 1:21), many voices other than that of God are heard in the Bible. Other voices include Satan, demons, false prophets, pagans, idol worshippers, liars, thieves, murderers, adulterers, betrayers, deniers, and fools. It is hard to imagine that all these disparate voices are speaking inerrant and infallible words of God.

A "more excellent way" of thinking about the plethora of human and even anti-divine personalities who speak and act throughout the Bible is to recognize that contrary to Calvin's teaching, God not only created human beings with genuine freedom but also allowed them to exercise their free will and express themselves accordingly. In doing so, God was not the least bit threatened by what they might say or do. God did not determine that the serpent in the Garden or Jacob or King David or anybody else lie. Rather, God took twisted strands of falsehood and foolishness and wove them with the truth about God's life into a wondrous tapestry of "God-breathed" revelation. This revelation brings glory to God's name. And it contributes to the overarching purpose of Scripture, which is the salvation of lost humankind.

Truth is multidimensional and many faceted. It is not only the red hue that makes a rainbow, but blue and green as well. Each color is distinctively different from the others. But working together, they form a breathtaking celestial display. So it is with the Bible.

2. The Bible must be read inductively and interpreted on its own terms.

The doctrine of scriptural inerrancy did not originate from a careful study of the Bible. It originated in a pitched battle waged by Calvinistic theologians against Enlightenment scholars who critiqued the Scriptures on supposedly scientific grounds. The first principle of scientific investigation, according to the seventeenth-century father of modern philosophy, Rene Descartes, was 'radical doubt." Everything must first be doubted before it can be proved.

While initial doubt works well when studying the physical universe, it is devastating when applied to the Bible. For Scripture, the first principle is not doubt but faith. Radical skeptics questioned the historicity of biblical events, ruled out all supernatural phenomena, and denied the deity of Jesus. In their hands, the Bible was reduced to just another sacred book among many in the history of religions.

Rather than respond to each point of the critics' attacks, it was easier for defenders of the faith. Charles Hodge and Benjamin Warfield simply declared that the whole Bible is the "inerrant and infallible word of God."

The problem with these early fundamentalists was not their intent. Like Christians everywhere, they desired to declare boldly their faith in *the essential trustworthiness of the Bible* in the story what it proclaims and all that it affirms. Rather, the problem was the questionable word they embraced and the fallacious argument they used to advance their cause.

The term "inerrant" works well with propositional statements that can, according to the normal rules of logic and empirical investigation, be verified or falsified. But it is grossly inadequate to deal with the diverse texture of human experience and the vast realm of spiritual reality that comprises most of the contents of the Bible. The adjective "inerrant," for instance, is appropriate when describing the computer printout of my bank statement (hopefully!). But it becomes nonsensical when applied to George Fredrick Handel's

Messiah, or Michelangelo's breath-taking panorama of *Creation* splayed across St. Peter's Sistine Chapel ceiling.

The overwhelming weight of biblical contents has much more affinity with art than with science. To tell its story, the Bible utilizes a diverse, rich, and wondrous collage of literary art: narrative, poetry, parable, drama, personification, metaphor, simile, analogy, history, genealogies, letters, fables, prophecy, apocalyptic, symbols, and every sort of figurative speech. When Isaiah says, "The mountains and hills will burst into song before you, and all the trees of the field will clap their hands" (Isa 55:12 NIV), it would be absurd to ask: Is that a true or false statement?

There is "a more excellent way" of looking at the Bible. Rather than superimposing modern technical notions about inerrancy upon ancient Scriptural texts—concepts utterly alien to the pre-scientific world of the Bible—we should read them as devotees have done throughout history. We should accept them as they are in all their vast, varied, and rich diversity. When we set out on this fascinating adventure, the often fallible, sometimes troubling, frequently surprising, but endlessly intriguing human-divine dance that leaps, soars, and sings throughout the Bible will captivate us. We discover that the Scriptures convey not only divinely revealed truth essential to salvation and holy living but also blend in the full coloration of the vast range of human experience in all its grossness and grandeur.

3. The Bible is not only divine but also human … *very human indeed.*

In the inerrantist's praiseworthy desire to take the "God-breathed" dimension of the Scriptures with absolute seriousness, they sacrifice the Bible's obvious and overwhelming humanness. Sacrificed is the *active role* that scores of diverse people played in its narratives, witness, writing, editing, and transmission. If the Bible were, as inerrantists claim, "wholly and verbally God-given," that can only mean that the human actors and mediators of that revelation were mere robots or automatons. This was what Calvin believed, at least implicitly. Humans are puppets dancing on the ends of divinely pulled strings.

All one has to do is read the Scriptures to see how wrong-headed this is. The human authors' unique personalities and distinctive theological voices, shaped by the dynamics of their spiritual communities as well as their constant interaction with the larger pagan world, are too obvious and far too numerous to be dismissed.

The Bible itself is testimony to the fact that God has mediated his message of love, grace, and salvation through imperfect and flawed creatures formed "out of the dust of the ground"—fallen and cursed ground at that (Gen 2:7; 3:17). Think of it: Abraham, hardly a praiseworthy exemplar of contemporary "family values," became the father of three great world religions as well as all who place their faith in Christ. Jacob the deceiver became progenitor of the twelve tribes of Israel. Into the hands of a killer was committed the Ten Commandments that included "You shall not kill." And what more shall we say of David the adulterer and murderer who wrote some of the world's most loved and treasured poetry? Or Saul of Tarsus who lay waste the church of God and yet penned nearly half of the New Testament books?

It is abundantly evident from the first verse of the Bible to the last that God was pleased to accommodate the "treasure" of self-disclosure to the sin-darkened minds and oft-fickle hearts of human "jars of clay." Why would God do this? Paul's insightful answer is "to show that this *all-surpassing power is from God* and not from us" (2 Cor 4:7 NIV; emphasis added). If there were such a thing as divine revelation totally free of the human element with all the risks that it entails, the temptation to "bibliolatry"—the worship of the Bible—would be overpowering.

We can rephrase Paul's word to the Corinthians in this way, "My message and my preaching were not with wise and [inerrant] words, but with a *demonstration of the Spirit's power,* so that your faith might not rest on *human wisdom*, but on *God's power"* (1 Cor 2:4–5 NIV; emphasis added). This very uncertainty about absolute truth delivers us from the insufferable 'arrogance of infallibility.' It helps us to be humble in the claims we make about the Bible. When we remember that we do not possess absolute certainty, we can remain dependent upon the Holy Spirit to lead us into all truth (John 16:13), always looking to Jesus who alone is "the author and finisher of our faith" (Heb 12:2).

4. We must read and interpret every part of the Bible in light of its overall purpose and message.

The Chicago Statement claims that the Bible is inerrant "not only in the whole but in every part." This statement seems to make it not only permissible but also praiseworthy to lift a single verse or even a part of a verse out of context and run with it. Logically, one may string verses together in any combination to say or prove whatever one wants. In practice, this 'mix and match' approach is the way many Christians read, preach, and teach the Bible.

Such 'proof-texting' is fraught with innumerable hazards. It invites all sorts of scriptural abuse. Biblical texts loosed from their contextual anchors have been used to promote strange doctrines and validate cultic claims. Christians have used context-less proof-texting to authorize bizarre practices from plural marriages to prosperity theology to snake handling to child abuse to genocide. We blush to admit it: the Scriptures are not only the divine source of light, life, and salvation. But people have used the Bible to distort, damage, and even destroy human beings. I offer just two of many such examples.

Spurred by a Mosaic injunction, "Thou shalt not suffer a witch to live" (Exod 22:18, KJV), a witch-craze swept sixteenth and seventeenth century Europe. It spilled over into colonial America in the infamous Salem witch trials. Conservative estimates suggest that over one hundred thousand women—mostly single, poor, ugly, elderly, physically or mentally handicapped and thus especially vulnerable—were unjustly arrested, cruelly tortured, and savagely executed. The *Christian* persecution of witches constituted, according to historians, the greatest mass killing of European people by a cause other than war. And all of that heinous destruction of human life was authorized by one verse of Scripture!

Or take slavery as an example. Slavery—what John Wesley decried as "that most vile of all human institutions"—was not only accepted by long generations of Christians but also stoutly defended as instituted by God and authorized in Scripture. It would be difficult to overstate the inhumanity, atrocities, and horrors visited upon generation after generation of slaves by Bible-believing slave holders. When abolitionists became serious about ending slavery in this country, biblical literalists on 'scriptural grounds' vigorously slapped them down.

> Recalling his own violent pre-Christian past, Paul writes of the very Hebrew Scriptures to which he was deeply committed and so often cited: "the letter kills" (2 Cor. 3:6). When a particular way of reading and interpreting the Bible lends itself to such inhumane and patently unChristlike beliefs and practices, clearly it must be questioned if not abandoned. *It is precisely because of my heartbreak over the continuing inhumane and abusive use of Scripture that I am addressing this topic of inerrancy.*

5. God has chosen to reveal himself fully and finally in Christ.

Few theologians have operated from the presupposition of the inerrancy of "all Scripture" as rigorously as Dutch Reformed theologian A. van de Beek. In his book, *Why? On Suffering, Guilt, and God,* van de Beek takes the received text of both Old and New Testaments as representing the literal words of God. All distinctions

between the testaments are erased, and the differing historical locations, perspectives, and personalities of the human mediators of
God's self-disclosure mean little. If all parts of the Bible have equal
weight of revelatory value, van de Beek must of necessity portray
God as not only good and faithful but also changeable, unpredictable, irrational, and even evil. "[The] way of God does not answer
to our norms of good and evil," he argues. "God is a rough God,
grim, and in our eyes even cruel. . . . God is not one you can figure
out. Majestically he goes his own way. . . . Good and evil both come
forth from his will."[2]

Belief in scriptural inerrancy logically leads to this: *we have
a perfect Bible but a grotesquely imperfect God*—a God who is
"rough," "grim," even "cruel." Sensing that the reader may well be
frustrated by such a monstrous view of God, van de Beek admits,
"We could perhaps restrict revelation to certain texts in Scripture."
In response to his own suggestion, he asks rhetorically, "But then
what is the criterion for our selection?"[3]

The New Testament answers with a shout: JESUS! He is the living Word of God made flesh. John exults, "We have seen his glory,
the glory of the one and only Son, who came from the Father, full of
grace and truth" (John 1:14 NIV). Paul adds that in Jesus "the whole
fullness of deity dwells bodily" (Col 2:9 NRSV).

Thus, to absolutize the Bible is to relativize Jesus. When all
the words of Scripture are elevated to the rank of being the very
words of God, the unique word of God embodied in Jesus (Col.
2:9) is reduced to just one source of divine revelation among
many. What Jesus had to say is, in principle, no more revelatory or
authoritative than the words of Moses, or the spiritually bankrupt
Solomon, or Balaam's 'ass' (KJV) for that matter. One never hears,
for instance, of anyone campaigning to get Jesus' two love commandments displayed in a public school classroom or engraved
on stone and placed in a courthouse vestibule. When it comes to
the commandments, Moses' robust ten are preferred over Jesus'

two love commandments (Mark 12:30–31).

From the very first verse of Matthew to the last paragraph of Revelation, the New Testament is all about Jesus. He alone was present and active with God the Father from before creation, and he is the one whom God will "exalt to the highest place." Jesus is the one before whom "every knee . . . in heaven and on earth and under the earth" will bow, and "every tongue [will] confess that Jesus Christ is Lord to the glory of God the Father" (Phil 2:5–11). Jesus is greater than Moses, greater than Joshua, greater than Solomon, and even greater than the angels. He alone is "the radiance of God's glory and the exact representation of his being" (Heb 1:3 NIV).

The whole purpose of the Scriptures, according to Paul, is to make you "wise unto salvation" (2 Tim 3:15 KJV). This salvation is found only in Christ. Early Christians and the Church Fathers valued the Hebrew Scriptures (our Old Testament) as an indispensable prologue to and preparation for the coming of Jesus. Without it, we would be unable to understand well the significance of his ministry, atoning death, and resurrection. As Augustine famously put it, "Jesus is in the OT concealed and in the NT revealed."

Our final authority not only in matters of faith and salvation but also in determining the true nature and character of God is Jesus. "The Holy Scriptures are a spiritual light far brighter even than the sun," said Martin Luther, "especially in what relates to salvation and all essential matters."[4] John Wesley typically spoke of the sufficiency of Scripture to accomplish its divine purpose. It is sufficient to announce the incredibly good news that "God was in Christ reconciling the world unto himself" (2 Cor. 5:19 KJV) and that "whosoever believes in him shall not perish but have everlasting life" (John 3:16). Millions of people across many centuries have experienced this truth in a life-transforming way. As Paul so succinctly put it: "Therefore, if anyone is in Christ, the new creation has come. The old has gone, the new is here!" (2 Cor 5:17 NIV).

"To attach our faith to the letter of Scripture," warns William

Greathouse, "may result in substituting the written word for Christ the living Word. The infallible Word of God in whom I put my trust for salvation is Christ, and Christ alone—the Christ revealed in Holy Scripture as the Word become flesh and made sin for us that we might become the righteousness of God in Him. . . . 'The letter kills, but the Spirit gives life.'"

C. H. Spurgeon, the great London preacher of the mid-1800's, said it well: "The Bible, like a lion, needs no defense. It needs only to be set free." Amen!

---

1. Benjamin Warfield and A.A. Hodges, Calvinistic Princeton Theological Seminary theologians, introduced inerrancy as an "article of faith" into the Presbyterian Confession of Faith in 1881. *This was the first time in Church history in which such an article had been articulated and adopted by any denomination.* Later, that same Presbyterian Church removed "inerrancy" language from its Articles of Faith, precipitating a major split in the denomination.
2. A. van de Beek, **Why? On Suffering, Guilt, and God** (trans. J. Vriend; Grand Rapids: Eerdmans, 1990), 274.
3. Ibid., 278.
4. Martin Luther, *On the Bondage of the Will* (trans. J. Packer and O. Johnston; Grand Rapids: Fleming Revell, 1957), 125.

— 7 —

What "Things" Are Included in "All Things Necessary to Our Salvation?"

Michael Lodahl[1]

We believe in the plenary inspiration of the Holy Scriptures, by which we understand the sixty-six books of the Old and New Testaments, given by divine inspiration, inerrantly revealing the will of God concerning us in all things necessary to our salvation, so that whatever is not contained therein is not to be enjoined as an article of faith.

2009 *Manual* of the Church of the Nazarene, Article of Faith IV. "The Holy Scriptures"

The Church of the Nazarene Article of Faith on the Scriptures, generally known to have been written by H. Orton Wiley, was composed in strokes of genius. While there are undoubtedly a number of Nazarenes who are discontent with the carefully delimited parameters that Wiley outlined for this statement—by which he reportedly hoped to create what he called "a little bit of elbow room"—I believe that he left for us a responsible, careful and profoundly *biblical* understanding of the nature and scope of the Bible's authority. There certainly are people who wish that this statement would say more than it does. But I contend that there are profound and good reasons for guarding Wiley's well-guarded language: "*inerrantly revealing* the *will* of God *concerning us* in all things *necessary* to our *salvation*."

There is no question that Wiley meant this carefully-crafted phraseology to be taken seriously. One often finds similar sorts of qualifications placed upon his affirmations of biblical authority in his *Christian Theology*. Here are a few examples (emphases added by this author): "inspiration signifies the operation of the Holy Spirit upon the writers of the books of the Bible in such a manner that *their productions become the expression of God's will*" (*CT* 1:167); "inspiration is the actuating energy of the Holy Spirit by which holy men chosen of God have officially proclaimed *His will* as revealed to us in the sacred Scriptures . . . through which holy men were qualified to receive *religious truth*, and to communicate it to others without error" (169); through divine inspiration "the Bible *becomes* the infallible Word of God, the *authoritative rule of faith and practice* in the Church" (171); it is thus "the infallible standard of *religious truth*" (173); this means "only that the results of that inspiration give us the Holy Scriptures as the final and authoritative *rule of faith* in the Church" (184); the end result is that "we must regard [the Canon of Holy Scripture] not only as *the Christian rule of faith and practice*, but also as the ultimate critical *standard of religious thought*" (185).

I believe that Wiley's careful wording hews closely to the ideas in one of the biblical quotations most often utilized to support an inerrantist position: "All scripture is inspired by God and is useful for teaching, for reproof, for correction, and for training in righteousness, so that everyone who belongs to God may be proficient, equipped for every good work" (2 Tim 3:16, NRSV throughout). Too often, though, critics of the Church of the Nazarene's official statement on the Holy Scriptures will quote the opening of 2 Timothy 3:16, "All scripture is inspired by God," and stop there. Perhaps the rest of the verse should be taken seriously.

The particular use or value of Scripture is carefully delineated in the rest of the sentence, where it makes no claim to be "useful" for teaching, say, astronomy or biology or history. We may grant that the passage does not say that Scripture is not useful for other purposes (such as being a science textbook or a history volume), but surely there is no need to go beyond what is written. This does not necessitate believing that the Scriptures are necessarily *wrong* about such matters all the time or even once; my point is the humbler one that this passage focuses very specifically on the Bible's function to "make you wise for salvation through faith in Christ Jesus" (2 Tim 3:15). That surely sounds like a soteriological function, which is a decidedly Wesleyan emphasis regarding Scripture.

Further, it seems to me that often those who might be discontent with the Nazarene Manual statement on the Holy Scriptures far too readily assume that the meaning and implications of the statement "all scripture is inspired by God" are self-evident. This passage does not explicate itself as having the implications that inerrantists typically claim for it. Rather, they *interpret* the passage to mean (or at least to imply) that because Scripture is inspired (or "God-breathed"), it must therefore speak with infallible authority on all subjects whatsoever that it might be construed to address.

The question is, Who informed such interpreters that this is what "God-breathed" implies? (Answer: a certain tradition of interpretation.) But it would surely be wise to consider what the word/concept "God-breathed" might entail when interpreted within the context of the larger sweep of biblical imagery. So, for example, Genesis 2 states that the human being (*adam*) was God-breathed (v. 7). But surely this did not entail, let alone necessitate, human infallibility. For that matter, Psalm 104:29–30 celebrates the perhaps surprising idea that all creatures, not just humans, are God-breathed.

These texts would suggest to us that to be "God-breathed" is to be creaturely and alive, living and breathing, sharing in the generously bestowed life of God. But they have precious little to do with absolute inerrancy in all matters. In this broader biblical context, the statement that Scripture is God-breathed would seem to imply that while it arises from and participates in the creaturely realm (and thus is *not* 'uncreated,' to employ a venerable theological term—and thus quite unlike the Eternal Logos or Son of God), this body of writings *lives*. The Bible is animated, by divine breath to be "useful for teaching, for reproof, for correction, for training in righteousness" (2 Tim 3:16).

Perhaps the important point arising from such considerations is that the act of reading any text, including any given passage of the Bible (such as 2 Tim 3:16), necessarily requires the hard work of interpretation. This matter of interpretation is a critical one. After all, there are plenty of people, both dead and living, who have claimed biblical inerrancy but have come to radically different doctrinal conclusions about the very same passage.

One radio preacher to whom I listen (far too often) who unapologetically proclaims the Bible to be God's Word direct from the very mouth of God, absolutely infallible in all respects. He claims to have also figured out from God's Word that the age of the church ended in 1988 and that the end of the world will occur precisely on May 21, 2011. And he is just one (very wacky) example. Another is the pair of Jehovah's Witnesses at your door, who also subscribe to the doctrine of biblical infallibility. Apparently belief in infallibility does not guarantee much of anything as far as orthodoxy is concerned. As Church of the Nazarene theologian, Ray Dunning, has written, "In the final analysis, . . the decisive question does not relate to one's theory concerning the nature of biblical authority, but to the way one uses the Bible."[2]

In any case, why should 2 Timothy 3:16 play such a large role in shaping our understanding of biblical authority? Given the idea of plenary inspiration, virtually any relevant biblical passage may, at least in principle, be consulted to help us understand the nature of the Scriptures.

I offer a suggestion that we take another passage as providing a critical contribution to our understanding of the Bible:

> Therefore, beloved, while you are waiting for these things [associated with the age to come], strive to be found by God at peace, without spot or blemish; and regard the patience of our Lord as salvation. So also our beloved brother Paul wrote to you according to the wisdom given him, speaking of this as he does in all his letters. There are some things in them hard to understand, which the ignorant and unstable twist to their own destruction, as they do the other scriptures. (2 Pet 3:14–16)

I submit that whatever understanding of divine inspiration and authority we uphold, it should be able to take into account this passage above (and others like it).

Notice that the author in this passage acknowledges that some of what Paul writes is "hard to understand," which seems to be at least a mild criticism (or so it may be interpreted). It is, to my mind, inherently interesting that one biblical author would offer such a judgment upon another biblical author's writing. It is not likely that the writer of 2 Peter is blaming God for the times when Paul is "hard to understand," even while granting that Paul "wrote . . . according to the wisdom given him." Instead, we encounter here one early Christian author observing that another's writing is difficult, and on no less important a topic than salvation itself. To repeat: "There are some things in [his letters] hard to understand" is hardly a ringing endorsement, especially since the eternal destiny of some of Paul's readers ("to their own destruction") is at stake. So we find also in this 2 Peter passage a distinct emphasis upon the necessity of sound interpretation, something presumably out of reach for "the ignorant and unstable."

Even more fundamentally, in this passage we encounter this somewhat surprising description of biblical writings: "Paul wrote to you according to the wisdom given to him." Perhaps this needs to be placed alongside of "all scripture is breathed by God" as mutually interpretive passages. According to 2 Peter 3:15, *Paul wrote his letters according to the wisdom given to him.* While I certainly think we should assume this wisdom to be divine wisdom, it is clearly also the case that a very human Paul wrote the letters—indeed, he wrote them in such a way (pardon my saying it one more time) that "some things in them are hard to understand!"

We should add, by the way, that as far as Paul himself was concerned, the "wisdom given to him" could be nothing other than "Christ crucified . . . the power of God and the wisdom of God" (1 Cor 1:23, 24). God "is the source of your life in Christ Jesus," says Paul, "who became for us wisdom from God, and righteousness and sanctification and redemption" (1:30). Paul's writings, even if "hard to understand," were intended to bear witness to the saving and sanctifying work of God through Jesus Christ. That was his purpose in writing to his churches—"all things necessary to our salvation," we might characterize it—and it is this purpose we should strive to discern through careful interpretation of his writings.

We can illustrate the critical difference between this soteriological purpose and whatever else may be found in Scripture by staying a little longer with this same Pauline epistle. In 1 Corinthians 1:14–16, we read, "I thank God that I baptized none of you except Crispus and Gaius, so that no one can say that you were baptized in my name. I did baptize also the household of Stephanus; beyond that, I do not know whether I baptized anyone else."

If I understand this text rightly, Paul corrects himself virtually in mid-thought. Suddenly he remembers the family of Stephanus and, given his awareness that he had temporarily forgotten them, acknowledges that he is not entirely sure whether perhaps in fact he had baptized some other forgotten Corinthians as well. For one thing, it's clear that this is *Paul talking here!* For another, Paul makes an error and, in the logic of many inerrantists, all it takes is one mistake and the whole house collapses. Granted, Paul immediately corrects himself, but the error stands: "I baptized none of you except Crispus and Gaius." Indeed, Paul is quite aware that he may still be making errors in the recollection of events by adding "beyond that, I do not know whether I baptized anyone else."

Is this a trivial error? Indeed it is. It does not hinder Paul from making his main point—his soteriological point—that Jesus Christ, and not Paul or Apollos or any other minister of the gospel, is the church's foundation (3:11). And we trust that Paul's letter to the Corinthians "inerrantly reveal[s] God's will concerning us in all things necessary to our salvation." Whether or not Paul baptized two, three or 18 people in Corinth is not necessary to our salvation. That Jesus Christ is the one foundation that has been laid for the church most definitely is. Thus, we probably are not troubled by Paul's lapse in memory, his error of recollection. But if one has set up an idealized "pure packaging" notion for the Bible as a kind of deductive truth (i.e., "the Bible must be this or that way in order to be trustworthy"), even a small "error" like this would presumably be disconcerting.

It seems exceedingly wise, then, that the Church of the Nazarene's Article on the Holy Scriptures counsels us to read the Scriptures as "inerrantly revealing the will of God concerning us in all things necessary to our salvation." To be sure, this raises the question still lurking in the background of this paper thus far: *What things are* necessary to our salvation? After we acknowledge the point already made—that God has laid the church's one foundation, Jesus Christ our Lord—is there anything else to be said?

This question is not terribly easy to answer. On the one hand, we might readily gravitate to John 3:16, and so claim that it is sufficient simply to believe in Jesus Christ as God's unique Son. Similarly, though not identically, Paul wrote, "if you confess with your mouth, 'Jesus is Lord,' and believe in your heart that God raised him from the dead, you will be saved" (Rom 10:9).

On the other hand, at the conclusion of the Sermon on the Mount we hear Jesus' warning, "Not everyone who says to me, 'Lord, Lord,' will enter the kingdom of heaven, but only he who does the will of my Father in heaven" (Matt 7:21). In the prelude to the famous Parable of the Good Samaritan (found only in Luke), Jesus tells a Torah expert that he is correct to cite the commandments to love God (Deut 6:4–6) and neighbor (Lev 19:18) as the path to eternal life (Luke 10:25–28).

But those are relatively easy, if not readily reconcilable, passages. Let us muddy the waters a little. Think of one of Paul's arguments, later in that Corinthian letter, for the resurrection of Jesus: "If the dead are not raised at all, why are people baptized on their behalf?" (15:29). Is Paul implying the possibility of post-mortem salvation for proxy baptizands? Christian interpreters have mostly scratched their heads on this one, while Joseph Smith's followers are busily being baptized for your ancestors. How are we to interpret such a statement from Paul? On a possibly related note—Latter-Day Saints certainly think so—2 Peter mysteriously proclaims that Christ "was put to death in the flesh, but made alive in the spirit, in which also he went and made a proclamation to the spirits in prison," identified as disobedient people from Noah's era (3:18–20). Were these "spirits in prison" given opportunity to repent and believe the good news? And if so, does this open the door of possibility for others who die without sufficient teaching or light from God to have made a responsible decision?

Perhaps we would dismiss these rather odd passages as not pertinent to our salvation. But that of course would be an interpretive decision not shared by all. How about Paul's declaration that "all Israel shall be saved" (Rom 11:26)? Context clarifies that he really does mean it when he writes "all Israel." Paul adds, "as regards the gospel they are enemies for your sake; but as regards election they are beloved, for the sake of their ancestors; for the gifts and the calling of God are irrevocable" (vv. 28–29). How is a Christian soteriology affected by Paul's words here, and how shall we best interpret them?

There are other examples. What of Colossians's claim that "God was pleased to reconcile to himself to all things, whether on earth or in heaven" (1:20)? Is it difficult to read this as gesturing toward universalism? (Karl Barth certainly did not think so.) On the other end of the spectrum, how shall we interpret the disconcerting words of 1 Timothy 2:15, that women "will be saved through childbearing," even if it immediately adds, "provided they continue in faith and love and holiness, with modesty?" Is the proposition that women "will be saved through childbearing" (however it might be interpreted) to be understood as one of the "things necessary to our salvation?"

Think, too, of the passage widely known as the Parable of the Sheep and the Goats, unique to Matthew's gospel. It certainly appears to be pertinent to Christian soteriology. Is Jesus really teaching that inhereting "the kingdom prepared for [us] from the foundation of the world" (25:34) is contingent upon our acts of mercy toward the hungry, the thirsty, the stranger, the naked, the sick and the imprisoned? John Wesley certainly thought so. In sermon four of his series, "Upon our Lord's Sermon on the Mount," he proclaims: "Whether they will finally be lost or saved, you are expressly commanded to feed the hungry and clothe the naked. If you can and do not, whatever becomes of them, you shall go away into everlasting fire."[3]

While I hesitate to gainsay Wesley, it is arguable that he (like many others) misinterpreted this passage. Much rides on who "the least of these my brothers" are. The Gospel of Matthew as a whole would suggest that Jesus refers here to his disciples, even and especially the most humble and youthful, i.e., the most vulnerable, among them. The passage is, after all, a portait of divine judgment of "all the nations." In other words, God judges all those (Gentile) nations or peoples to whom Jesus sends out his disciples with the Great Commission at the conclusion of this same gospel. In this scenario, the passage becomes about how all those "nations" have treated Jesus's emissaries in their missionary endeavors. Earlier in Matthew, Jesus specifically states that those who receive anyone he sends are in fact receiving him: "I was hungry and you gave me food" (Matt 25:35). My point is simply this: Even a passage as powerful as Matthew 25 is sufficiently ambiguous to yield multiple readings. And those variant interpretations would surely yield different understandings of "all things necessary to our salvation."

Such passages represent just a small sampling of the rich variety of New Testament observations about salvation. Taken together, it all sounds very much like a many-sided conversation. But perhaps the most dramatic intertextual example of this conversation is the 2 Peter passage to which we have already given attention. It soberly observes that Scripture requires careful interpretation if its saving message is to be understood and appropriated.

Admittedly, conversations about interpretation may get heated. We should recall that, while 2 Peter refers to "our beloved brother Paul," in his letter to the Galatians Paul minces no words in describing his run-in with Peter—"I opposed him to his face, because he was clearly in the wrong" (Gal 2:11). The issue at stake is nothing less than salvation (Gal 2:14–16). My point is that the early church was nothing if not a sustained and vigorous conversation regarding the manner of God's salvation of us through Jesus Christ. Christian tradition in all of its diversity, including patterns of liturgy, theology and biblical interpretation, surely embodies a rich and complex continuation of this conversation over the centuries.

I believe that Wiley's (and his Methodist predecessors') "dynamical theory" of inspiration applies nicely to this situation of ongoing conversation that is Holy Writ. This "dynamical" understanding of the work of the Holy Spirit gives a significant place to the human element in Scripture. That human element would include the whole "social world" of any particular biblical writer: the commonly held ideas in his or her culture about cosmology, anthropology, biology, history, Israel's God, and so on.

If the purpose of the Scriptures is to be "inerrantly revealing the will of God concerning us in all things necessary to our salvation," we need not expect that prophets or apostles would possess, or be given, unerring knowledge about other matters. Indeed, even in the matters of salvation, the dynamical theory of inspiration, if taken seriously, should imply that the biblical writers will not all write the same things. There will be differences. This is an extended and rich conversation with diverse participants.

The gospel of Jesus Christ was received, formulated, and communicated through the linguistic and cultural systems in which the early generations of Jesus' disciples participated. There are different cultures, different communities, that contribute to the New Testament's (to say nothing of the whole Bible's) proclamation about the salvation that has come to us from the God of Israel through Jesus Christ our Lord. Presumably we need all of its voices, all of its rich and diverse testimony—this is the basic implication of the doctrine of plenary inspiration—to appreciate sufficiently the wealth of God's grace through Jesus Christ in the presence and power of the Holy Spirit.

Does this rich, vast and varied conversation that is our Bible, then, yet offer a coherent theme? We ask, again, what *are* "all [those] things necessary to our salvation?" The sainted Bishop of Hippo offers perennial wisdom to this question, not to mention sage guidance in how we ought best to pursue its answer. In his classic wrestling with the opening passage of Genesis in Book XII of his *Confessions*, Augustine observes:

> Christ our Master well knows which are the two commandments on which, he said, all the law and the prophets

depend. . . . Let us not, therefore, go beyond what is laid down for us. . . . Let us love the Lord our God with our whole heart and our whole soul and our whole mind, and our neighbor as ourselves. Whatever Moses meant in his books, unless we believe that he meant it to be understood in the spirit of these two precepts of charity, we are treating God as a liar. . . . Do you not see how foolish it is to enter into mischievous arguments which are an offence against that very charity for the sake of which [Moses] wrote every one of the words that we are trying to explain?[4]

Similarly, in *On Christian Teaching* Augustine stipulated that difficult biblical passages "are to be elucidated in terms of the need to nourish love," for "scripture enjoins nothing but love." Any given passage should be "interpreted according to the aim of love," he argues, "whether it be love of God or love of one's neighbor, or both."[5]

Augustine, it seems to me, was on solid exegetical and soteriological ground here. As Wesleyans, we certainly understand and believe that the redeemed and sanctified life is a life of love made perfect by God who is Love and who therefore loves perfectly. If "all of the law and the prophets hang on these two commands" to love God and neighbor, surely we are to read Holy Writ always with an eye toward nourishing and nurturing greater, deeper, and wider love for God and for all our neighbors (including the ones who more readily fall under the category of "stranger" or even "enemy"). To adapt a point from Paul: the letter kills, but the Spirit gives life. And that life is always the life of love, a life growing by the grace of God through Jesus Christ. It is our Scriptures that tell us that Jesus taught that all divine revelation hangs upon those two commandments to love God and all neighbors. It is that life to which the Scriptures bear witness, and that life which those Scriptures inform.

That, I believe, is where the rich conversation that is the Bible inevitably takes us. In the light of this calling, may we heed Wesley's challenge to "run the race that is set before [us], in the royal way of universal love . . . keep[ing] an even pace, rooted in the faith once delivered to the saints and grounded in love, in true catholic love, till [we be] swallowed up in love for ever and ever."[6]

1. C.S. Cowles, who was among H. Orton Wiley's last graduate students in theology at Pasadena College, taught in the Department of Philosophy and Religion at Northwest Nazarene College from 1975 to 2001, but for a two-year period as pastor of Spokane, Washington First Church of the Nazarene (1984–1986). I was privileged to be his student during his first two years in Nampa, and his teaching assistant during the second of those years. Returning to my college *alma mater* in 1988 as a professor, I was blessed to be C.S's colleague at NNC for what would be eleven rich years of friendship and mutual support. It was a joyous serendipity, I am confident for us both, to be reunited as friends and teaching colleagues at Point Loma Nazarene University during his final decade of teaching, 2001–2010. My indebtedness to C.S. as teacher, friend, brother in Christ, mentor and guide goes far deeper than I could ever say or repay, and I offer this essay in his honor.

2. H. Ray Dunning, *Grace, Faith and Holiness* (Kansas City, MO: Beacon Hill Press of Kansas City, 1988), 73.

3. John Wesley, "Upon our Lord's Sermon on the Mount, IV," in *John Wesley's Sermons: An Anthology* (ed. A.C. Outler and R.P. Heitzenrater; Nashville: Abingdon, 1991), 204.

4. Augustine, *Confessions*, (trans. R. S. Pine-Coffin; New York: Penguin, 1961), 295, 302–3.

5. Augustine, *On Christian Doctrine* (trans. R. P. H. Green; New York: Oxford University Press, 1997), 76, 77, 79.

6. Wesley, "Catholic Spirit," in *John Wesley's Sermons: An Anthology*, 309.

John Wesley on the Bible: The Rule of Christian Faith, Practice, and Hope[1]

Randy L. Maddox

This essay surveys John Wesley's understanding and use of the Bible, as an instructive example for those in the Wesleyan tradition. It has become traditional to introduce this topic with an excerpt from Wesley's preface to the first volume of his *Sermons*:

> I want to know one thing, the way to heaven—how to land safe on that happy shore. God himself has condescended to teach the way: for this very end he came from heaven. He hath written it down in a book. O give me that book! ... Let me be *homo unius libri*.[2]

This proclaimed desire to be "a man of one book" could suggest that the best way to honor Wesley's legacy would be to say nothing more about him, and simply study the Bible. But Wesley also responded to the claim of some of his lay preachers, "I read only the Bible," with strong words: "This is rank enthusiasm. If you need no book but the Bible, you are got above St. Paul (who requested to be sent some books)."[3] As Wesley explained his stance more carefully in *A Plain Account of Christian Perfection* (§10), to be *homo unius libri* is to be one who regards no book *comparatively* but the Bible. Thus, my goal in this essay is to explore how Wesley read the Bible *comparatively* with other books and sources. In the process, I will also consider Wesley's approach to reading the Bible *comparatively* with other readers, and reflect *comparatively* on the reasons that Wesley read the Bible so regularly, and encouraged his followers to do the same.

The Bible That John Wesley Read

I begin with some brief comments on what Bible John Wesley read. As one would expect, Wesley owned, read, and most frequently cites the currently standard English translation of the Bible, commonly called the King James Version (KJV). But this use must be qualified in at least three ways.

The first qualification concerns the scope of the biblical canon. The KJV, as published through Wesley's lifetime, included the sixteen books commonly called the "apocrypha." Article VI of the Anglican Articles of Religion affirmed these works as worthy to read "for example of life and instruction of manners," though not as authorities for doctrine. Thus, we find occasional allusions to these books in Wesley's early years in this vein. But by the mid 1750s, Wesley had consciously adopted the narrower Protestant canon, eventually saying of the apocrypha: "We dare not receive them as part of the Holy Scriptures."[4] This helps explain why there is no record of Wesley preaching on a text from the apocryphal books, while we can document him preaching on texts from every book in the Protestant canon except Esther, Song of Songs, Obadiah, Nahum, Zephaniah, Philemon, and 3 John.

A second qualification is that Wesley did not confine himself to the KJV. When he cites from the book of Psalms, for example, he frequently uses the translation (by Miles Coverdale) that was part of the *Book of Common Prayer*. More broadly, it is clear that he studied earlier English translations of the whole Bible, as well as translations in German and French.

Perhaps the most important qualification is that Wesley valued the original Hebrew and Greek texts of the Bible over any translation, citing these texts throughout his life. Indeed, we can identify at least four versions of the Greek New Testament that he owned.

How John Wesley Read the Bible

Wesley's practice of reading the Bible in its original languages provides a good transition to our more central question: *How* did John Wesley read and interpret the Bible *comparatively*?

Read with the Standard Scholarly Tools

The first way in which Wesley drew upon other sources *comparatively* in reading the Bible was his use of standard scholarly tools. These included Johann Buxtorf's Hebrew grammar (1609) and lexicon (1613), and Richard Busby's similar tools for Greek (1663), along with some of the most recent alternatives.

One issue receiving significant scholarly attention in Wesley's day was textual criticism, particularly of the New Testament. Wesley shared this interest and understood the general issues involved. This is why he owned multiple versions of the Greek New Testament, including John Mill's two-volume version that gathered the most complete list at the time of variant readings in Greek manuscripts. Significantly, Wesley favored what is agreed to be the best critical Greek text of the day, that of Johann Albrecht Bengel (1734).

Bengel's Greek New Testament corrected the Textus Receptus (the Greek text used for the translation of the KJV) at numerous points. These and other issues had led to a growing number of calls for a new English translation of the Bible and scattered attempts to undertake this task. Wesley owned a copy of one of the most thorough defenses of the need for a new English translation.[5] This likely encouraged him to venture his own translation when he prepared his *Explanatory Notes upon the New Testament*. The English translation that Wesley provided there varies from the KJV in over 12,000 instances.

Most of the variants between John Wesley's translation of the New Testament and the KJV were modernizations of the English and minor in nature. But many reflected text-critical decisions that remain standard in biblical scholarship. That is not to say that current scholarship would concur with all of Wesley's textual judgments. To cite one case in point, Wesley followed Bengel in vigorously defending the phrase "these three are one" as part of the original text of 1 John 5:7–9. Scholarship that is more recent has persuasively discounted this possibility. Here as in other matters, Wesley's present heirs will want to appreciate his precedent in its historical context, then seek to be similarly engaged and discerning in our current scholarly settings.

Read as Scripture – the Book of God

While Wesley embraced the enterprise of textual criticism, his relationship was more ambiguous to early strands of *historical* criticism that surfaced in the later seventeenth century. Scattered scholars began to apply analysis used on other literary texts to the books of the Bible, which called into question traditional assumptions about authorship of some books, challenged the historical accuracy of certain biblical accounts, and highlighted human dynamics in the process of canonization. Some advocates of this agenda appeared to reduce the Bible to a mere collection of antiquated human texts.

The response of the vast majority of eighteenth-century Anglican scholars and clergy to these developments was defensive. Some marshaled book-length lists of evidence to defend the textual integrity of the Bible and its accuracy on historical and other matters. Equally prominent were manuals offering pastoral advice to laity on how to read the Bible as *Scripture*, as a book carrying divine authority. The third major means of defending the integrity of the

Bible, mixing scholarship with pastoral concern, was publication of accessible commentaries with notes to guide laity in addressing difficult passages and to point them toward unifying themes.

John Wesley generally reflected this Anglican response. While he welcomed studies of the customs of the ancient Israelites and the early Christians to enrich his reading of the Bible, Wesley retained traditional assumptions about authorship (such as Moses as author of the first five Old Testament books) and was quick to reject suggestions of errors in the Bible. His comments on this last topic can be quite sharp, such as insisting that "if there be one falsehood in the Bible, there may be a thousand; neither can it proceed from the God of truth."[6]

Some interpreters have taken such quotes to indicate that Wesley would align with the modern model of "biblical inerrancy," which insists that the Bible is accurate in every detail, including historical allusions and descriptions on the natural world. But Wesley never uses the word "inerrancy" (which was not in common use at the time), and his broader comments on the authoritative role of the Bible suggest a more nuanced stance. To begin with, his affirmations almost always focus on the Bible as the "rule of Christian faith and practice."[7] Wesley was following the lead of 2 Timothy 3:16–17, where the inspiration of Scripture is related to its usefulness for instructing in Christian belief and training in lives of righteousness. He frequently cites this text in teaching sermons, affirming the Bible as "infallibly true" on these matters. While he never provides a detailed account of what the *infallibility* of Scripture entails, Wesley did not think that it was undercut by mistakes on tangential matters like reproducing mistakes in the Jewish historical records the authors used, or quoting inaccurately Old Testament texts in the New Testament.[8]

More broadly, Wesley embraced at least some aspects of the principle, long held in Christian tradition, that God graciously condescended to adapt revelation to our human situation. He particularly stressed God adapting to our inability to understand fully matters like God's timelessness. At the same time, there is little evidence that Wesley joined Augustine and others in affirming that divine condescension included allowing the human authors of the Bible to articulate the truths of revelation in the specificity (and limitations) of their language, culture, and current "science." This is another place where Wesley's descendants may want to appreciate his example in historical context, while suggesting that his conviction about how God works in salvation—by undergirding and assisting our will, but not overriding our liberty—has broader implications than he realized. Applied to God's agency in inspiring the human authors of Scripture, this conviction would allow one to take with utmost seriousness the cultural specificity of the various books in the Bible that modern scholarship makes evident, while still affirming a robust sense of the authority of Scripture as the "book of God." For example, one would appreciate how God enables the authors of Scripture to convey the truths of revelation in terms of the "science" of their day.

The last point to make is that, while Wesley clearly believed that Scripture was infallible, he never took up the scholarly project of crafting an extended defense of this point. He focused his energy instead on the pastoral/practical task of enabling lay readers to engage the Bible as the trustworthy book of God. His most significant contribution in this regard was *Explanatory Notes Upon the New Testament* and the later parallel *Explanatory Notes Upon the Old Testament*.

Read Relying on the Inspiration of the Spirit

Part of the reason for Wesley's focus on this pastoral task was his recognition of the vital role of the "inspiration of the Spirit." His typical use of this phrase is broader than considerations of the production of the Bible. In the *Complete English Dictionary* (1753) that Wesley published to help his followers read Scripture and other writings, he defined "inspiration" as the influence of the Holy Spirit that enables persons to love and serve God. This broad use of the word trades on the meaning of the Latin original, *inspirare*: to breathe into, animate, excite, or inflame. The broader understanding is evident even when Wesley uses "inspiration" in relation to the Bible. For example, while his comments in *Explanatory Notes* on 2 Timothy 3:16 affirm God's guidance of the original authors, Wesley's focal emphasis is encouraging current readers to seek the Spirit's inspiring assistance in reading Scripture!

What assistance are we to seek? To begin with, "we need the same Spirit to *understand* the Scripture which enabled the holy men of old to *write* it."[9] Thus, in the preface to *Sermons*, immediately after stating his resolve to be "a man of one book," Wesley stressed that, when he opens the Bible, if he finds anything unclear, his first recourse is to pray for divine assistance in understanding.

While conceptual understanding of the teaching in the Bible is vital, Wesley's deepest concern was personal *embrace* of the saving truth in Scripture. The Spirit's inspiring work is essential at this point.Wesley was insistent that "true, living Christian faith … is not only an assent, an act of the understanding, but a disposition which *God hath wrought* in the heart."[10] Significantly, he included mere assent to the truthfulness of Scripture among those things that fall short of living Christian faith, reminding his readers that "the devils believe all Scripture, having been given by inspiration of God, is true as God is true," but do not embrace that saving truth for themselves.[11] As a gift of God, the disposition of true faith is not the result of rational argument alone. This is why Wesley never devoted significant energy to *proving* the inspiration of the Bible by appeals to its truthfulness or other such arguments. He could publish brief resumes of arguments by other writers. But Wesley valued such apologetic efforts for helping *confirm* faith born of the work of the Spirit, not as providing the foundation for that faith.

Read in Conference with Others

Wesley makes another significant point in his preface to *Sermons*, about how he was *comparatively* a "man of one book." We have already noted his recognition of the need for divine assistance in understanding Scripture. He goes on in this paragraph to describe how he carefully considers other relevant passages in the Bible. Then he adds, "If any doubt still remains, I consult those who are experienced in the things of God, and then the writings whereby, being dead, they yet speak."[12] The crucial thing to note in this concluding line is not just that an individual might turn to other books to understand the one book, but that we as individuals need to read the Bible *in conference with other readers*!

Several dimensions to this need deserve highlighting. Note first that Wesley identifies consulting particularly those "more experienced in the things of God." His focal concern is not scholarly expertise (though he is not dismissing this), but the contribution of mature Christian character and discernment to interpreting the Bible. Where does one find such folk whose lives and understanding are less distorted by sin? One of Wesley's most central convictions was that authentic Christian character and discernment are the fruit of the Spirit, nurtured within the witness, worship, support, and accountability of Christian community. This is the point of his often (mis-)quoted line that there is "no holiness but social holiness." As he later clarified, "I mean not only that [holiness] cannot subsist so well, but that it cannot subsist at all without society, without living and conversing with [other people]."[13] While the class and band meetings that Wesley designed to embody this principle were not devoted primarily to Bible study, they helped form persons who were more inclined to read Scripture, and to read it in keeping with its central purposes. Thus, the early Methodist movement provides an instructive example for those seeking today to recover appreciation for the role of community in interpreting Scripture.

I hasten to add, secondly, that Wesley's emphasis on the value of reading the Bible in conference with others was not limited to considerations of relative Christian maturity. It was grounded in his recognition of the limits of all human understanding, even that of spiritually mature persons. He was convinced that, as finite creatures, our human understandings of our experience, of tradition, and of Scripture itself are "opinions" or interpretations of their subject matter. God may know these things with absolute clarity; we see them "through a glass darkly." Wesley underlined the implication of this in his sermon on a "Catholic Spirit."

> Although every man necessarily believes that every particular opinion which he holds is true (for to believe any opinion is not true, is the same thing as not to hold it); yet can no man be assured that all his own opinions, taken together, are true. Nay, every thinking man is assured they are not, seeing *humanum est errare et nescire*: "To be ignorant of many things, and to mistake in some, is the necessary condition of humanity."[14]

Wesley went on in the sermon to commend a spirit of openness to dialogue with others, where we are clear in our commitment to the main branches of Christian doctrine, while always ready to hear and weigh whatever can be offered against our current understanding of matters of belief or practice.[15] His goal in this dialogue is clear—seeking the *most adequate* understanding of whatever we are considering.

The final dimension to highlight about Wesley's call for reading the Bible in conference with others should be obvious: it is vital that we do not limit our dialogue partners to those who are most like us, or those with whom we already agree. We should remain open to, and at times seek out, those who hold differing understandings. Otherwise, we are not likely to identify places where our understanding of something in Scripture (usually shared with those closest to us) might be wrong!

Read in Conference with Christian Tradition

Among those outside of his circle of associates and followers whom Wesley was committed to including in his conferring over the meaning of Scripture were Christians of earlier generations. As he noted, our primary means of hearing their voice is through their writings.

It is widely recognized that John Wesley valued highly the writings of the first three centuries of the church, in both its Eastern (Greek) and Western (Latin) settings. Wesley specifically defended consulting early Christian authors in a published letter to Conyers Middleton. He insisted that consultation with these writings had helped many Christian readers avoid dangerous errors in interpreting Scripture, while the neglect of these writings would surely leave one captive to misunderstanding currently reigning.

In both his formal definitions and his practice Wesley tended to jump from the early church to the seventeenth-century Anglican standards in his consideration of Christian tradition. But his reading of various commentaries and historical works passed to him an awareness of the major Medieval and Reformation debates over biblical interpretation, as well as a set of central interpretive principles. For example, he generally stressed the primacy of the literal meaning in interpreting Bible texts (a principle that the Reformers had adopted to counter the fluidity of allegorical and spiritual exegesis). In cases where two biblical texts appeared to contradict each other, he stressed that the more obscure text should be understood in light of the clearer one. Likewise, he was aware of the importance of context in interpreting Scripture—both the specific context of any particular verse or phrase and the overall context of the Bible. In fact, one of Wesley's most frequent objections to opponents' suggested interpretations was that they contradicted "the whole tenor and scope of Scripture."

Read in Conference with the "Rule of Faith"

One interpretive principle of earlier Christian generations deserves special attention. A good example can be found in St. Augustine's *On Christian Teaching*.[16] Augustine instructs his readers that when they find unclear or ambiguous passages in the Bible they should consult for guidance the "rule of faith" (*regula fidei*). He was using here the typical Latin translation of Paul's advice in Romans 12:6 for exercising the gift of prophecy according to the "analogy (Greek, "*analogian*") of faith." Augustine defined this rule of faith as the teachings in "the more open places of the Scriptures and in the authority of the church." The use of the term throughout Augustine's works and the broad early church makes clear that the two sources identified should not be considered as either separate or additive. Early baptismal creeds and related catechetical materials sought to provide a narrative summary of God's saving work as revealed in Scripture, with particular attention to the implicit trinitarian form of this work (the Apostles' Creed is a key example). The "rule of faith" gathered the early church's sense of what was most central and unifying in Scripture, to serve in part as an aid for reading the whole of Scripture in its light.

The topic of the "rule of faith" became a battleground during the Reformation. Some teachings and practices had been advanced on the "authority of the church" through the medieval period that the Reformers judged contrary to clear biblical teaching. In response, they championed "Scripture alone" as the rule of faith. But for most Protestants this did not mean rejecting the value of some communally-shared sense of the central and unifying themes in Scripture when trying to interpret particular passages. They changed the name for this shared sense to the "analogy of faith," reflecting Paul's Greek text, as one expression of their concern to stick close to Scripture. But they typically defended under this label the practice of consulting at least the Apostles' Creed when seeking to interpret Scripture correctly.

Wesley inherited through his Anglican standards this Protestant commitment to Scripture as the "rule of faith," interpreted in light of the "analogy of faith." He also inherited the impact of Protestant debates that elevated attention to topics of the dynamics of individual salvation in communally-authoritative guides to reading Scripture. These topics were particularly important for those Protestants concerned with piety and holy living, like Wesley. As a result, his specific articulations of the "analogy of faith" tend to focus on four themes: the corruption of sin, justification by faith, the new birth, and present inward and outward holiness.[17]

Wesley's focus on these topics has led some interpreters to fault him for a one-sided "personal-salvationist" reading of Scripture. If this charge is meant to imply that Wesley ignored or downplayed the redemptive work of the triune God, it must be rejected. It is true that Wesley devoted far fewer sermons to the Trinity than, say, to justification by faith. But this is because he assumed that his trinitarian commitments were generally shared among his Anglican peers; he was focusing on areas of misunderstanding and disagreement. As Geoffrey Wainwright has shown, Wesley's reading of Scripture was actually deeply shaped by his trinitarian convictions.[18]

Wesley's commitment to reading the Bible in light of the trinitarian (and other) themes affirmed in the Apostles' Creed is embodied in his advice: "In order to be well acquainted with the doctrines of Christianity you need but one book (besides the New Testament)—Bishop Pearson *On the Creed*."[19] John Pearson's volume was an exposition of the Apostles' Creed, which Wesley's parents had commended to him and was a text during his study at Christ Church in Oxford. This was the theological text that Wesley himself most often assigned to his assistants and recommended to his correspondents.

In other words, Wesley's description of himself as a "man of one Book" should not mislead us from recognizing that he generally read that Book through the lens of the broadly shared Christian "rule of faith" and his more specific high-church Anglican commitments. While some of Wesley's current descendants will consider this a limitation, many others will find it a helpful example of an approach to reading Scripture that needs to be recovered!

Read in Conference with the "Book of Nature"

One of Wesley's commitments nurtured by his Anglican upbringing was a higher emphasis than in some Protestant circles for studying God's revelation in the natural world (the "book of nature") alongside of studying Scripture. Wesley's stated and central interest in studying the natural world was to strengthen the faith awakened by Scripture and deepen our appreciation of God's power, wisdom, and goodness. But there is good evidence that his study of current science also helped him test and reshape inherited interpretations of Scripture.

For a fitting example, return to the preface of the first volume of *Sermons* and note Wesley's line: "I want to know one thing, the way to heaven—how to land safe on that happy shore." Wesley is reflecting here a long development in Christian history. Although Scripture speaks of God's ultimate goal in salvation as the "new heavens and earth," a variety of influences led Christians through the first millennium to assume increasingly that our final state is "heaven above." The latter was seen as a realm where human spirits, dwelling in ethereal bodies, join eternally with all other spiritual beings (a category that did not include animals) in continuous worship of God. By contrast, they assumed that the physical universe, which we abandon at death, would eventually be annihilated. Wesley was taught this understanding of our final state in his upbringing, and through much of his ministry it was presented as obvious and unproblematic. But in the last decade of his life, he began to reclaim boldly the biblical imagery of God's renewal of the whole universe, specifically championing the notion that animals participate in final salvation. What led to this change? A major factor was his study, in his sixties, of some current works in biology that utilized the model of the "chain of beings." Central to this model is the assumption that the loss of any type of "being" in creation would call into question the perfection of the Creator. Prodded by this emphasis, Wesley began to take more seriously the biblical insistence that God desires to redeem the whole creation.

As this instance suggests, when the mature Wesley confronted an apparent conflict between current science and Scripture, he did not simply debate which was more authoritative. He reconsidered his interpretations of *each*, seeking an understanding that *did justice to both*. In this way, he honored the authority of Scripture, while affirming the contribution of broad conferencing to our (human) understanding of Scripture. This is a balance worthy of emulation.

Read with an Emphasis on God's Universal Pardoning and Transforming Love

While all of the points that have been made so far were characteristic of how Wesley read the Bible, none of them was unique to him. Similar points could be made for Christian leaders and theologians throughout the history of the church. But this leaves the question of what was most *distinctive* in Wesley's general interpretation of the Bible.

As David Kelsey and others have shown, what most differentiates various theologians, or theological traditions, in their reading of Scripture is not divergence on its "authority," but their "working canon"—the group of texts to which they appeal most often, and present as the "clear" texts in light of which to read the rest of Scripture.[20] This was a reality that Wesley recognized:

> We know, "All Scripture is given by inspiration of God," and is therefore true and right concerning all things. But we know likewise that there are some Scriptures which more

immediately commend themselves to every [person's] conscience.[21]

So what was Wesley's "working canon"? In the quote just given he went on to cite as an example 1 Corinthians 13. He also highly prized the Sermon on the Mount in Matthew 5–7. But, as Robert Wall has argued, the biblical book that Wesley prized most highly was the First Epistle of John.[22] He referred to 1 John as "the deepest part of Scripture" and a "compendium of all the Holy Scriptures." He praised it as the best rhetorical model for preaching. And he favored the book in his own preaching, using 1 John for his sermon text much more frequently (comparative to the number of verses in the book) than any other biblical book.[23]

At one level, Wesley's preference for 1 John is surprising, since there is little evidence that his contemporaries held the epistle in special regard. But note Wesley's description of 1 John 4:19—"We love [God] because he first loved us"—as "the sum of the whole gospel."[24] Wesley is highlighting here the deepest conviction that he gained in his own spiritual journey. He had always longed to love God fully, and had sought to do so with utmost seriousness. But it was only in the events surrounding 1738 that he finally and fully grasped the truth of 1 John 4:19, discovering that authentic and enduring love of God and others is a *response* to knowing God's pardoning love for us. Wesley also valued 1 John because it stressed so clearly the goal of the Spirit's work: to transform our lives, so that we might be made perfect in love of both God and neighbor (4:7–18), ideally leading sinless lives (2:1, 3:6–9).

Wesley was aware that many read Paul's emphasis on being justified freely by grace (Rom 3:24) as rejecting the possibility of such sinless lives in this present world, and some read Paul in such a way as to downplay the very concern for holy living. His response was to insist that the possibility of Christian perfection, while perhaps still unclear even in the letters of Paul, was decisively settled by

John, "the *last* of the inspired writers."[25] He went on to summarize his defense of Christian perfection as "in conformity therefore both to the doctrine of St. John, and to the whole tenor of the New Testament." As the order of this claim suggests, Wesley read Paul (and the rest of the Bible) through the lens of the central convictions he found in 1 John, not to discount Paul's message but to highlight Paul's insistence on believers being set free from sin to be servants of righteousness (Rom 6:18).

Another emphasis that many found in the writings of Paul was predestination—in the sense of God's *unconditional* election of some for salvation and the others for damnation. Wesley's response was that this particular way of reading Romans 8:29–30 and other passages was that "no Scripture can mean that God is not love, or that his mercy is not over all his works."[26] In this insistence on God's universal offer of grace, we hear echoed the emphasis in 1 John that "God is love" (4:8, 16). But the specific point that this love is *universal*, or reaches over all God's works, is not particularly highlighted in the epistle. Wesley is invoking here Psalm 145:9, "The Lord is loving to every [person], and his mercy is over all his works." While he did not preach on this text often, it became Wesley's favored summary of his conviction that Scripture affirms God's saving concern for all persons. And this conviction deeply shaped his reading of specific scriptures.

To summarize, Wesley increasingly and self-consciously read the whole of the Bible in light of a deep conviction that God was present in the assuring work of the Spirit both to *pardon* and to *transform* all who respond to that inviting and empowering love (and *all* can respond!). This conviction was not something that Wesley thought he was imposing on Scripture. He was convinced that it was the most central and clear message of Scripture—as seen particularly in 1 John and related texts. At the heart of reading the Bible in "Wesleyan" ways today would be embracing Wesley's central interpretive lens, even as one continues to test and refine it by ongoing conference with the whole of Scripture and the range of other readers.

Why John Wesley Read the Bible

We come to one final question: What were John Wesley's reasons *comparatively* for reading the Bible, and encouraging his followers to do the same?

The Rule of Christian Faith

The initial answer would seem obvious: Because it is the rule or guide for determining Christian belief! Wesley strongly affirmed this purpose, insisting that he regulated his theological convictions by Scripture, and arguing that no pastor could be a good divine (i.e., theologian) without being a good textuary.

The Rule of Christian Practice

But Wesley would be the first to insist that more is at stake in reading the Bible than just seeking better *understanding* of Christian beliefs. He consistently highlighted as well its role as the rule of *practice*. Indeed, he more frequently focused on this second role, identifying at least three dimensions of practice. Consider this fitting example:

> From the very beginning, from the time that four young men united together, each of them was *homo unius libri* – a man of one book. God taught them all to make his "Word a lantern unto their feet, and a light in all their paths." They had one, and only one rule of judgment in regard to all their *tempers, words,* and *actions,* namely, the oracles of God.[27]

As the rule of our *words,* Wesley meant more than avoiding profanity. He believed that Christians should adopt the very language of Scripture, as far as possible, in their conversation.

As the rule of our *actions*, Wesley turned to Scripture not only for guidelines on moral issues, but also for testing supposed leadings of the Spirit, for deciding questions of worship practice, and so on.

Wesley's deepest concern was Scripture's role as the rule of our *tempers*. To appreciate this, one needs to recognize that Wesley used the word "tempers" to designate our fundamental character dispositions—the springboards of our words and actions. He discussed sin in this threefold division, stressing that sinful actions and words flow from corrupted tempers, so the problem of sin must ultimately be addressed at this deeper level. Correspondingly, his mature definition of Christian life placed primary emphasis on this inward dimension, the recovery of holy tempers, from which would flow holy words and actions.

What is the role of Scripture in this recovery of holy tempers? It was clearly more than just a "guide" to identifying sinful and holy tempers. Wesley considered attentive reading of Scripture to be one of the most central "means of grace"—one of the crucial ways that God has provided for receiving the assuring presence of the Holy Spirit that awakens and empowers our human response of love, and for nurturing our initial responses (by repeated practice) into enduring holy tempers. Thus, Wesley encouraged readers to come to the New Testament ready "to hear [Jesus'] word, to imbibe his Spirit, and to transcribe his life into our own."[28] And he worried about those who were quick to defend the authority of Scripture, while neglecting regular study of Scripture!

The Rule of Christian Hope

The last point that I would make is not one that Wesley stresses explicitly, but one that is embodied in his lifelong journey with Scripture. In addition to finding Scripture a sufficient and reliable guide to central Christian beliefs, a wise guide to Christian practice, and a vital means for nurturing Christian character, Wesley's engagement with Scripture over the course of his life served to sustain, challenge, and deepen his sense of the Christian hope!

Consider in this regard Wesley's appeals to Psalm 145:9, "The Lord is loving to every [person], and his mercy is over all his works." We have already noted that this is not just an incidental verse for Wesley; he prized it for articulating one of the themes that he considered most central to Scripture. What I want to suggest now is that Wesley's continuing engagement with Scripture, in the various dimensions of conference laid out above, led him to recognize and emphasize an ever broader scope of the "works" over which God's mercy reigns.

As we have seen, Wesley's initial appeals to Psalm 145:9 on topics of debate focused on predestination, insisting that God offers the possibility of eternal salvation to all humans. This was a broader sense of the possibility of salvation than his opponents held. But it could easily be charged with remaining a "personal-salvationist" reading of Scripture, this time in the sense of focusing only on human souls finding their way to heaven above. This personal focus remains almost exclusive for Wesley until his later years. But then, in 1774, we find him citing this verse again in a pivotal section of his *Thoughts upon Slavery* (as one of his few scriptural citations in that work).[29] Here he was invoking the breadth of God's mercy as a warrant for rejecting the slave trade *in this world*, not just defending the possibility of eternal salvation for those being sold in slavery. In 1781, Wesley invoked Psalm 145:9 again, in an even broader context, insisting on God's intention to *redeem animals* as well as humans, and encouraging his readers even now to "imitate the God whose mercy is over all his works."[30] With these added emphases on the breadth of God's saving mercy, and our participation in God's saving work, Wesley had clearly moved beyond a merely "personal-salvationist" reading of Scripture. He had come to embrace the cosmic scope of the Christian hope.

Through this process, Wesley also provided a demonstration

that a life of immersion in Scripture, read in the full range of conferencing, can reshape one's inherited interpretive assumptions and lead them into a deeper sense of the message of Scripture. May we who are heirs of his ministry take this example to heart!

1. This essay draws on and condenses Randy L. Maddox, "The Rule of Christian Faith, Practice, and Hope: John Wesley on the Bible," *Methodist Review* 3 (2011): 1–35 (online: http://www.methodistreview.org). See the longer online essay for more detailed discussion and documentation.

2. *Sermons on Several Occasions*, Vol. 1 (1746), Preface, §5, *The Bicentennial Edition of The Works of John Wesley* (Nashville: Abingdon, 1984–) 1:104–5. Cited hereafter as *Works*.

3. 1766 *Minutes*, Q. 30; also as "Large Minutes," Q. 32, *The Works of John Wesley* (ed. T. Jackson; Grand Rapids: Zondervan, 1958), 8:315. Cited hereafter as *Works* (Jackson).

4. *Popery Calmly Considered*, I.4, *Works* (Jackson), 10:141.

5. Charles Le Cène, *An Essay for a New Translation of the Bible* (London: John Nutt, 1702).

6. Letter to William Law (6 Jan 1756), *Letters* (Telford), 3:345–46.

7. E.g., "Thoughts Upon Methodism" §2; *Arminian Magazine* 10 (1787); *Works*, 9:527. See also *Plain Account of Christian Perfection*, §5, *Works* (Jackson), 11:366.

8. See *NT Notes*, Matt 1:1; Heb 2:7.

9. *Letter to Bishop of Gloucester*, II.10, *Works*, 11:509. See also *OT Notes*, Preface, §18, *Works* (Jackson), 14:253.

10. See Sermon 18, "The Marks of the New Birth," §3, *Works*, 1:418 (emphasis added).

11. Ibid., §2, *Works*, 1:418.

12. *Sermons*, Vol. 1, Preface, §5, *Works*, 1:105–6.

13. See respectively, *Hymns and Sacred Poems* (1739), Preface, §4–5, *Works* (Jackson) 14:321; and Sermon 24, "Sermon on the Mount IV," §I.1, *Works* 1:533–34.

14. Sermon 39, "Catholic Spirit," §I.4, *Works*, 2:84.

15. Ibid., §III.1, *Works*, 2:92–93.

16. Augustine, *On Christian Teaching*, Book III, par. 2.

17. E.g., *NT Notes*, Rom 12:6; *OT Notes*, Preface, §18, I:ix, *Works* (Jackson), 14:253; and Sermon 122, "Causes of the Inefficacy of Christianity," §6, *Works*, 4:89.

18. Geoffrey Wainwright, "The Trinitarian Hermeneutic of John Wesley," in *Reading the Bible in Wesleyan Ways: Some Constructive Proposals* (ed. B. L. Callen and R. P. Thompson; Kansas City, MO: Beacon Hill Press of Kansas City, 2004), 17–37.

19. Letter to Cradock Glascott (13 May 1764), *Letters* (Telford), 4:243. Referring to John Pearson, *An Exposition of the Creed* (London: John Williams, 1659).

20. See David H. Kelsey, *Proving Doctrine: The Uses of Scripture in Modern Theology* (Philadelphia: Trinity Press International, 1999), esp. 163–67, 193–96.

21. Sermon 91, "On Charity," proem, *Works*, 3:292

22. Robert W. Wall, "Wesley as Biblical Interpreter," in *The Cambridge Companion to John Wesley* (ed. R. L. Maddox and J. E. Vickers; New York: Cambridge University Press, 2010), 113–28.

23. Although extant records are not exhaustive, a list of all known sermon occasions (over 400 pages in length), compiled by Wanda Willard Smith, longtime assistant to Professor Albert Outler and now available on the website of the Center for Studies in the Wesleyan Tradition (CSWT) at Duke (http://divinity.duke.edu/initiatives-centers/cswt/research-resources/register), supports this conclusion.

24. *Sermons*, Vol. 5, Preface, §6, *Works*, 2:357.

25. Sermon 40, *Christian Perfection*, II.20, *Works*, 2:116 (emphasis added).

26. Sermon 110, "Free Grace," §26, *Works*, 3:556.

27. Sermon 107, "On God's Vineyard," I.1, *Works*, 3:504; see also Sermon 115, "Dives and Lazarus," III.7, *Works* 4:18.
28. *NT Notes*, Preface, §9, *Works* (Jackson), 14:238.
29. *Thoughts upon Slavery* (1774), V.7, *Works* (Jackson), 11:79.
30. Sermon 60, "General Deliverance," §III.10, *Works* 2:449.

The Bible in a Postmodern Age[1]

Terence E. Fretheim

The Influence of Postmodernism

The question of biblical authority is in the air these days. By "biblical authority," I mean the Bible's unique capacity to mediate God's word of judgment and grace. This word can affect life and salvation for individuals and communities. Scripture delineates Christian faith and identifies the basic shape of Christian life in the world.

The Bible's authority will only be acknowledged if, through its use, people see that it speaks to their needs of life, well-being, and flourishing of communities. The question of biblical authority, then, is an inside, churchly conversation. But this conversation can spill out into the larger culture and affect the church's witness either positively or negatively.

Some consider the issue of biblical authority to be a crisis in postmodernity. We might order this crisis in three overlapping spheres:

1. *Culture* One characteristic of our context is that people—both inside and outside the church—are suspicious of authority. This includes being suspicious of the authority claimed by leaders in church or society. And it includes being suspicious of anyone's claims to have a corner on truth. Too many monsters have been loosed in the world in the name of authority.

If one were to think in terms of a marathon, the Bible in the postmodern world has the same starting place as any other book. If it is going to win, it will have to prove its value for life and well-being in the heat of the day. One might lament this. But it is real.

Another important factor in our postmodern world is religious pluralism. The Bible's authority is contested by other claims to authority among our increasingly diverse neighbors. The Bible has to compete in a marketplace of authorities, and a buyer's market prevails.

A third factor in postmodern culture affecting biblical authority is the sharply individualistic orientation of our culture. We have lost the sense of an overarching community with a universal story. If the Bible claims to have a story that applies to everyone but that story does not fit an individual's or sub-community's story, many will consider the Bible's claim as suspect.

2. Churches The authority of the Bible is no longer a given among many Christians. Many are unfamiliar with the Bible and its often strange vocabulary.

Christians have sometimes alienated people from the Bible by the way they have used it. Christians who disagree about a host of matters—from homosexuality to the place of women in the church—often use the Bible more as an Uzi than as a source of life. Causes polemically pursued with Bible in hand often push to the edges what should be the central truth of what God has done in Jesus Christ.

3. Academy Recent developments within the biblical disciplines have complicated the issue of authority. One development is reader-response criticism. In this approach, the focus of authority shifts from the authors of texts to the readers. Such an approach (among others) brings a new level of awareness to how personal perspectives affect our readings of the Bible. Complete objectivity is a mirage.

Reader-response criticism notes that readers of the Bible have preunderstandings and predispositions—personal, social, cultural, religious. These affect how they interpret the Bible. For instance, it makes a difference whether a person is male or female, black or white, upper class or lower class.

This postmodern approach works differently from approaches assuming the Bible has an original, true, or intended meaning. No meaning is the final or absolute meaning of a text. Reading is a dialogical process in which the contributions of both text and reader are important. Readers themselves play a significant role in making meaning. In fact, meaning changes over time for the same reader, because each reader is a different person every time she reads the Bible.

In one sense, reader-response interpretation does a better job than other approaches accounting for the historical realities within the Bible. Many Old Testament texts in their present form are the result of centuries of revision at the hands of numerous ancient interpreters. In other words, numerous readings of the tradition over time now reside within the Bible. The texts themselves do not speak with one voice. To appeal to an original or intended meaning is simply not being true to the historical character of the Bible.

Christians who embrace reader-response criticism also speak of a third party at work in the interpretative process: God the Holy Spirit. God engages in the interaction of reader and text and contributes to the production of meaning. Meanings emerge within this text/reader/God encounter.

Some who hear that postmodernism acknowledges the validity of multiple interpretations of the Bible can sometimes become worried that *any* interpretation is therefore valid. But this worry is not necessary. There are limits to what we should consider valid interpretations. The text cannot mean anything just because it can mean many things.

One reason the text cannot mean anything at all pertains to the text itself. The never-changing words on the page provide constraints. Distinctive textual features (e.g., prose or poetry) influence readings in certain directions and not in others. The text was shaped by certain realities in the culture within which it was produced. These need to be taken into account. Readers are not in full control of meanings nor do they create them out of whole cloth.

Yet, we must admit that the text is not entirely stable. A text may include gaps, silences, polysemic words, or grammatical ambiguities. All of these can affect interpretation. Texts never stay still for readers. The proliferation of contemporary Bible translations reflects this reality.

A second constraining factor on the Bible's meaning possibilities is that both text and reader reside within communities. Texts only exist in a web of community beliefs about the Bible or about particular texts and their meaning. These realities shape our reading before we even pick up the Bible.

Of course, community experience may change. Certain texts may be given a diminished status. Take, for example, 1 Corinthians 14:35: "If there is anything they desire to know, let them ask their husbands at home. For it is shameful for a woman to speak in church" (NRSV). For communities that ordain women, this text can never again be seen in isolation from this churchly role for women. For this community, this text is now stuck in a secondary status. This illustrates my main point: texts reside in communities, and meaning possibilities are deeply affected thereby.

Finding a way between the two extremes of only one meaning and unlimited meanings requires us to speak of three realities: (1) the text, which is reasonably, but not entirely stable; (2) readers and their commitments, including their basic sense of Scripture and the Christian faith; and (3) the communities within which texts and readers stand, which shape them such that their readings are not quite so variable as is sometimes supposed.

The indeterminacy of meaning in biblical texts actually has the potential of enhancing biblical authority. It can provide avenues in and through which the Bible can address more people. Through these people, the Bible can enrich the life, health, and flourishing of our neighborhoods, nations, and world.

Biblical Portrayals of God

How we view the authority of the Bible depends closely on how we view God. Likewise, the way we relate to God will decisively shape how we relate to the Bible.

The doctrine of God is an important conversation in church and academy. The Bible's role in thinking through this doctrine arises repeatedly. Numerous Bible readers—from women to pacifists to environmentalists—have raised serious questions about some biblical portrayals of God.

Most Christians believe the Bible does not speak the full truth about some matters. For instance, for more than a century scientific discoveries and observations have raised issues about the Bible's authority when it speaks about the natural world. In most Christian communities, an understanding emerged: the Bible's authority does not pertain to physics, astronomy, geology, or the like.

Many Christians also do not believe they must affirm the historical value of every biblical story. The truth value of the Bible does not necessarily depend upon the happenedness of every report. For example, the narrator no doubt used considerable imagination in constructing a conversation between David and Nathan regarding David's sin with Bathsheba (II Samuel 12). Despite this imaginative construction, the truth value of the material remains. The story of David and Bathsheba tells us something true about sin, indictment, repentance, and forgiveness.

We also know that biblical literature that is not historical in character can convey truth. Jesus' parables speak the truth, for instance, even though they never happened. It is important, of course, that some events of which the Bible speaks do have roots in history (e.g., the Exodus or Jesus' life, death, and resurrection).

But not everything in the Bible must be historically true to be true.

In the eyes of some, developments regarding science or history threaten or diminish the authority of the Bible. They ask, How can the Bible be authoritative on one level but not another?

When responding to this question, we should remember the absent-minded professor argument: If a professor tells me the plane for Chicago leaves at noon when it actually leaves at 11:00 a.m., I do not conclude that her reputation as a scholar rests on fraud. She can be a faithful guide on some matters and not others.

Unfortunately, some people claim that if we question the authority of the Bible on any matter, we begin down a slippery slope. In their minds, everything in the Bible is called into question. I contend, however, that the Bible's lack of authority with respect to certain matters helps us focus on its central confession regarding God and its gospel proclamation.

Most Christians assume that whatever the Bible says about God is right, true, or somehow appropriate. They believe no biblical text contains or conveys a contorted view of God. Consequently, the church tends to block any challenges to biblical images for God, to screen out questions about divine accountability, and to defend the Bible's portrayal of God.

Unless one adopts a problematic view of biblical inspiration that disallows any real participation of the human mind in writing the biblical texts, however, one must be open to the possibility that sinful and finite writers did not always get theology straight. Not all biblical portrayals of God are accurate.

It helps to remember that questions and challenges to God are present within the biblical texts themselves. Think of Abraham's question of God in Genesis 18:25: "Shall not the judge of all the earth do right?" Abraham asks whether God's contemplated action to destroy cities conforms to standards of justice God himself built into the world. God honors Abraham's question by discussing the fate of Sodom and Gomorrah. God remains open to the possibility that this conversation will issue in a future for the cities different from that which God initially contemplated.

Or think about the challenge Moses raises with God in the wake of the golden calf debacle (Exodus 32). In the first exchange, God informs Moses that this people will be destroyed. God asks to be left alone. Moses does not obey this request and instead presents a case as to why God should not destroy Israel. Moses appeals to God's reason, reputation, and resolve. In response, God changes his mind about destroying the people.

Texts like these provide an inner-biblical warrant for the raising and pursuing questions about God in every generation. Postmodern people who challenge the God of certain texts stand in the shoes of Abraham, Moses, and others. Those who silence such questioning are being untrue to the biblical tradition.

This approach confirms what I said earlier: the type of relationship one has with God shapes one's relationship to the biblical text. If God is one with whom we can converse, this models the way in which we approach the Bible.

The way in which we often deal with biblical views of the natural world can help point the way. The view of the natural world in Genesis 1–2 is considered less than fully accurate in light of contemporary scientific understandings. At the same time, few have suggested these verses be discarded. Instead, we affirm the considerable truth about matters basic to the chapter, e.g., that God is the Creator of all that is. The truth about the Creator is mediated in and through the knowledge and language available at that time and place.

This way of thinking about the Bible provides a paradigm for our postmodern age. Interpreters should take the available knowledge of the world and, like their biblical predecessors, use that as a vehicle in and through which to convey other truths about the creation. For example, a person might use evolution as a vehicle to speak of the complexities of God's work as Creator.

Take as another example Leviticus texts having to do with bloody animal sacrifices. For the Christian community, animal sacrifices are no longer required. At the same time, these texts remain part of our Bible. They undergird a theology that informs Christian understandings of atonement and the Lord's Supper. In this case, we make distinctions within texts with respect to the nature of their authority.

This less-than-totalistic approach to biblical texts is more helpful. In it, we acknowledge both the value and/or problems each text poses. But we still must ask, on what grounds do we make distinctions *within* the biblical text?

Some scholars claim that when we evaluate texts with harsher images of God, we tend to domesticate God. We end up making God more palatable to current tastes.

I believe we are always in danger of doing this. We must move carefully, even reluctantly. We must learn to read the Bible against ourselves and not just for ourselves. But it is also dangerous simply to repeat, for instance, texts portraying God as an abuser and killer of children. We must evaluate these texts in terms of what they say about God and about how we should act, no matter what is currently fashionable.

The image of God as Judge, for instance, must be affirmed as valuable. At the same time, we must raise questions about the way in which divine wrath is said to have been exercised. When we do so, we follow the example of Abraham and Moses.

For example, some prophets say God lifts up Israel's skirts and exposes her genitalia (Isa 3; Ezek 16; 23). In this instance and others, the prophets describe God as one who uses sexual terror. God is sexually abusive. In response, we should ask whether every terrifying image the Bible uses is appropriate in our search for understanding God as fully as possible.

The image of God in the story of Nathan and David (2 Sam 12) might serve as another example. In verse eleven, God says, "I will take your wives from before your eyes, and give them to your neighbor, and he shall lie with your wives in the sight of this very sun" (NRSV). As punishment for David's sin, fulfilled later, God gives David's women to another man for the explicit purpose of rape.

We must be attentive when the Bible says something that is threatening, strange, or surprising, for that may be a word we need to hear. At the same time, we must not fall into the trap of assuming all biblical texts are theologically valid.

Most Christians affirm that God cannot be captured in any text, language, image, or system. But faith *does* seek understanding. It is potentially just as idolatrous to claim we know little about God as it is to claim we know much. Either way, we worship at the feet of a claim limiting God in some way. The Bible is indispensable in the search to understand God more fully. But it is not sufficient. Trinitarian formulations show us this.

The factors we use when evaluating Bible texts and their portrayal of God vary. These factors enable us to make distinctions within Scripture. I want to mention three of the most important.

1. Other biblical texts. We must bring to bear the witness of other material in the Bible when evaluating a particular text's portrayal of God. We can read difficult texts in light of the more extensive portrayal of God. The principle, "Scripture interprets Scripture," can be used in such a way that Scripture sometimes interprets itself *against* itself. Because problematic texts continue to be used in isolation from the broader biblical message, it is important to include this larger canonical picture.

For instance, in response to passages that portray God as abusing children, we might think of texts such as Isaiah 49:14–15, which present a maternal God who will not desert her children *ever*. Or we might think of the image of Jesus who takes children into his arms. These images might better describe the God-human relationship. The larger biblical portrait stands over against an image of God as an abuser of children.

Similarly, we can affirm the idea of a canon within the canon. This formula asks whether a central biblical theme or textual grouping can be used to critique what other texts say.

Not just any canon within the canon will do. We must discern an inner-biblical warrant as the basis for our choice, not a standard outside the Bible. This move is fraught with danger, of course, but so is every interpretive move. All interpreters function with such a canon, though many are unaware of it. Generally speaking, the canon within the canon is centrally located in the word of the Gospel, that which conveys or inculcates Christ.

2. Our new identity as people of God. The Bible has been shown to have a generative, life-giving quality. God uses it to create new identities for people—one of the basic reasons many consider it authoritative.

Having received such an identity, Christians now stand within the same community of faith as Abraham and Moses. They are drawn into a relationship with God that may include challenges and questions about God's own ways, including those found in the Bible. Persons of faith have authority to speak against whatever in the Bible may be life demeaning, oppressive, or promoting of inequality. The Bible itself gives permission.

In an age where some have caught a vision of peace, many peacemakers claim biblical texts generate and inform this vision. Some environmentalists pick up neglected biblical texts that show God's extraordinary care for nonhumans. Many female scholars continue to value the Bible in spite of the harm done to women over the centuries in response to its words. These uses witness to the Bible's ability to transcend its own limitations.

In other words, within the Scriptures themselves we find a basis from which we can bring a word against the text. This internal biblical capacity to be self-critical provides a paradigm.

These developing sensitivities, however, ought not to be credited to the Bible alone. Significant thought and action contributing to peace, ecological sensitivity, and gender equality have occurred outside the bounds of church and Bible. This is testimony to the work of God active in the world outside the church.

3. *Non-biblical knowledge.* By this, I mean knowledge gained both from academic study and from more general life experience. In this connection, it is important to remember that the Reformation call for *sola scriptura* was addressed against ecclesiastical authorities, not secular sources of information.

Scientific knowledge serves as a good example. We make our judgments on Genesis 1–2 partly based on knowledge gained from sources of truth other than the Bible. Such non-biblical sources must be examined critically, of course, but their potential for enhancing our knowledge about the world has been amply demonstrated.

Inner-biblical warrant exists for appealing to general life experience as generating new reflection about God. We might cite the instance of Hagar in Genesis 16 as an example. Hagar is a woman ostracized from the elect family of Abraham and Sarah and banished to the wilderness. In the midst of her suffering, God comes and gives her a word that enables a way into the future. In light of this experience, Hagar gives God a new name: *El Roi*. A slave, woman, and outsider uses her experience to shape new language for God.

The Authority of the Bible for Postmodern Theology

The God of much churchly tradition is remarkably similar to the generic god of the average person. God is given the traditional attributes of omnipotence, omniscience, immutability, impassibility, atemporality, etc. However, the Bible often gives testimony to a God who does not fit those categories. It speaks about God in ways the church has often ignored.

Take the God of the flood story as an example. In it, God expresses sorrow and regret. God decides to blot out every living thing and then does not do so when Noah finds favor with God.

God promises never to do this again, thereby placing eternal limitations on the divine response to human wickedness. Elsewhere in the Bible, we find God affected by people's prayers (e.g., Exod 32:11–14). Sometimes God tests people, because divine knowledge of future human behaviors is less than absolute (e.g., Gen 22:12).

In fact, the God of *most* biblical texts is not uninfluenced, not unchanging, not timeless, and not omnipotent or omniscient, at least in any conventional understanding of these terms.

But, if *some* biblical texts support traditional understandings, how does one work with these differences? If there are multiple meanings and even multiple theologies, do we pick and choose the theology we like and name it "biblical"?

Postmodern approaches to the Bible help us evaluate better the God-talk in the Bible. For instance, postmodern interpretation asks about the point of view offered in a text. When God is characterized, whose point of view is being expressed? Sometimes the narrator speaks of God, and these references express the narrator's own point of view. Sometimes God says certain things about God's self. While these words probably represent the narrator's view, that the words are placed in God's mouth gives them a special status. And sometimes a character, not the narrator, says certain things about God. The theology voiced by one character does not necessarily have the same value as that voiced by another. Think of the theology of Job's friends, or the serpent in the garden, or Jacob's uncle Laban. In such cases, the characters in the Bible may not tell the truth about God.

Postmodern literary criticism also asks us to pay attention to rhetoric. We must attempt to discern how best to interpret words by God or about God. Are these words meant to be literal, ironic, hyperbolic, or metaphoric? Take the songs of lament, for example. They are spoken in situations of deep distress. They may represent an understanding of God comparable to what we might say in a tight spot but would never say in a carefully formulated statement.

For instance, "God, if you get me out of this scrape, I will go to seminary!"

Literary criticism also reminds us that at least sometimes biblical characters, God included, are not "flesh-and-blood" personalities. Words on the page are not the same as characters in real life. Whom we meet in the pages of the Bible is not the actual Moses, the actual Jesus, or the actual God. The God portrayed in the text does not fully correspond to the God who is a living, dynamic reality who cannot be captured by words on a page.

Admittedly, it is difficult to discern the relationship between the *textual* God and the *actual* God. We should avoid two ditches as we move through the discernment process:

1. One ditch says that the real God is identical with the God embodied in the biblical words. This ditch claims that the text somehow captures or encloses God. While knowledge of God *is* mediated through the text, yet in some basic sense, the God in whom we believe is *not* the God portrayed in the Bible.

Because the textual God and the actual God are not identical, the *text itself invites* questions about God. The text invites us to imagine language and images more adequate for God, language more attuned to new times and places. This takes into account ongoing experiences with God and world under the guidance of the Holy Spirit. The text mediates that encounter, but the experience may enable one to imagine God in ways truer to the actual God than the textual God allows. Trinitarian formulations may serve as an example of this.

2. The second ditch to steer clear denies any relationship between God the literary character and the real God. One form of this position denies God's reality altogether. Another form says God is so radically transcendent that no text, in the final analysis, can say anything true about God.

I claim, however, that while God transcends the text, the text does convey some knowledge of the actual God. In seeking to portray this God, we must be aware of the inexact character of the enterprise. We must check our efforts with what other readers have discerned. And we must remember that the tradition and community in which we stand will shape our construal of God in ways beyond our knowing.

One way to avoid these ditches is to consider the role of metaphors in relation to God. All metaphors for God say both a "yes" and a "no." At the basic thrust of the analogy, metaphors correspond to the reality that is God (the "yes" of the metaphor). But they also bespeak a "no," for God outdistances all our images.

The task of discerning the 'yes' and the 'no' in the metaphor is difficult. Not all metaphors have the same value. For example, Hosea's use of "parent" for God (11:1) has more value than does his image of God as "dry rot" (5:12). Some metaphors say so much "no" that they obscure who God is (e.g., God is a child abuser). The negative images of divine judgment in terms of female sexuality, for instance, may be very important to say "no" to altogether.

These images have great impact on our thinking and feeling and being. They sink deep into our selves and shape us in ways beyond our knowing. But all metaphors, whether of high value or low, are only partial visions into the truth about God. No metaphor fully corresponds to the actual God.

Metaphors bring us one step further along in providing the groundwork for our task of understanding God. Certain ruling metaphors or generalizations provide a key place from which to assess the adequacy of other metaphors.

We determine which metaphors are primary by discerning (1) their pervasiveness, (2) the literary genres in which they typically recur, and (3) their ongoing role in tradition. Those images of God drawn into creeds and hymns have an especially high value. They make central truth-claims about God.

The most common creedal statement in the Old Testament is found in Exodus 34:6–7. This statement echoes throughout the

Psalms and elsewhere. It says,

> The Lord, the Lord, a God merciful and gracious,
> slow to anger, and abounding in steadfast love and faithfulness,
> keeping steadfast love for the thousandth generation,
> forgiving iniquity and transgression and sin,
> yet by no means clearing the guilty. (NRSV)

The underlying assumptions expressed in these words about God pervade the Bible. They inform and bring considerable coherence to biblical God-talk. We qualify other images of God by these generalizations. For instance, God is not simply father; God is always a *loving* father. Only such generalizations, irreducible to story form, enable one to discern continuities in the story. They help us spot something strange or new. They give internal directions for interpreting the kind of God present in the biblical narrative. While the God of the Bible could be characterized in various ways, these metaphors make truth claims that give specific direction to one's interpretation.

In the past, scholars have thought confessional recitals of God's mighty acts in Israel's history (e.g., Deut 26:5–9; Josh 24:2–13) provide the clue to Israel's God-talk. These are important, but they are insufficient. They do not often make clear what kind of God is acting. After all, a God who saves could also be capricious, unloving, and unjust.

Old Testament scholars have neglected the kind of Exodus statement above, perhaps because of its more abstract, even propositional character. But such truth-claims about God enable Israel to see the continuity in its own story and be carried across those times when the story seems to have broken off.

The book of Lamentations, which never appeals to God's actions in Israel's past, makes this kind of confession (3:20–32). In the midst of the great gulf between past and future, the hope of Israel is not to be placed in its own story. Its hope is in the kind of God it confesses. We should understand the God who is the story's subject in terms of such generalizations.

The crucial confession has to do with the kind of God God has been, is, and will be. God is faithful, loving, gracious, and righteous. Therefore, there is hope. This confession makes an intelligible and reasonably coherent narrative world possible.

The combination of these generalizations and historical recitals suggests that together they represent some kind of unanimity regarding the characterization of God amidst the Bible's theological pluralism. They constitute a metaphorical canon with the canon. Just as historical recitals confess those events in Israel's history constitutive of its identity, so also generalizations about God provide the confessional clue for determining the basic character of the God of the story.

In the midst of all that makes for process and pluralism, there is that which is utterly constant in Israel's claims about the God in whom it believes. The most fundamental continuity through the centuries is the history of a certain kind of God who will always, come what may, execute justice and love the stranger (Deut 10:18). God's salvific will is never diminished. God's righteousness is never compromised. God's faithfulness will never waver. God's steadfast love endures forever. God is love.

Some Christians today seek to show, directly or indirectly, that the God of many Old Testament texts is the God of classical theism. But increasing numbers of theologians are offering theologies potentially truer to biblical moorings than classical theology. The God described in the Old Testament often contributes positively to this postmodern task: Yahweh is a passionate God, who enters into lively conversations with people like Abraham and Moses, who gets jealous, who repents of something said or done, who is genuinely influenced by people's prayers.

Those who interpret the Bible have a responsibility, not simply to themselves, but to those who read and hear what they have to say. No reading is value-free. How we interpret in one way or another will promote the personal and social values we hold dear.

We must ask ourselves a series of questions: What will the effects of my interpretation be? What is at stake if I interpret the text in a certain way? What ideology might I be promoting? Will my interpretation contribute to the life and well-being of others?

When constructing theology in our postmodern age, we seem presented with three possibilities for approaching the Bible as our theological resource:

1. *Pick and choose among texts about God according to our own likes and dislikes or in terms of whatever tradition to which we belong.* The advantage of this option is that differing contexts may need differing theologies. Such diverse theologies aim to meet differing needs of people in various times and places. The disadvantage is that the result would be (and often is) a biblical- theological cacophony. Chaos reigns. A great deal of confusion emerges as to just who the Christian God really is. Will the real biblical God please stand up?

2. *Insist that biblical differences be consolidated to present a uniform and single picture of God.* One advantage of this option is that the church would present a coherent and unified theological front on such a fundamental issue as the identification of the God whom it trusts and worships. The disadvantage is the temptation to dismiss the diversity of biblical portraits of God. All contrary texts and opposing metaphors of God would be drowned out or ignored.

3. *Seek a unified portrayal of God, but with the understanding that some biblical texts will just not fit.* The advantage of this option is that marginal texts constantly challenge us to reexamine any theological construal. Another advantage is that keeping in play biblical differences has the capacity to spark theological imagination.

I find this third option most persuasive. It seeks to present a unified portrayal of God to the postmodern world. But it recognizes that the texts cannot so neatly be lined up behind such a portrayal as we might like. Perspectives not caught up in the prevailing theology may function as a gadfly or ongoing challenge. Or they may be given back-burner status, perhaps to emerge at another time and place. The ongoing struggle with difference leads us onward in our search for truth about God.

The Bible should function as an indispensable resource for generating ever new reflections about God in our postmodern age. But we should remember that God is greater than the portrayal of any biblical narrative, and bigger than the composite portrayal from the Bible as a whole.

The Bible's authority derives from the God to whom it witnesses. On the one hand, if God is perceived to be distant, aloof, removed from life, and absent in times of suffering and grief, the authority of the Bible may become authoritarian. In our postmodern world, authoritarianism diminishes authority. On the other hand, if we perceive God as genuinely engaged in relationship with us, our relationship to the Bible would be of the nature of a conversation or dialogue.

The church must witness to its God and articulate an understanding of God that strikes home in the hearts of people. It must witness to a God who engages in dialogue, mediated by the biblical texts. The church cannot prove the authority of the Bible. It can only issue a call to enter into a community where the gospel is preached. The postmodern church invites us all into an ongoing theological conversation.

---

1. This is a reduced version of Terence Fretheim's portion of the book, Terence Fretheim and Karl Froehlich, *The Bible as Word of God in a Postmodern Age* (Eugene, OR: Wipf and Stock, 2001).

10

Reading the Bible in a Postmodern Age: The Importance of Context for Interpretation

Kara J. Lyons-Pardue and Jason Sturdevant

The Word Became Contextualized

A lot of biblical interpretation happens in our churches and schools as if the meaning of the Bible was timeless and eternal. Interpreters seem to believe Scripture contains a *single* message stored within the pages of the Old and New Testaments. In this view, interpretation becomes an act of figuring out this abstract, timeless message, and decoding that message for contemporary Christians. This approach has helpfully led to our recognition that the study of the Bible is serious business. Moreover, it gives comfort that God's word will remain clear forever.

Yet postmodernity bristles at the notion that, if we simply apply the right technique, we can "decode" what God is really saying in Scripture. Some postmoderns tell us that words are not simple containers of meaning; people who read words in their various contexts make meaning out of words in ways that make the best sense for them. Throughout human history and across the world, people have understood the words of Scripture to communicate very different and even contradictory messages. If even interpreters with the "proper tools" fail to agree on the meaning of a text, perhaps we should ask if there really is a *single, timeless* meaning in Scripture.

To help with this question, we might find guidance in one of the central texts for our understanding of God's revelation, John 1:1–18. In these verses, John describes the miraculous event of the incarnation in poetic language. He states the eternal, timeless Word of God entered into our world.

John begins by making a strong differentiation: while the Word of God *was*, all other things *became* (John 1:1–3). This is an idea borrowed from Greek philosophy: all created things are constantly in the process of *becoming*, but only God truly *exists*.[1] Because human beings are creatures, they find themselves in this world of *becoming*, ever altered and changed by many different rhythms and contexts of life. Human understanding of truth, therefore, is limited, finite, flawed, and largely determined by individual perspective. Only the God who exists can know all things fully and truly, because God exists above the confines of the created world of *becoming*.

But here is the miracle of the incarnation of the Word: John writes that the eternal, timeless Word of God *becomes* flesh (1:14). The eternal Word chooses to reveal God's salvation in the midst of ever-changing circumstances. The Word in Christ is exposed to the varied contexts of human life. Jesus, the incarnate Word, experiences life as a Jewish male from a working-class background with a unique set of experiences. This incredible event indicates the amazing way God chooses to communicate to humanity: rather than express a timeless, eternal message, God in Christ speaks in a specific, context-bound way. To claim that we who are similarly context-bound can fully understand God's eternal Word is to forget the miracle of the incarnation. It is to forget God chooses the world of *becoming* as the place for telling us about Godself.

How does this shape biblical interpretation? When we recognize that the eternal Word of God chose to communicate to humanity in a specific historical, cultural, and social context, we can also affirm that God *continues* to communicate through our varying contexts. The Word speaks through Scripture and through our individual, limited perspectives to help us know and understand both God and ourselves more fully. We are called to listen to the perspectives of others to catch a greater glimpse of how God is speaking today. This view holds strong resonances with postmodern aspects of interpretation, and we will explore some of those aspects.

In this chapter, we mean to use the term "postmodern" very simply (and imprecisely). It has taken volumes to diagnose what a postmodern worldview means, multiple studies to diagnose how extensive a cultural shift "postmodernism" represents, and even more analysis of what it means for how we read Scripture.[2] But at its core, postmodernism recognizes that *context changes things.* Different contexts influence communication itself; the same words may convey dissimilar meanings when spoken by or to different people.[3] Postmodernism recognizes that people's cultures, ways of life, and individual experiences are not incidental. They deeply shape how people experience the world and who people are.

This worldview may threaten people whose faith is first and foremost about universal truths and ethereal absolutes. But Christian faith is rooted and grounded in the person of Jesus Christ. Christianity is at its core—in the person of Jesus—emphatic that context *does* change things. Jesus lived as a Jewish man in the first century AD, and our creedal confessions refuse to let us extract him from that context (i.e., "he suffered under Pontius Pilate"). He is at once a member of the eternal Godhead, the Word through whom creation came to be. At the same time, he lived as a native of Nazareth, a reader of the Torah, a son of Mary and Joseph, and a teacher and friend to his disciples. This life context forever changed and shaped the Second Person of the Trinity: Jesus of Nazareth is also Jesus the Christ, Son of God. The point is that postmodernism reminds Christians of something we should have known all along: context matters.

On the Page: Reading Biblical Texts in
Their Immediate, Literary Contexts

For anyone who has taken a college course on the Bible or engaged in-depth Bible study, this first step for reading the Bible will be no surprise. The first context that influences our interpretation of Scripture is its literary context. The words on the page or the pages that surround a verse or a passage are most important for understanding.

While this may be a *"no duh"* statement, frequently reminding ourselves of the purpose of reading within a literary context is vital. For example, in Exodus we find this statement from God to Moses, intended for all the Israelites: "The whole earth is mine, but you shall be for me a priestly kingdom and a holy nation" (19:5b–6a, NRSV). The reassurance of God's election and the implication to bring about good for God's people are beautiful. It makes for a good memory verse or inspirational placard on the wall.

When we look at the context in which these words are found, however, this "nice" verse has a little more bite. In context, God's words mean *even more* to us: we see that they were spoken after a series of trials in which Israel complained against God and against Moses (16:1–8; 17:1–7). Further, God's statement immediately precedes the giving of the Ten Commandments (ch. 20), signifying that election comes with covenant. Not much later in the Exodus narrative, this holy nation turns its worship toward a graven image, threatening the covenant altogether. But the Lord shows mercy even then. The isolated statement becomes more applicable and more moving when read in the context of God's interactions with the House of Jacob.

An exercise from the New Testament further emphasizes the importance of context. Read the following verses and imagine what practical application these verses might have:

We do not live to ourselves, and we do not die to ourselves.

If we live, we live to the Lord, and if we die, we die to the Lord; so then, whether we live or whether we die, we are the Lord's. For to this end Christ died and lived again, so that he might be Lord of both the dead and the living.

To what use might a minister or layperson put these verses? Perhaps they might provide reassurance to those facing imminent danger, knowing that living or dying we are in God's hands. Missionaries who take great risks to share the gospel could find comfort in the Lord's presence. These verses could be shared at a funeral, giving comfort to those who have lost a loved one.

The above passage exposes a deep confidence in God. But its application seems limited by the content to life-or-death situations. There is an expressed connection between Christ's death and resurrection and our own way of life. But the generalized terms restrict the situations to which we might apply these statements. The verses relate theological anthropology (i.e., how humans exist in relationship to God) to Christology, evidencing significant theological reflection.

We may be surprised to find that, in Paul's letter to the Romans, these verses serve as the theological groundwork undergirding very practical instructions, which lead to real-world consequences. In chapter 14, Paul talks about welcoming those who are "weak in faith" (14:1). Those weak in the faith have religious consciences that keep them from consuming certain foods (v. 2) and influence how they celebrate certain days as sacred (v. 5). Paul is addressing differences in ethics—how one's faith influences one's life—that have caused division, judgment, and condemnation among believers.[4] Paul is emphatic: the Lord is judge; it is not our job (whether weak or strong) to "judge someone else's servants" (v. 4). A more apt paraphrase for American culture might be: "Who are you to discipline someone else's child?" God is the parent/master in these analogies, and God is judge (this is rephrased and repeated in vv. 10, 12).

In this passage, Paul reminds his audience that believers' primary relationship is to God, not to please one another. Living and dying, a pair of terms repeated four times in verses 7–9, form the all-inclusive brackets that define our relationship to God. Thus, it is not only to life-or-death scenarios that Paul applies our allegiance to God (as we might suspect when viewing the verses in isolation). His point is that our ultimate duty is to please God in *every situation*. Whether the questions are mundane, as Paul's examples of diet and calendar seem to be, or serious, we are to reorient our pointing fingers to the Source of our salvation, the Lord.

Obviously, reading a passage in its literary context makes a big difference to our interpretation. There are simple steps that help to ensure we are vigilant in doing so:

Be wary of approaching Scripture in terms of memory-verse sized snippets. While Bible memorization is a vital element in spiritual growth, we should not reduce Scripture to sound bites.

Read a biblical book thoroughly before preaching or teaching *from* it. It may help to ignore the notes or introductions in a study Bible or comments from a commentator *until* you have read the book yourself.

We should not bend Scripture to be a mouthpiece for our own soapboxes. Take cues from the biblical authors in making ethical or real-world applications. Very often, ancient writers creatively apply profound theological insights to concrete situations.

Come to Scripture with an attitude of patient curiosity: you might be surprised where the text will take you. Approach the text in a different translation than usual. Or read it aloud. The "different" sound may trigger new pathways for interpretation.

Although the "work" of reading the Bible with literary contexts in mind may take real effort, it often saves us labor in the long run. No longer must our own creativity and organizational structure be in charge of making sense of Scripture. Instead, we can preach and teach within the logic and imagery of the text itself.

Looking Backwards: Reading the Bible within Its Historical and Canonical Contexts

A basic claim that postmodern biblical interpretation makes is this: *stories do not mean anything*, at least not in isolation. Like the lives of real human beings, stories only make sense when put into historical context. Biblical passages require us to get a sense for the historical settings to make sense of them. In academic biblical scholarship, this has been the "mainstream" assumption for well over a century. It still provides helpful guidance for interpretation.

Yet reading Scripture in a postmodern age helps us move beyond determining what a passage *meant* in historical context to determining what a passage *means* today.[5] Biblical stories have histories of their own. Various people have told the stories, retold them, reinterpreted them, and understood them in vastly different ways throughout history. *We are heirs of this interpretive history*. We also come to the task of interpretation with historically conditioned concerns.

The passage of Genesis 22:1–18 offers a useful example of how one text has undergone significant changes in meaning throughout history.[6] In interpretations of this passage, dramatic changes in meaning have occurred, between the earliest form of the story of which we know and how people read and understand the story today.

The canonical version of the "binding of Isaac" shows signs that an older, pre-canonical story of Abraham's sacrifice of Isaac once stood on its own, consisting of verses 1b–14.[7] The unit may have circulated as a fixed oral tradition. These verses convey the story of Abraham's near sacrifice of Isaac and offer a specific interpretation of the event. This older version is still visible in the canonical version; the last verses (vv. 13–14) describe the story's significance for the earliest Israelites. They indicate the reason why Mt. Moriah was a sacred site[8] to provide an explanation for why Abraham's descendants did not engage in child sacrifice.

Some radical changes took place, however, when this basic story became a "link" in a chain of stories about Abraham that eventually became Genesis 12:1–24:11. First, this story would have been read more closely in relation to the other Abraham stories, such as the covenant between God and Abraham and the gift of the child Isaac. In this context, there is much more at stake when Abraham agrees to sacrifice Isaac, the child of the promise. The story also has two editorial additions: one at the beginning and one at the end (22:1a, 15–18). These additions reinterpret the story. They suggest that God wanted to see if Abraham truly had faith. The new layer of meaning is that Abraham's willingness to offer up his son led God to reaffirm his promise to bless both Abraham and his descendants.

No one is sure exactly why these verses were added to the older story of Genesis 22:1b–14. But one interesting suggestion is this: If the Abraham stories were collected during the time of Israel's exile, this particular story may have been retold to emphasize Abraham's children as God's special and blessed possession. It would reaffirm God's ability to fulfill the promise of Israel's restoration and the importance of faithfulness in a context of intense testing. Here we can see ways in which changing historical circumstances alter what a story means. Importantly, the first version of the story with its meaning has not completely disappeared; it stands side-by-side with its revision and its newer meanings.

In the New Testament, the meanings of Genesis 22:1–18 took on more layers in light of Jesus. In Mark 1:11, 9:7, and 12:6, for example, many see the connection between the affirmations of Jesus as God's "beloved" with Genesis 22:2 and when God says to Abraham, "Take your only son Isaac, *your beloved*." The idea of a "beloved son" appears only in a few Old Testament texts, and nowhere more prominently than in the story of Isaac.[9] In this light, Mark's understanding of Jesus' death builds on the story of Abraham's willingness to offer up Isaac in sacrifice. A clearer example is Romans 8:32: "God did not spare *his only Son*." This echoes Genesis 22:16. It invites us to understand the Isaac story as a kind of prefiguring of God's gracious provision of Christ for our salvation. We can also look to James 2:21 and Hebrews 11:17–19. In both passages, the authors state how Abraham's faith serves as a model for the faith of early Christians. Both use the story of Genesis 22 to demonstrate Abraham's faith in spite of opposition, a faith needed also by early Christians.

The New Testament authors did not retell the original story. But they expanded the scope of meaning of the "sacrifice" of Isaac. Importantly, almost all of these earliest Christian writers retold the story in light of the new thing God had done through Jesus Christ. Connecting the story of Jesus with Genesis 22 added a new layer of depth to early Christian understanding of the significance of Jesus' life and death.

However, reinterpretation did not end with the last of the New Testament texts. In the early and medieval church, people frequently looked for Christ in Old Testament stories. Many saw the story of Genesis 22 as an example of Christ's own sacrifice as the Lamb of God, linking the passage with Isaiah 53.[10] During the Reformation and its strong emphasis on "faith alone," interpreters believed Genesis 22 gave an example of faith that looks to God alone for hope.[11] Recent interpreters have pondered the psychological dilemmas facing Abraham when asked to give up his only son.[12]

All of these interpretations emphasize different components of a single biblical story. As contexts and circumstances shift, so too has the way God's people have understood biblical texts. At the same time, people have not abandoned earlier understandings. They expanded those understandings. We stand today as heirs of this long history of interpretation. As our own circumstances change, a postmodern approach that recognizes the importance of historical contexts allows us flexibility and openness to new, multi-layered readings of texts like Genesis 22. These new readings may help Christians make sense of God's message of salvation for the world in which they live.

There are basic steps we can take to appreciate the historical contexts of scriptural interpretation:

Develop an awareness of broad historical developments in the story of Israel and the church. Being familiar with key events like the Babylonian exile, the birth of the church, the destruction of the Jewish temple, the Reformation, and the Holocaust can help us momentarily step into the shoes of earlier interpreters. This can help us see what they might have seen.[13]

Use resources for accessing what earlier Christian interpreters have said about a particular passage, such as *textweek.com*. This website has a Scripture search function and links to online sources for the commentaries of figures like Augustine, Luther, and Wesley. Such sources can give us a clearer sense of how earlier historical periods read and understood Scripture. They can help us identify assumptions about the text we have inherited.[14]

Develop and maintain your understanding of issues in contemporary society. This awareness can be as simple as keeping up on current events. It can be deepened when we take a theological view of what goes on in our world (e.g., where does God seem to be at work, and where in our culture do we hear people crying out for God's voice?). Such a view also helps us to explore how God might be speaking through a text to our new historical context.

Around Us: The Reader's Context

The above sections provide examples for ways in which contexts—literary and historical—make a difference in interpreting Scripture. The third context for interpretation is, perhaps, the most categorically "postmodern." It focuses primarily on the Bible's *readers*. The lenses through which readers view Scripture are as varied as the reading communities represented. Some postmodern approaches to the Bible are even antagonistic or come from a readerly perspective of skepticism and agnosticism. The perspectives designated here, however, are generally *believing*. Even among faithful interpreters, readers of Scripture start and end at different places, culturally, socially, ethically, and theologically.

a. Naming our own context(s)

People have used Scripture to justify terrible episodes in human history: American slavery of the 18th and 19th centuries, Christian failure to oppose Hitler, South African apartheid, just to name a few. We humans are often blind to our own prejudices and ignorance. In addition to praying for the Holy Spirit's illumination to see ourselves clearly, the practice of critical self-examination in the context of Scripture reading can help me us aware of "where we stand" when we engage a biblical text.

The parable of the prodigal son from Luke 15:11–32 is a classic test case for asking the "where do we stand?" question. Identifying with each character yields a divergent message. When we see ourselves as the younger, wayward son, the story comforts and encourages repentance. When we imagine imitating the father in the parable, we may—especially if we are parents—find ourselves wanting to emulate patience, graciousness, and forgiveness. For many devout Christians, the elder brother's shoes fit best: self-righteous people need Jesus' message of grace as much as more blatant "sinners."

James 2:1–7 provides another opportunity for readers to examine their context, but this time as it relates to James' ancient audience. The sermonic-letter[15] imagines its initial recipients as those welcoming a person into their "assembly" (v. 2). Clearly, the readers of James's letter are asked to consider how they treat guests in church. Do they treat everyone fairly, or do they favor the wealthy? The author reminds readers that they have more in common with the poor (cf. vv. 6–7): "Is it not *the rich* who oppress *you*? Is it not *they* who drag *you* into court? Is it not *they* who blaspheme the excellent name that was invoked over *you*?" A good reader of Scripture notices these identifications, which are part of the text.

As we become more aware of the context we bring as readers, we recognize that our context may be different from the idealized reader implied in the text. In James 2, there are analogies between the ancient readers and those of us who, as regular churchgoers or pastors, may be directing a newcomer where to sit. In this, we can show either deference or dismissal based on superficial judgments, just like James' intended audience.

However, in contrast to the earliest readers of James' message, the modern Western church often has more in common with the rich guest of James 2:2. Most Christians in the West are more like the rich in terms of power and bank accounts.[16] When welcomers are themselves rich, it can be more tempting to favor the wealthy. On a global scale, Western Christians can make our poorer brothers and sisters "sit on the floor," so to speak, saving the best "seats" (be it education, resources, foodstuffs, opportunities, pleasures) for ourselves. We can relegate what is *good enough* to those with drastically fewer resources.

A final example of allowing a reader's setting influence her or his encounter with the biblical text can be addressed only briefly. In the Old Testament prophet Hosea, we find a lived-out prophecy in the marriage of Hosea and the prostitute Gomer. Readers are asked to draw an analogy between Hosea's relationship with Gomer and God's relationship with Israel. In preaching and teaching on the titillatingly sinful Gomer, a current reality of our global context requires caution. We can bemoan the "whorish" behavior of Gomer, which surely applies to God's people throughout history. Christians have sometimes been an unfaithful bunch.

Unfortunately, reading this story as an accusation may lead us to look at the "Gomers" of our society and blame them for their position. We live in a global reality in which hundreds of thousands of women and children are annually sold into sex-slavery against their will.[17] Human trafficking is at record levels, even within U.S. borders. In an era in which so much of "prostitution" is actually forced slavery, Hosea's image of a willfully and egregiously sinful prostitute may not communicate the same message today. Christians may find it difficult to vilify Gomer and still fight against the exploitation of women and children that characterizes much of the modern sex trade.

To be good interpreters of Scripture for our context, we cannot have our heads in the sand. Awareness of current events on a global scale will only enrich our ability to read Scripture. A few steps take the form of introspective questions:

In *narratives*, look for characters: With whom do you want to identify? With whom do you share most in common? (These are not always the same.)

In *parables*, consider both the specified audience of the story and the characters in the story itself: Where do you fit?

In *didactic* or *epistolary* texts, compare yourself to the described audience: How alike are you? If there are good and bad examples, be careful not to picture yourself too quickly on the "winning team."

Finally, Scripture challenges both us *and* our contexts. If we are willing to question our individual and communal positions in relation to the biblical text, Scripture can speak prophetically to believers *and* to the larger cultures and subcultures in which we live.

b. Inhabiting others' contexts

One of the most profound claims made by postmodern interpretation is this: the experience of each reader or group of readers can radically challenge the "plain meaning" of a text. Usually, what we call the "plain meaning" is only plain to people who are like us! It is plain to people who share our experiences and assumptions. Postmodern interpretation helps give voice to people *not like us*, and this can challenge our understanding of Scripture. In many ways, this is an extension of the metaphor of the body of Christ: we must listen to voices too easily ignored or silenced. The body is healthiest when it listens to all its members.

We benefit not only from *listening* to other interpretations in contexts different from our own. We benefit even more from *inhabiting* those contexts. To see how this kind of "inhabited reading" works, we can turn to the so-called "parable of the tenants" (Mark 12:1–12). We can begin by reading this passage in light of some attitudes involved in naming our own contexts (section 3a, above). We can become more aware of our own tendencies: who are the character(s) with whom we find ourselves sympathizing? Reading from our own contexts serves as a baseline for inhabiting others' contexts.

Learning to read from the perspective of others takes a good deal of imagination. It may require that we set aside some of our assumptions about the "plain meaning" of the biblical text, if only for a few moments. When we try to see how others might read a text, it opens up new avenues for understanding a passage. And it gives us more compassion for others in general. When we ask the same questions from multiple perspectives, we quickly find out how other people might look at the same text from very different angles.

For instance, try to reread the parable of the tenants from each of the following perspectives, one at a time:

Scenario #1: You and your family work on a farm for low wages with a high risk of physical injury.

Scenario #2: You have recently lost your job to someone younger or smarter, and you are running out of resources.

Scenario #3: Your house has just undergone foreclosure. The police came to evict you.

Scenario #4: You recently received a promotion, because your supervisor was unfairly terminated.

Scenario #5: You are a Christian minister who has been wrongly accused of abusing his/her power.

In each of these varying scenarios, ask the following questions:

How does the experience of this viewpoint alter the way you read the story?

With whom do you identify?

What does this passage make you *feel*?

Does your perspective influence the way you read the portion about the son?

What injustices are in this passage? What determines who is right (according to Mark) and wrong? Do we have to accept Mark's view of things (or can we set it aside, even momentarily)?

Try to answer these questions as honestly as possible, and allow yourself to answer them in ways that may make you feel uncomfortable. However this makes you feel, return to the passage one last time from your own perspective. What parts of the story now stand out that you had not seen quite as clearly? What layers of meaning might you see at work in the passage?

In our reading of the parable of the tenants, most of us unconsciously side with Jesus, the landowner. And we side with those who get to work the land after the "wicked" tenants have been given the boot. This seems to be what Mark *wants* us to do. However, the reality for many in our churches and around the world is that various life experiences force people to raise questions about whether what takes place in this parable is just or unjust, whether it brings good news or bad. And even though we may ultimately still agree with Mark's point of view, our agreement will not be naïve or simplistic. The result of such practice is this: when we take account of postmodern attention to readerly contexts, particularly those different from our own, we can hear stories in fuller ways. And this will draw our attention to God's voice speaking in areas we have not heard.

Trying to inhabit the contexts of others invites a wide range of actions. These are geared not only for pastors with regular preaching responsibilities but also for those in other settings:

Begin by trying to interpret Scripture in community. Invite

various members from your congregation and have them help you think through a text from their perspectives and from the perspectives of people they know. If possible, talk to one or two people *outside* the church and see how they understand passages. More broadly, be in conversation with at least a handful of trustworthy, open-minded individuals who will lovingly challenge your own views of a passage.

Expand your interpretive imagination. Spend a few minutes developing some imaginary profiles of individuals in your church. Try especially to imagine yourself as those people who are least like you. Ask yourself what issues matter to these people. Wonder how they might interact with such a passage.

Narrate your own context. Write out a summary of your life, noting those events that seem to have had the biggest impacts on your own interpretive approach. Are the events you narrate common to most people in your congregation? Why or why not? Which ones have had the most positive impact and (if possible) can you help your congregants or students share a similar experience?

By the Spirit

We have sought to highlight diverse "contexts" for reading the Bible. These contexts anchor our interpretation to Scripture and open up new vistas for understanding. Wesleyan-Holiness believers, with our robust theology of the Spirit, expect that the same Holy Spirit who flows wherever the Spirit pleases can speak as we read the Bible.

Our high view of Scripture as the central element in our Wesleyan quadrilateral, however, does not mean the Bible can simply mean *anything* to anyone. The most serious abuses of Scripture are self-centered uses of the text to defend great evils. Most commonly lacking in these abuses of interpretation is an understanding of *context*. The contexts we employ in biblical interpretation have various implications and help us approach Scripture from different angles. Context simultaneously protects us from reading too much of ourselves into Scripture and reminds us of various ways texts can make meaning to different people in widely divergent contexts.

Ultimately, through our belief that the Spirit is at work inspiring both authors and readers, we can affirm that the Spirit speaks to us in our context. The Spirit uses our limited understanding to point us—as individuals and communities of believers—to Christ. In so doing, the Spirit leads to ever-deepening understanding and strengthens us as fellow members of the body of Christ.

---

1. See Raymond E. Brown, *The Gospel According to John* (Anchor Bible 29; Garden City, NY: Doubleday, 1966, 1970), 1:30–31.
2. For an accessible introduction, see A. K. M. Adam, *What Is Postmodern Biblical Criticism?* (Guides to Biblical Scholarship, New Testament Series; Minneapolis: Fortress, 1995).
3. E.g., calling God "Father" might carry vastly varied implications to the following people: (1) an unwed or single mother, (2) a person abused by one's father or a father figure, or (3) someone from a strongly patriarchal culture.
4. For further explanations of the "parties" in play, as well as the subjects that may have been debated, see William M. Greathouse with George Lyons, *Romans 9–16: A Commentary in the Wesleyan Tradition* (New Beacon Bible Commentary; Kansas City, MO: Beacon Hill Press of Kansas City, 2008), 201–12. Luke Timothy Johnson thinks these instructions reflect Paul's general approach to multicultural churches, rather than demonstrating a specific knowledge of problems or disagreements in the Roman church (*Reading Romans: A Literary and Theological Commentary* [Macon, GA: Smyth & Helwys, 2001], 209–12).
5. On the problematic contrast of "what is meant" and "what it means," see Ben C. Ollenburger, "What Krister Stendahl 'Meant': A Normative Critique of 'Descriptive Biblical Theology'," *Horizons in Biblical Theology* 8 (1986): 61–98.
6. These are not altogether different elements, since the formation of the canon itself was an unfolding, historic event, whose historical contexts we similarly need to understand. For a helpful guide on the process of the canonization of the New Testament, see the classic: Bruce M. Metzger, *The Canon of the New Testament: Its Origin, Development, and Significance* (Oxford: Clarendon, 1987). A recent collection of essays on both the Old and New Testament canons may also prove helpful: Lee Martin McDonald and James A. Sanders, eds., *The Canon Debate* (Peabody, MA: Hendrickson, 2002).
7. See the bibliography in Brevard S. Childs, *Biblical Theology of the Old and New Testaments: Theological Reflection on the Christian Bible* (Minneapolis: Fortress, 1993), 331.
8. In 2 Chr 3:1, Moriah is identified with the location of Solomon's temple.
9. Childs, *Biblical Theology*, 329.
10. Frequently, this is referred to as "typological" interpretation; see, e.g., Tertullian, *Against the Jews* 13; Origen, *Homilies on Genesis* 11–13.

11. Childs, *Biblical Theology*, 332.

12. Such psychologizing concerns, together with those of the Reformers, are addressed frankly in Terrence Fretheim, "God, Abraham, and the Abuse of Isaac," *Word and World* 15 (1995): 49–57. Most notably, such psychologizing interests find their initial expression in Søren Kierkegaard, *Fear and Trembling* (Garden City, NY: Princeton University Press, 1954).

13. One helpful resource is Justo L. Gonzalez, *The Story of Christianity* (Rev. ed., 2 vols.; New York: HarperCollins, 2010). A shorter, more accessible resource by the same author is *Church History: An Essential Guide* (Nashville: Abingdon, 1996).

14. See Thomas Oden, ed., *The Ancient Christian Commentary on Scripture* (29 vols; Downers Grove, IL: InterVarsity), as well as John Sawyer, et al., eds., *The Blackwell Bible Commentaries* (Malden, MA: Blackwell).

15. Luke Timothy Johnson classifies the genre of James as "protreptic discourse in the form of a letter" (*The Letter of James: A New Translation with Introduction and Commentary* [Anchor Yale Bible; New Haven, CN: Yale University Press, 2008; reprinted from Doubleday 1974 edition], 25). From his discussion on "protreptic discourse" (21), however, it is clear that an exhortatory sermon would be an equivalent, if less technical, description.

16. The U.N.'s 2006 study of wealth (using data from 2000) defines wealth as "net worth: the value of physical and financial assets less debts." So, *wealth* represents the ownership of capital. On a global scale, assets of $2,200 (U.S. $) per adult meant that a household ranked in the top half of the world wealth distribution. Assets of $61,000 defined the richest 10%. For global wealth and poverty statistics: http://www.wider.unu.edu/events/past-events/2006-events/en_GB/05-12-2006/.

17. The U.S. State Department releases an annual report on human trafficking on a global scale. See http://www.state.gov/g/tip/rls/tiprpt/2010/index.htm. The 2010 report numbers the "adults and children in forced labor, bonded labor, and forced prostitution around the world" at 12.3 million (7). Of course, sex-slavery comprises a smaller percentage of the total. Nonetheless, the numbers are staggering.

11

Pilgrimage of the Preaching Pastor:
Parish to Academy, Academy to Pulpit
Daniel B. Spross

From its inception, the Church of the Nazarene has believed in a 'God-called' ministry. While some well-meaning parents, grandparents, or pastors have tried to influence young women and men to become ministers, the church always has insisted that calling into ministry must originate with God.

This calling typically occurs within the broad context of the life of the local church. It may be dramatic and sudden, or it may gradually emerge from an increasing awareness of God's leading into service for the community. Conversations with mature Christians help shape a particular person's understanding of ministry and discernment of specific gifts.

The journey toward fulfilling this call typically begins within the local church. The local congregation grants the first minister's license. It gives opportunity to preach and serve. Licensed ministers then begin the educational process, which seeks to broaden, deepen, and widen the biblical, theological, and historical foundations upon which to build a lifetime of ministry. Often the person called into ministry pursues that education by means of a pilgrimage to an academic institution the broader church established to educate women and men. Such institutions exist to equip people to serve the church that raised them and provided a spiritual home.

Tension between Local Church and Academy

When future pastors leave the parish and enter the academy, they sometimes find a different world. The transition can be challenging. One of the first discoveries is a difference between the church and the academy when it comes to reading and interpreting the Bible.

Within the local parish setting, the congregation understands the Bible as the "Word of God." The people read it, refer to it, and revere it as such. Often, after the public reading of Scripture during worship, there is a declaration, "This is the Word of the Lord!" Although the Church of the Nazarene Articles of Faith make it clear that these sacred Scriptures come to us through *human* vehicles and voices, the emphasis within the worshiping local church is upon the Bible's *divine* inspiration.

Parish ministry also encourages the private reading of the Bible. Here, too, the emphasis falls upon the divine origins of the Bible and belief God continues to speak through these texts. Devotional reading has as its primary aim the edification of the soul and the encouragement of the heart. In both public and private, the parish reads the Bible primarily as the word of God or as sacred Scripture.

The academy introduces students to new tools for biblical interpretation. These tools have a variety of technical names and specialized concerns that open new horizons of understanding. Exegetical methods expand awareness of the world behind, within, and in front of the scriptural text. The vast array of historical-critical and social-scientific approaches shedding light on the world behind the text requires the potential pastor to focus on a world very different from the contemporary world. Other approaches, such as genre analysis, grammatical criticism, form criticism, rhetorical criticism, and narrative criticism, give tools to examine better the world within the text.

This broad selection of interpretive tools can easily overwhelm potential pastors. Even the methods that connect the contemporary reader with the world in front of the ancient text (e.g., structuralism, reader-response criticism, canonical criticism, and ideological criticism) sometimes create the impression the issues are so complicated there is little hope of mastering the academic disciplines of biblical interpretation. In the academic study of the Bible, the emphasis moves inevitably toward recognizing the limitations of human words as vehicles of that divine word of God. Such a move is not a denial of divine inspiration. But the change in approach can feel very strange and unsettling to the potential pastor.

This process leads to questions about the connection between the local church and the academy. Some students wonder if common ground exists between the parish they left and the academic world they entered. Some wonder if they can go back home once their educational journey is completed. To compound the problem, many students feel they do not yet fit comfortably within the academy. This critical examination of Scripture may cause these potential pastors to lose their "first naiveté."[1]

Students may wonder if they are the first to experience this tension between the local church and the academy. But this tension has been with the church for centuries. From the twelfth century forward, universities and colleges the church originally founded to advance the knowledge, training, and education of clergy and laity alike have shaped Western civilization. From epic struggles between Abelard and Bernard to the present, those representing the institutional church have come into conflict with intellectuals in the academy. A significant portion of that ongoing tension springs from the different perspectives, aims, goals, and objectives of the two domains.

The church originally created schools as adjunctive servants to the church. The primary purpose for creating universities, colleges, and seminaries was to establish institutions that would efficiently educate future ministers, teachers, and church administrators. By assembling many of the best thinkers from the church, the academy provided thoughtful contributions to the theology and practices of the church. It trained the church's future leaders beyond the levels the local parish could reach.

Education *within* the local church was designed primarily to inform and indoctrinate adherents. The local church understood the Bible to function as God's word. The church typically used the Bible as the "canon" or measure against which it governed all of life. That is, the church interpreted and explained the Bible in support of congregational life and ecclesiastical authority. The divine nature of the Bible's subject matter was the primary presupposition from which the church operated.

The church typically understood Scripture to be normative. What the Bible plainly says is what the people should clearly do. Within the church culture, loyalty to the tradition and careful adherence to the faith are what the church highly values. The people of the church learned, understood, and passed along the dominant meta-narrative.

Accepting guidance from mature believers on the faith journey is part of assimilation into the church family. Within the local congregation, the primary concern is having one's heart right with God. Here, the context for thinking theologically is typically the local neighborhood or community. In these local contexts, people engage the ongoing struggles of life, including jobs, schools, proximity to industry and business, health, and family dynamics. Many people in such settings value right relationship with God above right thinking about God. In a church context, people usually read the Bible with a hermeneutic of trust.[2] Women and men in the community of faith believe the Bible—when read carefully and in a spirit of humble devotion—will provide direction for life decisions. The Bible offers comfort in times of loss and need and encouragement in challenging situations.

The agenda in teaching settings within the church leans toward the practical. Many Bible studies and sermons are based on three simple questions: (1) What does the text say to us? (2) What does the text mean to us? (3) How can we use it in our lives?

This approach is experiential. People want something that speaks to them where they live. Within the local church family, the aim is to find the primary, unifying essence of the Bible that will keep the diverse body working, worshiping, and having fellowship. When differences of opinion arise on theological, social, or even cultural matters, the question raised to find a solution is typically, "What does the Bible say about this?" The church perceives the Bible as stable, solid, and unchanging.

By contrast, a very different perspective is often at work in the academy. The academy typically focuses attention on the human element of the Bible, which it can scrutinize, categorize, label, and identify. The academy understands biblical texts more in terms of their time-conditioned historical and cultural contexts than in terms of divine calls for faithfulness. Academic study examines biblical writers in terms of their literary techniques, moves, and devices. In the academy, the primary goal is education, not indoctrination.

The academy may emphasize right thinking about God most highly. Instead of standard answers given at church, the academy may raise questions and offer differing viewpoints. This can unsettle students in their educational journey. Instead of a single voice, a plurality of voices speaks to the students. Rather than focusing only on the heart of the student, the academy also focuses on the head of the student, challenging them to deeper, broader, and more critical thinking. Instead of receiving simple answers, a barrage of challenging questions faces potential pastors. Instead of finding immediate and direct solutions to difficult questions, the complex issues students face resist simplistic responses.

Many academic institutions operate from an educational philosophy that welcomes a diversity of approaches. This diversity broadens the horizons for students. When the educational institution is understood to be a laboratory, a wide range of options can enrich the scope of learning. The academy often measures success in terms of the mastery of the breadth and diversity of the wide spectrum of knowledge. But in the church success is measured differently. The church often thinks the primary purpose of the academic institution is training students to fit comfortably and uncritically within the church.

Education can be a major threat to the faith students once held secure.[3] When it comes to interpreting the Bible, the analysis essential to critical thinking within the academy may affect the perspective the potential pastor develops. If critical *thinking* gives way to a critical *spirit*, negative attitudes can damage the total personality of the potential pastor. We hear this dilemma in these lines from Chaim Potok's novel, *The Promise*: "How can we teach others to regard the tradition critically *and* with love? I grew up loving it, and then learned to look at it critically. That's everyone's problem today. How to love and respect what you are being taught to dissect."[4]

The academy allows and encourages divergence from mainstream understanding. The context of the ivory tower—a caricature many exaggerate—often produces imaginative discussions about the theoretical with little application in the "real" world. The academy rewards what is innovative and original. Even within classical disciplines of Bible, theology, history, and philosophy, research presented in the master's thesis and doctoral dissertation must be original.Furthermore, the push toward specialization and compartmentalization in the academy creates tension even within academic departments. In some institutions, what one scholar calls "the invisible 'iron curtain' between Old Testament and New Testament scholars" has developed. An even greater gulf can emerge between historians or theologians and Bible scholars.[5] In some settings, greater barriers separate Bible scholars, theologians, historians, and philosophers from those who teach Christian education, preaching, and other ministry courses. These attitudes spill over into the relationships of the academy with the church, even with the churches that brought the respective academic institutions into existence!

Despite the initial organic relationship between originating churches and academic institutions created *for* these churches, church and academy can drift apart. In some denominational traditions, nothing currently connects existing academic institutions with the churches that created them—except a history rarely remembered and seldom mentioned. Even within the Church of the Nazarene, where churches and academic institutions have intentionally maintained close, strong, and healthy ties, perceptible gaps have emerged, especially when it comes to biblical interpretation.

Potential pastors are sometimes given conflicting counsel. Before entering the academic world, many hear they should be wary of the liberalism and even heresy their professors would teach. They are told professors have no clue about life in the local church. The true faith of such professors is questioned. This attitude of suspicion often creates obstacles to learning, especially at the outset for the wary potential pastor. Professors require additional time and effort to education wary students. Professors sometimes say the hardest thing to open is a closed mind.

At the same time, the potential pastor may encounter attitudes of frustration and even arrogance within the academy. Professor can be critical of ecclesiastical officials or situations. When this happens, the potential pastor feels conflicted. Instead of mutual appreciation and respect for the distinctive roles played in both contexts, they find conflict.

Coming Full Circle

I believe that in most cases, the pilgrimage of the pastor must come full circle from the local church to the academy and back to the local church. We must work together to build, strengthen, or in some cases rebuild bridges between church and academy.

The first step toward working together should be an honest reappraisal of attitudes within both worlds. Humility instead of hubris, appreciation instead of suspicion, mutual respect and support in place of confrontation all make the transitional journey of the potential pastor much smoother. When those in the academy show respect for the work of the church, the student as potential pastor is the benefactor. When those in the church acknowledge that academic institutions can help them become more faithful and authentic to their mission, good things result for the potential pastor.

While many of the best and brightest the church produces serve within the academy, many also find a fulfilling place of service within a local church. And while many of the faithful and loyal the church produces serve in local churches, many also move to faithful service in the academy and thereby serve the larger church. Affirming this reality can help narrow the gaps between the two worlds and help change some of the perceptions that create tension between the two realms. Mutual appreciation can make these different worlds more compatible, even with their differing emphases, approaches, and understandings.

One of the best ways these two worlds can collaborate is to develop areas of mutual service and cooperation. This may include internships and mentoring opportunities, as well as expanding local church use of the academic resources. If mature parish pastors are more involved with potential pastors during their educational journey, greater connections can be forged between the differing worlds. Internship leaders can keep the student's feet firmly planted in the world of the local parish as they gain new insights and understanding in biblical and theological studies. Professors can share their expertise within local church settings. This demonstrates their great love for the life of the church. Professors can also become mentors for potential pastors, forging friendships that will last beyond graduation.

When the loss of that "first naiveté" emerges within the potential pastor, both mentor professors and pastors should have the expertise and wisdom to step into the picture. These mentors can encourage and challenge the struggling student to move beyond what she has left behind and to discover the delightful "second naiveté" ahead in the mature Christian pilgrimage.[6] Having made that journey themselves, these mentors can offer hope. When coupled with caring pastoral and professorial mentors, the potential pastor should find help transitioning between the two worlds.

Another positive step that those within the academy may take is to stress methods, approaches, and understandings of biblical interpretation that take seriously the context of the local church parish. Encouraging the potential pastor to pay closer attention to the components within the so-called "Wesleyan Quadrilateral" can provide strong bridges connecting the academy and the church.[7] The quadrilateral is a useful *methodological* tool.[8] It can introduce students to the idea that multiple factors influence the way they read Scripture. This kind of interpretation works best when we keep these factors in a healthy balance, so they mutually inform one another. The quadrilateral can help describe the best ways to develop holistic theology, because recognizes that biblical, historical, philosophical, and practical concerns must inform good theology. The church tends to emphasize the traditional and the experiential more. The academy tends to emphasize the philosophical, historical, and specialized interpretive tools. However, a balanced approach pushes the interpreter beyond any *single* emphasis into a richer context. The well-educated pastor should leave the academy equipped with tools and resources to provide quality ministry when they return to the parish. An understanding of the balance among Scripture, tradition, reason, and experience can ease the transition between the worlds of academy and church.

Another helpful approach to interpreting Scripture that embraces both worlds is canonical criticism. Canonical criticism draws from a variety of historical-critical methods. But it insists on giving close attention to the faith dimension that accompanied these sacred texts. After all, Israel and the church collected, preserved, and passed these texts along to shape the faith community.

Instead of limiting the meaning of these texts to the occasions to which they were written, a canonical approach seeks to reconnect these texts with their recurring use in the history of Israel or the church *in their canonical context*. This method explores the ongoing legacy of the history of interpretation led to the creation of a sacred canon, which in turn the community of faith continued to use in worship and life.

Canonical interpretation closes some gaps between the academic study of Scripture and the study of Scripture within the church. It does so by acknowledging both the faith dimension associated with Scripture and the reality that the church has always had the last word on what transforms the Bible into Christian Scripture.[9]

Recent interpreters have developed other exegetical models that are also integrative. The communal narrative model of Walter Brueggemann stresses the powerful role of speeches within ancient texts in addressing the contemporary church.[10] W. Randolph Tate's model of exegesis consists of an emphasis upon three worlds: the world behind the text, the world within the text, and the world in front of the text.[11] His work combines the best of the historical-critical work with some of the most helpful literary-critical work within texts for creating dynamic contemporary readings. Manfred Oeming's introductory work on hermeneutics is also a comprehensive and balanced analysis of the current approaches to biblical interpretation from a more philosophical perspective.[12]

Within the last decade, two significant movements have arisen within the academy to close significant gaps between academy and church. The first of these movements has emerged under the label "Canonical Theism." William Abraham, the chief architect of the program, calls for developing a theology of Scripture as a decisive means of grace.[13] Abraham argues Scripture is at the heart of Wesleyan theology. Using a robust pneumatology, careful reading in Canonical Theism makes it clear that the primary concern of the movement is a revitalizing of the church.[14] Jason Vickers, a key contributor to this movement, accentuates its commitment to the church by examining the dominant role of the Holy Spirit in the theological work of conversion. Of particular interest is the emphasis on the way the Spirit uses Scripture at crucial stages, both in the initiation of conversion and continuing life of faith.[15]

The second movement appropriates the title "The Scripture Project." This movement consisted of fifteen pastors, theologians, and Bible scholars who gathered at Princeton Theological Seminary over a four-year period to explore the most effective ways to read Scripture within the community of faith.[16] Several affirmations from the group reveal the concern for the same issues I have expressed earlier in this essay.

Three affirmations stand out most significantly. First, "faithful interpretation of Scripture invites and presupposes participation in the community brought into being by God's redemptive action— the church. Scriptural interpretation is properly an ecclesial activity whose goal is to participate in the reality of which the text speaks by bending the knee to worship the God revealed in Jesus Christ."[17] Second, "the saints of the church provide guidance in how to interpret and perform Scripture.... Guidance in the interpretation of Scripture may be found not only in the writings of the saints but also in the exemplary patterns of their lives. True authority is grounded in holiness; faithful interpretation of Scripture requires its faithful performance."[18] Third, "be entirely blatant and unabashed in reading Scripture for the church's purposes and within the context of Christian faith and practice."[19]

Both movements demonstrate the connection necessary between the academy and the church for proper interpretation and understanding of the Bible. Like the integrative models of interpretation considered previously, these two movements deliberately connect the rigorous academic examination of Scripture to the life of the church within the context of faith communities. Through this examination of the written word, God still speaks to these faith communities God has called together.

The church still needs a creative and healthy academy to enable the church to become healthier. These academic moves to include the church in the foreground of exegesis can suggest to the potential pastor that the move back from academy to the parish need not require leaving behind everything learned in the academy. Rather, with a grateful attitude for the contributions in that academic world, the potential pastor's pilgrimage can come full circle. The pilgrimage can take a different direction by becoming a partner with other pastors and professors who previously traveled a similar path. When that happens, the academy will have met its original purpose and the church will continue to be built up to the glory of God!

---

1. This language comes from James Fowler's *Stages of Faith* (San Francisco: Harper and Row, 1981), among others. It refers to an unquestioned acceptance and loyalty to a faith that has largely been unexamined from a critical thinking perspective.
2. For an excellent treatment of the hermeneutic of trust, see Richard B. Hays, *The Conversion of the Imagination* (Grand Rapids: Eerdmans, 2005), 190–201, esp. pp. 197–200.
3. See Robert W. Wall, "A Theological Morphology of the Bible: A Prescription for 'Spiritually Disabled' Students," in *Immersed in the Life of God: The Healing Resources of the Christian Faith: Essays in Honor of William J. Abraham* (ed. P. L. Gavrilyuk, D. M. Koskela, and J. E. Vickers; Grand Rapid: Eerdmans, 2008), 41–62.
4. Chaim Potok, *The Promise* (New York: Fawcett Crest, 1969), 312.
5. Brevard S. Childs, *The New Testament as Canon: An Introduction* (Philadelphia: Fortress, 1985), xv; idem, *Biblical Theology of the Old and New Testaments* (Minneapolis: Fortress, 1992), xvi.
6. See Mark I. Wallace, *The Second Naiveté: Barth, Ricoeur, and the New Yale Theology* (Macon, GA: Mercer University Press, 1995), esp. xiv–xv.
7. I am working from the basic premise of the Wesleyan Quadrilateral that *Scripture* is the starting point, supported equally by *tradition* and *reason*, and undergirded with *experience*. I am not interested in reviewing the history of the concept of the Wesleyan Quadrilateral or the debate as to whether or not Wesley himself used it. That debate can be traced through several issues of the *Wesleyan Theological Journal*, especially the Spring, 1985 issue. See Donald A. D. Thorsen, *The Wesleyan Quadrilateral: Scripture, Tradition, Reason and Experience as a Model of Evangelical Theology* (Grand Rapids: Zondervan, 1990); and W. Stephen Gunter et al., *Wesley and the Quadrilateral: Renewing the Conversation* (Nashville: Abingdon, 1997).

8. Albert Outler, "The Wesleyan Quadrilateral—In John Wesley," *Wesleyan Theological Journal* 20 (Spr. 1985): 7–18.

9. Brevard S. Childs, *Biblical Theology in Crisis* (Philadelphia: Westminster, 1970), 99. He says, "Scriptures must be interpreted in relation to their function within the community of the faith that treasured them ... not [as] archives of the past but [as] a channel of life for the continuing church, through which God instructs and admonishes his people." See also R. Wall, "A Theological Morphology of the Bible," 52–53, "Within its ecclesial setting, 'canon' typically indicated the use of a certain standard of accepted truth, of right conduct, of useful practices, and of those who exemplified or personified these things to others." Lest there be any ambiguity in what he thinks, Wall further declares, "The orienting concern of a biblical canon is not framed by an authoritative listing of books; rather, the concern is for a more dynamic and practical performance of the Bible during worship with the effect of cultivating right patterns of faith and life in its interested readers/auditors."

10. See, e.g., Walter Brueggemann, *Hopeful Imagination: Prophetic Voices in Exile* (Philadelphia: Fortress, 1986); idem, *Finally Comes the Poet: Daring Speech for Proclamation* (Minneapolis: Fortress, 1989); idem, *Texts under Negotiation: The Bible and Postmodern Imagination* (Minneapolis: Fortress, 1993); and idem, *Theology of the Old Testament: Testimony, Dispute, Advocacy* (Minneapolis: Fortress, 1997). See also Bruce C. Birch, Walter Brueggemann, Terence E. Fretheim, and David L. Petersen, *A Theological Introduction to the Old Testament* (2nd ed.; Nashville: Abingdon, 2005).

11. W. Randolph Tate, *Biblical Interpretation: An Integrated Approach* (3rd ed.; Grand Rapids: Baker Academic, 2008).

12. Manfred Oeming, *Contemporary Biblical Hermeneutics: An Introduction* (trans. J. F. Vette; Burlington, VT: Ashgate, 2006).

13. William J. Abraham, "The Future of Scripture: In Search of a Theology of Scripture," *Wesleyan Theological Journal* 46 (Spr. 2011): 7–23.

14. Jason Vickers, "Medicine of the Holy Spirit: The Canonical Heritage of the Church," in *Canonical Theism: A Proposal for Theology and the Church* (ed. W. J. Abraham, J. E. Vickers, and N. B. Van Kirk; Grand Rapids: Eerdmans, 2008), 11–26.

15. Jason Vickers, "To Know and to Love God Truly: The Healing Power of Conversion," in *Immersed in the Life of God*, 1–20, esp. 16–18.

16. See Ellen Davis and Richard B. Hays, "Introduction" and "Nine Theses on the Interpretation of Scripture," in *The Art of Reading Scripture* (ed. E. F. Davis and R. B. Hays; Grand Rapids: Eerdmans, 2003), xiv–xx, 1–5.

17. Davis and Hays, "Nine Theses on the Interpretation of Scripture," in *The Art of Reading Scripture*, 3.

18. Ibid., 4. It is further noted that "this chain of interpreters, the communion of the saints, includes not only those officially designated as saints by the churches but also the great cloud of witnesses acknowledged by believers in diverse times and places, including many of the church's loyal critics. This communion informs our reading of Scripture."

19. Robert W. Jenson, "Scripture's Authority in the Church," in *The Art of Reading Scripture*, 28.

12

The Role of Scripture in Christian Formation[1]

Mark A. Maddix and Richard P. Thompson

There should be little doubt about the role of the Bible among we who identify ourselves as ecclesial and theological descendents of John Wesley. After all, Wesley described himself as "a man of one book"[2]—a description that makes an emphatic declaration about the Bible's place in his thought and life. Wesleyans view the Bible as central to matters of salvation and Christian faith and practice. Such emphases regarding the primacy of Scripture shaped both the earliest Methodists and are part of the DNA of the Wesleyan theological tradition.

Although Wesleyans specifically and Christians generally assert the Bible's authority, in recent years the appropriation of the Bible in the church seems to have decreased. This is especially true of the Bible's use in church's formative practices (e.g., worship) and concerns for discipleship. The Bible is increasingly relegated only to the realm of Christian doctrine.

Some may point an accusing finger at general Christian apathy or the influence of postmodern culture as reasons for such trends. Some blame may fall on the church's preferred approaches to the Bible, approaches found in the biblical scholarship of the last two centuries. In particular, the general trends of biblical scholarship in the modern era have tended to focus on "what the text meant," because all biblical texts were written in and to particular historical contexts. Such emphases correctly seek to account for the intricate and complex webs of historical particularities making these texts what they are.

The interpretive approach to the Bible focusing on the search for a selected text's meaning as a historical entity shaped by its historical context, however, has often left the church wondering what the Bible might actually say to contemporary people. Modern biblical interpretation may guide the church to read biblical texts in light of their original contexts. And it may help interpreters glean important information about Christian faith. But always asking, "what did the text mean?" may leave the interpreter starving for a few crumbs of a message that enables us to hear from God today.

In this essay, we address these issues by focusing on the Bible's role as sacred Scripture within the context of the church. We explore how Christians may appropriate the biblical texts and how the texts function within that ecclesial context in terms of formation and transformation, not just information. We offer a redefinition of the role of Scripture consistent with its historic role, particularly as that relates to the Wesleyan tradition. This essay has two distinct parts: (1) a delineation of the historic role of the Bible as sacred Scripture within the church, and (2) an exploration into the ways the Bible as sacred Scripture forms and transforms Christians into faithful disciples within the church.

The Historic Role of the Bible as Sacred Scripture within the Church

There is a difference between interpreting the *Bible* and interpreting these same texts as *Scripture*. Yes, persons often use these two designations for the biblical texts interchangeably.[3] This difference refers in no small part to issues related to authority, with which the process of Christian canonization was concerned. Although the theological and historical notion of Christian canon typically contributes little to the interpretive outcomes of the professional guild of biblical studies, such a notion *is* critical to understanding the authoritative role of biblical texts *as canon* throughout the history of the church.

Many assume the role of the Christian canon is to define Christian doctrine. They assume the Bible functions primarily to provide theological *information* about the Christian faith. The canonical process, however, suggests that the incorporation of the biblical texts into the Christian canon had more to do with their *formative* role.[4] The early church appropriated and turned repeatedly to these texts because of the formative ways they (and not others) functioned within Christian community.

John Wesley understood the Bible primarily as a formative text. He read the Bible "to find the way to heaven."[5] Wesley did not focus on heaven as a goal or ideal *per se*. Instead, he focused on the "way" that one leads ... the way and life of salvation. The Bible functions as sacred Scripture to transform and shape the lives of those who comprise the church. The Bible is not written to support arguments about the reliability of the Bible. And its primary purpose is not to offer data.

Wesley often did not quote a particular Scripture passage when addressing specific pastoral or social issues. Instead, he often used the Bible's vocabulary and stories to reflect on such matters.[6] In so doing, his arguments arose from a general theological and ecclesial context of a people living with and engaging the Bible as Scripture. While specific biblical texts may or may not address a particular issue, both Wesley and Wesleyans after him have considered *any* matter that intersects with those seeking to live faithfully for God to be fertile soil for a sanctified imagination. The holy cultivation of this imagination occurs in light of ways biblical texts enable the church to envisage the world.[7] This Wesleyan understanding of the Bible as Scripture—to be pursued in functional and (trans)formational terms—is consistent with the place of the biblical texts within the pre-canonical early church.

There are three distinct but related ways we may further clarify Scripture's functional role. First, an understanding of the formative role of Scripture suggests that there is more to the interpretive process than discovering a historical meaning in the biblical text. Contrary to many interpretive ventures (particularly text-centered approaches), the criterion for acknowledging biblical texts as authoritative is not merely what these texts *state* (i.e., their information) but what these texts *do* (i.e., the ways these texts affect readers). As important as the biblical text before Christian readers may be, something essential—beyond the information of the text—must happen within these readers for the text to become *Scripture*. A convergence between the text and readers must occur to bring otherwise dead words to life.[8]

Although secular literary theory explains this phenomenon in terms of readers' evaluation of textual features, Wesley stressed the essential role of the Holy Spirit. The Spirit inspires Christian readers so that they might think about and discern the will of God through a particular text of Scripture.[9] We do not need to separate entirely the roles of the faithful reader and the Spirit when engaging Scripture, because *both* reader and Spirit are potentially at work. These co-operative partners in the reading of Scripture contribute to what we may describe as "inspired imagination." This imagination enables readers to envisage or discover potential meaning(s) about God and God's ongoing salvation.[10]

If the Bible functions as Scripture in these formative ways, there is no replacement for the active, consistent reading and engagement of these sacred texts by Christian readers. Like a joke that loses some of its effectiveness when explanation is required, Scripture loses its functional authority when persons appropriate it for information alone rather than engaging it in potentially formative and transformative ways.

Second, an understanding of the formative role of Scripture suggests the church as the location where these texts function authoritatively. In significant ways, the Christian Scriptures are related in the canonical process to the so-called "rule of faith." This rule assumes the confessional context within which reading and interpretation occur. These basic theological convictions contributed to the formation of both the Christian canon and the faith community. That community considered these texts as sacred Scripture before confirmation by any ecumenical council.

This interpretive context becomes a critical aspect for a Wesleyan understanding of Scripture. Because the primary authority of these texts lies in their formative function within the Christian faith community, the church returns to these and not other texts. These texts have a standing invitation to read them, listen to them, and reflect upon them. They are not merely static historical documents from a different time, place, and people. They are also sacred texts the historic Christian tradition has consistently revisited.[11] A given faith community may not fully recognize or appreciate all concerns of a respective passage written in a different historical context. But the contemporary community should approaches that passage with the hope that a fresh reading will speak to and shape that community in meaningful ways.[12]

If the church is to be faithful to her identity as the people of God, critical work on the Bible is still necessary. Such work engages biblical texts acknowledging the historical "otherness" of the texts.[13] And yet the interpretative context invites all who comprise the church —laypersons and scholars, leaders and theologians—to consider how the text may speak to the contemporary context.[14] It is in this interpretive context of the church where Richard Hays suggests an "integrative act of the imagination" occurs. The church places her faith and practices imaginatively within the world these texts present.[15]

Third, an understanding of the formative role of Scripture suggests the necessity of living out the church's engagement with these texts as Scripture. The ongoing life of the faithful Christian community becomes the standard by which we evaluate the functional role of Scripture.

The interpretive task as often understood involves re-articulating a possible meaning of a given passage: a new set of words explaining what the "old" words meant. However, this runs counter to what the canonical process suggests: that some texts were accepted and others were not primarily because of how these texts functioned within the church.[16]

For Wesley and his theological offspring, the authority of Scripture ultimately refers to the church's mission and practices that encourage holy living among her people. Therefore, the Bible functions in authoritative ways as sacred Scripture when the church engages the biblical texts so that she actively responds in faithful ways to the God about whom these texts speak and who speaks through them.

The ways the Christian faith community embodies her encounters with the biblical texts reveal how these texts have functioned formatively as Scripture. Interpreters must consider as possible realms for interpretation the actual authority of these sacred texts for the church's life and practice. If the church takes seriously the task of listening to the biblical texts as Scripture, *both* her vocal witness and life will reveal the formative role of these texts.

Bible as Scripture:
Forming Christians into Faithful Disciples

Christians believe that Scripture provides inspiration and guidance in Christian faith and practice. The Bible does more than inform; it also forms and transforms. We explore three major areas in which Scripture functions formatively: *lectio divina*, inductive Bible study, and worship (including preaching, Scripture reading, and communion).

Making the transition from reading Scripture as information to reading it as formation can be difficult. Common ecclesial practices have ingrained an approach to reading Scripture that focuses on the discovery of certain kinds of biblical ideas (i.e., information). These practices teach Christians to read the Bible to master the text.[17] Because Scripture is primarily formative, any person, regardless of biblical expertise, can read the Bible and encounter God. In this regard, formational reading includes opening oneself to the biblical text and allowing it to address one's life. Instead of mastering the text through study, formational reading invites sacred Scripture to master and form its readers.

Faithful readers come to the text open to hear, receive, respond, and serve. Biblical spirituality is a transformative process involving individual and communal engagement with the biblical text. The non-specialist can approach the biblical text -- not merely as a historical record or even as a literary medium -- as that through which God speaks.[18] Historical and critical analysis of the Bible does not always lead to transformation. But the reader may be transformed when God speaks through Scripture by the work of the Holy Spirit. When Christians read the Bible as formative Scripture, they may find new energy in the text they once viewed as boring and irrelevant.

Spiritual reading is a meditative approach to the written word. It requires time and an open heart. The purpose of reading is for God to address the faithful reader. It requires both the practice of attentive listening and a willingness to respond. One reason biblical authors wrote these texts was to convey something about God's will. Because spiritual reading opens oneself to God's address, these purposes interconnect.[19]

I. Lectio divina

The ancient practice of *lectio divina* (sacred reading) has re-emerged in recent years as a transformative process to engage Scripture. This practice originated with the desert fathers and mothers whose spirituality consisted primarily of prayerful rumination on biblical texts.[20] Monasteries ordered around the Rule of St. Benedict (c. 540) developed the practice further. John Calvin was among the Reformers who undertook this practice. Puritan pastor Richard Baxter advocated a method of reflective mediation with Scripture directly derived from Benedictine practice.[21] Today, Christians and faith communities are regaining the significance of this ancient practice as a means to make Bible reading meaningful again.

Lectio divina is a process of scriptural encounter that includes a series of prayer dynamics. The series moves the reader to a deep level of engagement with the chosen text and with the Spirit who enlivens the text.[22] The process begins with silencio (silence). The person approaches a biblical passage in open, receptive listening and silent reading. The next step is lectio (reading). The text is read aloud, slowly and deliberately, to evoke imagination. Hearing the text reminds the hearer of the spoken word of God. Following this reading is a time of meditation. To meditate is to think about or mentally "chew on" what has been read. In the past, this process often included the commitment of the text to memory. By internalizing the text in its verbal form, one meditates on its meaning (meditatio).

Because the text is engaged in experiential terms, meditation gives rise to prayer (ortio) or response to God. Ortio (praying) is talking to God as someone within a close relationship. One speaks to God, preferably aloud, or writes the prayer in a journal. Next, through fervent prayer one may reach that degree of interiority and union with God that result in contemplation. The participant is in union with God through the Spirit. In contemplatio (contemplation), the person stops and rests silently before God, receiving whatever the Spirit gives.

The final step of sacred reading is compassio (compassion), which is the fruit of the contemplation of God as love—love of God and neighbor. Insights, feelings, or commitments that emerge from time spent with Scripture are shared with others. *Lectio divina* is a practice that one may experience on a regular basis to transform oneself into the image and likeness of Christ encountered in Scripture.[23] *Lectio divina* may be a personal or corporate spiritual practice. In either case, *lectio divina* provides a direct encounter with Scripture that forms and transforms a Christian.

2. *Bible Study or Small Groups*

Small groups and Bible studies provide a context for deepening relationships and connectedness. Reflecting the very nature of the Triune God, humans are created as relational beings in need of acceptance, love, and care. Spiritual formation and growth take place within a social context. The Christian life is not a solitary journey; it is a pilgrimage made in the company of others.[24] Although small groups have a wide range of purposes and approaches, a primary resource for shaping the life of the church emerges from Bible study in small groups. Scripture shapes people's lives. A biblical spirituality represents a transformative process of personal and communal engagement with the biblical text.[25]

For people with a limited knowledge of the Bible, reading and studying the Bible as Scripture in the context of an intimate group give opportunities for learning and spiritual growth. People who will not read the Bible on their own may read it in the context of a small group. Studying the Bible in a small group helps people broaden and deepen their understanding of a given passage, while potentially guarding against misleading, individual interpretations. Studying the Bible in a group also helps people make meaning of their faith by verbalizing what the Bible means and how it applies to a life of faith. On their own, people easily ignore the relationship of biblical truth to their own lives. In a group setting, people talk about Scripture together, which helps them apply what they learn.

John Wesley's group formation provided a context for spiritual growth and development for Methodists. Some argue that his small group formation revolutionized early Methodism and that Wesley was the "father" of the modern small-group concept.[26] Wesley employed an approach to spiritual formation that focused on assisting participants to grow in holiness of heart and life. Wesley's interlocking groups included a hierarchy of instruction for each group, tailored to a specific function. Each group, society, class, and band had a specific educational mode.[27] Societies focused primarily on cognitive development, teaching Methodist tenets and doctrine. Classes focused on changing and transforming human behavior. Bands focused on growing in holiness and purity of intention.

Wesley's group formation incorporated Scripture as central to the small group process. The reading, interpretation, and proclamation of Scripture were normal aspects of society meetings. The use of Scripture to shape behavior and promote holy living was a formative aspect of classes and bands.

Studying the Bible in groups is a central aspect of Christian discipleship. Christians gather to study Scripture on a regular basis with a wide range of methods. One method to Bible study is a deductive approach. In this approach, the reader comes to the Bible with conclusions and then proceeds to the text to find proof for those ideas. The reader hopes to deduce a particular idea from the Bible. Such deductive approaches tend to dictate what Scripture may say rather than listening to the Scripture.

By contrast, an inductive approach to Bible study demands that a person examine the particulars of Scripture and then draw conclusions. An inductive approach to Bible study allows the reader to interpret the Bible through observation and reflection, by drawing out ideas and truths in Scripture. Inductive Bible study is an approach of inquiry in which persons learn by examining the biblical texts themselves and drawing conclusions about these materials from this encounter.

This inductive approach allows the interpreter to discover what God may say through the biblical text as Scripture. This tends to promote formation and transformation. Admittedly, the reader's life experiences, context, and personal bias affect the reader's interpretation of Scripture. A Wesleyan approach to Bible study does not begin with presuppositions *per se* and then logically deduce irrefutable conclusions. Rather, a Wesleyan approach seeks a creative encounter with God through Scripture.

As faithful disciples gather in Bible studies to struggle over the meaning and contemporary understanding of Scripture, the Holy Spirit is active to form and shape faithful disciples. Bible study incites readers to discern a meaning from the text and its possible implications for daily life. Learning to discern the meaning of the text does not give readers complete control of the Bible. It potentially prepares readers to hear what Scripture may say to challenge the church and faithful believers. Faithful discipleship includes the willingness to engage in the sound study of Scripture by giving oneself to the difficult, yet rewarding, task of disciplined Bible study.[28]

3. Scripture in Worship

Christians can encounter Scripture in worship through a variety of practices. First, Christians engage Scripture through the preaching of Scripture. Preaching in the early church preceded the writing of the New Testament texts. The eyewitnesses of the Christ-event testified to what they had seen and heard. When Scripture is preached today, the hope is that lives are changed and transformed through the work of the Holy Spirit. The proclamation of Scripture emphasizes the spoken word of God that bears witness to the incarnate Word of Jesus Christ. But there is more to this than bearing witness. Through the proclamation of Scripture, the spoken word becomes a fresh expression of the living and active God. In this sense, the spoken word becomes a "means of grace."

The preacher speaks *for* God, *from* the Scriptures, *by* the authority from the church, *to* the people. God speaks through the proclamation of the word, through the inspiration of Scripture, to provide healing and reconciliation.[29] As Marva Dawn writes, "Sermons should shape the hearers by bringing the transforming Word to nurture the development of the character and pattern of Christ."[30] When preaching is maintained as central, it can be the Scripture-driven, worship-centered act that makes meaning for a community's life.[31] The preacher interprets Scripture for the community by placing it within the larger narrative of the biblical witness. This helps congregants make meaning for life. Scriptural preaching allows the congregants to hear and discover their role in the broader narrative of God's redemptive work in the world.

Second, Christians encounter Scripture through the worship service or liturgy. It is God through Scripture—read, preached, and received—who calls the Christian community together to worship.[32] Without Christian worship, there would be no Bible. The Bible is the product of the early church's common prayer. The earliest Christian communities circulated among themselves and read in common worship stories of the life and ministry of Jesus and the early apostles. They wanted to hear these stories and respond to them.[33] Similarly, the interrelationship between worship and the Scriptures is evident today as Scripture is read, preached, and experienced in worship.

As the community of faith gathers in worship, Scripture comes to life. Congregations that follow the Christian calendar and lectionary readings provide unique opportunities to participate in the story of God. It is ironic that some evangelicals and Wesleyans who view Scripture as primary and authoritative for faith and practice do not practice regular reading of Scripture in worship. For Scripture to be powerfully formative in the life of the church, Scripture must be read, experienced, and interpreted as a central aspect of the worshiping community. Through responsive readings, hymns, and choruses (assuming they have a biblical basis), the faith community provides various avenues for worshipers to interact with God's message through Scripture.[34]

Third, congregations that participate in the Eucharist encounter God through active expressions of Scripture in terms of ritual. The concept of the word and table or word and sacrament is an expression drawn from a particular theology of worship that has roots deep in the early church. A service of the word and table is worship that emphasizes the dual aspects of the spoken word built around Scripture and the embodied Word centered on the celebration of the Eucharist or communion. Once the proclaimed word is preached, congregants respond to the spoken Word by participation in the embodied Word of communion.[35]

Word and table were central to Methodist worship during the time of John Wesley. But they are not as common today in many Methodist and Wesleyan congregations. Most evangelical congregations identify with the proclamation of the gospel through preaching. These congregations see Scripture as central to proclamation. This reflects the influence of the Protestant Reformation, which placed a high value on Scripture for proclamation. Many of these same congregations are less likely to participate in communion (or the eucharist) on a regular basis. Many evangelical and Wesleyan congregations consider themselves "low" church, with a diminished view of liturgy, lectionary readings, and sacramental theology. But participation in the eucharist on a regular basis provides balance to the proclamation through Scripture in worship. The table expands our understanding of God's grace by including a living sign of the gospel in tangible and visible form.[36]

For Wesley, the eucharist was an opportunity to experience Christ. Wesley taught that Christ was present in the elements, though he did not hold the Roman Catholic view of *transubstantiation* (the bread and wine becoming the actual body and blood of Jesus). Wesley invited everyone participate, believers and nonbelievers alike. Christ was present spiritually, immediately, and independently, interacting with the eucharist recipient. Wesley believed a person may receive forgiveness and reconciliation through obedient response to God's grace, including participation in the eucharist. He believed that something divine takes place when a person comes with an open heart to receive the life-giving gift of the bread and wine as the Word of God.

Wesley believed the eucharist was a converting element for those who confessed and believed *during* the Lord's Supper. He based his desire to see Methodist followers take communion regularly on obedience to Christ and the hope that blessing and holiness would follow. According to Wesley, the eucharist served as a channel of grace that formed and transformed the believer. As a means of grace, communion forms those drawn toward holiness and those sanctified. For those desiring growth in God's grace, communion is the ordinary means of such growth. The sacrament serves not only to preserve and sustain but also to further growth in holiness.

Conclusion

For some Christians, the Bible is irrelevant, boring, and disconnected from faith. This may be the result of the church's inability to educate and model for congregants that Scripture is less about information and more about formation and transformation. Christians who view Scripture in formative ways can newly experience Scripture. Congregations should develop practices of Bible reading, Bible study, preaching, and worship that promote Christian formation. When this shift in emphasis takes place, the church becomes the primary context within which Scripture functions to form and transform persons as the people of God.

A Wesleyan view of Scripture in terms of formation shapes the way we think about God and ourselves as the people of God. And it shapes the ways we respond to one another and the world. From a Wesleyan perspective, the Bible speaks as sacred Scripture by calling us to respond in faithful ways in light of biblical provocations to faithful living. The formative role of Scripture requires obedient response to its call for holy living. Congregations that view Scripture

THE ROLE OF SCRIPTURE IN CHRISTIAN FORMATION 189

in formative ways provide opportunities to encounter the text in fresh and new ways that can form and transform members into faithful disciples.

---

1. The original, longer version of this essay first appeared as "Scripture as Formation: The Role of Scripture in Christian Formation," *Wesleyan Theological Journal* 46/1 (Spr. 2011): 134–49.
2. "Preface" to *Sermons on Several Occasions*, in *Works* (Bicentennial ed.), 1:105.
3. Cf. Stephen E. Fowl and L. Gregory Jones, *Reading in Communion: Scripture and Ethics in Christian Life* (Grand Rapids: Eerdmans, 1991), 20; and Joel B. Green, *Seized by Truth: Reading the Bible as Scripture* (Nashville: Abingdon, 2007), 1–25.
4. See William J. Abraham, *Canon and Criterion in Christian Theology* (Oxford: Oxford University Press, 1998), esp. 1–56.
5. "Preface" to *Sermons on Several Occasions*, in *Works* (Bicentennial ed.), 1:105.
6. See Scott J. Jones, *John Wesley's Conception and Use of Scripture* (Nashville: Kingswood, 1995), 129–38, who describes Wesley's use of Scripture in five ways: textual, explanatory, definitional, narrative, and semantic.
7. Cf. Richard B. Hays, *The Moral Vision of the New Testament: Community, Cross, New Creation; A Contemporary Introduction to New Testament Ethics* (San Francisco: Harper San Francisco, 1996), 1–11, 291–312.
8. See Richard P. Thompson, "Inspired Imagination: John Wesley's Concept of Biblical Inspiration and Literary-Critical Studies," in *Reading the Bible in Wesleyan Ways: Some Constructive Proposals* (ed. B. L. Callen and R. P. Thompson (Kansas City, MO: Beacon Hill Press of Kansas City, 2004), 66–73.
9. See Wesley's comment on 2 Tim 3:16 in his *Explanatory Notes upon the New Testament* (London: Epworth, 1958), 794: "The Spirit of God not only once inspired those who wrote it, but continually inspires, supernaturally assists, those that read it with earnest prayer." See also R. Thompson, "Inspired Imagination," 62–65.
10. See R. Thompson, "Inspired Imagination," 57–79.
11. Cf. Max Turner, "Historical Criticism and Theological Hermeneutics of the New Testament," in *Between Two Horizons: Spanning New Testament Studies and Systematic Theology* (ed. J. B. Green and M. Turner (Grand Rapids: Eerdmans, 2000), 57ff.
12. Cf. Robert W. Wall, "The Significance of a Canonical Perspective of the Church's Scriptures," in *The Canon Debate* (ed. L. M. McDonald and J. A. Sanders (Peabody, MA: Hendrickson, 2002), 529–31.
13. See Stephen E. Fowl, *Engaging Scripture: A Model for Theological Interpretation*, Challenges in Contemporary Theology (Malden, MA: Blackwell, 1998), 75–83.
14. See Trevor Hart, "Tradition, Authority, and a Christian Approach to the Bible as Scripture," in *Between Two Horizons: Spanning New Testament Studies and Systematic Theology*, 196; and Stephen B. Chapman, "Reclaiming Inspiration for the Bible," in *Canon and Biblical Interpretation* (ed. C. G. Bartholomew et al.; Grand Rapids: Zondervan, 2006), 183.
15. Hays, *The Moral Vision of the New Testament*, 6.
16. Cf. A. K. M. Adam, "Poaching on Zion: Biblical Theology as Signifying Practice," in *Reading Scripture with the Church: Toward a Hermeneutic for Theological Interpretation* (Grand Rapids: Baker Academic, 2006), 28.
17. See M. Robert Mulholland, Jr., *Shaped by the Word: The Power of Scripture in Spiritual Formation* (Nashville: Upper Room, 2000); A. K. M. Adam, *Faithful Interpretation: Reading the Bible in a Postmodern World* (Minneapolis; Fortress, 2006); Marjorie J. Thompson, *Soul Feast: An Invitation to the Christian Spiritual Life* (Louisville: Westminster John Knox, 1995).
18. Sandra Schneiders, "Biblical Spirituality," *Interpretation* 56/2 (Apr. 2002): 136.
19. M. Thompson, *Soul Feast*, 19.

20. See D. Burton-Christie, *The Word in the Desert: Scripture and the Quest for Holiness in Early Church Monasticism* (New York: Oxford University Press, 1993).
21. M. Thompson, *Soul Feast*, 22.
22. Doug Hardy, "Lectio Divina: A Practice for Reconnecting to God's Word," *Preacher's Magazine: A Preaching Resource in the Wesleyan Tradition*, Lent/Easter 2009, 38–41.
23. Schneiders, "Biblical Spirituality," 140.
24. Roberta Hestenes, *Using the Bible in Groups* (Philadelphia: Westminster, 1983), 11.
25. Schneiders, "Biblical Spirituality," 136.
26. See, e.g., David Hunsicker, "John Wesley: Father of Today's Small Groups," *Wesleyan Theological Journal* 31/1 (Spr. 1996): 210.
27. David Michael Henderson, *John Wesley's Class Meeting: A Model of Making Disciples* (Nappanee, IN: Evangel, 1997), 83.
28. Dean G. Blevins and Mark A. Maddix, *Discovering Christian Discipleship: Foundations of Christian Education* (Kansas City, MO: Beacon Hill Press of Kansas City, 2010), 196.
29. James F. White, *Introduction to Christian Worship* (3rd ed.; Nashville: Abingdon, 2000), 167.
30. Marva Dawn, *Reaching Out without Dumbing Down: A Theology of Worship for the Turn-of-the-Century Culture* (Grand Rapids: Eerdmans, 1995), 211.
31. Debra Dean Murphy, *Teaching that Transforms: Worship as the Heart of Christian Education* (Grand Rapids: Brazos, 2004), 145.
32. Susan J. White, *Foundations of Christian Worship* (Louisville: Westminster John Knox, 2006), 15.
33. White, *Foundations of Christian Worship*, 15.
34. E.g., the Wesleyan tradition influenced by the hymnology of Charles Wesley (1701–1788), who wrote over 6,500 hymns and integrated Scripture in his hymns.
35. Dennis Bratcher, "Word and Table: Reflections on a Theology of Worship," Online: http://www.crivoice.org/wordtable.html.
36. Lester Ruth, "Word and Table: A Wesleyan Model for Balanced Worship," in *The Wesleyan Tradition: A Paradigm for Renewal* (ed. P. W. Chilcote; Nashville: Abingdon, 2002), 138.

Old Testament Chapters

13

How *Ever* Shall We Preach Genesis 1–11?!

Joseph E. Coleson

The Bible contains a number of potential minefields for Christian preaching. This is especially true for those of us who minister within the Wesleyan-Holiness tradition. We believe in the truth and authority of Scripture. However, we define "truth" more comprehensively than do many on the theological "right" and more comprehensively than those to our theological "left." In many parts of North America, those who listen to our preaching are not aware that Wesleyanism stands within the tradition of the English Reformation and the Anglican *via media*. Nor are they aware of the value of that positioning for accurate, effective, and deeply rewarding biblical study and understanding.

You know the minefields. Several lie hidden in Genesis 1–11, often titled, "The Primeval Prologue." Does it tell us *how* God created? Can one be a Christian and believe the "how" as the processes of evolution? (One group answers, "No.") Can one be intelligent and educated, and also believe the "how" produced an earth that still is very young, even now? (Another group answers, "No.") Was Noah's flood a historical event? A church will never run out of questions in these chapters. And believers never will outdistance their need to step carefully. They will need to be careful to be constructive and not destructive of people's faith in God and in one another. It is an awesome responsibility, but God's grace is even more awesome.

Ten Themes I Would Feature in Preaching Genesis 1–11

My recent work for the New Beacon Bible Commentary has focused primarily on Genesis 1–11. Among a hundred or more possibilities (really!) that emerge from living in these chapters, these are ten I would preach, if I still were in the pulpit regularly.

1. This book is well and truly named *Genesis*.

"Genesis" is a Greek word meaning "beginning." This book speaks a little of the beginnings of the cosmos, including our solar system and earth. It speaks more of the beginnings of humanity. It speaks of our self-chosen alienation from God and of God's prior choice not to give up on us. Genesis 6–9 records the de-creation of the flood and God's re-creation out of that temporary return to the primordial emptiness. Soon after, the book begins the account of God's moving forward on the promise of complete restoration/re-creation, narrating Abram's response to God's call, "Go . . . to the land I will show you" (Gen 12:1; *unless indicated, translations are the author's*). By the end of Genesis, the reader understands that God intended to fulfill God's eschatological purposes through Abram/Abraham and his family. God's initial call (12:3) and its re-iteration (22:18) even hint already that God intended to extend to all persons and all peoples this grace first offered to Abraham and his family.

2. God is both the transcendent and the immanent Creator.

Genesis 1 clearly teaches that God was and is before all else. Without God's intentional calling forth (however it was done), nothing else but God would exist. God is the uncaused Cause. This does not require the phrase *creatio ex nihilo* ("created out of nothing") actually to be in the text (in Hebrew, of course, not Latin!). Genesis

1:1 suffices, "In the beginning, God created the heavens and the earth." If one subscribes to the Big Bang theory as the mechanism for this beginning, God was and is the Cause of the Big Bang, whenever and however God did it. If one is a young-earth creationist, this verse still teaches that God brought everything else into being (cf. also John 1:3).

It is quite common for people to see Genesis 2 as a contrasting, even as a contradictory, creation account, as compared to Genesis 1. One supposed evidence for this is God's "immanent" creation of humans in Genesis 2, as contrasted with the magisterial, transcendent One of the, "And God said, 'Let there [be] . . .'" statements (Gen 1:3, 6, 9, 11, 14, 20, 24). Yet, a closer look at Genesis 1 reveals there also the immanence of God's creative work, as well as God's transcendent nature and character. Not only did God say, "Let there be," but God also "saw" (evaluated), "named," "made, and "set" in place various parts of the creation. God even privileged the waters, the skies, and the dry land to partner with God to "bring forth" both vegetable and animal life.

Similarly, we are quick to see Genesis 2 as the account of the immanent Creator "forming" the first human (who became the "man") and "building" the second (the "woman"), with equal love and care for both of them, the now-completed human species. This way of looking at Genesis 2 is not "wrong," yet it also does not do full justice to this account. The very distinction between "transcendent" and "immanent," although useful to the modern Western mind, would have seemed strange, perhaps even ridiculous, to the first millennia of hearers of these two accounts. In sum, "transcendence" and "immanence" can be convenient descriptors, but they really are two sides of the same coin, to use an imperfect metaphor. God is everywhere (one aspect of "transcendence"), but wherever God is, God also is "immanent."

3. Genesis 1 raises the question, "Why would we worship *any* of our fellow creatures?!"

The cultural setting of the Genesis creation accounts was the larger ancient Near East of which Israel was a part. This is true whether Genesis originated with quite ancient written and/or oral sources or was compiled as a monotheistic primer and polemic for exiled Judeans in Babylonia and beyond. (While over-generalized, these represent the spectrum-ends of current opinion on the origins/sources of Gen 1–11.) The dominant creation myth within their purview may have been the Babylonian cosmogony most commonly titled *Enuma Elish*.

The Babylonian version presents Marduk, patron deity of Babylon, as creator. However, Marduk was not pre-existent; he was the progeny of Tiamat, goddess of the primeval salt-water ocean (in that region, the Persian Gulf), and her consort, Apsu, god of the freshwater water sources. In brief, Marduk killed Tiamat in personal combat, and then split her body in two. From one half, he formed the earth; from the other, he fashioned the "firmament" (the same concept as in Gen 1:6–7). Marduk set the "great gods" in the heavens: sun, moon, planets, major stars, and constellations. Eventually, the defeated "gods" who had sided with Tiamat complained about the servitude imposed upon them. In this cosmogony, Ea, god of wisdom, found the solution. He created humans to take their place, i.e., solely and specifically to serve all the "gods."

Intentionally correcting this polytheistic cosmogony, Genesis 1 depicts everything as *God's* creation. The great deep (1:2)—*tehom*, from the same Semitic root as Akkadian Tiamat—is not a goddess. Most strikingly, the account of the fourth creation day (1:14–19) avoids even naming the "sun" or the "moon," major deities for all of Israel's neighbors. All other heavenly bodies, the "great gods" of the *Enuma Elish*, are subsumed under a single Hebrew word, "the stars." *Everything* that Israel's neighbors worshiped is included in the good creation of Israel's transcendent/immanent God. If any

could speak, it certainly would say, with horror at the thought of receiving our worship, "Do not deify *me*! Worship the One who made
both of us in wisdom and in love, *for* love and for our proper glory
as created beings."

I would remind us that worship of our fellow creatures did not
end in antiquity. We may find it easy to point our fingers at religious
traditions of other cultures. But some of our objects of idolatrous
worship are just as tangible: ostentatious homes, autos, boats, ap-
parel. Some may be less tangible but are no less real: devotion to
a favorite team, a favorite leisure activity, our work, a spouse or
other family members. Wisdom and discernment would be critical
in discussing it, but even our involvement in a local church, if done
for the wrong reasons, *can* be a form of worshiping the creature
instead of the Creator.

4. Genesis 1 presents a *functional* ontology of creation, not a material ontology.

I had paid scant attention to the "creation as cosmic temple
inauguration" work of some of my colleagues in Old Testament
and ancient Near Eastern disciplines. Then I came across John H.
Walton's recent work, *The Lost World of Genesis One* (Inter-Varsity,
2009), and used it in a creation theology course. I was instantly
impressed and wished I *had* been part of this discussion. It makes
sense in the world of the ancient Near East from which Genesis 1
came. This is the "literal" reading of the text, if by "literal" we mean
(as we should) something like, "starting with the meaning the text
itself was/is intended to convey." Just as important in our day, it offers a way out of the so-called "creation-evolution" debate. It never
has been true that the thinking believer must choose between
"faith" and "science." But this recent work presents and demonstrates solid reasons why that is so.

I cannot present Walton's entire approach here. In sum, however, Walton demonstrates that Genesis 1 is an account of God's

establishing and putting into motion the *functions* of the created order, preparing the earth to be and to function as God's cosmic temple. Put another way, in six creation days God established the various elements of creation in their *functions*. God then took up residence in God's cosmic temple, the earth, on the seventh (sabbath) day of the creation week. This *functional ontology* is of a piece with the cosmogonies of Israel's neighbors in *its* form and function. The crucial difference is that Israel's monotheistic account sets the record straight, following millennia of distortion and misapprehension occasioned by a universally polytheistic worldview.

This leaves no room for—and more importantly, no *need* for— understandings of Genesis 1 and 2 as accounts intended to present a *material ontology* of origins. *Material* origins are a Western, not an Eastern concern, and Genesis is an Eastern document. We have imposed our Western concerns for material origins (learned from our Greek intellectual forebears) upon the ancient Near Eastern Hebrew text. We hardly could have been expected to know better. But now, thanks to Walton and others working in this important comparative area, we *do* possess historical and cultural analogues to the Genesis cosmogony. Especially in our Anglican/Wesleyan/ Holiness stream of biblical and ecclesial tradition, we must begin to learn and teach this approach.[1]

How I would present this would require specific and detailed knowledge of the local setting. But I would find a way to plant and nurture the seed of this *accurate* understanding of the didactic purposes of Genesis 1. We lose too many of our intelligent youth as they leave for college and become convinced they must choose between "hard science" and "soft faith." We lose too many thinking and inquiring adults who see problems with these accounts when they are interpreted as a material ontology. We need to become prepared to inform our people, at least those who come to us with serious and sincere questions.

A final word here: this is not a choice between a "literal" reading and a "figurative/metaphorical/mythical" reading of Genesis 1–2. This *is* the "literal" reading of these chapters, because this is how they would have been understood in their ancient Near Eastern, Israelite (or early Jewish) context. To read a material ontology into texts intended to present a functional ontology is not to read those texts "literally." It is to misread them, transgressing the biblical instruction that we are consistently to be "expounding correctly the word of truth" (2 Tim 2:15). All of us who espouse a high view of Scripture are under obligation to interpret it correctly, even when that means modifying what we previously thought we knew.

5. God's creation intention was and is for gender (and other) equality among humans.

At issue for this point is the correct understanding of the Hebrew phrase *'ezer cenegdo* (A-zer ke-neg-DOE), which occurs only in Genesis 2:18, 20. Traditionally, it is rendered "a help meet for him" (KJV) or "a helper as his partner" (NRSV). Putting it bluntly, that translation is a mistake. We must lay it aside and adopt the meaning the text actually intends. That meaning is "a power like him, facing him as equal."[2] I am as confident about the correctness of this translation and of its necessary interpretive nuances as I am about anything I have ever researched in more than forty years as a student and professional biblical scholar.

God's creation intention was and is absolute gender equality: not gender *identity*, but gender *equality*. God's eschatological intention is the restoration/re-creation of all the created order. It follows that God seeks to restore gender equality where it needs restoration. God calls us to live even here and now in accordance with God's plans and purposes for this, *already* provided and begun in Christ. For the church, of all peoples and of all institutions, to teach that women are second-class members of God's family because our first mother ate first of the forbidden fruit is not only mistaken. It is *sin* of the first order. It is *rebellion* against the will and desire of God, revealed from the very beginning.

If any teaching of some segments of the church is currently more sinfully destructive, especially within the church itself, I am hard pressed to think what it may be. To put it positively, if the church would get this right, act on it consistently, and teach our families (including single members of the church family) all its ramifications in conviction and practice, the transformation of the church *and* the culture—every culture where the church is—would be the result. We as ministers of the gospel and grace of Christ *must* take this seriously. We must preach and teach it. We must examine and change our structures, both institutional and informal, to see that women and men equally have real voice, vote, and participation in all the life of the church. We must teach parents and families how to believe and live this in and outside their homes. We say we long for a revival of holiness in our churches and among our people. If we mean that, we must find ways to teach our people that everyone stands on level ground, not only at the foot of the cross, but in God's creation and eschatological purposes. Everyone has a seat at the table, and only Christ himself sits at the head of that table.

6. God's motive for creating is love; God's motive for sustaining creation is love.

As I have lived in Genesis 1–11, I have been amazed over and over by the large and small evidences of God's passionate love, both for humans and for the whole creation. I have mentioned already God's intimate loving care in "forming" the man and "building" the woman (Gen 2:7, 22). There is much more. Israel's neighbors thought they had to beg, cajole, bribe, and even threaten their gods to bless their families, fields, flocks, and fruit trees with fertility. Here, God specifically and emphatically blessed all living creation with abundant fertility, right from the beginning (1:11, 22, 28; 9:7). God evaluated and declared the entire creation "very good" (1:31). God delighted to meet the first couple daily in the garden in the most refreshing period of the day (3:8; even the verb form affirms God's delight). Seven times in God's declaration of covenant with Noah following the flood, God specified that this covenant was/is with *all flesh*, not only with and for human beings (9:8–17).

7. God is heartbroken at our turning away and our reluctance to come home.

God's nature and God's character do not and will not change. From eternity to eternity, God is good, and God is love. Some go further and teach that God is "immutable" in the sense of being "impassive," unaffected by feelings of any kind or to any degree. I think the child knows intuitively this is not true of God. But I was astounded by the strength and depth of the pathos of God's cry at our first parents' failure to keep the daily tryst in the Garden, "Where *are* you?!" Simple translation cannot do the single Hebrew word justice; it is like Twain's comparison of the lightning bug with the lightning itself. God was grief-stricken, heartbroken, at this first betrayal, though (as I believe) God knew it was coming.

God's pain and sorrow are evident in God's conversation with the wayward Cain. Then, God regretted—felt sorrow and pain— that God brought into existence creatures capable of such evil as to require the judgment of the flood. Grief and pain are evident centuries later in the prophet's cry on God's behalf, "When Israel was but a youth I loved him . . . How can I give you up, Ephraim?!" (Hos 11:1, 8). They reverberate in Jesus' lament, "O Jerusalem, Jerusalem, . . . how often did I long to gather your children, just as a hen gathers her chicks [under her wings], but you were not willing!" (Matt 23:37).

As it was with them, so it is with us. God feels pain at our rejection of God and God's overtures toward us. God longs for the reconciliation already provided in Christ to become a reality in the life, the mind, and the heart of every human, of everyone within the sounds of our voices.

8. To refuse God is to choose death; no other outcome is possible.

This principle permeates God's revelations (not arbitrary judgments) of the consequences of the first turning away (Gen 3:16–19). I have known that, but I was surprised to discover its clarity in God's announcement to Noah of the coming destruction. Genesis 6:12 reads, "But the earth was ruined before God, and the earth was filled up with lawlessness. Now God had seen the earth and, behold, it was ruined; for all flesh had brought to ruin its way upon the earth." Based on this, God said to Noah, "The end of all flesh has come/is coming before me, because the earth is filled up with lawlessness because of them. Now, behold, I am bringing them to ruin, [together] with the earth" (6:13). "To ruin/destroy" occurs again four verses later (v. 17).

Because the cultures of antiquity virtually required monarchical imagery, God's statements of impending judgment almost always sound to our ears like arbitrary judicial decrees. In reality, there is nothing arbitrary about them nor hardly anything "judicial," except as formal pronouncements that (given the circumstances) had to be proclaimed. Our first parents turned their backs on the Giver of life. How could they have expected anything other than the death of which God had warned them? By Noah's day, the earth's inhabitants had thoroughly corrupted it. How could they have expected anything else than that God would finish the job? That God would "wipe clean" the earth from the stain that creaturely corruption and violence had become upon it (6:7)?

As it was with them, so it is with us. The person who dies from a lifetime of substance abuse or even of a single overdose can hardly blame God for dying earlier than expected. If we refuse God's way of love and forgiveness throughout a lifetime, pushing everyone away, ought we to blame God when we face the end of life alone and embittered?

Of course, this is not the whole story. Living in the imperfect world our own turning away from God has fashioned, much evil, pain, and suffering falls on those who have not directly earned it. Ultimately of much greater import, though, God's grace and loving-kindness have the capacity to wipe all that away—will we but let God do it—as thoroughly as God's perfect justice wiped the earth clean for a fresh start in Noah's day.

9. The Bible is without peer in its literary artistry.

This one may seem strange, but I include it for a reason. A well-known television preacher wrote that he found it difficult to find new things to preach, new ways of keeping his preaching fresh and vital. I found *that* strange, barring the malaise that can afflict any-one temporarily. Constantly, I am amazed, astounded, overjoyed, satisfied, contented, challenged, amused, perplexed by the virtuos-ity of the biblical authors, wherever I am reading. I give you three examples from these eleven chapters; I *could* discuss several from every line of the text.

First, Eve's recorded words total eighteen in the Hebrew text. In 3:13, she told God, "The serpent deceived me, and I ate" (three words). At Cain's birth (4:1), she said, "I have acquired (or fash-ioned) a man [child] together with Yahweh" (again, three words). While perhaps not blameworthy, these words can strike the reader as arrogant, or even presumptuous. Eve's final speech (4:25)—at twelve words, twice as long as the other two combined—is filled with pathos, loss, and a chastened humility, "And she called his name 'Seth, because God [Elohim here, not Yahweh] has set for me another seed instead of Abel, because Cain murdered him.'"

Second, in the space of twenty Hebrew words (6:8–10a), "Noah" occurs five times. At the beginning of verse nine, "Noah" occurs twice in succession, "These are the accounts of Noah; Noah was . . . ." The statement of Noah's sterling character (v. 9) begins and ends with "Noah." "Noah" occurs in the middle of verse 10a, the report of his fathering three sons. In every way literarily pos-

204 THE BIBLE TELLS ME SO

sible, the narrator emphasized that Noah would be the human protagonist of this longest narrative of the Primeval Prologue.

Finally, the narrator has given us more than three chapters of God telling Noah what to do and of Noah doing it, with never a word from Noah's mouth reported. When at last we do hear from Noah, he is in a most unedifying situation, and his words are an enigma totaling two speeches, three lines, and only twenty-four Hebrew words!

The observant reader will notice and find ways to convey the joy and the pathos, the delight and the solemnity—what Lewis once called, "the serious business of heaven, which is joy"—present in (literally) every line of every biblical book.

10. God's call to Abram/Abraham is a call to holiness.

We are a Wesleyan-Holiness people. God evaluated Noah as "a righteous man of integrity (Hebrew *tamim*). I take "integrity" here as denoting Noah's holiness, as the end of the verse intimates, as well, "Noah walked with God."

Just so, God instructed Abram, on the occasion of changing his name to Abraham, "Walk before me, and be [a man of] integrity" (Gen 17:1). To be a person of integrity is to be "one," i.e., to be wholly dedicated, without division of loyalties, to one person, one cause, one way of life. That is the essence of the holiness to which God also calls us. This call to "adventure ourselves with God" permeates the Old Testament every bit as thoroughly as it does the New, will we but see it.

I would preach these themes in sermons and series wholly dedicated to them. I also would find ways to weave them into all my preaching and teaching. A sentence here, a verse or a half-verse there, often would be enough, but I would take every opportunity to remind my hearers that God created for loving, constructive purposes. Amazingly, God has not given up on those purposes nor on us—and never will.

Five Common Beliefs I Would Avoid in Preaching Genesis 1–11

I do not believe it is possible to be a faithful preacher/teacher of Scripture and to avoid addressing altogether these topics/issues that often are taken as what Genesis 1–11 is intended to teach. That is not what I mean here by using the word "avoid." For the first four of these, what I *do* mean is to avoid preaching/teaching them as the "real" message of Genesis 1–11. They are not. The last one falls into Paul's categories of "myths and endless genealogies" (1 Tim 1:4), of "foolish questions and genealogies and discord and strife about the Torah" (Titus 3:9).

1. I would not preach/teach any material ontology as "*the* Genesis view of creation."

Of course, I have touched on this above, in discussing what I *would* preach. To put it negatively here is to reiterate my conviction that the Genesis creation accounts simply do not address the Western understanding of a physical, material ontology of the earth and its origins. Genesis 1–2 (together with all other creation passages in Scripture) neither endorses nor opposes a young-earth creation *or* an eons-long age for the earth and the universe, the evolution of life upon the earth *or* a special creation of each species of life. All biblical creation passages simply are silent on these questions. We ought not to expect Scripture to address them. On the other side of this issue, no scientific inquiry, if pursued with integrity, poses a threat to biblical faith.

2. I would not preach/teach that Genesis 1–2 are contradictory accounts of creation or that these chapters are "only mythical" anyway.

Literarily, Genesis 1 and 2 *are* two different creation accounts, if you will. However, rather than being *contradictory*, they are *complementary*. Genesis 2 provides a (primarily theological) account that would be grossly out of place, if stuffed into its "proper" position, "chronologically," following 1:27. Developed fully as its own subsequent narrative, it eloquently and elegantly fills in important and fascinating details. In its literary artistry, it is fully the equal of Genesis 1.

On the scientific plane, this is the flip side of our first caution. By way of technical literary definition, of course, these texts *are* "mythological," inasmuch as they feature God as the Protagonist. But "myth/mythical/mythological" has an entirely different connotation in popular thought, including among those whose spiritual well-being is a part of our concern. To say these texts do not teach a Western, scientific, material ontology of the cosmos is not to say that that ontology is unimportant. It is to say that the concerns of these texts are not *those* concerns. We must encourage those entrusted to our care to learn to hear and read these texts for what they are intended to say, without belittling or embarrassing those who want to know the material ontology also.

3. I would not preach/teach that woman was created to be man's "helper."

On this issue, also, I have said my piece in many places, including above in this essay. Positively, this issue has the potential to transform the church truly into the image, likeness, and way of God's holiness—and following the church, all the cultures of the earth, if we ever were to take it as seriously as I believe God would have us take it. Negatively and in light of the whole of our biblical and Holiness heritage, no Wesleyan-Holiness minister ought ever to preach, teach, model, or condone anything other than the full biblical, creational, and eschatological equality of women with men, and men with women, *especially* in this present imperfect world. To be less than proactive is to be less than Wesleyan, and less than biblically holy. To be less than affirming, at least, should be to invite discussion with those appointed to see that our churches remain

Wesleyan and Holiness. Yes, this *is* that important an issue.

4. I would not preach/teach that humans, male or female, were or are "cursed" by God.

God cursed the serpent (Gen 3:14); God cursed the ground (3:17). "Cursed" means diminished in some way(s), as compared with previous existence and/or capacities. However, God did *not* curse either the man or the woman immediately responsible for the first transgression. For any minister of the gospel of God's grace and lovingkindness to state or imply that any daughter of Eve or son of Adam today is cursed by God because of *their* primordial rebellion is to pervert that gospel and belittle that grace. God's desires and designs are for redemption/restoration/re-creation, not for cursing.

5. I would not spend pulpit time on unanswerable questions.

Did either Adam or Eve have a navel? Where did Cain find his wife? What exactly did Ham (or Canaan?) *do* that Noah found objectionable when he awoke from his wine? Speculation is possible, but it always must remain speculation. Allow the emphases of the text to determine where to focus time and attention. When approached about such issues (as we will be), we ought not to treat the inquirer with anything less than courteous respect.

If you take an interest in these themes and issues, you soon will outstrip in your own studies all I have said here. May God give you that grace. It is a most delightful and rewarding journey!

---

1. I do not agree with Walton in every detail, but his overall approach is sound.
2. See the evidence in Joseph E. Coleson, *Genesis 1–11: A Commentary in the Wesleyan Tradition* (New Beacon Bible Commentary; Kansas City, MO: Beacon Hill Press of Kansas City, forthcoming).

14

Is There Anything to
Preach from Leviticus?

Thomas J. King

The stereotypical view of Leviticus rejects its laws as wearisome and irrelevant. At the same time, the church is drawn to Leviticus as the theological foundation for understanding atonement through the sacrifice of Christ on the cross. One can diminish this disparity by recognizing that Leviticus considers God's holiness and grace, not only in the divine provisions for atonement, but even in the most perplexing legislation.

Far from extraneous, Jewish tradition views Leviticus as the starting point for religious education. Jacob Milgrom puts it this way, "From earliest rabbinic times, Leviticus was the curricular foundation of the Jewish primary school: 'Why do young children commence with the Priests' manual (i.e., Leviticus) and not with Genesis?—Surely, it is because young children are pure and sacrifices are pure; so let the pure come and engage in the study of the pure' (*Midr. Lev. Rab.* 7:2)."[1]

We may approach the study of God's revelation in the book of Leviticus with the purity and innocence of children. As a sample of the significant insights that one may glean from Leviticus, this essay seeks to provide a brief overview of theological themes evident in the third book of the Pentateuch.[2]

God's Love as the Motive for Atonement

In an attempt to explain the purpose of the *burnt offering* (Lev 1), J. Hartley speculates that it must serve to atone for the general sinful disposition of the one who offers it. The reason for his conclusion is that Leviticus lists no specific sins in relation to this offering.[3] However, sin as a general disposition seems foreign to the legislation in the book. Even unintentional sins have added qualification of *doing* "what is forbidden in any of the Lord's commands" (4:2, 13, 22, 27). The need for atonement underscores the violation of a known law of God (as opposed to a general sinful disposition).

Baruch Levine, who acknowledges that no offense needing expiation required the burnt offering, claims that the need prompting the sacrifice is for redemption from God's wrath. He argues that proximity to God was inherently dangerous even when no violation occurred that angered the Lord.[4] This identifies the motivation for atonement as God's wrath, however, rather than love.

Christians make the same mistake by asserting that the satisfaction of God's wrath is the motivation behind the crucifixion and the atonement it offers. Such thinking would require the revision of John 3:16 so that it should read, "For God was so *angry* with the world, that he sent his only begotten son ..." In contrast, however, God's love and grace provide the means of atonement for ancient Israel through the sacrificial system, which the life, death, and resurrection of Christ bring to fulfillment. Certainly, the Bible describes God's *wrath* against sin and the brokenness it generates. However, God's great *love* for humanity motivates God's provision of atonement.

In addition to atonement, the sacrificial system provides for the expression of other significant *relational* concerns. For example, the functions of the burnt offering include the invocation of God's presence, a declaration of devotion to God, and a means of celebration in response to significant events. The dedication of first fruits to the Lord also reflects devotion to God (Lev 2:12, 14; Exod 13:11–13; 22:29–30; 34:19–20; Num 8:17; 2 Chr 31:5). The faithful worshiper acknowledges that everything comes from God and is therefore dedicated back to God by means of a token or representative "first fruit." The *grain offering* and the *well-being offerings* specifically demonstrate cherished relationship with God (Lev 2–3; 6:14–18; 7:11–21). Both bread shared between God and priests (grain offerings), and meat shared between God and offerers (well-being offerings), represent a theme of communion uniting God and humanity in intimate fellowship. Finally, the motivations for the various types of well-being offerings further reflect positive relationship with God. The *thanksgiving offering* provides for expressions of gratitude to the Lord. The *votive offering* depicts celebration upon the accomplishment of a vow; and the *freewill offering* represents spontaneous praise to God.

A serious investigation of the laws in Leviticus reveals much more than the messy and morbid business of bloody sacrifices focused on defeating sin and impurity. The sacrificial system represents a variety of expressions reflecting right relationship with God. As Jacob Milgrom concludes, "the freewill sacrifice makes a link between individual/communal joy and thanksgiving: in our moments of greatest happiness, the sacrificial system teaches us, we pause to appreciate the blessings in our lives and say thanks."[5] John Wesley recognized the range of relational functions among the sacrifices: "some by way of acknowledgment to God for mercies either desired or received; others by way of satisfaction to God for men's sins; others were mere exercises of devotion."[6] Such an emphasis on relationship with expressions of joy and praise make it evident that God's love and grace (above anger) motivate the sacrificial system, including its demand for atonement.

Reverence for Life

Explanations of the rationale behind the impurity laws often treat them as remnants of pagan influence, as if tolerated within God's greater written revelation. Such interpretations include concepts founded upon the following: (a) the need for order and wholeness in the face of a mixed and unmanageable creation, (b) the threat of supernatural powers emanating from unclean objects or persons, and (c) ancient taboos reflecting the fears of an ignorant society seeking to appease a pantheon of gods through ritual acts. In contrast, God's revelation acknowledges ancient Near Eastern influences, yet divests them of pagan belief and reforms them with God's theological message. Milgrom explains by saying, "Some benign skin diseases are diagnosed and quarantined, passing by the spate of known contagious diseases. Genital discharges are declared impure but not issues from other orifices. These are the subjects of the impurity laws . . . They sound bizarre. But as symbols they reveal deeper, basically ethical values that remain relevant to this day."[7]

The theological principle behind the impurity laws becomes evident upon consideration of the sources of impurity identified in the priestly legislation. The priests limited impurity to only three main sources: a corpse or carcass, genital discharges, and scale disease. This narrow inventory excludes a number of known contagious diseases in the ancient world and bodily secretions. The specificity of the priestly sources of impurity reveals the common denominator that they share: death in some manner. Clearly, a corpse/carcass reflects death. Genital discharges (semen and vaginal blood) represent forces of life, and therefore their loss represents death. The wasting away of the body is the common characteristic of a highly visible form of scale disease labeled impure in the Bible. It symbolizes the process of death. When scale disease (often translated leprosy) afflicted Miriam, Moses prays, "Oh, do not let her be like one dead, whose flesh is half eaten away when he comes from his mother's womb!" (Num 12:12 NASB). Leviticus 13–14 includes moldy fabrics and fungous houses as impure, not because they have scale disease but look like it. Milgrom concludes that the impurity laws symbolically call Israel to *choose life* by means of obedience to these commands of God.[8] Impurity, associated with death, stands in opposition to holiness that represents life. Consequently, in this symbolic system, holiness and life overcomes impurity and death. The system represents the victory of life over death! The impurity laws provide an expression of God's commitment to resurrection and life!

The impurity legislation also serves as a constant reminder of relationship with God. Even the most private, mundane, irritating, and embarrassing aspects of being human, such as seminal emissions and menstrual cycles, are subject to relationship with God. The impurity laws remind us to stop in the midst of the most tedious elements of life, acknowledge God, and recognize God's grace even in places where and at times when we would rather be left alone.

Sin's Disruption of Relationship with God

The defilement of the sanctuary because of sin and uncleanness is clearly expressed in the Pentateuch:

> Thus you shall keep the people of Israel separate from their uncleanness, so that they do not die in their uncleanness *by defiling my tabernacle* that is in their midst. (Lev 15:31 NRSV; emphasis added)

> I myself will set my face against them, and will cut them off from the people; because they have given of their offspring to Molech, *defiling my sanctuary* and profaning my holy name. (Lev 20:3 NRSV; emphasis added)

> If they fail to purify themselves after touching a human corpse, they *defile the Lord's tabernacle*. (Num 19:13 NIV; emphasis added)

> But if those who are unclean do not purify themselves, they must be cut off from the community, because *they have defiled the sanctuary of the LORD*. (Num 19:20 NIV; emphasis added)

The defilement of the sanctuary is a vital concern because God, who is holy, cannot abide impurity. For the priestly legislation, the place of God's presence is understood to be the holy of holies within the sanctuary (Exod 40:34–35; Lev 16:2). When impurity begins to penetrate the sanctuary (from courtyard, to holy place, and even into the holy of holies itself [re: the Day of Atonement, Lev 16:14–16]) a growing fear arises that God may abandon the sanctuary, and the presence of God may be removed from the midst of the community. Ezekiel's vision (Ezek 10:18–19; 11:22–23) reflects such a devastating event, and Lamentations mourns the thought of it happening: "The Lord has rejected his altar and abandoned his sanctuary" (Lam 2:7 NIV).

A primary function of the *purification offering* is to cleanse the sanctuary and keep it free of defilement from sin and impurity.[9] But abiding in a clean sanctuary is not God's foremost concern. Rather, God's greatest desire is right and holy relationships with the covenant community in whose midst God has placed the sanctuary of divine presence. The defilement that sin and impurity generate pollutes the sanctuary and represents the brokenness and alienation that sin afflicts upon relationships. That is what drives away the presence of God. Thus, in cleansing the sanctuary, the purification offering also serves to purge the unclean and the sinner with the goal of restoring relationship to God. Even though the cleansing agent of blood is not applied directly to persons, the goal of reconciling humans in relationship to God, expressed through purification and forgiveness, indicates that the purification offering also cleanses the offerer.[10]

Degrees of Sin and Implications for Accountability

The following chart summarizes the distinctive elements of the purification offerings described in Lev 4:

	Anointed Priest	Israelite Community	Leader	Member of Community
Type of Animal	Young Bull	Young Bull	Male Goat	Female Goat or Lamb
Blood Application	Inside Holy Place: In front of curtain On horns of incense altar	Inside Holy Place: In front of curtain On horns of incense altar	Outer Court: On horns of altar of burnt offering	Outer Court: On horns of altar of burnt offering
Disposal of Animal Flesh	Burn outside camp in a clean place	Burn outside camp in a clean place	Eaten by priests	Eaten by priests

The type of animal, the application of blood, and the means by which the animal flesh is disposed reflect the degree of impurity that a particular purification offering purges. The inadvertent sins of the anointed priest and the whole community (Lev 4:3–21) generate impurity that penetrates all the way into the holy place.[11] Thus, the requirement is for an offering of a young bull, the sprinkling of blood in front of the curtain in the holy place and on the horns of the incense altar within the holy place, and the burning of the animal's flesh outside the camp. In contrast, the inadvertent sins of a leader or a common member of the community (4:22–35) generate impurity that only penetrates as far as the outer altar in the courtyard of the sanctuary. The requirement for the purification offering is for a male goat (in the case of a leader) or a female goat or lamb (in the case of the common person). In addition, the blood is applied to the outer altar, and the priests would eat the animal flesh.

The class of animal required (from bull to female lamb) reflects the greater or lesser sense of consequence attached to the sins of the offerer. The sins of the priest and the whole community represent more serious offenses that require sacrifices of greater value. The sins of a leader or common person represent lesser offenses that require sacrifices of lesser value. The sacrificial system applies greater accountability to leaders, especially those exercising spiritual and moral influence (cf. Jas 3:1).

Gracious Provision of Atonement from All Sin

The Article of Faith regarding sin in the *Manual* for the Church of the Nazarene provides a helpful distinction between intentional sin and inadvertent sin. Paragraph 5.3 begins, "We believe that actual or personal sin is a voluntary violation of a known law of God by a morally responsible person. It is therefore not to be confused with involuntary and inescapable shortcomings, infirmities, faults, mistakes, failures, or other deviations from a standard of perfect conduct that are the residual effects of the Fall."[12] The sins addressed in Leviticus 4, which someone may commit unintentionally and are specified as violations of prohibitive commands of God, might be included among the "shortcomings, infirmities, faults, mistakes, failures, or other deviations" that should not be confused with "actual or personal sin." Lest one conclude that such "infirmities" should not be reckoned as sin, the sacrificial system proclaims otherwise. Although they may be unintentional, such sins still interfere with healthy righteous relationships and are therefore in need of atonement.

It sometimes *appears* in Scripture that willful, rebellious sins (actual or personal sin?) cannot be atoned, and the one who commits such must be "cut off; his guilt remains on him" (Num 15:30–31). However, atonement is possible, even for deliberate sins, through genuine remorse and confession. Numbers 5:6–8 (parallel to Lev 6:1–7 [Heb. 5:20–26]) stipulates that the offender "must confess the sin he has committed" (Num 5:7) before making restitution. Consequently, sincere remorse and confession serve to reduce deliberate sins to unintentional sins that sacrifice can thereby atone.[13] Milgrom cites the early rabbis as already acknowledging this principle: "R. Simeon b. Lakish said: 'Great is repentance, which converts intentional sins into unintentional ones' (*b. Yoma* 86b)."[14]

The sacrificial system calls God's people to be attentive and diligent even with respect to weaknesses and infirmities. God graciously provides a means to atone even our rebellious acts, if we turn to God with sincere repentance. For those with sensitive personalities who are anxious about "suspected" sins, God's love provides a means of easing the tender conscience through the *guilt offering* for unknown sins (Lev 5:17–19).[15]

Righteous and Inclusive Relationships

The sacrificial system serves to keep relationship with God constantly before God's children. The daily morning and evening burnt offerings (*continual* burnt offerings) are a perpetual reminder that the community lives in relation to God. Keeping the evening burnt offering smoldering all night suggests that petition on behalf of Israel continued through the night.[16] The pleasing aroma of burnt offerings (Lev 1:9, 13, 17) ascended continually and calls to mind the burning incense associated with the New Testament prayers of the saints (Rev 5:8; 8:3–4).

The sacrificial system reflects an inclusive concern for relationship to God. The evidence of such concern is the active participation of laypersons in the sacrificial rites in cooperation with the priests. Both the layperson or offerer and the priest would have alternating roles in offering a sacrifice such as the burnt offering. The offerer designates the sacrifice by laying a hand on its head and slaughters the bull; the priest then sprinkles the blood against the altar. The offerer skins the animal and cuts it into pieces; the priest arranges the pieces of the sacrifice on the fire and wood on the altar. The offerer washes the inner parts and the legs; the priest burns the whole animal on the altar. This partnership allows the layperson to be directly involved in meaningful interaction with God.[17] The tabernacle is not an isolated sacred space for the exclusive activity of the priests. It is a center for the community's expression of its walk with God.

The addition of the burnt offering of birds and the grain offering for the sake of those who cannot afford a large animal reinforces the relational and inclusive foundation of the sacrificial system. These provisions make it possible so that no economic limitations should prevent any member of the community from participating in the sacrificial expressions of genuine relationship with God.

Clearly, the sacrifices aimed at cleansing and atonement provide for maintaining right relationship between humans and God. The sacrificial system also demonstrates concern for maintaining right relationships among humans themselves. For example, the guilt offering atones for wrongs committed against one's neighbor. However, such atonement only follows upon appropriate acts of reparation and reconciliation. Thus, the sacrificial system does not merely provide release from sin and justification before God. Rather, its foundational aim is to establish and maintain right relationships with God and among humans.

The people of God do not express relationship with God solely through somber ceremony and meticulous ritual. The well-being offering serves to illustrate aspects of joy and celebration that also characterize the sacrificial system. The three types of well-being offerings (thanksgiving, votive, and freewill) express gratitude, achievement, and adoration through ritual.

The Offering of Life to God

The rite of laying a hand on the head of one's offering (see Lev 1:4; 3:2, 8; 4:4, 15, 24, 29, 33) provides initial insight into the profound connection intended between an offerer and the offered sacrifice. Too often, this is understood only symbolically in terms of substitution, such that the worshiper offers herself only through the victim.[18] In contrast, identification with the sacrifice is intended to compel the offerer to truly consecrate her own "life and labour to the Lord."[19]

The idea is not for the sacrifice to replace the offerer, but rather for the offerer to take on the representative consecration reflected in the sacrifice. Therefore, in order to fulfill the intent of an offering, the offerer must follow-up the act of sacrifice with behavior that is consistent with authentic relationship to God. As R. K. Harrison states, "the sacrifice consecrated to God by the donor must be matched by an intent to live an equally holy and consecrated life."[20]

The prophetic critique of the sacrificial system reinforces this very concept. The eighth century prophets do not reject sacrifices themselves. Rather, they reject Israel's hypocritical abuse of the sacrificial system by presenting their offerings to God while behaving in ways that deny their true intent. The prophets proclaim that proper fulfillment of the sacrificial system should result in justice, care for the needy, loyalty, knowledge of God, righteousness, kindness, and a humble walk with the Lord (Isa 1:11–19; Hos 6:6; Amos 5:21–24; Mic 6:6–8). W. Kaiser implies more than mere substitution is at stake: "At the core of Leviticus is a conviction that human life is most rich, beautiful, and free when, amid the confusion of life, people fashion themselves into offerings to God."[21] This is surely the intention of the Apostle Paul in relation to his exhortation to Christians in Rome: "I appeal to you therefore, brothers and sisters, by the mercies of God, to *present your bodies as a living sacrifice*, holy and acceptable to God" (Rom 12:1 NRSV).

The horns of the altar, upon which sacrifices are burnt, are recognized as symbols of "strength and force" or "power and might."[22] Interpreters have understood the horns as directing the thoughts of worshipers upward.[23] C. Keil and F. Delitzsch see the altar as the place of the manifestation of God's grace and salvation ultimately reflected in the power and might that the horns represent.[24] Gane sees the upward movement that the horns symbolize and the manifestation of divine grace and salvation as complimentary concepts.[25]

The foundational association of blood as life (Lev 17:11) reveals a significant feature of the purification offering. The application of blood to the altar (a primary act of sacrifices involving atonement) signifies the offering of *life* (not a substitutionary *death*) to God, which directs the worshiper's thoughts upward, and the worshiper renews fellowship with God by means of divine grace and salvation. Such an offering finds expression and fulfillment through a life committed to God through a renewed pursuit of holiness and righteousness.

The offering of life is one aspect of the *representative* character of the sacrificial system. The laying of a single-hand upon a sacrifice (Lev 3:1–2, 7–8, 12–13; 4:3–4, 13–15, 22–24, 27–29, 32–33) identifies the offering and designates it as representative of the offerer. This gesture indicates that the sacrifice belongs to the offerer as the one who presents it. This does *not* indicate that the offerer intends for the sacrifice to suffer in her or his place. The Old Testament *never* suggests that a sacrificial victim was to suffer a penalty.[26] Rather, in relation to the offerer, "the death of the victim symbolized his death to his sin, or to whatever stood between him and God, or his surrender of himself to God in thankfulness and humility."[27]

In parallel with gestures of primitive prayer and acts of prophetic symbolism, one may describe the sacrificial act as representative realism. The act of sacrifice affects change in the offerer's relationship to God, by representing the devotion and commitment of the worshiper.[28] The eighth century prophets declare that one must express such commitment through righteous living. Otherwise, one risks the invalidation of that sacrifice (Isa 1:11–19; Hos 6:6; Amos 5:21–24; Micah 6:6–8).[29] Wesley affirmed that the sacrificial system called worshipers to offer themselves entirely to God, with these words:

> The sacrifices signified that the whole man, in whose stead the sacrifice was offered, was to be intirely [sic] offered or devoted to God's service; and that the whole man did deserve to be utterly consumed, if God should deal severely with him; and directed us to serve the Lord with all singleness of heart, and to be ready to offer to God even such sacrifices or services wherein we ourselves should have no part or benefit.[30]

Further, Wesley said, "man, represented by these sacrifices, should aim at all perfection of heart and life, and that Christians should one day attain to it."[31] The representative character of the sacrificial system calls one to holy and righteous living, as seen through the offering of life to God.

All Powerful Grace of God

The disposal of the flesh of sacrificial animals reflects another form of gradation in relation to the purification offering (see above at "Degrees of Sin and Implications for Accountability"). The flesh of the sacrifice for the priest and the whole community must be burned outside the camp, while that for the leader or common person must be eaten by the priests. Priests cannot eat the meat from the offerings for the priest and community. The reason behind the prohibition is so they do not personally benefit from offerings related to their own sins or the sins of the community to which they belong.[32]

The priests *did* eat the meat from the offerings for a leader or common person, however. Milgrom points out that this act conveys a significant theological message. In the ancient Near East, the destruction of sacrifices after their use was to avert the exploitation of their remaining power for the purposes of sorcery. By eating the flesh of the purification offering, the priests of Israel proclaim that there is no magic power (dangerous for ingestion) in the ritual or sacrifice itself. Rather, the power to cleanse and purify are completely dependent on God's will.[33] Consequently, despite the common tendency to recognize "power in the blood," the sacrificial system affirms that the power for atonement rests in the grace and mercy of almighty God alone!

Furthermore, by ingesting the meat of the purification offering, the priest who represents holiness and life swallows up the sacrifice that evokes impurity and death. Thereby, the rite of the purification offering reflects the powerful theological theme of resurrection by portraying that "holiness has swallowed impurity" and "life can defeat death."[34]

Holiness and the Overwhelming Love of God

The strict separation between the sacred and the profane that the sacrificial system depicted emphasizes the holiness of God. One sees this in numerous ways: (a) the priest's change of clothes when entering or leaving the tabernacle, (b) the placing of the ashes from the burnt offering in a clean place (6:11 [Heb. 6:4]), (c) the eating of the most holy offerings in a holy place, (d) the warning against touching most holy offerings (6:16–18, 26–27 [Heb. 6:9–11, 19–20]), and (e) breaking the clay pot or scouring the bronze pot in which meat from a most holy offering is cooked (6:28 [Heb. 6:21]). The purification features of the sacrificial system further reveal the concern to maintain a resolute boundary between that which is holy and that which is common.

Despite this obsessive commitment to holiness, God reveals an even greater devotion to loving God's children. The pursuit of holiness seeks to enrich relationship to God, and therefore the expectation is that God's children pursue it meticulously. Nevertheless, even when idolatry and apostasy compromise holiness, these do not overthrow the love of God, as expressed so passionately in the words of Hosea:

> How can I give you up, O Ephraim? How can I surrender you, O Israel? How can I make you like Admah? How can I treat you like Zeboiim? My heart is turned over within Me, All My compassions are kindled. I will not execute My fierce anger; I will not destroy Ephraim again. For I am God and not man, the *Holy One* in your midst, And I will not come in wrath. (Hos 11:8–9 NASB)

God's overwhelming love finds its greatest expression in Christ, through whom God's holiness touches the unclean and associates with sinners. God's passion for right relations with God's creatures finds its most dramatic expression in the incarnation. This God, who cannot abide sin and impurity, and for whom the elaborate sacrificial system provides a means of cleansing in order to maintain divine presence in the midst of the community, reveals God's very self in Christ. And through Christ God encounters humanity even to the point of *defilement* by touching the unclean (Matt 8:1–3; 26:6; Mark 5:25–27) and associating with sinners (Matt 9:10–11; 11:19)! When the sacrificial system fails, contrary to abandoning humanity, God breaks the very stipulations that God revealed to Israel in relation to avoiding impurity, through self-sacrifice in Christ for the sake of restoring right relations with humanity.

---

1. Jacob Milgrom, *Leviticus 1–16* (Anchor Bible 3; New York: Doubleday, 1991), 3.
2. Much of the material in this essay relies on my forthcoming volume on *Leviticus* in the New Beacon Bible Commentary series (Kansas City, MO: Beacon Hill Press of Kansas City).
3. John E. Hartley, *Leviticus* (Word Biblical Commentary 4; Dallas: Word, 1992), 19.
4. Baruch A Levine, *Leviticus* (JPS Torah Commentary; Philadelphia: Jewish Publication Society, 1989), 6–7.
5. Jacob Milgrom, *Leviticus: A Book of Ritual and Ethics* (Continental Commentaries;

Minneapolis: Fortress, 2004), 29.

6. John Wesley, *Explanatory Notes upon the Old Testament* (3 vols.; Bristol: William Pine, 1765), 1:344.

7. Milgrom, *Leviticus: A Book of Ritual*, 101.

8. Milgrom, *Leviticus 1–16*, 45–47.

9. See Milgrom, *Leviticus 1–16*, 256–61.

10. See Roy Gane, *Cult and Character: Purification Offerings, Day of Atonement, and Theodicy* (Winona Lake, IN: Eisenbrauns, 2005), 129.

11. Milgrom, *Leviticus 1–16*, 263.

12. *Manual of the Church of the Nazarene, 2009–2013* (Kansas City, MO: Nazarene Publishing House, 2009), 30.

13. Milgrom, *Leviticus 1–16*, 365–78.

14. Milgrom, *Leviticus 1–16*, 373.

15. R. K. Harrison, *Leviticus: An Introduction and Commentary* (Tyndale Old Testament Commentaries 3; Downers Grove, IL: InterVarsity, 1980), 72.

16. John H Walton and Victor H. Matthews, *Genesis–Deuteronomy* (IVP Bible Background Commentary; Downers Grove, IL: InterVarsity, 1997), 149.

17. Milgrom, *Leviticus: A Book of Ritual*, 17, 22; see also Milgrom, *Leviticus 1–16*, 155, 163.

18. René Péter, "*L'imposition des mains* dans l'Ancien Testament," *Vetus Testamentum* 27 (1977): 52.

19. C. F. Keil and F. Delitzsch, *The Pentateuch* (Biblical Commentary on the Old Testament 2; trans. J. Martin; Grand Rapids: Eerdmans, n.d.), 283.

20. Harrison, *Leviticus*, 53.

21. Walter C. Kaiser, Jr., "Leviticus," in *The New Interpreter's Bible* (12 vols.; ed. L. E. Keck; Nashville: Abingdon, 1994), 1:1014.

22. Milgrom, *Leviticus 1–16*, 236; Keil and Delitzsch, *The Pentateuch*, 304.

23. Harrison, *Leviticus*, 62.

24. Keil and Delitzsch, *The Pentateuch*, 304–5.

25. Gane, *Cult and Character*, 62 n 70.

26. H. Wheeler Robinson, "Hebrew Sacrifice and Prophetic Symbolism," *Journal of Theological Studies* 43 (1942):130.

27. Harold H. Rowley, "The Meaning of Sacrifice in the Old Testament," *Bulletin of the John Rylands University Library of Manchester* 33 (1950–51): 88.

28. Robinson, "Hebrew Sacrifice," 135.

29. See Robinson, "Hebrew Sacrifice," 137; Rowley, "Meaning of Sacrifice," 88–93.

30. Wesley, *Explanatory Notes*, 1:344–45.

31. Wesley, *Explanatory Notes*, 1:345.

32. Milgrom, *Leviticus 1–16*, 264; Hartley, *Leviticus*, 58, 61; Gane, *Cult and Character*, 89–90, 98.

33. Milgrom, *Leviticus 1–16*, 637.

34. Milgrom, *Leviticus 1–16*, 638.

15

Judging Judges:
Theological Issues and
Homiletical Strategies

Robert D. Branson

We might view the book of Judges as an adventure in heroic narrative. God empowers individuals to perform extraordinary exploits in the name of liberation. Against overwhelming odds,God chooses a lone figure to rally the meager forces of Israel to throw off their yoke of oppression.

Such action heroes make good subjects for Sunday school classes for junior boys. Their rowdy nature delights in stories with exploits of heroism and violence.[1] For the serious interpreter of biblical texts,however, the book presents theological and ethical challenges. It records not only stories of liberation but also accounts of oppression and cruelty. And we are left to wonder: Are these actions examples to be emulated?Or are they accounts of barbarisms that enlightened believers should condemn?

From the opening chapter to its conclusion,the problem of violence, particularly the violence of war,confrontsthe reader: wars of conquest, wars of liberation, wars over kingship, wars of extermination. Such stories are the common experiences of humanity, not only of our history but of our present. What compounds the theological problem is the description of God, who delivers God's people into the hands of enemies and then raises up a deliverer who violently defeats the oppressors.

Introductory Issues

The book of Judges is part of a larger work stretching from Deuteronomy through Joshua, Judges, Samuel, and Kings. This work, commonly designated as the "Deuteronomic history,"took its final form during the exilic years, probably soon after Jehoiachin's release from prison (2 Kgs 25:27–30). Deuteronomy supplies the theological basis for the evaluations of the various leaders and rulers of Israel and Judah. God established his covenant with Israelat Sinai. Obedience brought blessing, and disobedience brought judgment (Deut 27:11–28:68).

The story describes Israel's successful conquest of the land, its failure to observe the fundamental command to worship Yahweh alone (monolatry or monotheism?), and the collapse of both political entities, Israel and Judah. In its final form,Deuteronomic historyexplains why exile occurred, first for Israel and then for Judah. Because of their disobedience, specifically worshiping other gods, the people of Israel lost the blessings of God: the land, the monarchy, and the temple.

The early part of the Deuteronomic historyis set in a three-generation sequence. The first generation experienced the exodus but proved unfaithful and perished in the wilderness (Num 14:20–24; Deut 1:34–38). The second generation entered the land under Joshua's leadership and remained faithful as long as the elders of that generation lived (Deut 1:39; Josh 24:31; Judg 2:7). The third and subsequent generations described in Judges turned away from following the God of the covenant. They intermarried with indigenous peoples of the land and served their gods (Judg 2:11–13; 3:5–6).

The book of Judges traces Israel's apostasy after Joshua's death. The first section (1:1–2:5) comes from the hand of the book's final editor, who worked prior to the fall of Jerusalem (586 BC). The account moves geographically from south to north and chronicles Israel's fading ability to possess the land. The section culminates with God indicting the Israelites for breaking the covenant and announcing the end of the conquest of the land.

The middle section (2:6–16:31) includes mostly stories of the exploits of six tribal heroes. These stories originally circulated in oral form. The Deuteronomic editor structured the stories in six repeating cycles: apostasy of the people, oppression of Israel by foreign forces, Israel's crying out to God for deliverance, and God's raising up a deliverer. The first three cycles—with their deliverers Othniel, Ehud, and Deborah along with Barak—have a theologically and literarily satisfying conclusion. Each judge liberated the people, leading to a period of rest.

Gideon is a pivotal character. Insecure and doubting, he haltingly followed God's commands. Finally, with decisive action he annihilated the oppressor's army. He then inflicted revenge on Israelites who did not provide the support his army needed. At the end, he set up a worship symbol that became an idolatrous snare for the people.

Although God used Jephthah, God never chose him as a deliverer. His victories included the liberation of Israel from the Ammonites and a slaughter of the warriors from the tribe of Ephraim.

The last judge, Samson, could only begin to deliver Israel from the Philistines (13:5). While he performed great personal exploits, he never led Israel's armies in battle, and he broke each of his Nazirite vows. The accounts of the last three judges move in a descending path of religious and social disintegration.

The final section (17:1–21:25) comes from the hand of the final editor. It describes Israel's continuing degeneration. The tribe of Dan was forced to relocate and in the process established an idolatrous shrine. The book ends with the account of an inter-tribal war that nearly led to the extermination of the tribe of Benjamin, the slaughter of an Israelite town to provide wives for some of the remnant of Benjamin, and the abduction and forced marriage of maidens from Shiloh for the remainder.

The book closes with a description of religious and social chaos. All were doing what was right in their own eyes (21:25), not what was right in the eyes of God.

Understanding the purpose of the book enables the interpreter to build sermons in keeping with its message. Although the judges do bring some but not complete relief from the oppression, the peoples' continual seeking after other gods led eventually to social and religious degeneration. The book is shaded in darkness with points of punctuating light. This light is insufficient to illuminate the future of the people.

Sermons Not to Preach

What are five sermons I would not preach from the book of Judges? And what are then sermons that I would? The choice of topics and manner in which one develops sermons need to take into consideration the purpose and structure of this book. In this case, Judges describes Israel's slide into religious and social disintegration. In addition, the location of a text in the progression of the story can impact how the interpreter will handle it. For example, how different sections of the book treat women should influence how one should deal with the topic of gender relationships.

I once heard about a sermon titled, "Samson, An Example of the Sanctified Life." True, the Spirit moved on Samson more than any other judge. It is also accurate that Samson performed more exploits of strength in fighting the enemy than any other judge. However, when one examines Samson's life, he falls far short of what we hope would be the moral pattern of a sanctified Christian.

Samson was committed to the vows of a Nazirite, specifically not to drink wine or strong drink (beer), not to eat any unclean food, and not to cut his hair (13:4–5). We assume that his vow prohibited contact with a dead body (Num 6:1–7) although, since he was a warrior, there would have been concession for times he was in battle. He broke all of these vows. From the carcass of a dead lion he took honey, which was unclean due to its source. He hosted a drinking party at his wedding feast. His barber Delilah shaved his head. His relationships with women were anything but exemplary, particularly his visit with a prostitute and his living with Delilah (16:1–21).

Samson was an anti-hero. He never led troops into battle. He never brought peace to Israel. He continued to pursue non-Israelite women, adominant issue in Israel's unfaithfulness to God. He is the antithesis of Othniel, the first and the most exemplary of the judges. In short, I would not preach a sermon on Samson as the ideal sanctified person.

A second sermon I would not preach is this:"God Is Punishing You for Your Sins."Yes, the text does say that when Israel broke the covenant by worshiping other gods, God sold them (3:8; 4:1; 10:1) or gave them (6:1; 13:1) into the hands of their enemies. God strengthened the hand of the king of Moab against them (3:12).

The purpose of the curses of the covenant was to bring the people to repentance and obedience. There is a cause-and-effect process in life. People who smoke often have breathing problems and throat or lung cancer. People who abuse drugs often have brain damage. Although the inspired writer identified God as the one who brought war as a punishment, I doubt many, if any minister, is so gifted today.

People do bad things and suffer for their actions. But I would not want to say that God specifically targeted them for punishment. Jesus *himself* rejected the identification of tragic circumstances as punishment for sin (John 9:2–3). We should follow his example.

The third sermon I would not preach is similar to the second. Contrary to the opinion of some, the United States of America is not in covenantal relationship with God. Thus, we cannot claim our wealth and successes in war as blessings of God. Nor can we claim

disasters or losses in war as the direct punishment of God that calls
us to repentance for breaking covenant.

America's founding fathers were knowledgeable of the teachings
of Christianity. Some may actually have been Christians. But most
were deists, a few Unitarians, and all children of the Enlightenment.
They incorporated some concepts of Judeo-Christian beliefs into
the foundational documents of our country. But God has not chosen the United States of America as an elect people destined to
reveal a divine political purpose to the rest of the world.

As an American, I pray that God will bless my country by giving our leaders wisdom. But God does not favor Americaany more
than Ireland, Kenya, New Zealand, or Chile. Therefore, I would not
preach from Judges that we can test our spirituality by reading or
viewing the daily news.[2]

The fourth sermon I would not preach relates to Gideon. This
Israelite leader represents a turning point in the story of the judges.
The earlier judges were decisive in their leadership. They successfully rallied tribes to throw off the yoke of oppression and brought
rest to the land.

By contrast, Gideon lacked boldness in his obedience. He
needed repeated assurances from God that his mission would be
successful (6:36–40; 7:10–15). Although he was successful in battle,
he unwisely created an ephod that became an object of worship for
Israel (8:27).

When preaching from the stories of Gideon, I would avoid
holding him up as an example to follow when it comes to dealing
with those who oppose us. Although God was patient with him,
Gideon took fearful revenge upon Israelites who did not support
him (8:13–17). Vengeance belongs to God (Deut 32:35; Rom 12:19;
Heb 10:30), not us. Jesus taught us to love our enemies and pray for
them (Matt 5:44). Gideon's example in victory is not one to follow.

The final sermon I would not preach deals with gender. Israel
was a patriarchal culture, and the social position of women was

one of subordination to fathers and husbands. The treatment of women in Judges reflected the spiritual and social health of the society.

At the beginning of the book, several good models for women do appear (material for a positive sermon about women in the Bible). Achsah was forceful in dealing with her husband and father (1:14–15). Deborah gave commands from God to Barak (4:6–9, 14) and Jael was praised for her actions in behalf of Israel (5:24).

As the book progresses,however, the treatment of women degenerates. The mother of Samson, who demonstrated greater wisdom than did her husband Manoah (13:23), remains unnamed. The concubine of the Levite was sexually abused and her body dismembered (19:25–29). There were the forced marriages of women with Benjaminites (21:12–14, 20–23). I would caution a pastor about taking Judges as a guide for what God intends to be the societal structure for gender relationships.

Sermon Suggestions

Turning from the negative to the positive, I want to suggest some topics and themes that a pastor could use for sermons from Judges. This list is not exhaustive, only illustrative. I will not develop a full outline for each. But I deal with each in a suggestive manner. Although the topics are applicable on a broader scale, a pastor tailors sermons to fit a specific congregation. My hope is that these examples will enable pastors to see more possibilities for preaching from the book of Judges.

I. "Women Who Fought the System"

Althoughone should not affirm some examples of how Israel dealt with women as guides for today, there are some positive examples that one may use. In the background of these texts is the problem of patriarchal culture. This was a problem in Israel and most ancient cultures, including the Greco-Roman culture that forms the setting of much of the New Testament.

The theological question that arises is this: Did God intend for a society to be patriarchal, or did God use what was the culture of the time as the setting for revelation, without placing God's stamp of approval? Wesleyan theologians have been unanimous that the culture was a vehicle through which God spoke. As a result, Wesleyan churches have ordained women and placed them as pastors of churches.

While we have the examples of Achsah as a woman who stepped outside the constrictions of her society and Manoah's wife as one more spiritually astute than her husband, perhaps the best example of a woman providing leadership is that of Deborah (chs. 4–5). She was a judge and prophet (4:4–5) who gave the commands of God to Barak and was willing to accompany Israel's armies into battle. The text for the sermon would be 4:1–9. One could draw supporting texts from 2 Kings 22:14–20, the story of Huldah who also prophesied, and Luke 24:1–10, the account of the women who were the first to proclaim Jesus' resurrection.

This sermon could emphasize that gender does not limit God and whom God chooses as leaders for the community of faith. Young women as well as young men should be sensitive to the leading of God when it comes to seeking God's will for their future.

2. "Don't Keep Foolish Vows"

I first thought about including a sermon on foolish vows as one I would not recommend. On further reflection, I concluded that Christians should be warned not to make foolish vows to God. And if made, they should not be kept.

The primary example in Judges of making a foolish vow is Jephthah's vow to sacrifice whatever came first out of his house, which unfortunately was his daughter (11:29–40). Other examples are the vows Israel took not to give their daughters to the Benjaminites and that whoever did not come up to Mizpah for the war would be put to death (21:1–7). Unfortunately Jephthah and Israel kept their vows. To keep Israel's first vow yet to void it somehow, they destroyed an Israelite town but saved the maidens as brides for the Benjaminite survivors. Then they instructed the remaining Benjaminite men to kidnap women from Shiloh and force them into marriage. (The involvement of the elders was more direct than merely condoning the actions of the Benjaminites.)

While one should not enter into vows lightlyand should generally keep them (Eccl 5:4–6), such is not the case with a foolish vow. An example of the appropriate breaking of a vow or oath can be found in 1 Samuel 14:24–46, when the Israelites refused to let Saul kill Jonathan.

Peopledo make vows they cannot or should not keep. Swept away emotionally,some make pledges beyond their financial means and threaten the financial stability of their family. If they do not keep the commitment,they feel guilty for failing God.

The theological issue has to do with the nature of God. What kind of God would be pleased with the sacrifice of a daughter? Only a demonic one. This is not the God and Father of our Lord Jesus Christ. Nor is God pleased with vows that hurt others, disrupt a family, or in some manner destroy or harm relationships with others. The pastoral emphasis should be on mediating forgiveness. And the preacher should portray God as one who knows our good intentions yet understands our frailties and failures.

3. "When Soldiers March to War"

Judges brings to the forefront a serious theological issue we too often neglect:Is it permissible for Christians to join the military? Or should Christians be pacifists?

In the history of the church, voices have been raised advocating both pacifism and the notion that Christians may join the military. Those who advocate pacifism cite Jesus' teachings in the Sermon on the Mount, specifically Matthew 5:38–45 and his teaching on the two greatest commandments, particularly that Jesus' followers must love their neighbors (Matt: 22:34–40).

Those who hold that fighting a war is sometimes permissible draw upon many Old Testament war accounts in Israel's history, including those in Judges. From the New Testament,they note that when soldiers inquired of John the Baptist what they should do, he did not tell them to resign from the military (Luke 3:14). Neither Jesus (Matt 8:5–13) nor Peter (Acts 10:24–48) said to the centurions they met that their profession was displeasing to God. Paul was not hesitant to call on the military for protection (Acts 23:12–25).

The storey of Ehud (3:12–30) presents a good launching point. In this story, God remains in the background while others act. Israel had been oppressed for eighteen years. Having devised a cunning plan, Ehud delivered Israel and gave the peopleher longest recorded time of rest, eighty years or two generations.

Two items are noteworthy when considering the topic of war. First, a foreign king oppressed Israel. If Christians forsake the use of any violence, how then will they help the oppressed?[3] The evils of Hitler's death camps or the worldwide practice of slavery would not have been stopped without the threat or actual use of violence.

Second, the wars the judges waged were defensive wars. They took up arms in response to attacks. To be sure, it is anachronistic to invoke the just war tradition to justify this. But people have the right to defend themselves.

4. "Caution! You Might Find What You Seek"

The story of the Levite who migrated from Bethlehem and found employment in the house of Micah (17:7–13; 18:14–20, 30–31) illustrates how even good people can be seduced into serving the wrong god. There was nothing wrong in accepting a good position or even leaving it for a better one. The Levite who was trained as a priest would have known, however,the prohibition against using graven images in worship. Yet he accepted Micah's offer. When the

Danites took him as their priest, the Levite stole Micah's images.

One can make two main points here. First, when our priorities are not right, we can be seduced into unethical and immoral practices. We can be tempted to justify these practices as necessary to succeed. Second, our actions can have long-range effects. The Levite established an illegitimate shrine for Dan that later led to the destruction of the city and the exile of the people.

5. "God Delivers Us into the Hands of Our Enemies"

This sounds like a contradiction of what I wrote earlier (see second sermon I would not preach). Here, however, the emphasis is on choice. Israel chose to serve the gods of the land, Baal and Asherah, who promised to increase the fertility of the land. In an agricultural setting, this meant bountiful crops and economic security. They also violated their covenant with Yahweh, who protected them from their enemies.

Because of their actions, God had a choice: allow Israel to follow a path of ultimate destruction or allow the harsh realities of their choices. God did not create the enemies of Israel: Ammon, Midian, or the Philistines. They were already in the land. God gave Israel into their hands. That is, God allowed them to invade and oppress Israel.

The text from Judges 10:6–9 could be paired with Mark 10:17–22, the inquiry of the rich young ruler. As Jesus did not violate the man's freedom and coerce him to become a disciple, neither does God violate our freedom and force us to obey.

The turning point of the sermon comes when discussing the purpose of God. The curses of the covenant were always remedial (Deut 30:1–5). They were meant to call Israel back to repentance and obedience so that God might bless them. A parallel text is 2 Peter 3:9, which emphasizes the patience of God. God does not want to see anyone perish. The closing portrait of God is of a loving God who calls to repentance and life.

6. "Removing Idols to Follow God"

The stories about Gideon's victories stir the imagination. His weaknesses help people identify with him. God used Gideon to deliver Israel, even though he was hesitant and insecure. He repeatedly needed assurances that God would give him victory (6:36–40; 7:9–15).

The text for the sermon comes from the call of Gideon (6:11–27, esp. vv. 25–27). New Testament companion texts are Acts 19:11–20, which recount the burning of books of magic at Ephesus, and Mark 5:1–15, the healing of the Gerasene demoniac. The sermon should emphasize that the peoples' turning away from sin, idols, and the like accompany the power of God to deliver from sin.

God called an insecure Gideon to deliver Israel from the oppression of Midian (6:11–16). After receiving assurance of God's presence, he responded in worship (v. 24).Gideon's first task was to destroy the town's temple of Baal. This took place at night, because he was afraid of both his family and the townspeople. If he tried to destroy the altar during the day, the people would have stopped him.

After conversion and by the Spirit's prompting, a new Christian begins to confront his or her own idols. The spiritual struggle of confronting treasured values often takes time. The Spirit remains faithful and eventually, when complete consecration takes place, the Spirit fills the void with the abiding presence of Christ. The Christian becomes empowered to explore the heights and depths of the love of God (Eph 3:14–19).

7. "Remaining Faithful in the Midst of Change"

The text for this sermon is Judges 2:6-10, with supporting passages in John 15:1–11 and 1 Timothy 1:3–14. The topic deals with changes in life. The conquest under Joshua's leadership had been successful in giving Israel control over much of the land west of the Jordan. Yet many of the original peoples still occupied fortified cities and fertile valleys (3:3–5).

When Joshua dismissed the people, they went to the areas that were their inheritance and continued the conquest. The leadership changed from one person over all the people to the elders over the tribe. In the midst of changes, the people continued to be faithful to God.

It was the third generation (see introductory remarks) that followed after other gods and forgot the Lord. They knew neither the Lord himself nor what he had done for Israel.

Changes challenge our values and behavior patterns. We cannot continue in the same old ways. They also provide tests for us to determine our core values: what we are unwilling to give up, the values and actions that define who we are. The ever-faithful God calls us to be faithful in the midst of change and not give up commitment to Christ.

Our obligation is not to our own generation. We must also win the next generation by helping them experience the grace of forgiveness and cleansing. We must be faithful to the next generation by telling them the stories of what God has done and what he will do in their lives. We must be faithful to God, our generation, ourselves, and the next generation.

8. "Responding to the Call of God"

The primary text for this sermon is Judges 3:7–11, which briefly recounts the exploits of Othniel. Companion texts are Romans 5:6–11, which describes our redemption through Christ's atoning sacrifice, and Hebrews 4:1–11, which speaks of God's rest for God's people. Othniel was the example of what a judge should have been. He had a proper Israelite marriage to Achsah (1:13). God had called him, and the Spirit motivated him. He was successful in delivering Israel from oppression.

The Israelites sinned by worshiping other gods and suffered the consequences of their disobedience. However, the God of Israelcould not ignore the cry of God's people. Sin and punishment are not God's final word. God is the God of hope and deliverance for those in bondage due to their sin.

The second movement in the story begins when God raised up a deliverer, Othniel. Although he was a mighty warrior, he was not sufficient for the task. The spirit of the Lord came upon him and enabled him to defeat Israel's enemies.The end result was rest for the people of God. They were no longer oppressed, and they had peace with God. They could carry on the normal activities of planting and harvesting crops without the worry of raids or invasions.

9. "When God Becomes Angry"

Judges 2:20–23 portrays God as angry with Israel. We find it difficult to reconcile the image of an angry God with that of the loving, compassionate Jesus. Yet even Jesus became angry with the cities that reject his message and pronounced woes or courses on them (Matt 11:21). The scribes and Pharisees were also the objects of his anger (Matt 23:13–36). He was angry with those in a synagogue and grieved over theirinsensitivity to the plight of the man with a withered hand (Mark 3:5).

In Judges, God is not only angry but also vulnerable. Israel was God's chosen people. God liberated them from Egypt and entered into covenant with them. When Israel pursued after other gods, their actions caused God pain (Hosea 11:8–9). His anger was like that of a betrayed spouse.

Yet God is still divine, not human.God is always willing to overcome the anger and pain through forgiveness. That is the message of the cross. While we are in sin, God's love seeks us.God is "slow to anger,and abounding in steadfast love and faithfulness" (Exod 34:6NRSV). Only our rejection of his offer of forgiveness and reconciliation keep us from experiencing redeeming grace.

10. "Overwhelmed by Evil"

The end of the book of Judges (19:1–21:25)recounts one horror after another: rape, deception, perverting justice, wars of genocide, kidnapping of women, and a total breakdown of moral discipline (21:25). The final editor added these stories to show the end result of continued disobedience to God. Contrary to popular opinion, sin does not only affect the individual. It destroys the foundation of society itself. The suggested text is Judges 19:22–26, the account of the rape of the Levite's concubine. But others in this section could work as well.

This would be a difficult sermon for a pastor to preach. It is not an uplifting, positive message. It deals with the darker side of life. One could take illustrative material from several literary and movie seriesthat deal with the theme of good versus evil: Lord of the Rings, the Matrix, Harry Potter, and Star Wars. Historical illustrations abound including the Axis powers of World War II, the drug wars in Mexico, and tyrants such as Saddam Hussein and Idi Amin.

A positive conclusion could be based on the story of Jesus healing the Gerasene demoniac (Mark 5:1–13). Or it could be based on Jesus' call to his disciples to impact society through their lives (Matt 5:13–17). Or one could point to Jesus' parables of the mustard seed and leaven/yeast (Matt 13:31–33) in which the kingdom of God will continue to grow, even in an evil world. A conclusion which looks forward to ultimate triumph could be drawn from passages from Revelation 19:1–8 or 21:1–8.

---

1. Such teaching strategies do not work with junior girls. They may be "hard wired" differently and find such violence abhorrent.
2. Before the author is accused of being anti-American or some type of subversive, the reader should know that he has demonstrated his love for his country by serving for twenty-five years as an U.S. Army Reserve chaplain, retiring with the rank of colonel.
3. Donald E. Gowan, "Amos," in The New Interpreter's Bible (12 vols., ed. L. E. Keck; Nashville: Abingdon, 1996), 7:167.

Love in the Old Testament: Insights from Ruth and the Song of Solomon

Sarah B. C. Derck

R uth and the Song of Solomon each have a great deal to say about love. Love in many forms—family love, romantic love, divine love—dominates almost every page. These themes are part of what makes both books so attractive to readers. Not many other books in the Old Testament play on love quite so positively from start to finish. No great violation or pollution of love, no violence, no warfare or oppression stains the pages. But neither are these sappy romances. The portrayed relationships are poignantly human, and thus their appeal. Most readers can identify with some element of the love in these books.

Readers connect with the book of Ruth because of their familiarity with the story. Most Christian weddings include a reading of Ruth 2:16–17, "Where you go, I will go . . . ."[1] The story of Ruth and Boaz is one of the great love stories of the Bible. However, there is more to the story than its happy ending. This essay will consider some of the elements our 'fairy tale' readings of Ruth miss.

It might be more accurate to describe the Song of Solomon as notorious: most believers know the nature of the book without having read it much. The Song also doesn't get much 'air time' in pulpits, presumably because of its explicit content. However, this evocative book has some incredibly redemptive things to say to our culture about love. It deserves careful attention.

We will consider Ruth first, with five things worth saying about the book, and two that are not. Then we move to the Song, with five things worth saying about it, and three that are not.

Five Things Worth Saying about Ruth

1. A declaration of loyalty, not romantic love

The most familiar passage from Ruth, used in weddings the world over as an illustration of commitment to one's spouse, is not directed at a spouse. Ruth makes this phenomenal vow, not at the end of the story to her new husband, but at the beginning, to her old mother-in-law! The butt of jokes since time began, the daughter-in-law/mother-in-law relationship, is the surprising context of this declaration. This is perhaps our biggest clue that the book of Ruth is not *primarily* a love story. The focus of this passage is the determination of one widow to stick with another. The continuing story is not about finding love but about securing their futures.

The theological insight from Ruth's declaration of loyalty is a welcome one: the people of God owe this kind of loyalty *to one another*, as our spiritual family. Ruth had other options besides moving to enemy territory with her destitute mother-in-law. Naomi even pushed Ruth and Orpah to take this option: "Go back each of you to your mother's house" (Ruth 1:8). It would presumably have been more comfortable for Ruth to return to her parents' home, find another husband, and settle into a new life in her own homeland. Instead, Ruth took responsibility for her mother-in-law, made a dangerous journey with her, and settled in a foreign land. Ruth pursued loyalty, not security.

Can you imagine if our congregations pledged Ruth's vow to one another, if we literally agreed not to leave one another and to live and die together? Jesus certainly had this kind of relational loyalty in mind for his followers when he said, "For whoever does the will of my Father in heaven is my brother and sister and mother" (Matt 12:50). The boundaries of believers' family relationships are not to be drawn by blood and marriage, but by faith and obedience to our Father's will.

Finally, love in God's family must be as concrete as Ruth's care for Naomi. It dare not be merely theoretical. What if Ruth had made that stunning declaration but then allowed Naomi to convince her to return to Moab? She would have missed her part in the lineage of David and consequently the birth of Jesus. Likewise, if our love for one another is only theoretical or only declared but never demonstrated, we will miss our part in bringing Christ into this world. Concrete and demonstrated love leads to life. Ruth's love for Naomi led to the life of her child Obed and ultimately to Jesus' birth. Our concrete love for one another leads to the life of Christ lived in our midst.

2. Ruth is about Ruth

This seems obvious. But many sermons and devotions from Ruth focus on Boaz: his noble protection, faithfulness, and mercy in marrying a foreigner. These descriptions of Boaz are certainly accurate. But we need to adjust the balance of the focus here.

The focus of this book is boldly, shockingly, and unrelentingly on its heroines. *Naomi* and *Ruth* made the grueling journey back to Judah. *Ruth* gleaned in the fields and continued this backbreaking work through the whole harvest season. *Naomi* recognized the need to force the issue with Boaz. *Ruth* got up the gumption to go to the threshing floor. Finally, *Ruth* agreed to marry an older foreigner to secure her first husband's legacy. The careful reader must acknowledge three main characters in this story, but only one of them is in the book's title. Highlighting Ruth (not to mention Naomi) gives our congregations a comparatively rare opportunity to identify with a faithful *woman* in the Bible.

3. A shocking choice for David's ancestor

It is impossible to overstate the scandal in ancient Israel over the fact that David's great-grandmother was a hated Moabite. Moab neighbored Israel on the eastern shore of the Dead Sea. According to Genesis, they descended from Lot's incestuous coupling with his daughter (Gen 19:30–38). As such, the Israelites despised the Moabites, and further encounters did nothing to dispel this hatred.

Just before entering the Promised Land, the Israelite men had sexual relations with the women of the Moabite city of Shittim and succumbed to idolatry; 24,000 people were killed for this apostasy (Num 25). Throughout Israel's residence in the land, Israel and Moab clashed (Judg 3:12–30; 1 Sam 14:47; 2 Sam 8:11–12; 2 Chr 20, etc.). In direct violation of Yahweh's command, Solomon married a Moabite, who demanded a place to worship her god. Solomon seems to have gone so far as to worship with her (1 Kgs 11). Finally, Ezra 9 and Nehemiah 13 record the command to Israelite men to divorce their Moabite wives, in order to secure commitment to Yahweh in the community returning from exile. The relationship between Israel and Moab was complex and often sexually charged.

Given this history, a young Moabite widow willing to follow her Israelite mother-in-law, worship Yahweh, and marry an Israelite to preserve an Israelite heritage is remarkable indeed. Ruth's actions were almost unbelievable to an Israelite. How could a Moabite possibly act so nobly? The story of Ruth's incorporation into the family of Yahweh is dangerous. Scandal lurks around every corner. We can almost hear the whispers, "A woman from the *enemy* returned with Naomi. And Boaz let her glean! She even spent the night with him!"

In God's redemptive scheme, however, these are minor obstacles to be overcome. The woman from the enemy showed unbelievable loyalty, worked hard, and took risks for the mother-in-law for whom she vowed to care. Such a woman is worthy of God's family, Moabite or not. This message from Ruth is crystal clear: God's love is bigger than our love, extending to the foreigner, those we hate, those we would exclude.

4. A bitter, old woman

It is evident from the opening of the story that Naomi suffered a great deal of pain. Famine drove her and Elimelech to Moab (Ruth 1:1). This circumstance alone is enough trauma for any lifetime. But Naomi also buried her husband, then her two sons (1:3, 5). And neither son had children. This must have been difficult in a culture that expected offspring within a year of marriage. Finally, the famine followed her to Moab, and Naomi was forced home, a penniless widow robbed of her children. The pain in Naomi's life story is overwhelming.

By the time we meet Naomi, her pain has manifested itself in bitterness. The only two people left in her life wanted to stay by her side. But Naomi pushed them away, preferring to return alone (Ruth 1:8–14). At first, it sounds as though Naomi was trying to advise them with wisdom and care, trying to be the bigger person. She sounded as if she would sacrifice her own needs for the sake of her daughters-in-law. But the harsh cry of verse 13 jumps off the page, "No, my daughters, it has been far more bitter for me than for you, because the hand of the LORD has turned against me." Comparing one's own pain with another's is almost always a sign of resentment.

The bitterness continues with Naomi's greeting to the women of Bethlehem, "Call me Mara [Bitter], for the Almighty has dealt bitterly with me" (Ruth 1:20). Naomi obviously believed the Lord had taken active steps to bring her grief and had actually turned against her. Naomi is not a warm and comforting old woman! This Naomi is in pain, bitter and defeated, dragging herself home with nothing.

Recognizing the pain and bitterness in Naomi is valuable for

246 THE BIBLE TELLS ME SO

two reasons. First, cozy idealizations of the Bible's people do nothing for a reader in the long term. They present nothing with which to identify, nothing on which to build one's involvement with the story. They turn the Bible into an irrelevant book of fairy tales, deserving the dust it collects on many shelves. By contrast, honest descriptions of the flawed and troubled folk in the Bible give a reader something to grasp, someone about whom to say, "She is just like me!"

This leads to the second reason to highlight Naomi's pain: every person we encounter will face deep pain. Many carry with them the same levels of bitterness toward God as Naomi did. It is startlingly redemptive that in the face of Naomi's pain, Ruth stuck by her. The people of Bethlehem embraced her, fed her, and provided exactly what she was hoping for: a child for Elimelech's lineage.

In chapter 1, Naomi declared that God had left her empty. At the end, the people declared right back to her, "Blessed be the LORD, who has not left you this day without next-of-kin" (Ruth 4:14). We should acknowledge Naomi for who she really was, because it shows God for who God really is: not the destroyer Naomi claimed, but the restorer of life.

5. A scandalous rendezvous

We hinted at the potentially sexual nature of the encounter on the threshing floor (Ruth 3). On the one hand, some readers desperately want to acquit Ruth and Boaz of the charge of premarital sex. On the other hand, several narrative elements unabashedly set the scene for a sexual encounter: the secrecy of meeting at night in a place culturally associated with trysting; Ruth's preparations with a bath and oils (v. 3); her laying at his "feet," a noun sometimes used in Hebrew as a euphemism for genitals (vv. 4, 7–8, 14). As with every other scandalous rendezvous in human history, we may never know the truth of what happened that night.

The real question is not "Did they or didn't they?" but "What's really going on here?" The clue comes in the phrase "spread one's cloak over" (v. 9), which is a Hebrew idiom meaning, "to take a woman as one's wife." When Ruth asked Boaz to spread his cloak over her, she was not asking for a blanket. She was asking him to marry her. What we have here is a betrothal scene: Ruth proposed marriage (v. 9), Boaz agreed (vv. 10–11), they conferred about the legalities (vv. 12–13), and then spent the night together (v. 14). Boaz sent her off with proof of his pledge—the barley he measured into the cloak (vv. 15–18)—and went to the gate to have their betrothal ratified by the concerned parties (ch. 4).

One must understand that the point at which a couple was considered married and intercourse permissible was different in the ancient world than in Christian communities today. Israel's law tacitly acknowledged that men and women sometimes slept together before the public wedding ceremony. It was more concerned to keep a man from abandoning the woman after physical union or from having sex with a woman betrothed to someone else (Deut 24). Therefore, sleeping with one's betrothed was not in quite the same moral category as it is for most Christians today.

We may consider Ruth and Boaz as having acted honorably within the moral constructs of their own day, whether or not intercourse occurred that night. The important point is that Ruth asked Boaz to marry her. He agreed and made all the necessary arrangements to protect her and provide for Elimelech's lineage. Ruth was faithful to Naomi's instructions and courageous in a nerve-wracking situation. Therefore, she ultimately was the recipient of a future full of hope and a place in the lineage of Christ.

Two Things Not Worth Saying about Ruth

1. Boaz the kinsman-redeemer

When preaching and teaching about the book of Ruth, it is helpful to avoid assigning Boaz the title "kinsman redeemer," as translated in the NIV. The title has come to encompass some idealized and imprecise ideas (like "knight in shining armor"). Much preferred is the NRSV's "next-of-kin" or simply "kinsman," which are both accurate translations of the Hebrew participle *goel*. This avoids the confusion that seems to have arisen by combining and applying two different laws to the situation in Ruth.

The first law definitely applies in Ruth: "If anyone of your kin falls into difficulty and sells a piece of property, then the next of kin shall come and redeem what the relative has sold" (Lev 25:25). In Ruth 4:5ff, Boaz asked Naomi's next-of-kin in Bethlehem to redeem the field she was forced to sell. The sale would raise needed money. At the same time, the field would remain within the holdings of Elimelech's larger family until Naomi raised enough to buy it back or until the year of Jubilee, when it would revert to her.

The confusion comes when interpreters mistakenly apply a second law to the situation: "When brothers reside together, and one of them dies and has no son, the . . . brother shall go in to her . . . and the firstborn whom she bears shall succeed to the name of the deceased brother" (Deut 25:5–6). This law does *not* directly apply to Ruth. The first clause lets Boaz off: he was not Ruth's brother-in-law, and they did not reside together in the family home. Therefore, neither Boaz nor the unnamed next-of-kin was *required* to produce offspring for Ruth's deceased husband. Ruth asked Boaz to marry her because as a kinsman (one of several), he was a safe option. Also, it was in the interest of the larger family that kinsmen had right of first refusal, when a widow needed marrying. Boaz admirably accepted the duties of Deuteronomy 25:5–6, but they were not required of him.

Ruth's marriage and future offspring are separate issues from Naomi's field. However, Boaz cleverly tied the two together to manipulate the nearer relative into refusing Ruth, thereby leaving Boaz to marry her free and clear. It would have been problematic, after all, for Boaz to have children with Ruth, with another family member having purchased their inheritance (the field). Likewise, the nearer kinsman did not want to dilute his own wealth by producing and providing for Elimelech's heirs.

Referring to Boaz as "kinsman" or "next-of-kin" is more precise and less confusing. But what is the point of making this distinction? Besides greater clarity in translation (always an admirable goal), this distinction allows us to highlight the intensity and nobility of Boaz's desire to marry Ruth. He was not required to marry her, to provide an heir for Elimelech, or to redeem Naomi's field. However, he did so at great cost. It is evident that Boaz was coming to care for Ruth, and he went out of his way to arrange the situation in his own favor. He stepped into the gap of his own accord, not because the law required it. The free will of Boaz's love for Ruth increases its significance and poignancy.

2. A story for women

Ruth is a story about love in many forms: a stubborn love between Ruth and Naomi, a tender love between Ruth and Boaz, God's love for Naomi through the Bethlehemites. In Western cultures, however, a 'love story' connotes mere romance, a predictable formula of "boy meets girl, boy loses girl, boy marries girl."

Describing a book as a love story sometimes relegates it to the realm of 'chick lit,' to borrow a pop-culture term. Unfortunately, Ruth has suffered that fate as well, in some circles being studied only by women's groups. The story has so much to say to the whole church, however, with significant theological implications. Let's not sequester it.

Five Things Worth Saying about the Song of Solomon

1. Whatever else it *might* mean, it *first* means "that."

For centuries, Jews and Christians interpreted the Song of Solomon with all manner of labored metaphors and some-times-tortuous allegories and symbolism. The most prevalent interpretations cast God and Israel as the Song's lovers, or Christ and the church, or Christ and the individual believer. Some read-ers have acknowledged the book's erotic nature, but still deduced only spiritual applications. As Roland Murphy points out, it is not difficult to discover why, "When one realizes . . . that most of the Christian exegesis on the Song until the Reformation was pro-duced by clerics and monks, it becomes understandable that a mystical interpretation thrived."[2] With his tongue planted firmly in his cheek—Murphy himself was a member of the Carmelite order—he is not surprised that celibate men and women had trouble expounding the Song's eroticism.

A Wesleyan approach to Scripture insists that we first deter-mine the plain meaning of a text and allow that plain meaning its full voice before moving onto more symbolic, allegorical, or mystical interpretations. The plain meaning of the Song is clear. It describes the loving relationship between a young woman and her beloved in terms both stunningly beautiful and unabashedly arousing. A Wesleyan interpretation of the Song acknowledges that, whatever else the Song might evoke in terms of theological insight or spiritual application, it must first be allowed to exercise its sensuality.

To what end, this sensuality? The simplest answer is also per-haps the most profound for our time and place. This holy book, included in the canon of Scripture for both Jews and Christians, is essentially and most obviously a flamboyant celebration of conjugal love. It elevates the value of human sexuality, giving it a significance that generations of readers have missed by imposing symbolic meanings. Perhaps more than at any other time in Western history, the church needs the witness of the Song of Solomon to help us recover an attitude of celebration regarding sexual love.

2. The participation of friends

If one accepts the plain meaning of the Song, one element appears in stark relief: the friends of the lovers are thoroughly involved in their erotic discourse. This is no clandestine tryst, carried out in the fear of discovery. The friends are called upon to help the lovers find each other (Song 4:8; 6:1), to admire the lover's beauty (5:9-16), and even to adorn them for the lovemaking (1:11). In other words, the lovers' relationship is carried out in full view of their friends and with their input and protection.

If a contemporary writer were to rewrite the Song, it might strike them as vulgar to think of including other people in the lovers' encounters. To modern sensibilities, sex is private, and to proclaim desire as enthusiastically as the Song would be bawdy or lewd. However, the participation of friends is perfectly in keeping with a culture that arranged marriages and lived in multi-generational households. Marriages were communal affairs, affecting the lives and livelihoods of entire communities. The benefits of such involvement are apparent. When desire can be discussed with friends, the likelihood of violating moral boundaries is diminished. When others are supporting a relationship, it stands a better chance of surviving the storms of life. Lovers today would be well advised to take a page from the Song and to invite trusted friends and family to influence their relationship.

3. Obscure metaphors

Throughout the Song, descriptions of the lovers include metaphors that resist immediate understanding by today's readers. For instance, "I am black and beautiful, O daughters of Jerusalem, like the tents of Kedar, like the curtains of Solomon" (Song 1:5). What is it about tents and curtains that likens them to a beautiful woman?

We may guess, but in the end, a twenty-first century reader cannot be certain of knowing what the author was trying to highlight about the woman's beauty. The description of the young man as a leaping gazelle and young stag is similarly unclear (2:8–9). Very few readers in our churches have any personal experience of a gazelle or stag. We may rightly deduce that vitality and agility are being praised in the young man, but our own distance from these animals renders the metaphors less vivid.

We could multiply the examples, but the point is this: cultural references we cannot make out sometimes obscure the plain meaning of a passage. It is wise, then, to proceed with caution, reserving judgment in interpretation, rather than imposing symbolic meaning. For instance, interpreters have sometimes used the stag as 'evidence' that the male lover was Solomon himself, as stags were sometimes associated with royalty. However, that interpretation is certainly more than this one text alone can bear. And we must restrain ourselves from such conclusions until we can be certain we understand a metaphor.

4. Part of a larger genre

Faithful readers have struggled to allow the explicit sexuality of the book its full voice, in part because it is an anomaly. Nothing else like the Song exists in the Bible. Likewise, today's societies generally keep such literature hidden if not forbidden or even outlawed in some places. How can it possibly be Scripture, and still be about sex? We simply do not know what to do with this oddity!

However, this love poetry was not an anomaly when it first appeared. Texts like these abound in the canons of ancient Near Eastern literature—from Egypt to Babylon, from Sumer to Mesopotamia—and they evidently played an important role in social life. We know they were read aloud in the New Year celebrations of some cultures. They may also have been sung at weddings to encourage the bridal couple as they went off to consummate the marriage. The materials of the Song itself may have originated as such wedding songs, later compiled into its present form. As one of many, the Song seems less shocking. It is helpful to remember the ancient context from which it comes.

5. A holy book

There was significant debate over the canonical status of the Song. After all, it is obviously sexual, and God's name does not appear anywhere in the book. Astonishingly, some Jewish rabbis decided the Song was not only holy, but *extra* holy! Rabbi Aqiba said, "The world was never as worthy as on the day that the Song of Songs was given to Israel, for all the Writings are holy, whereas the Song of Songs is the holiest of the holy" (*m. Yadayim* 3:5). That is quite a recommendation from one of the most influential rabbis in Judaism!

The canon not only included the Song but, more astonishingly, it became one of the texts read annually during Passover. The celebration of the foundational event of Israel's history includes the reading of this erotic Song! One modern rabbi has said this is perfectly understandable, because it expresses the second element of Israel's freedom: the first is freedom *from slavery* in Egypt, but the second is freedom *to love* wholly and holy.[3]

This opinion of the Song was firmly established by AD 100, before the metaphorical interpretations gained a foothold in either Jewish or Christian tradition. We can likewise regard the book as authoritative for our own lives, although we have argued for its plain meaning to have priority. We can acknowledge it as Scripture precisely *because* it speaks to human love, not *in spite* of that fact. Human love is holy, especially love as euphoric and free as the Song represents it, precisely because that is how God created it to be.

Three Things Not Worth Saying
About the Song of Solomon

1. For adults only

Here we depart from the rabbis, who recommended that no one under the age of 30 should read the Song (some said 45!). Christian believers sometimes espouse this sentiment too. They want to protect innocence and take earnestly the Song's own admonition, "Do not stir up or awaken love until it is ready!" (Song 2:7). However, anyone with a thought to spare would readily admit that the obsession with sex in Western society and our children's daily exposure to explicit images and ideals of promiscuity would make the Song's lovers blush.

We can respond in one of two ways. We can keep quiet about sex, maintain our privacy and propriety, and assume that will protect our children until they are safely married. Some churches take this approach. But what they have done is remove the Christian voice from the conversation flowing all around (and sometimes within) them.

The other option is for the church to take the opportunity presented by the Song to proclaim joyfully the value and virtues of holy, human love. By acknowledging the Song's plain meaning and reading it as part of our holy Scriptures, we can set this boisterous and blissful portrayal before our people as the best of what love can be. We can and should be reading it together, as the people of God, all ages and stages of life, to set the standard of human love.

2. Not in my pulpit

Some pastors rarely leave the New Testament in their sermons, let alone choose the Song. This is mostly a default position, rather than a conscious choice. But I have actually heard pastors say they would never preach from the Song on a Sunday morning. Several challenges can be made to that opinion.

The first is that public proclamation of a biblical passage creates corporate accountability to that passage. When we preach from the Sermon on the Mount, we imply that our congregation should follow its precepts. Marriages in every congregation need the accountability that would be provided by preaching from the Song, by proclaiming the value and virtue of holy, human, sexual love. The many hidden sexual issues in our churches find root in an opinion of sex that is much too low, rendering it dirty and shameful. The Song shatters that image from the second verse and clamors for a high view of human sexuality, created by God for pleasure and purpose.

Second, we teach that love is selfless, pursuing the good of the other in every situation. Many children and young people in our congregations are witnesses to marriages that prove precisely the opposite. They will never see an actual human marriage in which the spouses actively pursue one another. The Song can give them a glimpse of that kind of love, but only if we preach from it.

Of course, we should know our audience and choose our sermon texts appropriately. But we should never allow caution to rob our people of hearing the good news as it affects every aspect of human life. Redeemed love between a man and a woman should be carefree, jubilant, and rejoicing in one another's sexuality. How dare we leave that out of our gospel, just because it makes us squirm?

3. Nothing spiritual here

Obviously, this author gives priority to the plain meaning of the Song, as the sensual depiction of young lovers in the prime of life. We have not argued for this interpretation simply for the sake of deconstructing older ones or for shock value. Rather, the plain meaning has vital importance for the church, which is desperately in need of a restored vision of love between the sexes.

This is not to say there is nothing spiritual about the Song. The writers of Scripture acknowledged the role of human love in teaching us about God's love. This is why marriage and the parent/child relationship are primary biblical metaphors for the relationship be-tween God and God's people.

To be precise, we learn to love by being loved. When a marriage, friendship, or parent/child relationship is at its best, it *will* highlight how God loves us and wants us to respond with love. It is neither surprising nor wrong that as we read the Song, our thoughts are eventually drawn to the Great Lover of our souls. We have argued merely that we first allow our blushing hearts to contemplate the depiction of lovers in paradise that is actually on the page.

---

1. All Scripture quotations are taken from the New Revised Standard Version.
2. Roland E. Murphy, *The Song of Songs* (ed. S. D. McBride, Jr.; Hermeneia; Minneapolis: Fortress, 1990), 12.
3. Shefa Gold, "Initiation onto the Path of Love," n.p. [cited 15 January 2011]. Online: http://www.rabbishefagold.com/SongOfSongsArticle.html.

17

Preaching from 1–2 Kings:
Guidelines for the Faint of Heart
Karen Strand Winslow

I suspect many pastors avoid teaching and preaching from the Old Testament because of the difficulties it presents. Their people miss its lessons about God and humans *and* its delightful, earthy, troubling stories. If we open the Old Testament for our people, we savor with them the flavors of these ancient stories while taking to heart their lessons. We help people realize these Scriptures help us tell our own stories.

I admit teaching the entire library of the Scriptures is no easy task! The brave who do are tempted to smooth rough edges, explain away incongruities, and recast rogues as good guys. But the Bible presents very human characters that are bad as well as good. Like us, many start good and then turn complacent, compromising, and finally all out bad.

Some reasons given for avoiding the Old Testament are valid. We should not read some passages to children or those immature in the faith. We could rate each passage, not only for violence, sex, language or drug use, but also according to levels of theological and moral difficulty:

X: Mature Audiences (no admittance to the young, in age or faith)

R: Restricted to those with theological training

PG: Parent or guardian guidance (step-by-step interpretation)

G: Welcome to all general audiences.

Although I state this somewhat tongue in cheek, I seriously think some biblical narratives are not for children. We should introduce these only as people mature in their faith.[1]

And yet all Scripture has been given for the church's education, transformation, correction, and training in righteousness (2 Tim 3:16). Romans 15:4 states, "whatever was written in former days was written for our instruction, so that by steadfastness and by the encouragement of the scriptures we might have hope" (NRSV). The "Scriptures" here refer to what we call the Old Testament. These Scriptures are able to make us wise for salvation through the faithfulness of Christ. So how shall we preach the Old Testament?

In this essay, I recommend ways for pastors to interpret these Scriptures in the life of the church. After offering general guidelines for using the Old Testament, I turn to the early chapters of 1 Kings and provide suggestions for a sermon series. Palace intrigues, divisions, coups, and apostasy riddle this book. God rarely shows up. Although there are a few heartwarming passages, most of 1 Kings is difficult to preach. But guidelines for preaching 1 Kings will not only yield insights for it. These also provide examples for dealing with other biblical books preachers are tempted to sidestep.

Five General Guidelines for Preaching the Old Testament

The Bible is a witness to God events and to how storytellers and sages of Israel interpreted Israel's encounters with God. Because those who produced the Bible belonged to Israel, it is almost as much about Israel as it is about God.

And yet Israel's own sacred texts say God works for the peace of the entire world. Israel's traditions reveal God's hope for everyone. God encountered these people, who then humbly transmitted their understanding of these God events to later generations with an eye to the whole world. Clearly, the storytellers enjoyed telling stories, and audiences enjoyed hearing them. The people who shaped and handled these stories had an agenda, which usually involved building faith in and obedience to one God: the LORD, the God of Israel.

1. We must read and listen closely to each passage in the Bible.

If we do not hear the message the first time, we should re-image and re-imagine it. We will eventually hear what the Holy Spirit is using this passage to say. When we wallow in it, we will gradually absorb what God means for us to internalize.[2] As Scripture, these stories are refreshed and re-inspired when we dwell upon them to interpret and apply them. God uses these stories to speak to us today when we have "hearing hearts" (1 Kgs 3:7).

2. Recognize that few biblical characters are all good or all bad.

This is partly what makes the story true to life. However, this is also a warning against complacency, fear, lust, and greed. That is, biblical authors and editors included the failures of the stories' heroes and brought them down to earth or, more specifically, down to us.

For example, the stories about Israel's kings show that Saul, David, and Solomon (and others) ignored the premises that undergirded their reign. They ignored what was laid down for them by the God who raised them up to lead Israel. The books of Samuel and Kings do not protect us from the news that Saul went mad with jealousy. The do not hide the fact that David got fat, lazy, and lustful. They do not avoid the truth that Solomon became concerned with commerce, political alliances, and peace at all costs.

Although the first three kings were at first humbled by their new role, they later misused their power with devastating results for their families and for the nation. The storytellers rarely put it so baldly. Instead, they told stories to let their readers draw these conclusions. Perhaps as preachers, we should learn from this. Simply *reading* the Old Testament lesson on Sundays without telling what the story means can sometimes be effective.

3. Read the/an Old Testament lesson regularly, even if you do not preach on it.

Let your congregations appreciate the sophisticated storytelling techniques that draw in the listener, provoke curiosity, and illustrate the themes of the larger theological framework within which the lesson stands.

4. Your familiarity with the whole Bible will make your preaching sing.

Show the parallels and intertextuality between your passage and the rest of the Scriptures. Without using footnotes, the Bible has ways of reminding us of other characters and situations, other times and places.

But do not strain to make the connections. When you know the whole Bible well, you can make thematic links and see that each narrative is about far more than itself. The Bible is full of allusions to its other stories.

For example, what happened in the Garden of Eden is repeated in Kings: God's provision was thwarted by disobedience, which led to exile. Loss is interwoven with mercy and hope for restoration. You want to lead your people into knowing the whole Bible well so that they can see these allusions and intertextuality for themselves.

5. Consider why particular narratives or other texts were included in the Scriptures.

We confess that God inspired or guided our Old Testament lessons. But we also confess that people transmitted these and not other stories for a reason. What were those reasons? Do similar needs and conditions exist today? If not, how do these stories remain instructive in hope and righteousness?

These guidelines for teaching the Old Testament also apply to the books of Kings, to which we now turn.

Ten Guidelines for Preaching Kings

1–2 Kings reads sometimes like history (using annals and other records), sometimes like a novel, and sometimes like sermons. It talks about the king that reigned in the Northern Kingdom (i.e., Israel) corresponding with the reign of the king in the Southern Kingdom (i.e., Judah). These formulae are interspersed with anecdotes and longer narratives about certain kings and prophets. The narrator restrains himself from drawing too many conclusions. However, when he does, he pulls no punches. In light of this, how shall the preacher begin his sermon series?

1. Survey 1 Kings and make an outline, noticing the literary units—here one pericope ends and another begins.

The layout of the stories is often similar to a drama with acts and scenes. The narrator may provide a clear transition with a change of location, character, or circumstance. The story may begin with a summarizing or introductory formula, such as "after these things." Once you have completed your outline, compare it with one found in a commentary. This helps to give you a feel for the entire book and how the plot unfolds. This will inform your preaching from the outset.

2. Show that the books of Kings rest within the "the Former Prophets" division of the Hebrew Bible.

The position of Kings within the "Prophets," the second division of the Hebrew Bible, has theological significance to which you should allude throughout your sermon series.[3] The name of this division—"Prophets"—underscores the theological significance of prophecy for Israel's story in Kings. Prophets guide kings to the covenant and to warn them of impending disaster if they fail to obey. These books recount Israel's story from a prophetic viewpoint.

For incidents within the narrative, these books offer both a po-litical and a *prophetic* cause.[4] These stories were shaped to support this theme: Israel and her kings must keep God's laws.[5] Consistent disobedience will thwart God's provision of land, king, and temple.

3. Read these stories closely as you prepare to preach.

"Close reading" is based on the recognition that everything matters: details, nuances, implications, what is said and what is left unsaid. For example, when a retelling of an incident or a message is different from the initial report, the messenger (via the narrator) is purposefully making new meanings. Changes in reports are not mistakes. They are economical ways for the writer to signify dispo-sitions of different characters. Make your own sets of observations and then turn to scholars for help. The scholars might have noticed things you missed, especially since they are reading the story in its original languages.[6]

4. Provide background to the story of 1–2 Kings.

Kings continues the story started in Samuel, Judges, Joshua, Deuteronomy, and so forth. You can sketch the Exodus-through-Judges story briefly.[7] The books of Samuel are essential background for Kings, as are Deuteronomy 17:14–20 and Joshua 1:7–9.[8] David's story begins in 1 Samuel and comes to a conclusion early in 1 Kings 1–2. Since Kings begins by focusing on David's last days, review the high and low points of David's life to which 1 Kings 1–2 alludes, es-pecially 2 Samuel 7, the Davidic Covenant, and 2 Samuel 11–12, the Bathsheba story and its fallout. If possible, teach 2 Samuel 11–12 in the same sermon as 1 Kings 1. Teach 2 Samuel 7 with 1 Kings 2. Consult scholars who have studied these chapters in depth.[9]

To understand these stories of David and Solomon, re-read Genesis carefully because of parallels with the stories of Isaac,

Jacob, and Judah. Ask, why did the author portray David like these patriarchs and his children to look like their children? (For example, David/Jacob, Tamar/Dinah, Absalom/Simeon and Levi; Solomon/ younger brothers).[10]

5. Review Deuteronomy 17:14–20 and Joshua 1:7–9 after you have preached 1 Kings 1–2, where Solomon is established as king.

Deuteronomy 17:14–20 is the mandate for kings by which Solomon was evaluated. We should always keep this passage in mind. It shows us that even when the narrator describes his policies favorably or neutrally, Solomon was breaking this mandate for kings.

6. Preach Solomon's story as found in 1 Kings 3–11.

As you reflect closely on this account, you will see, especially in chapter 11 that Solomon did everything a king should *not* do, according to Deuteronomy 17:14–20. Solomon (and many other kings) ignored the stipulations of the Mosaic covenant as described in Deuteronomy and other places throughout the Torah. These covenant conditions prohibit graven images, worshiping at shrines in the high places outside of Jerusalem, and syncretism (worshiping other gods together with the Lord).

As Kings proceeds, the narrator evaluates all the kings of Israel and Judah by these means. Ask questions of the text: Did the king keep a copy of the law before him and read it all the days of his lives? Did he learn to fear the Lord? Did the king observe all the laws and statutes, neither turning aside from it nor exalting himself above the members of his community? Did he acquire many wives, or silver, or gold, or horses from Egypt? Did the king make slaves out of his fellow Israelites for one month of every year? Did he show favoritism? Was he frightened or courageous, strong or dismayed?

7. Throughout your series on Kings, point out the opportunities God continued to provide for living people, both inside and outside the family of David. These opportunities included receiving promises, obeying the law of the LORD, and leading the people.

For example, highlight Jeroboam's covenant with the LORD at the end of chapter 11, and compare it to the Davidic covenant of 2 Samuel 7. Let your listeners absorb the promises to Jeroboam and the brief biography the narrator gives us, because Jeroboam's unfaithful response to God's gracious covenant marks the Northern Kingdom for the next 200 years. While God promised Jeroboam an enduring dynasty under the condition that he obey God's commands, his fear and dismay provoked him to maneuvers that became the downfall for the northern kings. This offer of a lasting dynasty to Jeroboam in 1 Kings 11 introduces the story in 1 Kings 12 about the loss of the tribes of Israel to Solomon's son Rehoboam, who chose to continue Solomon's oppressive policies. This was the political cause of the divided monarchy. But the prophetic reason for the split was Solomon's idolatry (1 Kgs 11:29–40).

8. Order your forays into the history and geography of this period according to the storyline and your audience's need to know.

After preaching through 1 Kings 12, provide a succinct lesson in the history of this period. Your listeners should notice the references to princesses from outside Israel, other kings and queens, natural resources exchanged in the building of Jerusalem and providing for Solomon's enormous household, and taxation and forced labor levies for outsiders and Israelites. They are now ready for a lesson on geography and history! If you give a history lesson at the beginning, your listeners may not care or remember.[11]

9. For especially troubling passages, consult scholars.

Turn to your professors and friends for leads. For example, 1 Kings 13 depicts an account about prophecy that you as the preacher must understand before you speak about it to your people. It is a very important "parable" intended to have profound effect on King Jeroboam and later leaders of Israel. This passage, interpreted properly, will throw light on the significance of prophets and prophecy throughout the rest of Scripture.[12] Although we may distinguish poems and songs in the Psalms collection and in other obvious places, it is harder to accept the poetic or parabolic nature of some other biblical texts.

10. Conclude your series with a scintillating summary of the themes of Kings you encounter elsewhere throughout the Bible, including the New Testament.

What theological meanings in Kings reinforce major biblical claims about God and humanity? Here are some examples:

Covenant — The covenants given to kings are like the implicit covenant (through an explicit command) given to the man and woman in the garden of Eden. When God's people disobeyed the commands, God exiled them from the land. Yet God's presence of mercy and love followed them. Even though they deserved execution, God gave them life and hope for the future. What happened in Eden is a refrain repeated in later narratives, both on the micro and macro levels: covenant, broken covenant, exile, interwoven with mercy and promise.

Divine providence and human free will — The books of Kings illustrate the mix of God's providence, i.e., God's plans for people and their free will. Human choice can thwart the loving purposes of God. God must move to other strategies and other people, always hoping women and men will agree to help accomplish God's loving purposes for the entire world.

Moses and the law of the LORD — Throughout Kings, the narrator mentions repeatedly the significance of Moses and the law of the Lord. As Solomon's story shows, the law is more important than wisdom to govern Israel. After all, this did not keep Solomon from breaking the law.

The judgment of Israel's leaders — A repeated message of Kings is that leaders are judged severely as an example to later rulers and leaders. Recall that when Saul, David, and Solomon ignored God's laws, they suffered. Their stories shadow Moses, and this should be demonstrated. When Moses flamed with anger and hit the rock without acknowledging God, God forbade Moses to enter the land of promise (Num 20). This seems like an overreaction, but the message to leaders is clear: be fully obedient to the words of God. They could not ignore them, waffle, cheat, or fail to give God the glory for provision. The laws applied, first and foremost, to leaders. The kings discover this again and again.

Your outlining, close reading of biblical texts, and consulting scholarly resources will expose other themes as you preach your way through Kings.

Five Ideas to Avoid When You Preach 1 Kings

What ideas should you avoid in your sermon series on Kings? This question is as important as the previous one, and your answer should come from the same background regarding Kings noted above.

1. Do not expect the narrator to condemn explicitly the evil he is showing.

The reader should figure out the narrator's negative perspective through his tone or a "neutral" statement that sums up a debacle (e.g., "In those days there was no king in Israel; everyone did what was right in his own eyes" [NASB]). Clearly, such a statement is not neutral. It suggests the requirement of a king to implement the law.

If the ruthless manner by which Solomon avenged his father's friends and enemies (1 Kgs 2) appalls you, the author likely hoped for that reaction, even though we do not read, "and the thing Solomon had done was displeasing to the LORD." Often, the narrator silently judges the proceedings of Kings from the perspective of Mosaic Law.

2. Do not endorse brutality *even if* the text appears to endorse it.

In the above example, the text summarizes Solomon's first bloody moves as king with the statement: "In this way the kingdom was established in the hand of Solomon" (1 Kgs 2:46; author's translation). Is this approval of Solomon's moves? Hardly. Avoid the temptation to explain how this was good, even if it seems bad. Struggle with the tension. Recognize that our texts emerged after the story itself. The story depicts two sets of worldviews: one of the characters in the story, and one of the storyteller. *Both* may be may be at odds with dominant biblical perspectives about justice, mercy, and love.

3. Do not use Chronicles to interpret Kings.

The Chronicler made earlier traditions relevant to his post-exilic community. The Chronicler did so through revisions and excisions of his primary source, Kings. As a post-exilic commentary on Kings, Chronicles demonstrates scribal agendas of the restoration period. Chronicles may also transmit some historical memories unknown to Kings. Consult current commentaries.[13]

4. Although commentaries and books are useful, avoid using scholarly terms like "redactional layers."

As helpful as redaction and other such concepts are for understanding the history of the biblical text, the final canonical form has carried the theological interpretation of this portion of Israel's history for centuries. Explanations about editions of Kings and "redactor/authors" may help us understand textual transmission, but to use such terms when preaching can steer you away from the meaning of 1 Kings as Scripture for the church today.

5. When teaching and preaching from Kings, do not ever say: "It's just a story."

Stories convey God's story as well as our own. We need stories to survive. We need the Scriptures to tell our own stories. Remembering Solomon's story, what shall we say we have asked from God? Remembering Jeroboam's story, what shall we say is the covenant God has made with us? Have we responded in fear or faith? Has not God through Jesus commanded us to ask? Did Paul not say that, with the gift of God's son, all other things are freely given (Rom 8:32; cf. Matt 7:7)?

Conclusion

The guidelines above do not exhaust the theology of 1 Kings. Rather, these are ways to wallow in the story, while perceiving what it says to you and your church. They provide methods for preachers and teachers to recognize the meanings stories make, with no intention of leaving any story behind. The story of Israel and Judah, woven through the collective memory preserved in 1–2 Kings, provides the context for theology.

Knowing this helps us understand the nature of biblical historiography. These Scriptures express human experiences with God as they happened in a particular place and time (history), interpreted with inadequate but profound words (story and theology). Although the producers of Scripture belonged to the collective Israel, traditions reveal God's hope for everyone.

As believers, we confess that the Bible leads to divine encounters. God uses the language of Scripture to communicate with us and to meet us. Our own walk with God is living and present, not confined to the past or pages of a book. As precious and unique as the Scriptures are for kindling and nourishing our faith, our faith is not in the Bible. It is not in codes or concepts developed about the Bible (such as "inerrancy"). Rather, our Bible directs us—our faith—in particular ways.

And what does the Bible tell me? The Bible always points to the love of God and God's son. The Scriptures affirm our dependence on God and on God's ways of love and mercy. The Scriptures say: look what God has done and can do. And this is for you too!

---

1. When I taught families in our church's education program, I came to the decision not to teach Gen 19 or 22. I knew 6–9-year-olds are not ready for the theology of these stories. These are for mature audiences.

2. See Robert Alter, *The Art of Biblical Narrative* (New York: Basic Books, 1981), 46: "The Bible presents a kind of literature in which the primary impulse would often seem to be to provide instruction . . . not merely to delight. If, however, we fail to see the creators of biblical narrative . . . took pleasure in exploring the formal and imaginative resources of their fictional medium . . . capturing the fullness of their subject in the very play of exploration,

we shall miss much that the biblical stories are meant to convey."

3. The division "Prophets" follows the "Torah" division and precedes the "Writings" division in the tripartite Hebrew Bible. These divisions are older than those in our Protestant Bibles. The Prophets division has two parts: Former and Latter. The "Former Prophets" includes the books of Joshua through 2 Kings. The order of the books is similar in the two communities' canons.

4. Kings provide the contexts for the messages of pre-exilic prophets: Amos, Hosea, Isaiah, Micah, Nahum, Habakkuk, Zephaniah, and Jeremiah. The books bearing their names make sense only when read with the background that 1–2 Kings provides.

5. Scholars since Martin Noth call the Former Prophets "The Deuteronomistic History" because it bears out the covenant obligation theme of Deuteronomy: obedience brings blessing; disobedience brings disaster.

6. The Word Bible Commentary, the Interpretation commentary series, and the forthcoming New Beacon Bible Commentary provide excellent examples of close reading. See also Marvin A. Sweeney, 1 and 2 Kings: A Commentary (Old Testament Library; Louisville: Westminster John Knox, 2007).

7. God promised Israel's ancestors to make from them a great nation (Gen), and then used Moses, the greatest prophet and servant of the LORD, to deliver their descendents from Egypt (Exod). God eventually brought them into the land of Canaan (Lev–Josh). Because they broke the covenant and people groups still living in the land oppressed them, God raised up local deliverers for them (Judges) until they asked for a king (1 Sam 8).

8. You may provide an expanded version of this: When the people asked for a king, God selected Saul, who was humble and a champion for the oppressed. But he failed to obey particulars given by Samuel, the prophet and priest who had anointed him, and was set aside. This rejection led Saul to crazed attempts to kill David, his replacement, whom Samuel also anointed king. David ruled a kingdom that he procured from Saul's supporters, and which he united through negotiations, political astuteness, and shrewd local marriages, as well as successful battles. Despite his failures as a father, covenant keeper, and ruler, David is acclaimed as the ideal king of Israel throughout the Scriptures.

9. For 1 Kings 1–2, use "Gaps, Ambiguity, and the Reading Process," in Meir Sternberg's The Poetics of Biblical Narrative (Bloomington, IN: Indiana University Press, 1985), 190–221; James A. Wharton, "A Plausible Tale: Story and Theology in 2 Sam. 9–20, 1 Kings 1–2," Interpretation 35 (1981): 349–52.

10. Gary Rendsburg, The Redaction of Genesis (Winona Lake, IN: Eisenbrauns, 1986).

11. The following is a historical sketch that your own research may supplement: Kings explains why Saul, David, and Solomon ruled all the tribes, but Solomon's son Rehoboam and his descendents ruled only Judah, absorbing Benjamin and Simeon. Jeroboam, seemingly from nowhere, became the king of the northern tribes, "Israel," and was promised a dynasty every bit as stellar as David's. Archaeological excavations of settlements, texts, and artifacts demonstrate that the Northern Kingdom, Israel, was wealthier, more centralized and more of a contender among the nations than Judah until the eighth century BC.

At that time Ahaz became king of Judah and submitted to Assyria, buying time to grow, prosper, and gain autonomy. Jerusalem grew from ten acres to 150 acres and its population from 1,000 to 12,000. With Assyria's protection and the influx of southern Israel refugees, Judah expanded. The thriving economy and widespread literacy during this period left evidence in the archaeological record of Judah's centralized government and its building programs. The reform of his son, Hezekiah, which led to his rebellion against Assyria, is confirmed by the excavation of dismantled sanctuaries and altars in the countryside and settlements outside of Jerusalem. This nationwide religious reform would have integrated the refugees from Israel with Judah's population, a literary compilation of traditions about David made possible by royal scribes and priests. Eventually, the reform led to revolution against Assyria. Hezekiah paid dearly with the loss of people, towns, and fields. Jerusalem remained, and Hezekiah was forced to pay tribute, as both 2 Kgs 18 and Sennacharib's Prism attests. During the reign of Hezekiah, workmen hewed the Siloam

Tunnel and inscribed the story of its completion on its bedrock wall.

In addition to excavated artifacts and inscriptions, texts from other nations help us understand the history of the 400-year period portrayed in Kings. Some events described in the
books of Kings correlate with the same events mentioned in tenth through sixth century
BC Egyptian, Assyrian, and Babylonian texts, which are then used to date the dynasties
and wars of Israel and Judah. You may want to save portions of this or repeat pertinent
particulars when you come to the respective narratives, for example, of Israel's fall to
Assyrian and of Ahaz and Hezekiah, kings of Judah.

12. Angel Hayyim, "When God's Will Can and Cannot Be Altered: The Relationship Between
the Balaam Narrative and 1 Kings 13," *Jewish Bible Quarterly* 33/1 (2005): 31–39; James
K. Mead, "Kings and Prophets, Donkeys and Lions: Dramatic Shape and Deuteronomistic
Rhetoric in 1 Kings XIII," *Vetus Testamentum* 49.2 (1999): 191–205; D. W. Van Winkle,
"1 Kings xiii: True and False Prophecy," *Vetus Testamentum* 39 (1989): 31–43; idem, "1
Kings XII 25-XIII 34: Jeroboam's Cultic Innovations and the Man of God from Judah," *Vetus
Testamentum* 46 (1996): 101–14; Jerome T. Walsh, "The Contexts of 1 Kings 13," *Vetus
Testamentum* 39 (1989): 355–70.

13. J. C. Endres, W. R. Millar, et al., *Chronicles and its Synoptic Parallels in Samuel, Kings, and
Related Biblical Texts* (Collegeville, MN: Liturgical, 1998).

18

Conceiving the Implausible: What Would It Take to Render a Ten-Sermon Series on Chronicles Intelligible?

John W. Wright

I t is extremely interesting to conduct a thought experiment, "What ten things I would say and five things I would avoid saying if I desired to present a sermon series on the book of Chronicles." Such a scenario presupposes many things that may not currently exist. It presupposes a contemporary congregation that would gather to hear the proclamation of the gospel of Jesus Christ from this late Persian period historiography. It also presupposes a congregation that would hear it so that the Holy Spirit would shape their lives as the body of Christ and each individually as members of it.

There are many reasons a ten-sermon series on Chronicles is profoundly implausible in the current North American Protestant context. Nonetheless, what makes this so interesting is that it really is conceivable. The church has shown the good of gathering for the ministry of the Word to bring about the justification of sinners and the sanctification of believers. Running commentaries of an elder or virtuous reader of Scripture for the upbuilding of the body of Christ is a practice that the church catholic has embraced from the late second century onward.

The book of Chronicles finds its place within Holy Scripture.

We find the book in all variations of the Bible. Even if Chronicles does not occupy the centrality of the Gospels, Christians still study Chronicles for its witness to all things necessary for salvation. It is part of that larger book to which the church has continually turned for its witness to Jesus Christ. Chronicles is known, says John Webster, for "its role in God's self-communication, that is, the acts of Father, Son and Spirit which establish and maintain that saving fellowship with humankind in which God makes himself know to us and by us. The 'sanctification' of Scripture (its 'holiness') and its 'inspiration' (its proceeding from God) are aspects of the process whereby God employs creaturely reality in his service, for the attestation of his saving self-revelation."[1]

A ten-sermon series on Chronicles can be part of that unique and particular sanctified creaturely reality that God has raised and perfected for human beings to participate in the very life of God through the Son by the power of the Holy Spirit. To explicate Chronicles within a gathered congregation to guide its formation and witness to Jesus remains a possibility, a practice that the Holy Spirit can use for the sanctification of a concrete congregation as the body of Christ within the world.

Preaching from Chronicles:
Ten Preconditions and Typological Structures

A ten-sermon series on Chronicles presupposes the ecclesial context in which the church catholic has read Chronicles as one particular text within the larger Christian Scriptures. We do not ultimately approach Chronicles as an autonomous book from the fourth century BC. Rather, we approach this Judean/Jerusalemite historiography with a particular book, the Holy Scriptures. On the one hand, Genesis through 2 Kings precede it. On the other hand, the New Testament follows it.

I. We read Chronicles within the whole of the biblical narrative.

Preaching from Chronicles requires us to see the full, concrete placement within Christian Scripture. 1–2 Chronicles follows Genesis through 2 Kings (including Ruth). The Bible narrates the story of creation and Israel past the quote of Cyrus that exhorts Israel to "go up" following the destruction of Jerusalem. In this placement, it comprises what contemporary scholarship calls "the secondary history" or, in the Old Greek, the *Paraleipomena*, "the things left out."

The placement represents the narrative logic of Chronicles. The structure reviews the Genesis narrative to the return to Jerusalem, though with very different emphases. The genealogies look chronologically past the end of the book. The listing of the Davidic genealogy goes long past Cyrus and Zerubbabel into the first third of the fourth century BC (1 Chr 3:9–24).

Placed within the context of the Old Greek Scriptures, the reader approaches the text following the narrative of Genesis through 2 Kings. However, Chronicles repeats some things, emphasizes others, and even changes some things. It ends with the narrative open, looking forward to a Davidic line upon which it has already focused: "Whoever is among you of all his people, may the LORD his God be with him! Let him go up" (2 Chr 36:23 NRSV). The text opens the reader to a story that is yet to come.

This story continues in and reaches a certain initial closure in Matthew 1:1: "The book of the genealogy of Jesus Christ, the son of David, the son of Abraham" (RSV). Jesus Christ is the hinge and the goal of this narrative. The narrative moves from creation to its lessening through disobedience to the promise to Abram and the election of Israel to the giving of the Torah, the gift of the land and the promise to David. The "wisdom books" presuppose the narrative, moving from the setting of Job in the pre-Abram time of Genesis 10, to a Davidic (Psalms) and Solomonic literature setting (Proverbs, Song of

Songs, Ecclesiastes) that presupposes the narrative given in Genesis though 2 Kings. Finally, the prophetic books participate in this movement from the judgment to salvation of Israel.[2]

To preach ten sermons from Chronicles, the pastor must see how this book, like a panel in a narrative mural, participates in what Irenaeus called the "rule of faith." To read Chronicles within the Christian book is not to deny the significance of the text's original production. However, it recognizes the Spirit's sanctifying work that has taken up this text and placed it within a new material context. This does not annul that original meaning. It perfects that meaning within the biblical narrative as it witnesses to Jesus Christ and the life of the church. The narrative structure of Scripture renders Jesus Christ and the life of the church intelligible.

2. The pastor and her congregation must find their life within the text as a member of Israel, whose story in Chronicles is theirs.

In preaching, the pastor stands before a particular people. These people have gathered from distinct locations into a common space. Perhaps they sing songs of praise, repentance, or assurance to God. These may be songs of testimony for salvation in Jesus. They share a common experience of baptism. The perceived integrity of Scripture weighs on how the congregation and its individual members receive the call to live their baptism.

In their baptism "into Christ Jesus," the pastor and the congregation now find themselves explicitly within the biblical story. The Holy Spirit has pulled the pastor and the congregation explicitly into the biblical narrative. The congregation looks back over its story in order to look ahead to God's future, to sustain the integrity of its witness for the sake of the world.

To render this time between the times intelligible, one must recognize that Jesus Christ presupposes a story that makes him intelligible. The gospel depends upon reading the death and resurrection of Christ according to the Scriptures (1 Cor 15:1–3). Jesus does not appear as an autonomous individual to bring salvation to the world as an abstraction. To quote John's Gospel, "Salvation comes from the Jews" (4:22). The titles "Lord" and "Christ" applied to Jesus presuppose the body of texts that now comprise that portion of the Scriptures known as the Old Testament.

If this is so, the congregation must affirm that the story of creation and Israel has now become *its* story. In baptism and through faith in Israel's Messiah, the congregation is part of Israel. As Gentiles, in Christ they are the wild shoots grafted into the holy root and life of the Jews (Rom 11:17–24). By participating in Christ through baptism, Israel's story becomes the congregation's story.

The pastor does not seek to make Chronicles relevant by finding parallels between the congregation and the text. The pastor must type the congregation into the form of Israel given by the structure of Chronicles as that narrative itself has found its goal in Jesus Christ. The pastor renders the congregation's life relevant to the text. In Jesus, the typological and allegorical nature of Chronicles becomes a story into which the church has been grafted to live by the power of the Holy Spirit. The pastor does not stand as the "expert" outside the text. She stands with the congregation within the text to help herself and the people understand the world in which they live truthfully through Jesus Christ.

3. The genealogies of Chronicles represent the people to whom the congregation belongs.

North Americans live in a political culture where genealogies supposedly have only private significance. In this culture, the individual thinks genealogical ties have no claim on his or her life. What matters are the "borders" in which he or she lives.

In Chronicles, by contrast, genealogies determine loyalties of the people. As the chronology of the text develops, the geographical sweep slowly swirls to encompass the "whole" world from

Jerusalem's perspective (1 Chr 1:1–54). A geographical space lays open at the center, filled by the "sons of Israel" (1 Chr 2:1–8:40) who belong to the land.

At the center of this world is Jerusalem; at its center is the temple. In Jerusalem, chronology laps into a time that incorporates other times. The setting is given following the return from the exile (1 Chr 9:1–2). The post-exilic temple becomes merged with the tabernacle in the wilderness, as Levites take their position in the tabernacle gates (1 Chr 9:19–22). The temple pulls Israel from various points of history into its own life as the center of the genealogical families of Israel, amid the world.

As part of Israel, the pastor understands that, through Christ, the congregation also participates in this new/old Jerusalem. The families of Israel take their orientation from the center: their roles in the temple in Jerusalem under the direction of the Davidic king that brings all Israel together from various times and settings. The genealogies map the people's lives into a new Jerusalem that includes even Gentiles. These witness to the God of Israel to a watching, surrounding world.

The genealogies do not have a private significance. They map the congregation's life at its center in Jerusalem and the temple in its midst. The genealogies represent the people and world into which the congregation—as part of Israel in witness to the world—has been grafted in Christ. With the center of the temple and Jerusalem in which all Israel finds their place together, one sees that Israel has orders of faithfulness within its own family.

4. The genealogies show intricate relationships within Israel and form an extended web of participation in Israel's end in the world.

The framework of the genealogies in Chronicles shows an intricate web of relationships within Israel. The genealogies do not merely differentiate between "insiders" and "outsiders," the "descendants of Israel" and "the nations." They differentiate relationships within Israel itself. The genealogies tell stories of faithfulness and unfaithfulness in subtle ways. The genealogies describe various levels of participation in Israel through the genealogical framework.

The predominance of Judah, with the Davidic line at its center, comes at the very beginning of the genealogy of Israel's descendants (1 Chr 2:3–66; 3:1–23; 4:1–23). Even within Judah's descendants, not all is well. Descendants from Judah and the Canaanite daughter of Shua represent a family line whose future is cut short (1 Chr 2:3). Those who come from the line of Judah and Tamar, Judah's daughter-in-law, are not drawn to assimilation to the nations through marriage. This line within Judah proves productive and enduring, and the royal family will arise from it. All are family, but not all interact to the same degree with the main line of Israel's witness among the nations.

Such relationships exist throughout the genealogies. The genealogies provide a form of Israel, a typology within which to find our lives. Israel has three main families in whom its mission goes forward: Judah (1 Chr 2:2–4:23), Levi (1 Chr 5:1–6:81), and Benjamin (1 Chr 7:6–8:40).[3] Wedged into these three families are the Transjordanian tribes (1 Chr 5:1–26) and Issachar (1 Chr 7:1–5). The first group ends in exile early under the king of Assyria (1 Chr 5:26). Issachar constitutes a large military force, but the family lasts only two generations after David's reign before fading into obscurity (1 Chr 7:3–5). The genealogies provide a typology of Israel, the depth in which a certain family tree opens Israel to their future. One must read these fascinating texts in how they typologically map Israel in its openness to the future. The congregation finds herself within the mapping the texts provide.

5. "Not all descended from Israel belong to Israel" (Rom 9:6)

So far, I have argued that the sermon series should help the congregation map itself within the world drawn by Chronicles through Jesus Christ. More particularly, the congregation should map itself into the form of Israel presented in the genealogies. The genealogies provide distinct types of "belonging to Israel." In many cases, the text affirms what seems a paradox: (1) a family is part of Israel by birth; and (2) a family is no longer part of Israel.

The last generation of biblical scholarship has emphasized "all Israel" within Chronicles[4] and the "inclusive" nature of Chronicles.[5] While rightfully drawing attention to one aspect of Israel in Chronicles, this emphasis overstates Chronicles' "inclusiveness." In the narrative world of Chronicles, to be part of Israel is not necessarily to belong to Israel.

Three examples will suffice to show the nuance in the form of Israel in Chronicles. First, as noted above, the three Transjordanian tribes are part of Israel. Because of their idolatry, they lose their place within the land granted them and remain in exile "to this day" (1 Chr 5:26). They play no role in the future to which the text witnesses.

Second, the family of Reuben has a profoundly tragic status in Chronicles. Reuben, the firstborn, explicitly loses his birthright. It passes to Joseph while primacy of status moves to Judah (1 Chr 5:2). Reuben's family is a story of defeat and disaster. Although having times of victory during the time of Saul (1 Chr 5:10), only exile waits for them (1 Chr 5:6, 26). Why? 1 Chronicles states, "because he defiled the bed of his father his birthright was given to Joseph" (1 Chr 5:1). The text suggests that Chronicles understands that the story of Reuben sleeping with his father's wife in Genesis results in Joseph's birth—the birthright passes to his oldest firstborn. Joseph's family never gets grounded. When Joseph's family reappears (1 Chr 7:29), the implication of exile becomes apparent. Joseph has no territory but must live in fortified cities under Manasseh's control, a group with no direct genealogical tie with Israel. Is Reuben Israel? Yes and no. Is Joseph Israel? Yes and no. Not all Israel belongs to Israel.

We find a third example in Hezekiah's Passover in 2 Chronicles 30. After the cleansing and rededication of the temple in 2 Chronicles

29, Hezekiah invites all Israel, Judah, and even the rebellious tribes, Ephraim and Manasseh, to come to the Jerusalem temple to celebrate Passover. The decree goes out to "all Israel" from Beer-sheba to Dan (2 Chr 30:5), with couriers especially addressing those "who escaped from the hand of the kings of Assyria" (2 Chr 30:6). They are called past the faithlessness of their ancestors to participate in the Passover out of the graciousness and mercy of "the LORD your God" (2 Chr 30:9). Those who left the Davidic king and the temple are still Israel.

Yet they are not Israel. Pride isolates them from their election as Israel. Hezekiah's invitation is rejected by all but a few (2 Chr 30:11). These still are Israel. Even if they had not properly prepared for the festival, Hezekiah, the Davidic king, intercedes for them (2 Chr 30:20). Only those who continually participate in "all Israel" are "all Israel," even if they remain in another sense "all Israel." Potential inclusivity in the form of Israel is not the actuality of participation in the form of Israel. Full participation in Israel ultimately takes place only under submission to the rule of the Davidic king.

6. God gives the rule over the kingdom of God to the line of David forever.

Chronicles looks beyond itself into a future that is intimated, but not explicated. The "primary history"—Genesis through 2 Kings—ends after the tragedy of exile. The slim notification of the release of the Davidic king sustains the faint heartbeat of the promise that God will "establish the throne of his kingdom forever" (2 Sam 7:13). The promise to David in 1 Chronicles 17 binds David with God's kingdom: "I will set him over my house and my kingdom forever; his throne will be established forever" (1 Chr 17:14). David's line rules forever over the kingdom of God. When the final words from Cyrus call for the Judeans to rebuild the temple and return to Jerusalem, the reader must peer into a future that lies beyond the story to a coming of a king from the line of David over God's kingdom.

Whether one speaks of it as "messianic," "royalist," or "Davidic," the centrality of the Davidic king's rule over "all Israel" represents a main theme in Chronicles. Prominence within Israel's descendents moves from the firstborn Reuben to Judah's family (1 Chr 5:2). David's descendants represent the center of Judah (1 Chr 3:1–24) that goes generations past "Jehoiachin the captive" (1 Chr 3:17). No human places David over the kingdom following Saul's debacle; the Lord "turned the kingdom over to David son of Jesse" (1 Chr 10:14). After all of Israel comes to him, David realizes that "the Lord had established him as king over Israel and that his kingdom had been highly exalted for the sake of his people Israel" (1 Chr 14:2). Note the ambiguity here over the word "his." Is it the Lord? Or David? Or both?

Chronicles never questions the indispensability of David and his line. David establishes the place for the temple and the altar for sacrifice (1 Chr 22:1). David offered his life to redeem Israel from the plague that Joab's disobedience (1 Chr 21:6–7) had brought upon the people.[6] David establishes the priests and Levites in their positions around the temple before it is built (1 Chr 23:1–5). David dies "at a good old age, having enjoyed long life, wealth, and honor. His son Solomon succeeded him as king" (1 Chr 29:28). The story comes from the perspective of divine election of the Davidic kingship over God's kingdom of Israel.

The Chronicler's picture of David looks forward to a fulfillment beyond its pages, found in Jesus Christ. Chronicles helps Jesus Christ become intelligible, the "son of David, the son of Abraham" (Matt 1:1), "who as to his earthly life was a descendant of David" (Rom 1:3 NIV). In the role of David, one understands the narrative background for Jesus' fulfillment of the text to which it points within the Christian Scriptures. Chronicles images the relationship between Jesus Christ and the kingdom of God over which he rules. The concreteness of this Davidic type fulfilled in Jesus is seen in the particular role the Davidic king plays in Chronicles.

7.The Davidic rule over all Israel in Jerusalem types Christ's rule over the church.

David does not stand as an isolated figure in Chronicles. David's significance arises in his place within the Chronicles narrative. We cannot abstract the character of David and the ideal Davidic king from this textual constellation of persons and institutions. This "form" of the Chronicler's David, read within Scripture, opens a Christological reading for preaching. This reading does not annul its original Davidic emphasis. It takes that text and *completes* it in light of a larger whole. With the congregation as "Israel," one sees that the typological/allegorical reading of the Old Testament that characterized early Christian readings presupposes a concrete setting often lost to modern reading habits. The literary logic of the relationship between the Old and New Testament requires such an interpretive move.[7]

The Davidic king stands in a necessary relationship with Jerusalem. The movement to actualize the kingship that the Lord has already given David (1 Chr 10:30) begins in Hebron (1 Chr 11:1–3), but it moves immediately to Jerusalem (11:4–9). Following the establishment of David as king of all Israel (1 Chr 11:1–14:2), the middle section of the David narrative (1 Chr 14:2–22:1) centers in Jerusalem. In Jerusalem, David comes to his full reign (1 Chr 18:14). The final movement of the David narrative (1 Chr 22:2–29:30) centers on him gathering material to build the temple and organizing personnel to run it.

David provides the royal, personal center over the kingdom of God. Jerusalem provides the setting for the formal gathering of Israel to unite the kingdom for the succession of the Davidic kingship to Solomon (1 Chr 28:1–29:30).[8] In Jerusalem, the unity of the people witnesses to their loyalty to the king and the Lord who appointed him. A structural relationship exists between the two: Davidic rule is exercised over all Israel in Jerusalem; Jerusalem's centrality depends on the Davidic rule exercised there.

Chronicles types Jesus' enthronement as "king of the Jews" in the triumphal entry into Jerusalem in the synoptic Gospels. Such a typological reading does not annul the conditions of the text's production. This reading takes up and fulfills these conditions. It completes them as the text finds its place within the larger textual framework of the Christian book. Israel reads this book, as the Spirit sanctifies it in its witness to Jesus. The structural relationships between the Davidic king and Jerusalem provide the control for typing this text by opening into a future that calls for its completion.

8. Davidic authority rules over the temple personnel as a participant and provider.

As already seen, Judah's descendants occupy the primary place within Israel, implicitly through their first place in the genealogies (1 Chr 2:3–4:23) and explicitly in the genealogy of Reuben's descendants (1 Chr 5:2). Likewise, Levi's descendants occupy a central place in the genealogies (1 Chr 6:1–80). Rather than a distinct territory, the Levites receive farmlands scattered throughout Israel (1 Chr 6:54–80).

The exemplary Davidic king stands over the priests and the Levites. They serve in their positions under the Davidic king's direction. The priests and Levites represent the king, the Lord's representative within the temple. Consistent with royal responsibility, Hezekiah later rehabilitates the temple properties through his reemployment of the priests and Levites (2 Chr 29:3–31). Hezekiah follows David's precedent by providing the essential sacrificial materials, both through his own goods and through motivation (2 Chr 31:2–8). The combined roles of Davidic king and priest—providing sacrificial *means* and sacrificial *practice*—belong together for the continued operation of the temple in praise of God.

As Chronicles opens into the New Testament, the preacher and the congregation can jointly see how Jesus, the Davidic king, takes authority over the temple personnel and even the temple properties in the Gospels. Christ makes atonement because he *is* atonement. The church as part of Israel *itself* becomes the temple, the gathering of the people by the Davidic king, to participate in the sacrifice, the Lord's Supper. Jesus, as the fulfillment of the Davidic line, *both* provides sacrifice *and* sacrifices as priest. The church's worship takes up the temple worship but instead of annulling it, re-embodies it.[9] Chronicles provides the structure of the Davidic king as the head of the temple and sacrificial apparatus in Israel.

9. The Davidic King has authority to interpret the Jewish law to insure that Israel achieves the end (*telos*) of the law.

The Davidic king's role as priest re-embodies the figure of Moses, who also conducts sacrifices (see Lev 8:14–21). The Jewish law does not state that the king has authority to conduct sacrifices. To accomplish the purpose of the law, the Davidic king takes personal responsibility to participate in the sacrificial system and the distribution of goods to Israel in praise of their God. The law's end is holiness: Israel's difference from the nations as a witness to their God (Exod 19:6). Obedience to the law is not a moral duty *per se*. God gives Israel the law for the formation of a particular people. These people allow themselves to be set apart from the world for God's good end and for the sake of the world.

At least twice, the Davidic king takes authority to redirect the law for its true purpose. Actually, the body of the king *is* the law. In the first instance, David revises the age requirement for Levites to serve. In 1 Chronicles 23:2, the minimum age requirement for Levitical service is thirty years of age, which corresponds with the age given in Numbers for the Levites who served in the tabernacle during the wilderness period (e.g., Num 4:3, 23, 39). However, David drops this age to twenty years and above for the temple in Jerusalem (1 Chr 23:24–27). The king revises the requirement, because the age in the wilderness required older members in a more dangerous situation (1 Chr 23:25–26).

In the second instance, Hezekiah calls for a Passover celebration. However, two legal stipulations seemingly came into conflict: to celebrate Passover at a certain time or with as many Israelites as possible (2 Chr 30:2–5). The Davidic king rules that the gathering of Israel was more important than that the celebration occur within the first month as the law specified. Hezekiah interprets the law so that the law might achieve its purpose: to make Israel a holy people. The Davidic king does not annul the law. The king has authority to interpret the law for its good end: the formation of Israel in its sacrificial worship of the God of Israel alone.

The structural relationship between king and Torah in Chronicles renders Paul's statement that Jesus Christ is the end or *telos*, of the law intelligible: "Christ is the end [*telos*] of the law so that there may be righteousness/justice for everyone who believes" (Rom 10:4). Jesus does not nullify the law in its divine election of Israel. He takes it to its true end in the incorporation of non-Jews into the holy root. In doing so, a people are formed to witness in their embodied life to the goodness of God. Unfortunately, the life of congregations today find themselves typed, not in the unified Israel of David and Solomon, but in the broken and fragmented Israel that receives God's judgment.

10. The contemporary witness of the church catholic participates in the sin of the division of Israel that denies God's election and mutes Israel's witness to the world.

The story of Israel after Solomon's reign deals with the tragedy of the division of Israel that arises from Jeroboam's sin. Whereas 1–2 Kings blames the northern tribe's split from Jerusalem on Solomon's apostasy, Chronicles mentions no such apostasy.[10] Jeroboam exploits Rehoboam's youthful ineptness to assault Israel's divinely mandated unity under the Davidic king in the Jerusalem temple.

Jeroboam returns from exile in Egypt to disrupt Rehoboam's succession. Jeroboam claims grievances against Solomon that have no basis in the Chronicler's Solomon narrative (2 Chr 10:3–4). The democratically elected northern king refuses the divinely ordained Davidic king. Using public pressure, he instead tries to negotiate a contractual relationship with him (v. 4). Jeroboam concocts things to try to disrupt the continuity of the Davidic line. The results are tragic, leading only to rebellion (2 Chr 10:19). Rehoboam is not without fault; he does not display the virtues necessary to hold the kingdom together. The personal gain of Jeroboam and those who follow him become more important than the unity of the kingdom. While priests, Levites, and some others subordinate themselves to the Davidic king at the Jerusalem temple, the division of the kingdom leads to divine judgment, which diminishes the witness of the people to the God of Israel.

Unity in witness under the Davidic king, witnessed mostly in the visible, bodily worship at the temple under the Davidic appointed personnel, becomes confined to the time of David and Solomon. While wise Davidic kings seek to re-unite all Israel in the temple (see, e.g., Josiah's Passover in Jerusalem in 2 Chr 35, esp. v. 18), the fragmentation of a united Israel diminishes Israel's witness among the nations. Even if the north is truly Israel, it also fails miserably. As Abijah states to Jeroboam, "Don't you know that the Lord, the God of Israel, has given the kingship of Israel to David and his descendants forever? . . . Now you plan to resist the kingdom of the Lord, which is in the hands of David's descendants" (2 Chr 13:5, 8). The failure of all Israel to remain united under the Davidic king remains a great failure of faithfulness. It leads to violence among the people who are really one and divine judgment against all. The Lord uses the non-Judean king Cyrus to re-start the people at the end. While the people are not faithful, God is.

If a congregation will identify with Israel within the narrative world of Chronicles, it will also need to identity with Israel as it develops in 2 Chronicles. We live under continued divine judgment as we live in a fragmented, rebellious Israel. We can see that the market competition between congregations inhibits the church's witness today. This lack of unity comes in competitive congregationalism and mindless localism of congregations today in working to tap market niches. It also cuts off the congregation from its long past and participation in the only Israel/church that is one, holy, catholic, and apostolic. "Emergent" and "traditional" become labels that are more important as new Jeroboam's rise to create new offenses that new Rehoboam's do not have wisdom to quell. The tragedy goes on.

Five Items to Avoid to Turn Implausibility to Potentiality

The above ten statements attempt to retrieve the book of Chronicles for preaching to local congregations. They point the way to a Christologically-based ecclesiology that renders the Scriptures as the sanctified creaturely reality that the Spirit has given to form us into a holy people, the body of Christ. The following points of avoidance are the other side of the preceding affirmations.

1. Avoid thinking that you are reading the Hebrew Bible.

Recent biblical scholarship has "naturalized" a new text for academic study from its own concrete textual history. What is called "The Hebrew Bible" is actually a shortened phrase for Biblia Hebraica, a family of contemporary editions that take their fundamental form from an earlier printed text, the Rabbinic Bible.[11] The Hebrew Bible presents to students a very different textual structure than a book that moves from Genesis through Revelation in the same language, beginning with our earlier textual witnesses in Codices Vaticanus and Sinaiticus.

More importantly, the place of Chronicles stands in different places within the particular material realities. In the Christian canon, it stands as a "secondary history:" it repeats what goes before, and opens up to what follows. The Biblia Hebraica closes its text with 1–2 Chronicles. It ends with a type of nineteenth Zionist century call "to go up" to the land. The framework of these texts produces very different texts, representing related but different histories and political contests that have often raged since the Reformation. We have yet to narrate this history fully, but the *Hebrew Bible* is a different material reality from the *Christian Scriptures*. That is, their different arrangements and the inclusion of the New Testament make the Old Testament, quite empirically, a very different text from the Hebrew Bible.

2. Do not say that the historical context of production of the text determines Christian preaching.

One need not deny the significance of the historical production of Chronicles for its proclamation. Knowledge of it is helpful. But the attempt to recover the "intention" of the author becomes a hopeless and needless task. The Spirit has sanctified the book of Chronicles. We need to broaden our understanding of inspiration from merely the production of Scripture to include the incorporation of these scrolls into a new and broader material reality to witness to God. This particular book renders God's presence in the hypostatic union with the human, Jesus of Nazareth.

3. Avoid saying that Chronicles is an accurate historical description of pre-exilic Israel.

Even a casual reader can discern that Chronicles presents a related but also profoundly different story from that found in Genesis through 2 Kings. Critics such as Wilhelm de Wette have shown that the harmonization of Chronicles with the "primary history" encounters profound problems. So-called "conservative responses" that attempt to preserve Chronicles' historicity in its presentation of pre-exilic history ironically contribute to the text's fragmentation.[12] These attempts to render Chronicles as history actually *diminish* its witness as Christian Scripture.

The history to which Christian Scripture testifies is Jesus Christ.

The rule of faith takes up the various histories and finds their end in Jesus. In other words, Christians confess that Scripture reveals all things necessary for salvation, that is, Jesus Christ. The history *in front of the text* provides the historical justification for Chronicles, not the history *behind the text*. The intention of the author can be helpful, but it is not determinative for how Chronicles works in and as Scripture. Likewise, the historical references to the past may also be helpful. But these are not determinative for the Spirit's work in the church's proclamation of this text in light of Christ. The text itself gestures into the future for the One who is to come, who was crucified for our sins and raised bodily from the dead according to the Scriptures. God has given us this text to open up a future that would free us from the closed history of the past.

4. Avoid saying that God justifies war to remedy injustice in the world.

The God of the Old Testament and war has become a hot issue in the twentieth century. On the one hand, critics attack the Old Testament as justifying violence. We must supersede it by "universal" ethical reason.[13] On the other hand, persons have used the Old Testament to justify military interventionist policies. Such readings share common presuppositions that often render preaching the ten-sermon series on Chronicles implausible.

Warfare plays a major theme throughout Chronicles, as does the normative status of peace under a Davidic king.[14] Solomon rather than David builds the temple because of David's involvement in war (1 Chr 22:7–10). Peace for Israel is the ideal under the Davidic king, the norm for which Israel aspires.

In Jesus Christ, the type of the ideal Davidic king is established. Under the reign of the resurrected Davidic king over the kingdom of God, Chronicles moves past its own narrative limits and finds its fulfillment. Jesus' teaching against retaliation and his advocating of love of enemy (Matt 5:38–47) brings his followers into perfection

as the Heavenly Father is perfect (Matt 5:48). In the fulfillment of
Jesus' life of non-retaliation by absorbing the sin and violence of
the world into his body on the cross, God defeats sin, death, violence, and Satan in the resurrection of Jesus. Christian commitment
to non-violence is not a liberal response to try to make the world
better. It is grounded in the conviction that the resurrected Jesus
fulfills the Scriptures as the Davidic king over all Israel.

The violence of Israel, God's deliverance, takes on a new typological significance. As the congregation understands itself within
Israel, we recognize that the nation-states in which the church dwells
represents the nations. Biblical Israel, not a particular nation-state,
represents God's elect. In Chronicles, Israel dwells amid the violence of the nations. Israel never joins one nation against another.
When Judah or Israel defeats its enemies, their trust in God to
deliver them always trumps violence. In Jesus, the new Israel no
longer participates in the world's violence.

5. Avoid saying that God wants to expand your borders.

Perhaps the most famous contemporary passage from
Chronicles is the so-called "prayer of Jabez" (1 Chr 4:10). Bruce
Wilkinson turned this text into a spiritualized version of the pros-
perity gospel for American evangelical Protestants.[15]

When we look at Jabez's place within Judah's genealogy, however, we see that Jabez has no direct genealogical tie. Moreover,
puns fill the text. In Hebrew, the name "Jabez" puns with the word
for "pain"—that which his mother experiences because of his
"honor"—a word that has a double meaning for weight, the cause
of his mother's pain at birth. The name itself represents a village in
southern Judah. God's response to Jabez's prayer to increase the
village's land to protect it from its own "obesity" both recognizes
the "honor" of the village within Judah and satirizes it (1 Chr 4:10).[16]
"Jabez" receives a place within Judah, even given his foibles.

Jabez is far from the Davidic line through which the story continues into a future about which the text does not yet speak. Only by refusing the typological function of the genealogies can Wilkinson type the passage into the mappings of social and spiritual upward mobility of late capitalist culture. The mistake is not Wilkinson's typologizing or allegorizing of the text; it is how he types through the text. He takes the text outside of the genealogical form of Israel that Chronicles provides within the biblical narrative that finds its climax in Jesus Christ.

Conclusion

Despite its implausibility, we may conceive a ten-sermon series on the book of Chronicles. These sermons move a congregation to repentance and faith in Jesus Christ. The congregation might become a visible witness in the world to this restored Israel, gathered by the Messiah. The congregation might become an Israel into which Gentiles have been incorporated because the messianic age has begun in Christ's death and resurrection. The Scriptures, including Chronicles, reveal themselves as the written Word that renders the Incarnate Word intelligible. Scriptures reveal a people called into this new Israel as believers in Him, to be made holy into his likeness.

---

1. John Webster, *Holy Scripture: A Dogmatic Sketch* (Cambridge: Cambridge University Press, 2003), 8–9.
2. See Brevard Childs, "The Canonical Shape of the Prophetic Literature," *Interpretation* 32 (Jan. 1978): 46–55.
3. The Benjaminite genealogy seems to enclose other tribes in its midst as subordinated to Benjamin as representative of the "northern tribes" as a whole.
4. See, for instance, H. G. M. Williamson, *Israel in the Book of Chronicles* (Cambridge: Cambridge University Press, 1977).
5. See, e.g., Gary N. Knoppers, "Intermarriage, Social Complexity, and Ethnic Diversity in the Genealogy of Judah," *Journal of Biblical Literature* 120 (Spr. 2001): 5–30.
6. See John W. Wright, "The Innocence of David in 1 Chronicles 21," *Journal for the Study of the Old Testament* 60 (Dec. 1993): 87–105.
7. See Henri de Lubac, *Scripture in the Tradition* (New York: Crossroad, 2000).
8. For the narrative structure of the David narrative, see John W. Wright, "The Founding Father: The Narrative Structure of the Chronicler's David Narrative," *Journal of Biblical Literature* 117 (Spr. 1998): 45–59.
9. See Margaret Barker, *Temple Themes in Christian Worship* (New York: T.&T. Clark, 2007).
10. See Gary N. Knoppers, "Rehoboam in Chronicles: Villain or Victim?" *Journal of Biblical*

Literature 109 (Fall 1990): 423–40.

11. Emanuel Tov, *Textual Criticism of the Hebrew Bible* (2nd rev. ed.; Minneapolis: Augsburg/ Fortress, 1992), 78: "The second Rabbinic Bible became the determinative text for all branches of Jewish life and subsequently also for the scholarly world. All subsequent editions, with the exception of a few recent ones, reflect this edition, and deviate from it only by the change or addition of details according to manuscripts, or by the removal or addition of printing errors."

12. See John W. Wright, "From the Center to the Perphery: 1 Chronicles 23–27 and the Interpretation of Chronicles in the Nineteenth Century," in *Priests, Prophets, and Scribes: Essays on the Formation and Heritage of Second Temple Judaism in Honor of Joseph Blenkinsopp* (Sheffield: JSOT Press, 1992), 20–42.

13. See John J. Collins, *Does the Bible Justify Violence?* (Minneapolis: Fortress, 2004).

14. See John W. Wright, "The Fight for Peace: Narrative and History in the Battle Accounts in Chronicles," in *The Chronicler as Historian* (eds. M. P. Graham, K. G. Hoglund, and S. L. McKenzie; Sheffield: Sheffield Academic, 1997), 150–77.

15. See Bruce Wilkinson, *The Prayer of Jabez: Breaking through to the Blessed Life* (Sisters, OR: Multnomah, 2001). Wilkinson's book provides a vintage example of what Christian Smith in *Soul Searching* calls "moralistic therapeutic deism," or more accurately "moralistic therapeutic relational theism," a contemporary version of American cultural Protestantism.

16. See Rodney Clapp and John W. Wright, "God as Santa," *The Christian Century* 119/22 (2002): 29–31.

19

Preaching the Preacher:
The Wisdom of Ecclesiastes
Stephen J. Bennett

The book of Ecclesiastes is both enticing and puzzling. It presents reflections from a wisdom teacher. But it challenges and nuances core wisdom teaching found in the book of Proverbs. Ecclesiastes targets a more sophisticated audience, young adults who have noticed that simplistic teachings such as "you reap what you sow" do not always apply in the real world. The author of Ecclesiastes, Qoheleth, wants to relate to the reader's realism or skepticism, while also help readers negotiate uncertainties of life such as economic reversal, war, and death.

Scientific and technological advances have not removed the uncertainty of life in contemporary society. Market crashes, natural disasters, political elections, and terrorist attacks contribute to uncertainty. In light of this, Ecclesiastes remains remarkably relevant for preaching. One could preach numerous sermons from the book written by "The Preacher" (ESV) or "Teacher" (NIV). The challenge is to decipher and communicate Qoheleth's message with clarity and power, while avoiding distortions.

Distortions to Avoid

1. Solomon repented?

There is a temptation to preach Ecclesiastes as a record of Solomon's repentance from idolatry later in life. He is familiar to most as the wisest man who ever lived. Ecclesiastes paints the picture of a king who ruled in Jerusalem (1:12), "increased in wisdom" (1:16 NIV), and "became greater by far than anyone" before him (2:9 NIV).

However, the idea of a repentant Solomon does not fit statements in Ecclesiastes or 1 Kings. Nowhere does the Bible say that Solomon repented. Instead, Ecclesiastes presents a king who reflected unhappily on a life wasted in chasing wisdom, wealth, and pleasure. Qoheleth uses Solomon as a negative example, the opposite of true wisdom. The assumption that Solomon mended his ways actually weakens this negative example.

There are legitimate reasons to think that Solomon did not write Ecclesiastes (e.g., the nature of the Hebrew vocabulary and statements about kings). The author uses Solomon as an example in the first two chapters, then moves on to other observations not related to Solomon (although the first-person tone continues throughout most of the book). So sermons on Ecclesiastes should avoid the suggestion that Solomon repented.

2. A time for *everything*?

"For everything there is a season, and a time for every matter under heaven" (Eccl 3:1 ESV). Biblical interpreters have portrayed the famous poem on time in Ecclesiastes 3 as a "panoramic view of life" or as events that are "common to all men."

On closer observation, however, this is inaccurate. Although everyone will die, laugh, weep, and speak, there is not a legitimate time to kill (although war may be a major exception). The last line of the poem refers specifically to war and peace, which seem to be the poem's real focus (this is the only line based on nouns instead of verbs). Ecclesiastes was likely written in a time when the threat of war was very real (Persian or Hellenistic periods), and this poem juxtaposes images of war with those of peace. The point is that the audience had no way of knowing when a war would come and take away day-to-day activities.

Rather than suggesting that there is a time to hate and kill in everyday life, sermons on Ecclesiastes 3 should promote the recognition of the uncertainty of disasters such as war that can snatch away laughter, embracing, planting, and building. One should relish these positive aspects of life while they are accessible. They are a gift from God (3:13).

3. Is there no pleasure in old age?

"Strong men are bent," "the grinders cease," and "those who look through the windows are dimmed" (Eccl 12:3 ESV). Almost all sermons (and commentaries) interpret these images from Ecclesiastes 12 as an allegory for old age. This implies a very negative attitude to old age as well as an unusual literary device (there are very few allegories in the Old Testament).

The chapter begins with a call to remember one's "Creator in the days of your youth" (Eccl 12:1 ESV). However, the author does not give this advice because there may be difficulties in old age. Regardless of one's age or difficulties, one should always remember God (Eccl 11:9; 12:1). Old age was not viewed as a hardship in Old Testament times. It was considered a blessing to reach old age and to live out life in peace (see Gen 15:15; Job 5:26).

Instead of reading Ecclesiastes 12 as an allegory for old age, one should take the imagery literally as a description of a city during or after wartime. Rather than preaching a negative view of old age, sermons on this chapter should emphasize the importance of serving God while there is opportunity, because war or other uncertainties could remove that opportunity without warning (see 2 Cor 6:2).

4. Mourning is not better than rejoicing.

Is sorrow better than laughter? Some preachers take seriously the statements in Ecclesiastes 7:2–3 that sorrow and mourning are better than laughter and rejoicing. While difficulties in life can be great teachers, they should not be preferred nor wished on anyone.

Ecclesiastes uses sarcasm in chapter 7 to show the futility of an extreme pursuit of reputation. Since reputation often increases after death, Qoheleth says that persons who live for reputation do, in effect, prefer death over life. This goes against the whole tone of Ecclesiastes, which recommends enjoyment of the life that God has given.

Rather than preaching that sorrow is better than joy, sermons should show that an extreme pursuit of reputation could rob joy from one's life. It is good to have a healthy respect for reputation, but not to be consumed by a desire for fame.

5. Life is not meaningless.

On September 18, 2010, 35-year-old Mitchell Heisman posted a 1,904-page manuscript in which, in the spirit of Ecclesiastes 1–2, he proposed to "design and conduct an experiment to test the proposition of the meaninglessness of life."[1] His suicide on the same day was the logical conclusion of his view that life is meaningless.

Many preachers characterize the Hebrew word *hebel* (ESV: "vanity") as "meaningless." They do so largely because the NIV translates that term as "meaningless" for every occurrence in Ecclesiastes (but translates the term with seventeen different words outside this book). This leaves the impression that life is meaningless, although the term *hebel* has a broader range of meaning. Life for most people in ancient Israel was not meaningless. During times of peace, life was quite fulfilling, although temporary and sometimes incomprehensible.

Unlike Mitchell Heisman, Ecclesiastes does not advocate suicide. It does not state that life (without God) is meaningless. It states that life is brief, often incomprehensible, and ultimately outside human control. Therefore, we must enjoy life with confidence in God's sovereignty and control.

Topics to Preach from Ecclesiastes

While the preceding topics are inappropriate for preaching, Ecclesiastes is rich with wisdom for relevant and helpful sermons.

1. *Carpe diem!*

Horace wrote 2,000 years ago, "Seize the day, trusting as little as possible in the future." Ecclesiastes has a similar message. The future is uncertain. Life is short. We should make the most of the time we have.

Ecclesiastes communicates this through the Hebrew word *hebel*, which the KJV translated as "vanity." The famous phrase, "Vanity of vanity ... all is vanity" (Eccl 1:2 ESV) is the first thing that comes to many people's minds when they think of Ecclesiastes. But what is vanity? It sounds like the description of a narcissistic person staring into the mirror! But another meaning of vanity is "futility." If something is ineffective or futile, it is *in vain*. The English word comes from the Latin for "emptiness." The Hebrew word, *hebel*, literally means a "breath" or "vapor." Vanity (*hebel*) is essentially a metaphor, which can have different nuances.

One of the nuances is "meaningless" (the NIV translation). Some things in life are meaningless, like the pursuit of excessive wealth (Eccl 5:10). Another nuance is "incomprehensible." Some things in life do not make sense, like the people of a city forgetting that a wise man had saved them from attack (Eccl 9:15). Perhaps the most important nuance of *hebel* is "temporary." Many good things in life do not last. The breath that gives us the word *hebel* is brief, but it is important and meaningful. Life itself is very short.

As I write this, the college where I work is grieving the sudden death of 21-year-old student, Anne Jackson. Her life was full of meaning. She had a beautiful voice and sang opera. Anne was training to teach music to children. She ran for the cross-country team. She volunteered in an inner-city ministry in New York City. Her smile brightened the day of everyone she met.

Anne died after collapsing during a running practice. On the day she died, she handed me an assignment quoting Isaiah 40:6–8. She added these words: "Life is short, and humanity will fade away."[2] Although Anne did not know that she would die that same day, she understood the wisdom of Ecclesiastes, which advises us to make the most of the short time we have.

2. How to be wiser than Solomon

This seems impossible. Most people know Solomon was the wisest man who ever lived and who ever will (see 1 Kgs 4:30–31; 10:23)! This is the impression that comes from reading the account in 1 Kings 1–11. Solomon was a political genius. He outmaneuvered his brother for the throne so that "the kingdom was established in the hand of Solomon" (1 Kgs 2:46 ESV). He famously asked for discernment in judging his people, and he proved his wisdom with the example of two prostitutes and one baby (1 Kgs 3). He organized his kingdom and established an empire, ruling over other nations and increasing wealth so that his subjects "ate and drank and were happy" (1 Kgs 4:20 ESV). He ran a massive building campaign, including the majestic temple of the LORD (1 Kgs 5–8). This showed his commitment to worship along with multiple sacrifices, with as many as 22,000 oxen at a time (1 Kgs 8:63).

Ecclesiastes uses a slightly different set of achievements to display Solomon's majesty. The king acquired great wisdom and knowledge (Eccl 1:16). He built houses, vineyards, gardens, parks, and pools. He acquired slaves and possessions, cattle and sheep, and silver and gold (Eccl 2:4–8).

But Ecclesiastes offers a negative assessment of Solomon's achievements. He chased wisdom, wealth, and pleasure. He did not really enjoy life. He lacked contentment. Even 1 Kings concludes that Solomon went astray when he worshiped idols, constructed temples to these idols, and married foreign (idolatrous) women so that "the LORD was angry with Solomon." He receives blame for the division of the kingdom (1 Kgs 11:9, 11 ESV). Solomon broke every guideline for kings listed in Deuteronomy 17:14–20.

Ecclesiastes gives advice on how to be wiser than Solomon: "There is nothing better for a person than that he should eat and drink and find enjoyment in his toil. This also, I saw, is from the hand of God" (Eccl 2:24 ESV). Instead of striving for more knowledge, wealth, and control, the better part of wisdom is to work hard and enjoy the gifts that God has given.

3. What wisdom can do for you

In the Bible, wisdom is more than intelligence. It is making godly choices. Such choices lead to good consequences. The book of Proverbs is full of advice about how to act in family relationships, personal habits, treatment of the poor, speech, and work.

Ecclesiastes is a wisdom book in the Old Testament, like Proverbs and Job. Yet Ecclesiastes is sometimes critical of traditional wisdom. How can this be? The trouble is that some people try to use wisdom to control life. However, life is uncertain, and we cannot control it. Unforeseen events may come along that change everything.

One can see clearly the limitations of wisdom when Solomon tries to use it as a means to wealth and power in Ecclesiastes 1–2. Wisdom is ineffective to control outcomes, because outcomes are subject to God's will. Corruption (Eccl 7:7) and a lack of knowledge (Eccl 6:12; 7:14) also limit wisdom. Wisdom is not a reliable path to wealth (Eccl 6:10–7:14), which itself is not a worthy goal (Eccl 5:10–6:9). Wisdom is inadequate for discerning the work of God (Eccl 8:17). If wise words are spoken, they will be ineffective unless the community remembers and implements them (Eccl 9:15–16). And one sinner or fool can destroy much wisdom, just as a fly can make a pot of ointment foul (Eccl 9:18; 10:1). So is it worth pursuing wisdom at all?

Yes, wisdom is still valuable as a practical principle in life. Ecclesiastes says the contrast between wisdom and folly is like night and day (Eccl 2:13). Imagine that you are on a path in the woods at night with no moonlight. If you have no light with you, you will stumble and lose your way. But with God's word, you have a light or lamp to show you the way through choices in life (Ps 119:105). Making choices with wisdom is like walking in the daylight.

Although godly choices cannot guarantee a good result, wisdom can lead to the surprising promotion of someone in debtor's prison to the position of king (Eccl 4:13–14). It can save a besieged city (Eccl 9:14–16). The rebuke from a wise person is more valuable than compliments from fools (Eccl 7:5). Wisdom can brighten the face. The skill of wisdom can make up for a dull ax (Eccl 8:1; 10:10). Even though wisdom is elusive and cannot guarantee "the good life," it is good (Eccl 7:11, 24). It is an expression of a right relationship with God and can draw a person closer to God.

4. You reap what you sow!

"You reap what you sow" is almost a motto of wisdom literature in the Old Testament (Job 4:8; Prov 22:8). This principle is sometimes known as the "doctrine of retribution." However, retribution can be either good or bad. If choices are good, the consequences will be good (with limitations).

Scott, a Christian surfer, stood on the beach waiting for friends who had agreed to meet him. They arrived with a new wetsuit and a new surfboard. Wondering how his friends could afford such a purchase, Scott asked the obvious question: "Where did you get the new gear?"

"We found it," they replied.

"You mean you stole it?" asked Scott, and added, "You'll reap what you sow!"

Actions have consequences. More specifically, righteousness and wisdom lead to blessing and success, while wickedness and folly lead to personal disaster. For example, the roof of a lazy person will leak because of lack of maintenance (Eccl 10:18; see Prov 6:10).

Qoheleth attempts to nuance this doctrine because, as he observes, it is not always reliable. Sometimes a wicked person lives a long life (Eccl 7:15; see Eccl 10:7–9). Even when the righteous do live longer, their death is just as final as the death of the wicked (Eccl 2:15; 9:1–6).

The doctrine of retribution is open to abuse. A person can think gaining wealth is the ultimate goal and righteousness merely the means of attaining that goal. Qoheleth says such an approach to life could lead to further problems, such as the loss of one's entire investment or even destruction (Eccl 5:13–14; 7:16).

Qoheleth nevertheless affirms the value of the doctrine of retribution, despite its limitations (Eccl 3:16-17). Even while observing the long life of the wicked (Eccl 7:15), he gives the assurance that they will die before their time (Eccl 7:17; see 8:6, 8, 13, 14; 11:9). Consequences are important, even though retribution is not a guarantee and is not completely predictable (since God is still sovereign over outcomes). Nevertheless, other things being equal, you reap what you sow.

5. Just a little bit more

That is the reported reply given by a famous billionaire when he was asked how much money would be enough. Just a little bit more. The quotation is ascribed to John D. Rockefeller. Ecclesiastes might have accredited it to Solomon. Ecclesiastes 2:1–11 portrays Solomon as accumulating hoards of wealth, but the wealth did not satisfy him. Qoheleth declares this pursuit to be "vanity and a striving after wind" (Eccl 2:4–8, 11 ESV). Solomon did not find any lasting gain in his accumulation of wealth.

Solomon is like the wealthy landowner in one of Jesus' parables. That man continued to build bigger barns to store his wealth. But suddenly his life was taken from him and all his wealth meant nothing (Luke 12:18). The accumulation of wealth does not lead to a satisfying life.

Ecclesiastes 5–6 extend this thought. Hoarded wealth leads to desire for more (5:10), additional consumers (5:11), lack of sleep (5:12), harm (5:13), loss (5:14), frustration, affliction, and anger (5:17), lack of ability to enjoy (6:2) and lack of satisfaction (6:7). Joy that is found in the LORD leads to lasting satisfaction (5:18–19).

The illustration in 1:7–8 underscores the same principle: "All streams run to the sea but the sea is not full.... The eye is not satisfied with seeing, nor the ear filled with hearing" (ESV). Hoarding wealth will never lead to lasting satisfaction because it is open-ended. However, one's current possessions are finite and, if enjoyed with contentment, will offer immediate satisfaction.

6. To see good in everything

Is the glass half-full, or half-empty? For Ecclesiastes and for people who are content, the glass is half-full. There are uncertainties in life, and some things are puzzling. But for those who are content, there is much to cause rejoicing. In Ecclesiastes, the recurring advice is to enjoy life (5:18). The literal Hebrew phrasing means "to see good."

Qoheleth advises his audience to see the good in simple pleasures such as food, drink, work, and relationships. A constant desire for more only leads to dissatisfaction. Contentment comes from accepting what one has as a gift from God (Eccl 2:24; 3:13; see Matt 7:11).

Like the rest of the Old Testament, Ecclesiastes does not promote a developed view of the afterlife. Death is universal and inevitable (Eccl 3:19). Without the possibility of resurrection or an eternity in heaven, Qoheleth concludes that people should enjoy the present life and rejoice in their work, which is their portion from God (Eccl 3:21–22; 9:10). Although Christians have a hope in the resurrection which Qoheleth did not, they should still enjoy the present life as a gift from God (see, e.g., Phil 4:4, 11–12; Luke 3:14). Qoheleth advocates a joy that is found in simple pleasures, "for this will go with him in his toil through the days of his life that God has given him under the sun" (Eccl 8:15 ESV).

7. Whatever my lot...

> When peace, like a river, attendeth my way,
> When sorrows like sea billows roll;
> Whatever my lot, Thou has taught me to say,
> It is well, it is well, with my soul.

This famous hymn by Horatio G. Spafford catches the essence of an important theme in Ecclesiastes. The book advises enjoyment of life. This leads to satisfaction and contentment, whereas striving for more profit leads to sleepless nights and a lack of joy.

Ecclesiastes makes a contrast between *profit* and *portion*. The pursuit of excessive profit is unsatisfying. Accumulating wealth can even be harmful. The loss of wealth in a high risk venture can leave a family destitute (Eccl 5:13–14). Indulgence is unsatisfying because the one who overeats spends the night struggling with indigestion. The hard work of a manual laborer ensures a good night's sleep (Eccl 5:10–12).

Instead of chasing excessive profit, Qoheleth commends the acceptance of one's portion or lot. This vocabulary calls to mind the division of the land of Israel during the time of Joshua (Josh 18–19). Each family received a fair proportion of the land. In the time of Qoheleth, a monetary economy superseded the agricultural economy, which meant that wealth could be accumulated and hoarded more easily. Qoheleth warned against this (Eccl 5:10). An orientation around endless accumulation does not lead one to say, "It is well with my soul."

8. Who can straighten what God has bent?

Have you ever tried to straighten out a paper clip? It works a little, but it will never be perfectly straight. The wisdom teachers of Old Testament times believed that they could give advice that would lead to a straight or easy path. But all the wisdom in the world cannot straighten what God has made crooked (Eccl 7:13). Even Proverbs 3:6 acknowledges that only God can make one's path straight.

Ecclesiastes develops this theme in a number of ways. One can see the limitations of human control in the unreliability of the doctrine of retribution. Qoheleth also specifies that knowledge of the future is unavailable to humans, thus making future outcomes beyond their control (Eccl 6:12; 8:7). By contrast, God *does* know the future and has the power to accomplish his will. Ecclesiastes 6:10 states, "Whatever has come to be has already been named, and it is known what man is, and that he is not able to dispute with one who is stronger than he" (ESV), namely God.

As the events of the future are under God's control, so is the timing of those events. Humans cannot control the time of their death (Eccl 8:8) or the timing of national events such as peace and war. This is emphasized in the famous poem on time (Eccl 3), which gives couplets of activities that are appropriate for either peace or war. The possibility of war severely limited individual human control of outcomes. Later in the book, Qoheleth states, "for you know not what disaster may happen on earth" (Eccl 11:2 ESV).

9. Be afraid, be very afraid!

Preaching has changed a great deal since 1741 when Jonathan Edwards preached his famous sermon, "Sinners in the Hands of an Angry God." Despite the popularity of horror films, people do not like to think of God as scary. This is good. God is loving and kind. Yet the fear of the Lord is a biblical concept and an important theme in Ecclesiastes (used four times in Eccl, and sixteen times in Prov; see Rom 13:4).

The expression seems to draw from royal vocabulary (see Prov 20:2; 24:21).[3] In the ancient Near East, there was good reason to be afraid in the presence of a king. But the subjects of a good king did not live in terror.

By analogy with the divine-human relationship, the fear of God expresses the proper posture in the presence of God. It is wisdom literature's way of expressing a right relationship with God. A profound sense of the power and sovereignty of God accompanies healthy religious devotion. One may describe this depth of honor and respect as the fear of God, but it is not a debilitating fear that comes from living under an abusive authority or tyranny.

The fear of God is connected with God's sovereignty in Ecclesiastes 3:14, which declares that the actions of God last forever. Nothing can be added to or subtracted from them. This is why "people fear before him" (ESV).

The fear of God leads people to be faithful to their vows (Eccl 5:6–7, see 5:1–2) and to avoid excessive wickedness (Eccl 7:16–18). Someone who fears God would avoid the trap of pursuing righteousness and wisdom for the purpose of material gain (Eccl 7:16). Righteousness and wisdom would be pursued appropriately and for the motivation of a right relationship with God. In this case, *everything will come out fine* (Eccl 7:18, AT; *yetse' 'et-kulam*).

Qoheleth promotes the fear of God as an important key to a successful life, despite his usual critique of a simplistic doctrine of retribution (Eccl 8:12–13). In any case, the fear of God and keeping his commandments are "the whole duty of everyone" (Eccl 12:13 NRSV).

Preaching the fear of God is not very popular in a culture that prefers to emphasize love. Yet one should not neglect the fear of God when preaching from Ecclesiastes. It is an important expression and aspect of a right relationship with God, the benevolent, yet sovereign, king over all.

10. But wait, there's more!

"All go to one place. All are from the dust, and to dust all return" (Eccl 3:20). In the thought of the Old Testament, belief in the afterlife was restricted to the place of the dead known as Sheol. Old Testament writers did not understand Sheol to be a place of eternal torment. It was understood as the place everyone, both righteous and wicked, went after death. In Hebrew understanding, no one lived in heaven except God and God's council.

While Qoheleth agrees with the general Old Testament view of afterlife, he seems dissatisfied with it. He mocks the idea that a good name after death is satisfying. What satisfaction can one have after death (Eccl 7:1–2)? His observations of the failure of the doctrine of retribution also hint at the need for a judgment after death, although he also suggests a qualified acceptance of the doctrine of retribution (in this life).

Qoheleth promotes enjoyment of this life, especially in the light of his limited belief in an afterlife. But he also expresses a sense of loss or even bitterness in the finality of death and in the inequity that both righteous and wicked receive the same fate (i.e., death). People die just like animals. A live dog may be better than a dead lion, but a live lion would be even better (see Eccl 9:1–6)!

But wait, there is more! The New Testament doctrine of resurrection answers Qoheleth's dissatisfaction with the incomprehensible brevity of life. "For Christians, the resurrection of Jesus of Nazareth gives hope to all who anticipate God's work of raising up the dead—from 'perishable' to 'imperishable', from 'a natural body' to 'a spiritual body' (1 Cor 15:42–44)."[4] So Ellen Davis can call Ecclesiastes "a kind of preface to the New Testament."[5]

Preaching from Ecclesiastes should promote Qoheleth's advice to enjoy this life. But it should also move beyond Old Testament categories to the New Testament revelation of the resurrection.

Concluding Remarks

Qoheleth's advice to enjoy life is important. While Christians need not despair at the anomalies of retribution, neither should they orient their lives around accumulating wealth. Paul's attitude toward wealth and contentment resonates with Qoheleth: "I have learned in whatever situation I am to be content. I know how to be brought low, and I know how to abound. In any and every circumstance, I have learned the secret of facing plenty and hunger, abundance and need. I can do all things through him who strengthens me" (Phil 4:11–13 ESV; see Luke 3:14).

There is much wisdom to preach from Ecclesiastes. Sermons based on the book written by "The Preacher" will help Christians orient their lives around an appropriate fear of God (a healthy relationship with him) and his sovereignty. Sermons on Ecclesiastes will help believers recognize the proper place of wisdom and wealth. These sermons will also lead hearers to wrestle with the complexities of retribution (why bad things happen to good people). Most of all, these sermons can guide listeners to enjoy faithfully and gratefully the life God has given us here on earth. For that is our portion.

---

1. *New York Post,* 25 September 2010. Online: http://www.suicidenote.info/, page 29, accessed October 7, 2010.
2. Anne Elisabeth Jackson, "Isaiah Journal Reflection Nine," Assignment submitted to Stephen J. Bennett, Nyack College, Nyack, NY, 16 November 2010.
3. See Antoon Schoors, *I Am God Your Saviour: A Form-Critical Study of the Main Genres in Is. XL–LV* (Leiden: Brill, 1973), 40.
4. Stephen J. Bennett, *Ecclesiastes and Lamentations* (New Beacon Bible Commentary; Kansas City, MO: Beacon Hill Press of Kansas City, 2010), 92. See also Matt 6:19–34.
5. Ellen Davis, *Proverbs, Ecclesiastes, and the Song of Songs* (Westminster Bible Companion; Louisville: Westminster John Knox, 2000), 169.

20

"I Never Understood
A Single Word He Said:"
Ten Things to Preach and Five Things to
Avoid in Jeremiah

Mitchel Modine

Introduction

The rock song, "Joy to the World," popularized by Three Dog Night decades ago, has a strange first line: "Jeremiah was a bullfrog." The song probably has nothing to do with the biblical Jeremiah. But the song never identifies the referent of "Jeremiah" in its opening verse.

The book of Jeremiah is certainly difficult to read. The reader can come away from reading the book claiming not to understand anything "he" said. In addition, there are several references to wine in this book. Most interesting among them is the cup of the wine of God's wrath: "This is what Yahweh, God of Israel said to me: 'Take this cup of wrathful wine from my hand and make all the nations to whom I send you drink from it'" (Jer 25:15; see also 51:7).[1] In what follows, I hope to alleviate at least some of the confusion with Jeremiah. I will alternate between interrelated themes, with two positive statements followed by a negative.

1. Recognize that the book was written to address a particular situation.

The book's historical context ranges from the thirteenth year of King Josiah (626 BC) through the eleventh year of King Zedekiah (586 BC) to the release of King Jehoiachin from prison (around 560 BC). These sixty or so years were very important. Although the size of the Babylonians deportations in two or three different waves (in 598, 587, and 582 BC)[2] was small—around 5–10 percent of the total population of Judah—these events had significant psychological effect. At the same time, a high degree of creativity marked this period, resulting in the creation or collection of many texts that eventually would form the Bible.

The central event in Jeremiah's ministry was the destruction of the temple. Jeremiah used threats against the place where God had chosen (particularly in Deut 12:5, 11; 14:23; 16:2, 6, 11) to express God's ultimate anger with the nation of Judah. In the famous Temple Sermon in chapter 7, Jeremiah invites hearers to consider the destruction of Shiloh, the place that God had previously chosen for the dwelling of the Name (7:12). Just as Shiloh was destroyed for the wickedness of Israel, so Jerusalem will be destroyed. Although the note at the end about the release of King Jehoiachin from prison (Jer 52:31–34; see also 2 Kgs 25:27–30) is hopeful, the hope is ambiguous. Jehoiachin was no longer in prison, but he was still in exile. The book ends like most parts of the Old Testament—outside the promised land.

2. Take a comprehensive view of its inconsistencies.

To say that the Bible, and especially a book like Jeremiah, has inconsistencies in no way threatens God's purpose for the Bible: to bring humans to salvation. The book exhibits both internal and external inconsistencies. One inconsistency has to do with whether judgment and punishment for sin are unavoidable or avoidable. For example, the book exhibits the doctrine of inevitability in the discussion of the droughts (Jer 14:1–12) or the inability even of great faithful ones from the past to intercede on Judah's behalf (15:1–4). By contrast, it also exhibits the possibility of turning away punishment in, among other places, the Temple Sermon (7:1–20) and in Jeremiah's vision in the potter's house (18:1–12).

We can deal with these inconsistencies in three different ways. First, we can explain them away by appealing to supposedly errorless autographs, which are conveniently unavailable for critical study. This is the approach taken by twentieth-century fundamentalism. Second, we can explain them away by blaming different authors, editors, and/or sources, a solution that grows more complex with each contribution. This is the approach taken by historical-critical scholarship. Finally, we can appreciate them as together creating a veritable work of art. Such an approach recognizes that people may have differing, inconsistent, or even contradictory opinions about a given subject at various times in their lives. Moreover, a person or a group might even hold contradictory opinions at the same time.

3. Do *not* imprison the text in its original history.

In biblical interpretation and preaching, it will not do to ignore the author's intent. The person who moves from the attempt to recover authorial intention to an insistence that the Bible cannot mean what it never could have meant, however, faces philosophical and theological difficulties. Such insistence renders not only preaching, but also the New Testament's reuse of the Old Testament, impossible (see below). Instead, a sufficiently robust theology of biblical inspiration should include the ability and the willingness of God to inspire the *readers* as well as the *writers* of the biblical text. This means that interpretation not only may, but must, go beyond the "original meaning." In this vein, Jewish scholar Shaye Cohen notes, "The most radical function of scriptural exegesis was that it allowed Jews to affirm undying loyalty to a text written centuries earlier for a very different society living under very different conditions. They could claim loyalty to the sacred text even as they freed themselves from it by interpreting it."[3]

Yes, the original meaning of the text is important. It provides a kind of "control" over interpretation. But it need not be an overbearing control. Because the text of Scripture is inspired, no interpretation—not even the most fanciful—can harm it. As Cohen puts it, "The canonization of Scripture set free the wellsprings of the imagination."[4]

4. Affirm the message of comfort to the oppressed (and judgment on the oppressors).

Jeremiah contains both a hopeful word for the oppressed and a word of judgment for the oppressors. Bearing in mind earlier comments about embracing inconsistencies as part of what makes the book a work of art, one should be sure to affirm both ideas.

The turn from judgment of sin to hope for the punished is not as dramatic in Jeremiah as in Isaiah 40. For *this* particular prophet, hopefulness comes more often in the midst of suffering. It will not do to return to old characterizations of Jeremiah as the weeping prophet, for these are only slightly helpful in interpretation. Two places in particular where punishment and promise seem to overlap are chapters 16 and 29. Associated with the promise is a confession of faith built around the return from exile.

Important in the present context is chapter 29, which reports the exchange of a number of letters between Jeremiah and those whom the Babylonians carried off in the first deportation. The key line is the admonition to "look after the prosperity of the city to which I have exiled you, for in its prosperity will be found your prosperity" (Jer 29:7). Even in the midst of more-or-less difficult circumstances brought about as punishment for sin, God is still with the faithful. This is a much-encountered note in the overarching symphony of Old Testament theology. For comparison, see how God makes clothing of animal hides for Adam and Eve, after expelling them from the Garden of Eden (Gen 3:21).

Regarding punishment for the oppressors, the key text is the oracle against Babylon in chapters 50–51. This lengthy diatribe proclaims that the great destroyer will get what is coming to it. By announcing Babylon's term is up (see the note of 70 years in Jer 25:11–12; 29:10), the tide is turning in favor of Judah. Any curse on Babylon is an equivalent blessing for Judah. The book and Hebrew theology in general are unconcerned what benefit other nations might derive from Babylon's downfall.

5. Testify to God's direction of history.

Jeremiah and most of the prophets have an overwhelming concern to see God as the director of history. One should take note here about the beginnings of cementing monotheism within the general "system" of emerging Jewish theology, both in the land of Israel and throughout the Dispersion. Although Israel did not achieve the final victory of monotheism until the Maccabean Revolt in the second century BC—around the time of the Book of Daniel—the prophets lean in that direction. Understanding that God is in control of the events of human history is a key component of this theological shift.

The principal way in which the major prophets enforce this point is through theological reflection on the successive human empires vying for control of the ancient Near East. Isaiah's ultimate conclusion is that all of these empires—Egypt, Assyria, Babylonia, and others—are but "a drop from a bucket" (Isa 40:15), not worth going back and retrieving when they drip off, even supposing one could do so.

Jeremiah says God decreed a certain time for Babylonia's reign (Jer 25:11–12; 29:10). Jeremiah develops this in chapter 29 to suggest that, if God has control over the nations of the world, the faithful community can trust God to provide a helpful and hopeful future for them. This seems to be the ultimate point of the justifiably famous injunction of 29:11. Apart from its striking insistence that Babylonia is a tool in the hand of God (see also 25:9; 27:6; 43:10), this prophetic word suggests that, regardless of the pain currently being experienced, there will be opportunities for new life after the exile. Because the exile will be long, in fact, the people should maximize the opportunities presented to them for new life *during* the exile. In other words, exile was not only punitive (punishment for sin) but also purgative (burning off unfaithfulness).

6. Do *not* oversentimentalize and trivialize the hopeful word.

As with any Scripture, one can misuse and sentimentalize Jeremiah 29:11 in such a way as to destroy anything approximating its original significance. A former coworker of mine once said she committed this particular error, though of course she did not perceive it as an error. Having gone to the grocery, she selected a collection of items totaling $29.11. This caused her to remember the "promise" of 29:11: "'I know the plans I have for you,' declares the LORD, 'plans to prosper you and not to harm you, plans to give you hope and a future'" (NIV).

I did not say this at the time, but I believed she was cheapening Jeremiah. Aside from the reality that the promise of Jeremiah 29:11 was given in specific historical and literary contexts—neither of which, of course, pertained to my friend—this seemed to me, at best, a serendipitous circumstance and, at worst, a pseudo-magical demand upon God. Although no interpretation, regardless of how fanciful, can do irreparable harm to the Scriptures, interpretations that border on the magical should have no place for Christians. We, as preachers and teachers, have a fundamental obligation to dissuade the people in our various charges away from such alarmingly simple—and specious—interpretations of Scripture.

7. Understand the function of the oracles against the nations.

A difficult section of Jeremiah, in terms of both interpretation and application, is the oracles against the nations in chapters 46–51. Of course, difficulty of understanding is neither excuse for avoidance nor reason for despair!

A short examination of the context of these oracles will go far toward revealing their meaning. On the one hand, the basic theological and philosophical affirmation of this material is that "the fortunes of the nations are a zero-sum game. That is, benefit or blessing for one nation requires an equivalent curse or calamity for another nation, or a cumulative series of them for several other nations."[5] On the other hand, the book affirms through these oracles that God controls all human history. God is able to raise and lower the fortunes of the nations in accordance with the divine will.

This second point has a particular connection with what I stated earlier: the assertion of God's control over the fortunes of the world is the foundation of Israel's hope. Readings of the Bible from the standpoint of oppressed peoples—for instance, those who live in various forms of economic or political oppression—may find in this material a source of hope in the midst of their difficult situation. Although there are admittedly some theological and ideological pitfalls that we must avoid—like, for example, making God the originator of Auschwitz—it still can be a powerful assertion of God's direction of human history.

8. Appreciate the ideological and theological importance of the land of Israel.

One must also emphasize in preaching from Jeremiah the ideological and theological importance of the land of Israel. The most jarring aspect of exile is the loss of key symbols of national identity. In the Bible, the land of Israel (or Judah, after the fall of the Northern Kingdom) is of indispensable importance. However, it is

noteworthy that major sections of the Bible end with a setting outside the land. The book of Jeremiah ends with Jehoiachin's release
from prison. But he remains in exile, at best a note of only ambiguous psychological benefit (Jer 52:31–34; see 2 Kgs 25:27–30).
In short, the story of the Old Testament seems, at least in respect to
the promised land, one of searching for the fulfillment of promise.

The children of Israel never seem to be in the land for long or
hold the land independent of various foreign influences. This fact
enhances, rather than reduces, the ideological and theological importance of the land. While it is true that Israel was never "there"
very long. Throughout most of their history, "someone" dominates
them. It is also true, historically speaking, that those who returned
from exile had never lived in the land themselves (at least most of
them). However, they still believed they belong in that land. They
still believed God's promise that they will live there in safety and
security.

9. Do *not* equate ancient Israel with modern Israel.

This item seems to be a particular temptation many evangelical
preachers face. While this issue is more germane to issues surrounding the exodus and conquest, it certainly also applies to the
exile and return.

While the 1948 document establishing the modern State of
Israel used language regarding return from exile,[6] the situations are
really so different that equating them leads to gross error and misunderstanding. There are complex political and philosophical issues
involved in the struggles facing the modern State of Israel, many
of which it has created. As such, a simplistic appeal to biblical authority for Israel's claims is not defensible. Failure to observe this
caution may confuse parishioners over a particular political stance.
One must be careful that those who hear the sermon also hear
the message that arises out of Scripture, rather than one's political
leanings.

10. Receive the "new thing" represented by Jeremiah.

Beyond the famous "new covenant" passage in Jeremiah 31:31–34—doubtlessly because Christians appeal to it during Advent and associate it with Jesus—Jeremiah voices other decidedly new things. One such idea, expressed in two parallel texts, holds particular interest in terms of developing Hebrew/Jewish thought. This idea speaks of a new kind of confession of faith to develop in the aftermath of exile: "Surely, days are coming—Oracle of Yahweh—when they shall no longer say, 'As Yahweh lives who brought up the children of Israel from the land of Egypt,' but 'as Yahweh lives who brought up the children of Israel from the land of the North, and from all the nations to which he had exiled them, and brought them back to their own land which he gave to their ancestors'" (16:14–15, with slight variations in 23:14–15).

The Ten Commandments are one of the foundational documents of Hebrew religion. They are based directly upon the liberation from Egypt. Given this, it is striking a prophet like Jeremiah could develop the tradition in the way described in the verses above. In the strictest terms, Jeremiah's prophecy in these verses did *not* come true. The history of the Jewish people in no way indicates they forgot the exodus. However, as the character of the declaration establishing the State of Israel demonstrated, the idea of return from exile has played an important role in Jewish self-identification since Jeremiah's time.

11. Consider how the book fits within the "evolution" of religion.

The relative place of prophetic, Mosaic, and priestly "religions" (i.e., aspects of Yahweh-religion) in the development of the Hebrew/Jewish traditions has long been a topic of discussion. Older scholars such as Julius Wellhausen tended to downgrade priestly religion as formulaic and ritualistic. They considered the prophets to be the closest to God, or at least the closest to the purest expression of the ideals of Hebrew religion.

The various strands of Hebrew/Jewish religion, however, co-existed throughout ancient Israel and on into the "Jewish period," which roughly began with the Babylonian exile and the subsequent return of some, but not all, Jewish communities. Diaspora Judaism is certainly not profitably characterized as ritualistic, formulaic, "dead," and so on. Rather, the biblical books represent a vital conversation going on about significant events like the exile.

It is important to note that prophecy in general and Jeremiah's prophecy in particular had a limited "shelf life" in Hebrew/Jewish religion. Prophecy seems to have begun a rather slow but inexorable decline during the Babylonian period, eventually to be replaced by apocalyptic. Israel began to hope for drastic measures from God, in part as a priestly/prophetic/wisdom response to a dramatically changed world. Their situation was marked by chaos, persecution, and the difficulty of maintaining contact and continuity with ancient religious traditions. Reinterpretations of both prophecy and apocalyptic in particular, of course occurred up to the present day. But even this is "nothing new under the sun" (Eccl 1:9).

12. Do *not* make Jeremiah into a Christian prophet.

With regard to the fulfillment of prophecy, John Wesley wrote: "A passage of Scripture, whether prophetic, historical, or poetical, is in the language of the New Testament fulfilled when an event happens to which it may with great propriety be accommodated."[7] This seems to mean that there may be many fulfillments of a specific prophecy, all of which are noted after the fact and many of which may be foreign to the significance attached to the original prophecy. A famous non-Jeremianic example of this occurs in the reinterpretation in Matthew 1 of the sign of the birth given in Isaiah 7. In Isaiah, the baby is the sign of deliverance. In Matthew, the baby is the agent of deliverance.

When considering Jeremiah 31:31–34, one could easily get the mistaken impression that because Christian interpreters from earliest days read it in light of the new covenant inaugurated by Jesus, this must have been what Jeremiah had in mind. Such an understanding robs Jeremiah (or Isaiah) of his original significance as the bearer of the word of the Lord for the particular situations in which he preached. Undoubtedly, there is significance for Christianity in Jeremiah's prophecy. But Jeremiah could not possibly have had Jesus (much less the eucharist) in mind when he wrote with new covenant language. Jeremiah preached for *his* immediate situation. Once that immediate situation passed and Jeremiah's words had been preserved, new situations were bound to arise by which those words could be fulfilled.

13. Consider the problem of true and false prophecy.

Contemporary readers of Jeremiah are in a much better situation to evaluate his prophecy than Jeremiah's original hearers, not to mention his original readers (see Jeremiah 36 for the transition from prophetic speech to prophetic writing). They had to make the decision then based on limited information. Later readers have the advantage of knowing the rest of the story. The book of Jeremiah is preserved because he was right, because he spoke the word of the LORD. But it would not have been possible to know that immediately.

One way to deal with the problem of true and false prophecy is the "dueling banjoes" scene of chapter 28. A comparison of the Septuagint (Greek) translation of Jeremiah with the Masoretic (Hebrew) Text yields interesting results. The Masoretic Text identifies Hananiah, Jeremiah's opponent in this story, as simply "the prophet." But the LXX consistently refers to him as "false prophet." Although he turned out to be a false prophet, preachers should recognize that truth and falsity in prophecy is determined, by and large, on the accuracy with which it is fulfilled (cf. Deut 18:15–22).

Those who originally heard the prophecy had to decide between one and the other; there was no third option. They did not know which was right. In fact, they would not know until Hananiah's word was proven wrong two years later. In short, preachers today should note that contemporary hearer/readers possess more complete information that makes the right decision somewhat easier to make.

14. Relate ethics and theology in a consistent manner.

For Jeremiah, ethics were every bit as important as proper worship practices, avoiding idolatry, and so on. One place where we see this idea is the Temple Sermon in Jeremiah 7, with the accompanying narrative of its delivery in chapter 26. This was clearly delivered some years before the destruction of the first temple in 586 BC and later recalled by Jesus in the cleansing of the second temple. The sermon struck at the heart of some of the cherished traditions and institutions upon which official Hebrew religion was built. Like Hosea (Hos 6:6) and Micah (Mic 6:6–8) before him and Jesus (Matt 12:7) and James (Jas 4:15–17) after him, Jeremiah is concerned with ethics. He is particularly concerned that Israel treats well those who have no one to look out for their interests (resident alien, orphan, widow—the poor and disenfranchised in society). Such right treatment takes precedence over perfection in the religious sphere. Ethical behavior and religious correctness are inseparable.

Christians should work to enhance justice and to eliminate injustice. This is especially the case in the local communities where our churches serve, for that is where we can have the greatest influence. Theological formulations and the precise articulation of them are fine, but such activities are not the true essence of religion. If we confess we love God and hate our neighbor, what credit is that? Holiness must naturally include both the vertical dimension (righteousness before God) and the horizontal dimension (righteousness before humanity). Consider the Ten Commandments: on the first tablet were written four commandments for the proper respect of God, and on the second tablet were written six commandments for the proper respect of other persons.

15. Do *not* look for literal fulfillment of prophecy.

I dealt with this topic briefly above in the discussion of true and false prophecy, as well as in the injunction not to make Jeremiah a Christian prophet. I turn now to yet another strange, paradigmatically enigmatic phrase predicting, "those nations [whom Nebuchadnezzar destroyed] will serve the king of Babylon seventy years. When the seventy years are over, I will punish the king of Babylon and that whole nation—Oracle of Yahweh—for the iniquities, and I will make it a desolation forever" (Jer 25:10–11; see 29:10).

For Jeremiah, this phrase indicates that the time in Babylon will be lengthy but not forever. As it turns out, the time between the destruction of the first temple (586 BC) and the opening of the second temple (515 BC) was 71 years. Preaching should not make too much of the almost-but-not-quite-correct prediction. What is most important here is that God set limits for Jerusalem's devastation and Babylonian's dominance: God promised to destroy the city of Babylon.

This last part of the prediction—the destruction of Babylon after seventy years—did not occur. This inaccuracy led two other Old Testament books to reinterpret this prophecy of seventy years in interesting ways. 2 Chronicles 36:22–23 links the rise of King Cyrus of Persia with the fulfillment of the prophecy. The apocalyptic vision in Daniel 9:1–2 extends the "time of Jerusalem's desolation" from 70 to 490 years! Neither one of these inner-biblical interpretations of Jeremiah is "literal" as we usually think of this term. This phenomenon is actually a good working model for the reinterpretation of Scripture to consider those other things that could not have been on the minds of its writers. Such reinterpretation also happens every time we step into the pulpit with a word from the Lord.

Conclusion

The book of Jeremiah is certainly complex! But it need not appear hopelessly daunting. On the one hand, like all biblical materials, it will yield rich insights for the thoughtful reader and preacher when treated carefully. On the other hand, misinterpreting Jeremiah can lead to the worst kinds of error. However, careful working through the issues of this book will be rewarding for both the serious lay reader and the nurturing preacher. The inspiration of Scripture continues beyond the production of Scripture into its reading, both now and into the future.

1. Unless otherwise indicated, all translations are the author's.
2. Note that the last of these is only reported in Jer 52:30.
3. Shaye J. D. Cohen, *From the Maccabees to the Mishnah* (2nd ed.; Louisville: Westminster John Knox, 2006), 195, 197.
4. Ibid., 203.
5. Alex Varughese and Mitchel Modine, *Jeremiah 26–52: A Commentary in the Wesleyan Tradition* (New Beacon Bible Commentary; Kansas City, MO: Beacon Hill Press of Kansas City, 2010), 270.
6. "The Declaration of the Establishment of the State of Israel: May 14, 1948." Online: http://www.mfa.gov.il/mfa/peace%20process/guide%20to%20the%20peace%20process/declaration%20of%20establishment%20of%20state%20of%20israel (accessed 2 December 2010).
7. Quoted in H. Ray Dunning, *Grace, Faith and Holiness: A Wesleyan Systematic Theology* (Kansas City, MO: Beacon Hill Press of Kansas City, 1988), 572.

21

Preaching Daniel:
Delivering Daniel from the Den of Distractions
Jim Edlin

Introduction

I hesitate to tell people I wrote a commentary on Daniel. When the subject comes up, people get nervous. They seem to be waiting for me to pull out a six-foot chart that maps the end of human history. I do not have such a map. Nor do I think Daniel intended to give us one.

I understand the uneasiness of folk. The dreams and visions in Daniel are strange. Like many people, for years I focused on certain stories in Daniel but did not know what to do with the prophet's bizarre experiences. I assumed only a few highly informed experts could figure them out. I thought a person must make complex cross-references to other obscure passages in various biblical books to make sense of things. Even then, I was not sure they made sense.

Through choices I did not make, I ended up working with the book of Daniel and discovered something amazing. The message of Daniel is not very complicated. At its core, the book is an intense study of the sovereignty of God and its implications for the life of the believer. Through both entertaining stories and surreal visions, Daniel affirms God overrules the rulers of this world. Therefore,

God's people can risk remaining faithful in an unfriendly world.

Unfortunately, we can obscure this simple but profound message when we attempt to preach the text. The bedazzling images passing before our eyes quickly confuse us. Much worse, a mixture of scholarly and not-so-scholarly discussions can entangle our thoughts and distract us from the text. But if we maintain focus, we will discover a gold mine of spiritual riches that can shape lives for an eternity.

In this essay, I present five things I avoid when preaching from the book of Daniel. Then I suggest ten points I include in a sermon series over this book.

Distractions for Preachers of Daniel

First, let me identify some pitfalls to avoid as the preacher deals with Daniel. These can be distractions that keep us from proclaim God's message clearly.

1. The quest for the original author and audience

Normally, we encourage expositors to explore the world of the original author and audience of a text when preparing for a sermon. This enables us to gain perspective by "living in the text" prior to living it out. First ask, "What did it mean?" before asking, "What does it mean?"

Daniel is a book that eludes a definitive answer on this issue, however. For several centuries, scholars have debated who wrote the material and to whom it was written. One can give solid arguments on behalf of both a sixth and second century BC dating. Neither date offers definitive proof for rigorous scholarship or scriptural conservatism or liberalism. A person can hold either date with intellectual integrity *and* maintain a high view of the inspiration of Scripture.

One's position on this debate does color interpretation of certain passages. For example, a sixth-century dating considerably enhances the element of predictive prophecy in the book. Likewise, a second-century dating diminishes that element. But the book is about more than whether God can and does predict future events. Of course, he can and does. The rest of prophetic literature clearly affirms God's knowledge of the future. This truth does not depend on the book of Daniel.

Rather than become enmeshed in arguments of dating, one might do better observing the parallels between the settings of sixth century and second century BC Judaism. Both experienced the rise and fall of earthly kingdoms. Both knew the intense hostility that such kingdoms displayed toward the people of God's kingdom. This is the essential setting of the book's first recipients. They live in a world unfriendly toward God and his people. The hostility is certainly more intense in the second century under the Seleucid rule of Antiochus IV. But sixth-century Judaism also experienced strong opposition from surrounding entities and felt the heavy hand of a dominating empire in the Persians.

2. The identification of each image

A second distraction to avoid is attempting to match each image of the text with historical realities. Occasionally, the text does this for us, as in Daniel 8:20–22. Most of the time, images leave interpretation open. This is the nature of apocalyptic literature. It paints pictures in broad strokes and does not define details.

The four kingdoms of chapters 2 and 7 are a good example. Scholars disagree over how to assess these images. They offer three plausible ways of reading the kingdoms, if one wants to make the identification. However, one can lose the bigger message while defending one position over another. The point of these chapters is that earthly kingdoms come and go, each perpetrating its own kind of violence. None stands forever. The kingdom of God overcomes each in turn and outlasts them all.

3. The calculation of numbers

The most tempting distraction from the message of the book of Daniel is the exercise of calculating numbers. This is fascinating business. Many efforts have *almost* produced remarkable correspondences to key points in human history. But one needs to admit that none of the mathematical computations of the numbers in Daniel is without problems. At the end of each formulation is a qualification or exception of some kind. Nothing fits perfectly.

The failure of centuries of calculations should teach us a lesson. Maybe the point of the book is not the addition and subtraction of numbers. Perhaps we should hear these numbers instead as symbols. This is what one would expect of numeric references in apocalyptic literature: the literature saturated with surreal images and symbols.

4. The quest for detailed future predictions

The calculation of numbers is usually associated with another pitfall: the desire to discover details of the future. Daniel certainly speaks of future events, but not in the kind of detail that some might hope. Even when scholars construct complex explanations of Daniel's words in reference to Ezekiel or the book of Revelation, the particulars of future events do not become clearer. Reading Scripture over against Scripture is an important principle of exegesis. In this case, it does not provide the clarity about specific future events some might imagine. The reason for this is that people read obscure passages in reference to other obscure passages. A sounder approach is to read *obscure* passages in light of *clearer* ones.

The many failed predictions of the end of the world erroneously based on Daniel should deter us from this path. The words of Jesus should guide us: "About that day or hour no one know," he says about end times, "not even the angels in heaven, nor the Son, but only the Father" (Matt 24:36 NIV). On another occasion, Jesus told his disciples, "It is not for you to know the times or dates the Father has set by his own authority" (Acts 1:7 NIV). In light of Jesus' words, one would assume the purpose of a book like Daniel was not to provide a map of end-time events. It is the affirmation that God is in the midst of God's world right now. It is only secondarily about the end of human history. Exactly what things might look like in those final days is sketchy. Daniel only tells us the most important fact clearly: God will win in the end.

5. The pessimism of fatalism

The fifth pitfall I avoid when preaching from Daniel is the implication that this world is inevitably deteriorating toward evil. The message of Daniel is much more positive than that.

Daniel presents striking images of perverted world systems and their demented evil leaders. But it also reminds us that faithful followers need not wait until the end of time to witness God's kingdom on earth. God reigns over all creation now. There is never a time when God's kingdom is absent from this earth. God's dominion is an "eternal dominion; his kingdom endures from generation to generation" (Dan 4:34 NIV).

Daniel affirms human choice in each generation matters. Everything is not predetermined. God's people are not victims of evil rulers in this world. This is why the book urges believers to take a stand—like Daniel and his friends—and change the course of events in this world. Refuse the food that defiles. Do not bow to foreign gods. Keep praying to the one true God. If necessary, be like Daniel's friends who "were willing to give up their lives rather than serve or worship any god except their own God" (Dan 3:28 NIV).

Such choices alter the outcome of life on earth. God's people play a significant role in the unfolding of human history. We dare not succumb to the pessimism of fatalism. We must embrace the optimism of God's sovereignty and grace that Daniel encourages.

Ideas for Preachers of Daniel

This brings us to consider major ideas in Daniel upon which the preacher might focus. The book contains profound theological insights as well as practical material for 21st century believers. Ironically, through fantastic stories and cryptic images it gets at the core of life for a follower of Christ. It speaks to the struggles believers face every day as they attempt to live faithfully in a world hostile toward God and the people of God.

The first six chapters present six stories of life from ground level. They portray life as we see it on earth. The final six chapters relate four visions from heaven's perspective. In both, we find people living in a world like our own. These people face challenges we must encounter.

1. The challenge of cultural engagement

The first chapter establishes the setting of an unfriendly ancient world that looks very familiar to us. A secular government appears to hold all the power. Babylon rules and seemingly suppresses the effects of God in that world. Education, religion, housing, vocation, and even diet fall under the control of an anti-God state.

We must note two points from this chapter. First, God's kingdom moves forward in spite of outward appearances. God is at work behind the scenes. God delivered Judah into Nebuchadnezzar's hands (Dan 1:2), moved the heart of a Babylonian official (1:9), and gave knowledge and understanding to Daniel and his friends (1:17).

Second, while God is at work, Daniel must navigate the turbulent waters of cultural engagement. Daniel must decide how to deal with the culture. Will he live within it, apart from it, above it, or beneath it? In some way, he does all of these. He identifies points of connection with the culture, but also draws lines of distinction from it. At one point, he "resolved not to defile himself with the royal food and wine" (Dan 1:8 NIV). He models what it means to be holy in an unholy world.

2. The challenge of intimidating human powers

Chapter two presents the story of a king's dream about a multi-metal image. As I suggested before, the point of this dream is not to map out events about the end of human history. Rather, it proclaims the truth that God overpowers the political systems of this world. No matter how spectacular they may be—gold, silver, bronze, or iron—God brings the kingdoms of earth down with a crushing blow.

This chapter also highlights the superiority of God's wisdom over human wisdom. Questions that the earth's wisest minds could not solve find answers in the One who "reveals deep and hidden things" and "knows what lies in darkness" (Dan 2:22 NIV). God outwits the wisdom of this world.

3. The challenge of the siren call to conformity

In chapter three, the impressive yet pretentious worship of pagans creates an alluring illusion. It calls God's people to mindless conformity with the masses. But Shadrach, Meshach, and Abednego stand against its seduction. They prefer a fiery furnace to the false fervor for a fake deity. Their bold testimony is a model for believers. After declaring their God can deliver them, they say, "But even if he does not, we want you to know, Your Majesty, that we will not serve your gods or worship the image of gold you have set up" (Dan 3:18 NIV).

For their faithfulness, God delivers the three *in* the fire not *from* it. They experience the horror of being thrown into the flames. But they also know the ecstasy of divine rescue.

4. The challenge of arrogant leaders

Chapters four and five help believers who live under the oppression of arrogant leaders. In chapter four, we meet the epitome of hubris in Nebuchadnezzar, one of the most powerful rulers of the ancient world. His own testimony reveals that God hates human arrogance, in large part because it fails to recognize God's sovereignty. Human haughtiness also disrupts the Creator's designs for the world. God ordered things so that leaders might care for creation. In the image of the king's dream, leaders are to be like a mighty tree that stretches to heaven, nourishing and protecting those under the leaders' domain.

God deals decisively with leaders who do not fulfill their God-given role. Ironically, the most powerful of humanity joins the lowliest creatures scavenging for life in the fields. The one who upsets the order of creation experiences the personal effects of disorder. By his own testimony, Nebuchadnezzar admits that God can humble the proud (Dan 4:37).

5. The challenge of trivializing the sacred

In a sequel to chapter four, chapter five tells of the downfall of another arrogant leader, Belshazzar. He should have learned from Nebuchadnezzar's experience, but he did not. His mishandling of the sacred displays his arrogance. He treats the things of God as if they do not matter. Such sacrilege carries devastating personal and national consequences. Leaders who do not appropriately ac-knowledge God bring down an entire nation as well as themselves.

God responds swiftly to sacrilege. With an ominous message from a disembodied hand, God declares that God *alone* numbers, weighs, and divides the lives of those who do not acknowledge what they hold in their hands (Dan 5:23). So that very night, the arrogant king dies, and God hands over his kingdom to his enemies.

6. The challenge of oppressive human law

Without a doubt, the most popular story in Daniel is the lions' den in chapter six. This dramatic story tells of God's deliverance and the rewards for those who remain faithful. But there is much more to this story!

Chapter six also focuses on the problem of human law. It can create an illusion of permanence and stability that earthly kingdoms do not really possess. False claims lead to oppression. The king's decree in this story blocks even the king from what he knows is right. And it endangers the state's most faithful citizen: Daniel. Thankfully, in the end, the laws of the Medes and Persians, which were not repealable (Dan 6:8), are overturned. Only the kingdom of Daniel's God offers real stability. It is the dominion that truly "will not be destroyed" and "will never end" (6:26 NIV).

7. The challenge of chaos of human governments

With chapter seven, the genre shifts to apocalyptic styled visions. These visions offer a heavenly perspective of human kingdoms rather than an earthly perspective. However, the message of the visions remains the same. God holds absolute control over earthly kingdoms. Believers can remain faithful to the end.

The vision of chapter seven stands as the centerpiece of the book. It sketches a broad overview of human history for which later visions will give more detail. It completes the Aramaic section of the book that began in Daniel 2:4 and reaffirms the key messages of the stories in chapters 1–6.

The vision's portrayal of beasts emerging from a turbulent sea illustrates how human rule apart from God creates chaos. Violence, terror, and destruction mark earthly kingdoms. Under such domains, God's people suffer. They struggle not only with the challenges identified in earlier chapters, but also with the confusion perpetrated by tyrannical rulers whose governments resemble grotesque monsters.

In striking contrast to the chaotic earthly systems, God's kingdom exudes order and tranquility. The eternal God, appropriately called "the Ancient of Days" in this vision, sits enthroned over his creation in control of everything. He strips earthly kingdoms of their authority and turns this authority over to "one like a son of man, coming with the clouds of heaven" (Dan 7:13 NIV). The assurance for God's people is that God judges evil and brings order out of the chaos. One day God will establish a new, messianic kingdom "that will never be destroyed" (7:14 NIV). In New Testament terms, this is the kingdom that Jesus Christ came to establish. He is the Son of Man who has come and will again be "coming on the clouds of heaven with power and great glory" (Matt 24:30 NRSV).

8. The challenge of deluded leaders

The vision of chapter eight expands upon the previous vision. It portrays in more detail the terror that human governments cause by comparing the Persian and Greek empires to two combative animals: a ram and a goat.

This vision emphasizes the violence created by deluded rulers who imagine they are divine. Each ruler pursues his goal of greatness and reaches it, only to fall as the next power brings him down. The last king in this vision, undoubtedly Antiochus IV, displays the extreme absurdity by trying to set himself up against the forces of heaven. By doing this, he stands as the quintessential antichrist. Such a foolish illusion exacts a heavy toll upon God's people and will result in "astounding devastation" (Dan 8:24 NIV).

The promise of the vision is that God will end this turmoil. In whatever way one might interpret the exact amount of time conveyed by the 2,300 evenings and mornings of Daniel 8:14, God has numbered the days of these rulers.

9. The challenge of corporate sin

Chapter nine begins with a prayer of confession that affirms one of prophetic literature's most fundamental points: the choices of the people of Israel brought about the exile to Babylon. God is merciful and forgiving (Dan 9:9). But God is also righteous in all that God does (9:14). Therefore, God judges the sins of a nation.

This prayer establishes the context for one of the most misunderstood visions of the book. Daniel pleads for God's mercy while acknowledging that God's people still have been disobedient (Dan

9:14). God's response to Daniel's prayer comes in a cryptic vision. An angel announces an extension of the judgment of exile. It will continue for a period of "seventy sevens," an indefinite amount of time into the future (9:24).

How long will that time be? According to the vision, this will be until people, among other things, "put an end to sin" and "bring in everlasting righteousness" (Dan 9:24 NIV). The point is that human choices matter. They play a major role in how history will unfold. Sin extends judgment. Righteousness ends it.

The vision sketches a general movement of history in mysterious phrases and terms. There are three periods: "seven sevens," "sixty-two sevens," and "one seven" (Dan 9:25–27). Again, readers should not calculate these numbers but interpret them as symbols. They promise periods of rebuilding and a coming messiah. But they also warn of eras of war and desolation.

10. The challenge of temporal focus

The final three chapters of the book contain an extended vision. This vision emphasizes the comforting thought that spiritual realities lie behind physical realities and actually hold greater significance. What happens in heaven does not stay there. Heavenly activities influence earthly endeavors.

These are important words to remember in the midst of a tumultuous world. As the vision reminds us, God's people live in a world continually at war with itself. Kings of the earth, like Ptolemaic and Seleucid rulers in chapter eleven, persist in constant conflict. On occasion, very contemptible kings like Antiochus IV appear on the scene. At such times, it is comforting to know that suffering only lasts for a season and is not God's last word for believers.

The hope of life beyond this world found toward the end of this vision is one of the clearest in all of the Old Testament. The angel proclaims in Daniel 12:2–3, "Multitudes who sleep in the dust of the earth will awake: some to everlasting life, others to shame and everlasting contempt. Those who are wise will shine like the brightness of the heavens, and those who lead many to righteousness like the stars for ever and ever" (NIV). These words of hope and warning encourage believers never to give up on an eternal focus.

The book ends with a personal word of hope for Daniel. An angel says, "You will rest and then at the end of the days you will rise to receive your allotted inheritance" (Dan 12:13 NIV). Daniel knows that, with God, there is more beyond this life. This is the hope the book conveys to all those who must live under the oppression of hostile world systems.

Conclusion

The book of Daniel clearly has much to say to our contemporary world. Communities of faith over the centuries have searched its pages for spiritual nurture. My hope is that preachers and teachers today will continue to proclaim its God-inspired messages. More than ever, our people need to rest in God's sovereign rule and remain true to their commitments to him. We need to be assured repeatedly that God's "dominion is an everlasting dominion that will not pass away" and that God's "kingdom is one that will never be destroyed" (Dan 7:14).

22

Selected Themes from Seldom Heard Prophets: Proclaiming Nahum through Malachi

Laurie J. Braaten

Not many can say they have heard or preached a sermon on Nahum. Even fewer would consider preaching on the book. The same goes for Habakkuk through Malachi. Only a few have ever heard a sermon on one of these book that was not connected with a building program or tithing. And who knows anything about Zephaniah? Perhaps Zechariah comes up in discussions about the first or second advent of Christ, but little else is known about the book. It is a shame how much we ignore these books, because they contain rich teaching.

Some Historical Background

Before exploring these six prophets, a little background would be helpful. These books are part of a larger work, the Minor Prophets, whom the ancient Hebrews called the "Book of the Twelve." This is an inspired work in its own right, probably arranged and theologically shaped in the late post-exilic era (fifth through fourth centuries BC). When interpreting books within the Book of the Twelve, we must place them within this broader historical and theological context.

The prophets under discussion fall into two natural groupings. The first three—Nahum, Habakkuk, and Zephaniah — generally belong to the seventh century BC (see 2 Kgs 21–25). This era is marked by Judean submission to Assyria, idolatry under Manasseh and Amon (687–40),[1] the reforms of Josiah (640–609), the ministry of Jeremiah (627–580) and a relapse under Josiah's successors (609–586). During this time, Assyria fell (612) and Babylon began to intervene in Judean affairs (604).

The second group—Haggai, Zechariah, and Malachi—falls in the post-exilic period (ca. 520–450; see Ezra–Nehemiah). Returnees from exile attempted to rebuild their religious and political community. Setbacks, discouragement, and relapses characterized this time.

Some Themes from the Book of the Twelve

1. Avoid hasty correspondences.

When proclaiming material from the Book of the Twelve, draw ancient and contemporary comparisons carefully. This means avoiding simple one-to-one correspondences, however appealing and obvious they might seem. One thing to avoid is viewing God's people as the "good guys" and outsiders as the "bad guys." The Book of the Twelve has more to say about the sins of God's people than the sins of outsiders. Even in Nahum, the prophet's condemnation of Assyria's idolatry and violence includes a condemnation of the nations who helped Assyria or tried to be like her. Sometimes, this included Judah. Kings like Manasseh and Amon submitted to imperialistic policies of this evil Assyrian empire and adopted its idolatrous worship.

We must remember this when attempting to apply these passages today. God's people from time to time need correction, because they have adopted the idolatrous or imperialistic qualities of ungodly nations. Sometimes the nations or outsiders get it right, while God's messengers fail due to their desire for punitive justice (see especially Jonah).

Likewise, there is no simple straight-line connection between nations mentioned in these prophets and any group today. Judah or Israel of the Bible is not the nation of Israel today, nor is the temple in Jerusalem a current local church. Assyria, Babylon, and Persia are not current nations. The occupation of the same geographical space does not result in the occupation of the same biblical place.

We must make even rough identifications with caution, such as the equation of Judah/Israel with God's people today. Israel of the Bible was a Yahwistic theocracy. No such nation, religion, or political group, party, or movement can claim such status today. Throughout the biblical period, it was apparent that religion and politics made strange bedfellows. Much of the history of late biblical prophecy is a testimony to the fact that the desired theocratic rule of the LORD, presided over by divinely appointed kings and priests, would not work in the present age as long as sinful humanity had a hand in it. Only in the new Age—on the other side of the resurrection—can God's ideal messianic rule succeed on earth. Until then, no nation, political party or movement, or Christian group can claim to represent God fully on earth without a trace of skewed or self-serving motives.

2. It's not about revenge, God's or ours.

A quick reading of Nahum might leave us with the impression that God is vindictive. We might think there is scriptural justification for revenge for wrongs against God or God's people. Others might look on this book with disgust as another example of the Old Testament "God of wrath."

Both responses are unjustified. One should not compare God's vindication to petty human revenge. Nor is it merely a matter of "justice served" or "getting even." The word translated "vengeance" in Nahum and elsewhere should not be construed as revenge. A better translation is "vindication" or the divine act of setting right. It is the restoration of God's people, all peoples, and the entire creation to the *shalom* God intended from the beginning. This positive goal of vindication often involves divine removal of corporate evil that works against God and creation's *shalom*. Vindication is an expression of corrective justice as restorative love.

We should not understand God's vindication expressed as judgment against the nations as a reward to Judah for its faithfulness. The track record of Judah at the time was rather dismal. God is acting to vindicate the divine name and release creation from an oppressive power.

These books do not provide justification for human revenge or for a nation to set things right. Vindication is *God's* job. Nations have mixed motives inconsistent with God's concerns. There is no direct biblical justification for us to implement God's wrath or exercise righteous anger. Like Nahum 1:2, Leviticus 19:18 describes God as a vindicator and keeper of anger. In Leviticus, God explicitly forbids humans from vindicating and bearing a grudge against a neighbor. Instead, the command is to "love your neighbor as yourself" (quoted by Jesus in Mk 12:31 and parallels). When the psalmists pray for God's wrath to be poured out upon the ungodly, they release their plans for revenge and allow *God* to act. When God answers such a prayer in Psalm 12, God's response is not couched in the language of revenge. Rather, God will act for the sake of the oppressed (Ps 12:5).

Jesus also taught non-retaliation in the Sermon on the Mount (Matt 5:38–48). Paul's comments in Romans 12:14–21 allude to Jesus' teaching. He advises Christians to bless persecutors, not to repay evil for evil, and never to avenge oneself. After all, the Scriptures (the Old Testament!) say vengeance belongs to God (Deut 32:35; perhaps also Nah 1:2). Rather, Christians should feed their enemies (Rom 12:20). The reason for such radical behavior is that evil will overcome those who use evil (i.e., retaliation). The best way to overcome evil is with good (Rom 12:21). The Christian's obligation is to love one another (Rom 13:8–10, which includes a citation of Lev 19:18). When the words "anger" and "righteousness" appear in the same sentence in James 1:20, it states that human anger does not produce God's righteousness. Justifying one's wrath as "righteous anger" would not cut it with James. (See the discussion concerning revenge above.)

3. It's a call to worship, not a call to arms.

When prophets in Israel announced judgment on other nations, Israel often expected to go to battle. *False* prophets often issued such calls to arms (e.g., 1 Kgs 22). But there is clearly no call to arms in Nahum, but only a call to worship (Nah 1:15).[2] Yes, there will be celebration in the world because of the release of the oppressed and the alleviation of suffering (Nah 3:19). But this is a far cry from the smug gloating of victors. One may avoid such gloating by acknowledging that God's honor is at stake and giving God the glory for vindicating those who suffer. We ask humbly that God's work against sin continue, even if it includes purging the church.

4. God's corrective justice is important.

We live in a world where bad things happen to good people. Life is not always fair. The prophets all agree God desires a fair and well-ordered world. They agree God will take corrective steps (divine judgment) when things go wrong (Nah; see also Hab 1:2–4; 2:6–19; Amos; Mic; Isa). This concern goes beyond defending God's people or individual believers from the world's evil doers. God cares about all who suffer unjustly.

God will eventually judge oppressive powers for their idolatry and abuse of others. But one should not construe this as an outmoded portrayal of the Old Testament "God of wrath" against wrongdoers. This does not mean God's anger opposes love. Rather, God's wrath and corrective justice are one side of the coin; God's love is the other side of that same coin. God's goal is to set right or restore a broken world.

5. God's redemption is far-reaching, and so is sin.

In the Book of the Twelve, God's concerns embrace all areas of life. The word "salvation" means "deliverance." It refers to God setting right the whole creation and maintaining a just social order (Hab 2:6–16). This is what the Old Testament describes as *shalom*, often translated as "peace," but more properly rendered as "well being" or "wholeness." Salvation is not just about individuals getting saved and going to heaven, to which this section of Scripture only faintly hints. Salvation is comprehensive. It extends *throughout* God's creation.

In the Bible, sin works against God's salvation or *shalom.* When the prophets mention sin, the worship of other gods is usually first on the list. A list of failures is usually given to show resistance to God's *shalom*: lack of justice in legal proceedings (e.g., Amos 5:10–12; Hab 1:4), failure to care for the suffering and marginalized in society (widows, orphans, Levites, and resident aliens; e.g., Isa 10:2; Zech 7:10; Mal 3:5; cf. Jas 1:27), taking advantage of and cheating people (Amos 2:6–8; 8:4–6; Mic 2:2; Hab 2:6–8), and the (direct or indirect) destruction of God's creation (Isa 24:4–8; 33:9; Jer 12:10–11; Hos 4:1–3).

This last one is the most surprising to many Christians. God cares about creation and judges those who abuse the earth. Habakkuk associates destruction of the earth with sins against humanity (Hab 2:8, 17). Babylon, like Assyria, pillaged the earth for grandiose building projects to glorify king and empire. They plundered the land to meet insatiable desires. They destroyed field and forests to build lavish palaces for their kings. Such anti-creation policies are condemned (e.g., Isa 14:17–22).

We find similar concerns in the New Testament, where we read all creation groans for salvation (Rom 8:22). Christ's work is comprehensive; the cross reconciles the whole created order to God (Col 1:19–20). The book of Revelation, like the prophets, says God will judge those who destroy the earth. God seeks to bring God's kingdom to the earth (Rev 11:18; see 11:15). While we often seem primarily concerned with our personal ethics (e.g., maintaining a pure character before God), the Bible moves beyond personal piety to concern for the welfare of others and God's creation.

The church sometimes stands up for the powerless. But it often does not. The views of Christians are often inconsistent. We may express concerns for the innocent lives lost in abortions, but we express less concern for innocent lives lost in wars. Some Christians provide for children whose mothers chose not to abort them. But many protest abortions but do not support services for new mothers.

Sadly, sometimes Christians determine the importance of an issue based on monetary rather than moral matters. When we discuss caring for creation, for example, the focus often shifts to the cost (money, jobs) of protecting the environment. Instead, the Christian should consider the Creator's will concerning creation. Regrettably, the major influences to Christian views on these and other issues are typically political parties or media personalities rather than scriptural teaching. The biblical teaching regarding God's concern for the world transcends such human ideologies.

6. God's slowness to act is an expression of divine mercy.

By Nahum's time, Judah had been waiting nearly a century for the fulfillment of God's promise to judge Assyria for its sins against the world (Isa 10:12). Sometimes God's response to injustices seems *very* slow. But I don't think we would want it any other way. If God responded quickly to all sin, none of us would have hope. We would only have the prospect of certain judgment. God's patience and kindness are for *all sinners* so that all might possibly repent (cf. 2 Pet 3:9; Rom 2:4–5). Sinners among God's people do not get a special deal. If anything, God's people are held to a higher standard, because they should know better (Amos 3:1–2). If we ask God to give people "what they deserve," we ask God to suspend mercy, both for others and ourselves.

7. God's use of an agent does not imply God's unqualified approval.

The entire sweep of biblical history shows that God uses Israel and the church despite their frequent lapses into sin and backsliding. God can also use pagan nations. Habakkuk was shocked when he realized God was going to employ the Chaldeans (Babylonians) to judge the wickedness of Judah—and so quickly after God freed Judah from Assyria. Perhaps the prophet forgot the earlier warnings to Judah: that God would use Assyria to judge them for their sins (Isa 7:18–20; 8:4–8; 10:5–6). However, God did not approve of Assyrian brutality or claim that Assyria was trying to follow the LORD. Rather, Assyria was condemned for carrying out its arrogant and idolatrous agenda. It later fell under divine judgment (Isa 10:7–19).

During the past several decades, several scandals have rocked the church. Revelations have exposed the private lives of popular ministers as grossly immoral or even criminal. During such times, people wonder: Were the ministries of these ministers the work of God or the Devil? If God used these people, does that suggest divine approval of their behavior? Habakkuk struggled with questions like these.

God's answer to Isaiah regarding Assyria provides a way out of this conundrum. Although people do evil and immoral things, God can transform these things for the benefit of God's people (see Gen 50:20–21; Rom 8:28). This does *not* suggest that God *causes* bad things or approves of evil doers. But it does suggest God can *use* them.

8. We can be honest with God.

Habakkuk is an example of a prayer warrior who is not afraid to tell God exactly what he thinks about God's actions. He is not alone. We also have the prayers of complaint of the psalmist, the prayers of Jeremiah (see Jer 12–20), and the cries of Job. It is refreshing to see such honesty among God's people.

Life seems unfair and out of control to Habakkuk. He is not afraid to question and challenge God; he gets in God's face. God seems to have ignored Habakkuk's repeated prayers to deliver the oppressed from the wicked (Hab 1:2–4). As soon as God delivers Judah from Assyria, things worsen. Habakkuk wonders, Doesn't God want to help the righteous and punish the wicked? God's answer does not help (1:5–11). How can a good God use a wicked nation against God's own people (1:12–2:1)? Does not working with evil nations impinge on the character of a righteous and holy God?

God's answers to the prophet are revealing. God ignores the prophet's impropriety. God reveals that the righteous will endure the crisis through faithfulness (Hab 2:2–5).[3] As we read Habakkuk, we may wonder why God does not rebuke the prophet for his disrespect. We cannot imagine doing this today. The key seems to be the prophet's surrender to God's will. Although hard to swallow, the prophet continues announcing God's judgment on the wicked (2:6–20), knowing that the innocent will suffer in the process. He does not like what God is about to do, but the prophet maintains his hope that God will set things right despite current circumstances (3:17–19).

One type of challenging denies God's authority and persistently refuses to submit. But this is not what Habakkuk does. His life is testimony that God's people can challenge God when life seems unfair or when God does not seem to make sense. God can handle such challenges. Besides, God knows that some of us are hardheaded!

9. God's judgment often brings collateral damage.

God's judgment against evil institutions is often with collateral damage. God does not remove evil by surgically removing it from society without touching the innocent. Apparently, this is what Habakkuk expected. Due to human social networks, what affects one affects another. Often, the innocent suffer when the guilty are judged. Jesus' parable of the tares (weeds) makes a similar point. Some things are best left for God to sort out (Matt 13:24–30).

We should be careful about our prayer requests. Asking for God's cataclysmic judgment against evildoers could result in more than we imagined. Jeremiah 29 offers a good model. The prophet told the Judean exiles to pray for the enemy, Babylon, because the wellbeing (*shalom*) of God's people was tied to the wellbeing of this despised empire (Jer 29:7). Similarly, the New Testament advises Christians to submit to and pray for rulers to assure a peaceful life (Rom 13:1–7; 1 Tim 2:1–2). The subjects hated most of these rulers. The choice seems to be between God doing some good through the present system or a divine judgment that would cause suffering to guilty and innocent alike.

The recognition of collateral damage during judgment helps make sense of some passages that anticipate the destruction of creation (Zeph 1:2–6, 17–18; cf. Hag 1:10–11). The issue at stake is not the ultimate divine destruction of a sinful creation. The issue is that human sin destroys creation (e.g., Hos 4:1–3). God uses this damage as divine judgment (as in the flood; see Gen 6:11–13).

10. Don't let our theology block our view of God.

Our theological formulations about God's character can prevent us from understanding God's work. Habakkuk is confused, because God contradicts Habakkuk's theology: God is not doing what the prophet thinks proper (Hab 1:12–14). How can God use a wicked nation to punish God's own people? Habakkuk formulated a reasonable view of how God works, so what appeared as divine inconsistencies shocked him. But what the prophet does not consider is that God always enters the sinful world of humanity. God often gets dirty in the process. Of course, when God's association with sinners benefits *us*, we have no problem with that! But if it brings judgment on us, we cry for consistency, fairness, and God's purity.

Theological formulations are necessary and usually helpful. But they also hinder us when our system fails to recognize that we cannot always fit God into our neat categories. They can even be counterproductive if we form our theology according to what *we want to believe*, rather than according to what God wants to show us.

The Bible sometimes gets in the way of what we believe or want to believe about God. I always find it surprising when I read a passage in class and a student blurts out, "Wait a minute! How can that be? Don't we know that God is _____ (fill in the blank)?" I usually point out that this is pitting a theological formulation against the Bible. I find that students rarely abandon their theological formulation over the Bible, because it is discomforting when God suddenly jumps out of a cherished theological box. But if we are going to mature spiritually, we must remain open to Scripture and allow for divine transformation of our views.

11. God's grace is consistent.

After pondering the discussions above, we should not conclude that God is inconsistent. God's apparent tolerance of sinners and evil in the world is completely in character for a God of mercy. The delight of Nahum's audience over God finally judging Nineveh, the dismay of Habakkuk that God would use a sinful nation, and the mixed feelings of Zephaniah's hearers over the salvation of a remnant after a horrifying judgment all have their roots in the experience of this God of grace (see section 15 below).

The words of Malachi sum this up. His audience had charged God with lack of concern, injustice, and inconsistency. Malachi replied that they could observe proof God had not changed in the fact that God had *not* destroyed Judah (Mal 3:6–7)! That is, God is a God of grace. God often does not punish evil as quickly as we would like, certainly not soon enough for Nahum's audience. God sometimes gives the most outrageous sinners a chance to repent (see Jonah) or may even use them to accomplish divine goals (see Isaiah, Jeremiah and Habakkuk). God often spares God's people from the judgment they deserve.

12. Lack of inner commitment can hinder God's work.

At times, it seems God is slow to fulfill promises. This leads some to doubt God cares. This was the situation during the Persian period (Hag, Zech, Mal, Isa 56–66). But the problem often has another source. Lack of commitment can affect how God works. When the people suffered hardships in Haggai's time, for instance, the LORD challenged the people through the prophet to "direct your heart toward your paths" (Hag 1:5, 7).[4] The people lacked inner motivation for doing God's work, including rebuilding the temple and responding to the covenant God made with them when God brought them out of Egypt. This covenant included commands that the people repeat God's redemptive acts toward others by caring for the oppressed: the widow, orphan, and alien among them (Zech 7:9–10; compare Isa 58).

The building of the temple would enable them to gather as a people to worship and glorify the Creator. This would grant opportunities to invite the marginalized to sacrificial meals (Deut 14:28–29). It would also provide means to attract the nations to see God's glory and justice at work (Hag 2:6–9; Mic 4:1–4). In other words, God is not just concerned about a building. After all, it could not "hold" God (1 Kgs 8:27). The structure should bring honor and glory to the Creator, both in terms of the people's corporate worship and their response to God's love by showing the same love to others.

13. It is not by power or might, but only by God's Spirit.

We can only do God's work properly in the power of God's Spirit (Hag 2:4–5; Zech 4:6).[5] The solution to the problem of self-centeredness is not trying harder, another form of self-centeredness. When we operate under our own power or live according to the flesh (Rom 7–8; Gal 5:17–21; 6:7–8), we run a greater risk of infusing our personal agenda, pride, or sinful desires into the project. Abuse, hurt feelings, and broken relationships often follow (1 Cor 3:1–4). God's Spirit brings God's power and resources into the situation. The result is spiritual healing and the extension of God's grace to a broken world.

14. God does not run a retribution/rewards racket.

There is no retribution or reward formula here, neither in Haggai's association of God's blessing with the building of the temple (Hag 1:7–11; 2:6–9) nor in Malachi's mention of blessing with the paying of tithes (Mal 3:8–12). Haggai promises God's *shalom*, "well being."[6] Furthermore, both prophets associate God's blessing of Judah with the nations seeing and responding to God's glory.

To reduce passages like these to a formula for riches is a perversion of Scripture. The promise of God's financial blessing in Scripture is usually associated with an assurance that God will give resources to fulfill divine commands (e.g., Deut 14:29; 15:4–10, 18). This is probably Zechariah's meaning when he says that God will not pour out divine blessing when God's people withhold their blessing from the less fortunate (Zech 7:9–10; cf. Isa 58).

We would do well to put to rest the idea that God will give us more money if we give ten percent of what we earn. Although this idea is not consistent with the Bible, popular Christian speakers and writers continue to proclaim it. If we would focus on how God commands us to live for others rather than how God can make us prosperous, we would then truly be a blessed *and blessing* people.

15. God will purify a remnant for divine purposes.

By the time the reader reaches Zephaniah, one wonders if there is any hope for God's people. The prospect of judgment for repeated failures seems to paint a bleak future. After the exile, the people hold onto hope, fanned by the prophecies of Isaiah 40–55. Yet the great expectations for the future do not pan out. If anything, life seems even harder. For some, life in exile was preferable.

In the midst of trying times of judgment, however, the prophets preach that God will redeem those who remain faithful (Hab 2:4). This does not mean that they will not feel the effects of judgment; they are part of the social and physical network of their sinful neighbors. They will suffer with the rest of the nation, but they will not suffer without hope (cf. Rom 5:3–5). This faithful waiting in hope is also Habakkuk's final word. In the face of devastation, he looks forward to the fulfillment of the divine purposes for God's people (Hab 3:17–19).

Zephaniah and Malachi look forward to a purified remnant emerging out of God's judgment (Zeph 2:1–3; 3:12–13; Mal 3:1–4; 4:1–3). The processes of earthly judgment are painful, like the purification of metals or the burning of chaff. But there will be justice, not only for God's chosen, but for all who call on God's name.

After such judgments, there will be a purified remnant that includes some surprises. God's aim is to restore all creation. Malachi mysteriously speaks of other nations that offer proper worship to Israel's God (Mal 1:11). And although God's judgment sometimes affects creation (Zeph 1; Hag 1:10–11; Joel 1), the Scriptures also depict creation glorifying God and as objects of God's renewal (e.g., Joel 2–3; Jonah 3–4; Ps 104). Such processes of judgment and renewal anticipate the final judgment, when God will make all things new (Rev 21:5).

---

1. All dates are approximate. For further discussion see biblical histories, commentaries, and academic study Bibles (e.g., *New Oxford Annotated Study Bible*).

2. Verse numbers from the English versions are used in this essay when they differ from the Hebrew.

3. The ancient versions are divided as to whether this faithfulness belongs to God, the righteous, or both. In Romans, Paul uses this passage (Rom 1:17) to illustrate both God's righteous act of setting things right through Christ's faithfulness (Rom 3:22) and the faith(fulness) of believers towards Christ.

4. Author's translation; rendered "Consider how you have fared" (NRSV, NIV).

5. "Spirit" is capitalized here, but without suggesting that the teaching regarding Spirit found has progressed into the more developed conception of the Holy Spirit in the New Testament or later church teaching.

6. See discussion on *shalom* above; translated "peace" in NIV, unfortunately as "prosperity" in NRSV.

New Testament Chapters

23

Proclaiming Theological Themes in 2 Corinthians

Frank G. Carver

"So if anyone is in Christ, there is a new creation: everything old has passed away; see, everything has become new!" (2 Cor 5:17).[1]

Introduction

Paul writes with passionate concern for the welfare of "the church of God that is in Corinth" (2 Cor 1:1). All he says is captive to his inner drive for the integrity of "the gospel of Christ" (Gal 1:7). A biblical theology informs and forms his proclamation.

Paul wrote with power (2 Cor 10:10). The secret of his power was in part that he lived in the Scriptures. The Law, the Prophets, and the Writings shaped his outlook on the world, his understanding of himself, and the situation in the Corinthian church. The language of the Psalms was in his blood stream.

For Paul, "God in Christ" sums up the entire history of God's dealing with humankind. His interpretation of Exodus 34:29–35 in 2 Corinthians 3:7–18 reveals his hermeneutic. Reflecting on the text, the Spirit of God overwhelms him with insight into the living Christ. Caught up in the creativity of fulfilled hope, he writes with fresh boldness, "Now the Lord is the Spirit, and where the Spirit

of the Lord is, there is freedom. And all of us . . . are being transformed into the same image from one degree of glory to another"
(3:17–18). The same Spirit that first gave the Exodus passage inspires Paul's fresh reading of this scriptural passage.[2]

Paul knows the Scriptures and the situation in Corinth. Listening
to the Spirit and the church's needs, he understands the Scriptures
in relation to that situation. As he brings the witness of Scripture
to bear on the church, we can infer that the key to our reading of
the Bible *as* Scripture is Scripture itself. *There* we find the primary
interpretive stance for our proclamation of its message.

The role of the church's sacred text in the lives of God's people is
the Bible read as *Scripture.* Second Corinthians is designed to speak
in our personal reading, in our understanding of our calling, and
in the preaching task as the Spirit illumines a transforming word.
This Spirit-inspired function constitutes the authority and power of
Scripture, as it has for the church through the centuries. The Spirit
actualizes and authenticates the Bible as Scripture in faithful communities of discipleship.[3]

We learn from Paul's Spirit-empowered witness to the person
and work of Christ as he applies this witness to every aspect of church
life: its ministry and the lives of its people (see John 16:13–15). The
Scriptures face us with "the arduous task of interpretation,"[4] as we
relate them to life. Paul says, "the Lord is the Spirit, and where the
Spirit of the Lord is, there is freedom" (2 Cor 3:17). Inherently, this
"freedom" involves a Christological-ethical imperative.

When we proclaim Jesus Christ as Lord, God shines "in our
hearts to give the light of the knowledge of the glory of God in the
face of Jesus Christ" (2 Cor 4:5–6). Scripture does this when proclaimed in the same Spirit that gave them. Nothing can better teach
us the nature and meaning of inspiration than personal experience
of it! We can have confidence in the Bible *as* Scripture to speak in
transforming ways to us and through us in the church and to the
world!

Ten Things to Proclaim in a Sermon Series
on 2 Corinthians

1. Proclaim Christ as pre-eminent for our Christian faith.

For the Apostle Paul, Christology was primary. He was concerned that the Corinthians would embrace a different Jesus than the one he proclaimed to them (2 Cor 11:4). The person and work of Christ were indispensable for Paul's life, his gospel, and his ministry (1 Cor 3:11). Paul proclaims that Jesus Christ was "the image of God" in whose face one can see "the light of the knowledge of the glory of God" (2 Cor 4:4–6).

Paul's all-penetrating theme is Christology: "For the love of Christ controls us" (2 Cor 5:14 NASB). Paul sees everything he faces in his apostolic calling in the light of Jesus the Christ, even the humiliations and hardships. He never strays from Christology, whether probing the work of the Holy Spirit or defining his ministry for those who denigrate it.

For Paul, all God's promises are affirmed in Christ. "For this reason it is through him that we say the 'Amen,' to the glory of God" (2 Cor 1:20). If the divine and the human are united in Christ, he is central for all Christian thought and life. Jesus becomes the key to the pattern that organizes the whole.[5] Where is this Jesus, this Christ, and how does he function in our proclamation?

2. Proclaim the life, death, and resurrection of Jesus as central to our life in God.

Here is Paul's gospel: "God was in Christ reconciling the world to Himself" (2 Cor 5:19 NASB). It encompasses the entire life and ministry of Christ: his incarnate life and death, and his resurrection and exaltation in and through which God carries out his redemptive activity in the world. He is "the Lord Jesus Christ" (1:2).

Paul's theology of Christian life and ministry comes to climactic expression as he concludes, "For he was crucified in weakness, but lives by the power of God. For we are weak in him, but in dealing with you we will live with him by the power of God" (2 Cor 13:4). The mysterious and profound deed of the crucified and risen Christ transforms all it touches in Paul's proclamation.

Christ was crucified "in weakness" as one like us who was physically born, lived, and died. This was no apparent weakness. Yet he "lives by the power of God," the "God who raises the dead" (2 Cor 1:9). Jesus' death was not merely a past event followed by a resurrection (4:10). The two are one, continuing event. The risen One remains the crucified One![6]

The incarnate, crucified, and resurrected Jesus is the key to what God is doing everywhere. We proclaim this kind of God, the Christ of the biblical witness. Our witness to Christ crucified and risen is where we supremely touch the holy in proclamation and meditative reflection!

3. Proclaim a new covenant life in and of the Spirit.

Paul speaks of his competence from God through Christ (2 Cor 3:4–5) as a minister of a new covenant characterized by spirit rather than letter, for "the Spirit gives life" (3:6). God's covenant was with the age-long people of God—Moses and the people of Israel (3:7)—with whom the church lives in continuity. This new covenant fulfills the eternal purpose of the God of creation and the LORD of the exodus. To this new people, God gives the Spirit in their hearts as a first installment (1:21–22). Thus, in contrast to the former covenant, accompanying this new covenant is the transformation that comes from the Spirit (3:17–18).

As those "engaged in this ministry" (2 Cor 4:2), we are privileged to announce a life constituted and being transformed by the Spirit of God. This is resurrection life in which we are liberated to "practice the resurrection."[7] Thus "if anyone is in Christ, there is a new creation: everything old has passed away; see, everything has become new! All this is from God" (5:17–18a).

4. Proclaim the way of the cross in Christian life and ministry.

For Paul, Christ provides the pattern for Christians: "you are in our hearts, to die together and to live together" (2 Cor 7:3). The sufferings of Christ (1:5) are indispensible for his ministry in Corinth. Paul's sufferings bring them the comfort of the resurrected Christ (1:6).

Our redemptive participation in the life, death, and resurrection of Christ constitutes what Paul describes as being "in Christ." This participation determines the manner of our personal relationships and ministry to others. By faith, we identify with the cross so that resurrection life might be released in the lives of others (2 Cor 4:10–12).

Paul expresses this way of the cross with the great paradoxes of the Christian life: "afflicted in every way, but not crushed; perplexed, but not driven to despair; persecuted, but not forsaken; struck down, but not destroyed" (2 Cor 4:8–9). He identifies with the physical weakness displayed in the life and death of the earthly Jesus. He sees himself as "carrying in the body the death of Jesus, so that the life of Jesus may also be made visible in our bodies" (4:10).

The harsh realities of life may partake of the redemptive presence of God in Christ and have meaning when we open our lives to the resurrection life of Jesus (2 Cor 4:10–11). This also allows us to view our human vulnerability as an opportunity for God to work (4:12). With Paul, ministry is in essence "power made perfect in weakness" (12:9). We Christians possess a freedom to be and a release to speak (4:13–15) as we share the "same spirit of faith" as the psalmist: "we also believe and so we speak" (4:13; Ps 116:10).

5. Proclaim the hope of life after death.

Inherent in "cross-and-resurrection" faith is the assurance of life after death (2 Cor 4:14). The resurrection of Jesus reaches all who conduct their lives in the "faith-light" of the cross. Otherwise, life is tragic, containing suffering without purpose or meaning.

Paul repeats the declaration—"we do not lose heart" (2 Cor 4:1, 16)—in the context of chapter 4, where he contrasts the temporary nature of human, earthly life with the hope of life after death. His outer nature is failing, but his inner nature is "being renewed day by day" (4:16). Paul's "momentary affliction" prepares him for "an eternal weight of glory beyond all measure" (4:17). Paul focuses on the unseen and eternal rather than on what is seen and temporary (4:18). That is, he directs our attention on a heavenly home that comes from God (5:1–10). God prepares us for the fulfillment of this hope by giving the Spirit as "a guarantee" (5:5). Even "while we are at home in the body . . . we walk by faith, not by sight" (5:7). God's work in us connects us to the next life.

Our motivation is that, "whether we are at home or away, we make it our aim to please him" (2 Cor 5:9). Life after death brings our final accountability to God: "For all of us must appear before the judgment seat of Christ, so that each may receive recompense for what has been done in the body, whether good or evil" (5:10).[8] We proclaim a gospel of ultimate accountability to God for the ethical and spiritual quality of our lives.

6. Proclaim the final triumph of the holy.

Paul expands his "aim to please" God to include cleansing "ourselves from every defilement of body and of spirit, making holiness perfect in the fear of God" (2 Cor 7:1). The expression "the fear of God" reaches back to Paul's declaration that everyone "must appear before the judgment seat of Christ" (5:10). There we will give an account of ourselves as a holy people (6:14–18) and will each receive "what has been done in the body, whether good or evil" (5:10).

For Paul, what we receive at the judgment is the result of the moral and spiritual quality of our lives. Our reward is the kinds of persons we have chosen to be! A direct continuity between the temporal and the eternal exists. God's judgment is not arbitrary. The reward or punishment persons receive will be to live throughout eternity as those persons they chose to be!

"God is holy" means that we live in a universe in which moral and spiritual values triumph in the end! In 2 Corinthians 6:14–7:1, there is no "partnership . . . between righteousness and lawlessness," no "fellowship . . . between light and darkness," and no "agreement" of "the temple of God with idols." Rather, the church is "the temple of the living God" (6:16). God has said, "I will live in them and walk among them, and I will be their God, and they shall be my people. . . . and I will be your father, and you shall be my sons and daughters, says the Lord Almighty" (6:16, 18). Thus, Paul's reaffirmation to "touch nothing unclean" (6:17) declares the ultimate worth of the ethics of the holy. The sanctification of life is an eternal matter. We proclaim the final victory of the holy in God's universe.

7. Proclaim reconciliation for all humanity in Christ.

Paul declares to the Corinthians that "Jesus Christ is in you" (2 Cor 13:5) and that they are "in Christ" (5:17). The latter assertion is at the heart of 2 Corinthians 5:16–6:1, where the controlling theme is that, when a person is in Christ, "there is a new creation: everything old has passed away; see, everything has become new!" (5:17). Paul describes God's work on humanity's behalf as reconciliation, which God accomplished in Christ (5:19). Paul's understanding of God's reconciliation is central to his own life and ministry (5:20). Therefore, a "new creation," a new world-order in Christ, emerges from Christ's death and resurrection. The connotations are both individual and corporate: "everything has become new!" The Christ-event creates a *new* humanity! God's future people have arrived! These folk "are being transformed into the same image from one degree of glory to another" (3:18), with a renewal that prefigures the renewal of the cosmos (Matt 19:28; Rom 8:19–23).

The reconciliation—the overcoming of humankind's alienation from God through Christ's death—began in an objective change (Rom 5:10). God *in Christ* had already dealt with human sin and its devastating effects in such a way that compromises neither the justice nor the holiness of God (2 Cor 5:21). With Jesus' death and resurrection, we proclaim the advent of the new creation *in Christ*. In him, God acted eschatologically and placed the world under his rule.

8. Proclaim the sacramental nature of all God's creation.

Scripture is all about this divine new creation (2 Cor 5:17; Gal 6:15) as constituted by God's holy presence through Christ in the world. However, Paul exhorts the church as "the temple of the living God" in the world to "be separate from them, says the Lord, and touch nothing unclean" (2 Cor 6:16–17). This distinction is against the world's idolatry. Idolatry misuses the good things God created (see Gen 1:31).

God promises the church as "the temple of the living God" that "I will live in them and walk among them, and I will be their God, and they shall be my people" (2 Cor 6:16). God lives among God's people in the incarnate, crucified, and risen Christ. On earth where he lived and yet lives, we seek to make "holiness perfect in the fear of God" (7:1). With the present Christ, we seek to avoid all "quarreling, jealousy, anger, selfishness, slander, gossip, conceit, and disorder" as well as "the impurity, sexual immorality, and licentiousness" (12:20–21) that accompanies idolatrous living.

We proclaim the privilege of treating all of life as sacred as we live in the presence of a holy God. All in life is sanctified in "spiritual worship" (Rom 12:1).

9. Proclaim stewardship as grace.

The Apostle Paul sometimes mentions money. The offering for the economic needs of the Jerusalem church is significant to his ministry (Rom 15:22–28; 1 Cor 16:1–4). Paul applies "the grace of Christian giving" to this project as he plays rhetorically on the Greek word for grace, *charis*, throughout chapters 8 and 9 (2 Cor 8:1, 4, 6,

7, 9, 16, 19; 9:8, 12, 14, 15). "Grace" (*charis*) is one of the theologically significant words that Paul uses to convince the Corinthians that their participation in this offering was essential to them being "Christian." A theology of grace informs Paul's understanding of the stewardship of resources (8:2, 4, 20; 9:5, 12), which originates in the graciousness of God, revealed in Jesus the Christ, who "graces" people to be gracious and generous. Theology informs giving!

Therefore, when Paul mentions grace (*charis*) with regard to the offering, it is a privilege or a "generous undertaking" (2 Cor 8:6, 19). When he urges the Corinthians to be generous and cheerful givers, grace enables them to serve others (9:8).

The entire scope of God's revelation in Christ motivates the stewardship of our resources as grace. The grace of God in Jesus Christ is the measure of all our giving. God has graced us to proclaim this!

10. Proclaim the Trinitarian "fullness of God" (Col 1:19) in the life of the church.

From the beginning of his letter, Paul establishes the Christian life and ministry in a Trinitarian God (2 Cor 1:19–22). His concluding benediction expresses his desire that the church enjoy the blessing of this Trinitarian God in all its ethical implications: "The grace of the Lord Jesus Christ, the love of God, and the communion of the Holy Spirit be with all of you" (2 Cor 13:13). Jesus the Christ is the source of grace. Love comes from God. The "fellowship [*koinōnia*] of the Holy Spirit" (NASB) designates the Corinthians' participation in the life and power of the Holy Spirit, a personal relationship with Christ the Son, God the Father, and the Holy Spirit. The redemptive reality in the person of Jesus by virtue of his crucifixion, resurrection, and exaltation becomes experiential in the life of the church.

The Trinitarian mystery of salvation vibrates with life. Each term—grace, love, fellowship—has theological and transformative implications for the ongoing life of the church. These are as relevant to the churches in today's cities as to the ancient church in Corinth! Although not developed with nuanced precision as in succeeding centuries, these terms call the church to experience God to a fullness or a new depth in relationship beyond what we can even imagine!

Five Things *Not* to Proclaim in a Sermon Series on 2 Corinthians

All five things flow from Paul's concern in 2 Corinthians 11:3–4. All these are based on Paul's reference to "another Jesus . . . a different spirit . . . a different gospel" from what he *himself* had received and proclaimed and what the Corinthians had received from him—the apostolic gospel (1 Cor 15:1–11).

1. Do *not* proclaim a mystical relationship with God that minimizes an incarnate Jesus.

Although Paul's knowledge of Jesus as a historical figure was not his last word, he did know Christ from a human perspective (2 Cor 5:16). The name "Jesus" conveys his humanity, including his suffering and death—flesh and blood. Paul refers to the "meekness and gentleness" but little else of Jesus' life (10:1). Still, *this* incarnate Jesus, whom God raised from actual death, was indispensible for the apostle's gospel. Paul proclaims that God gives "the light of the knowledge of the glory of God in the face of Christ" (4:6). Thus, the incarnate Jesus as the Christ mediates a "Christian" knowledge of God.

A theocentric God-mysticism that has little need for an incarnated Jesus is for Paul a different gospel. I would not proclaim a mystical relationship to God in which that One who "was revealed in the flesh" and "taken up in glory" (1 Tim 3:16) is not front and center.

2. Do *not* proclaim a resurrected, triumphant Lord apart from a suffering, dying Christ.

Paul warned the Corinthians against submitting to "another Jesus than the one we proclaimed" (2 Cor 11:4), that is, Jesus crucified and risen (1 Cor 15:3–4). His Corinthian opponents objected to his apostolic ministry in which "power is made perfect in weakness" (2 Cor 12:9). Their objection suggests they held to a triumphal interpretation of Jesus' ministry, which minimized his humiliation, suffering, and death by crucifixion.

At stake is a theology of the resurrection divorced from a theology of the cross. Thus, the cross becomes only a past event and the church lives in a consistent "resurrection-type" victory. Rather than being two separate events, the resurrection is a chapter in the theology of the cross. "The exalted Christ still bears the nail-marks of the earthly Jesus, but for which he would not be identical with Jesus."[9] The cross is not merely the last stop on his earthly journey. It remains integral to any theology of resurrection.

The implications of a triumphalist misperception of what it means to be "in Christ" of such "another Jesus" are deadly for authentic Christian faith. They result in a "different spirit" and a "different gospel" from the one the church learned from Paul. There would be such a sense of having so fully arrived spirituality that ethics would no longer be an issue. Thus, what one does is automatically right. Moreover, there would be a triumphalist approach to human suffering and tragedy. True Christians have the victory, not just *in* and through, but *over* such!

As to ministry, when Paul wrote that God "in Christ always leads us in triumphal procession" (2 Cor 2:14), the image would be that of a conquering Roman general in the lead rather than a captive staggering in chains at the rear. However, it is the latter Paul intended as "the aroma of Christ to God [as] . . . a fragrance from death to death [and] . . . a fragrance from life to life" (2:15–16). The methodology of a fully Christian ministry is the weakness of the crucifixion releasing the power of the resurrection (13:4)—a "treasure in clay jars" (4:7).

Christian salvation is determined by the person and work of the Christ, who "became poor, so that by his poverty [we] might become rich" (2 Cor 8:9; cf. 5:14–15). Basic to spiritual life and service is that for our sake God "made him to be sin who knew no sin, so that in him we might become the righteousness of God" (5:21). Christ fully participated in our sinful alienation from God throughout his entire life, leading to his death and resurrection (Phil 2:8). God treated Christ as sin, aligning him so completely with sin and its consequences that Christ became indistinguishable from sin itself. Jesus in his life and death became more than a loving example for us to emulate and interpret as we please. *He became sin for us before a holy God!* The suffering and death of Christ continue to constitute who we are as those who live in the power of his resurrection.

I cannot proclaim a triumphant risen Lord apart from a dying Christ, a theology of the resurrection unbalanced by a theology of the cross. Any triumphal Christian life and ministry are characterized by "we are weak in him" and "live with him by the power of God" (2 Cor 13:4). Christology is so crucial that I would be terrified of preaching "another Jesus" than that of the canonical biblical witness!

3. Do *not* proclaim a saving grace independent of character transformation.

When Paul writes about "seeing the light of the gospel of the glory of Christ," Christ *was* and *is* "the image of God" (2 Cor 4:4). Into this image, by "his Spirit in our hearts" (1:22) we who look openly to him in life "are being transformed into the same image from one degree of glory to another" (3:18). To live otherwise is to receive a different spirit (11:4). The ongoing transformation of personal character is an inherent part of devotion to Christ (11:3).

I could not proclaim a reception of the grace of God that does not liberate us for moral and spiritual transformation: "where the Spirit of the Lord is, there is freedom" (2 Cor 3:17). Biblical salvation is thoroughly ethical. Forgiveness of sins and cleansing of heart and life from sin (1 John 1:7, 9) are inherently related. Justification and sanctification *are* a unified "grace-full" work of God in Christ through the Spirit in us (Rom 3:21–8:39). Here is no mere bookkeeping, no hiding of the human condition from the eyes of God (Heb 4:13).

4. Do *not* proclaim a view of Christian living with implications only for this life.

A fully realized eschatology is a different gospel (2 Cor 11:4). It partakes of a future-less eschatology and eliminates any hope beyond this life. The benefits of salvation are pushed into the present with no need of any future transformation: one has "arrived" spiritually, here and now. This does not acknowledge the impact of this life on the next. The purpose of salvation is more therapeutic than moral and spiritual. Such seek to live "by sight" and not "by faith" (5:7).

Rather, Paul's articulation of the gospel focuses on the transformation of life that has implications extending beyond the end of human existence. The inner renewal now happening will be "an eternal weight of glory beyond all measure" (2 Cor 4:17) because it originates in the eternal. By faith, "we have a building from God, a house not made with hands, eternal in the heavens" (5:1). In addition, the eternal significance of the moral dimension of present existence is never far from Paul's mind: "So whether we are at home or away, we make it our aim to please him" (5:9).

I would not proclaim a salvation in which character transformation has no implications for future life. Because our participation in the image of God carries the culminating promise of full transformation into the likeness of Christ (2 Cor 3:18), our present spiritual lives have eternal significance. Christian life has a future! At the judgment seat of Christ, our eternal fate is to exist forever as essentially the kind of persons into which our moral and spiritual choices in this life have formed us. In our kind of world, where the present cries out for future consequences, we will receive "what has been done in the body whether good or evil" (5:10).

5. Do not proclaim your inner spiritual experiences as definitive for others.

Paul knew the joy of inner spiritual experience or the raptures of a mystical life (see 2 Cor 12:1). One report of such an exhilarating moment ironically appears between him mentioning his humiliating escape from Damascus (11:32–33) and his weakness from his debilitating thorn in the flesh (12:7–10). Paul himself was uncertain of the exact nature of this experience. "I do not know; God knows" (12:2–3). He mentions it with great hesitation.

Paul's spiritual experiences apparently gave him the encouragement he needed for his strenuous ministry. But these were so sacred that he kept them between God and himself (see 2 Cor 12:5). Did Paul's power in ministry lie in this hesitancy? In Corinth, there were those of "a different spirit" (11:4) in their spiritual bravado. Rather, Paul refrains from even truthful boasting, "so that no one may think better of me than what is seen in me or heard from me, even considering the exceptional character of the revelations" (12:6–7a). Two dangers accompany our mention of inner spiritual experiences. First, we may call more attention to ourselves than to Christ. Second, we may speak beyond what others can observe in our conduct and hear in our speech. We risk the credibility of our witness.

The French priest, Jean Nicolas Grou (1731–1803), speaks about seeking the "Divine Light" which "is given to do a special work at the moment" and renewed in times of need: "It is well to make a rule to yourself not to speak of these lights to other men, under the pretext of giving God glory or of enlightening them. . . . we waste our grace by too readily pouring it out around us."[10] It is spiritually dangerous for us and for others, except with extreme caution, to instruct them from inner, intimate experiences of the Lord meant for our affirmation and strengthening alone. They are pearls to be closely guarded (cf. Matt 7:6).

Conclusion: Christology!

What I would proclaim from 2 Corinthians for the life, ministry, and even the theology of the church, must be rooted in Paul's view of God "in Christ." I would not proclaim for Christian faith anything that obscures or perverts Paul's witness to what he sees in "the face of Jesus Christ" (2 Cor 4:6).

---

1. Unless otherwise noted, this essay uses the NRSV translation.
2. See Wesley's comment on 2 Tim 3:16 in his *Explanatory Notes upon the New Testament* (London: Epworth, 1958), 794: "The Spirit of God not only once inspired those who wrote it, but continually inspires, supernaturally assists, those that read it with earnest prayer."
3. Joel B. Green, *Seized By Truth: Reading the Bible as Scripture* (Nashville: Abingdon, 2007), 3, 164.
4. James F. Kay, *Preaching and Theology* (St. Louis: Chalice, 2007), 120. See also pp. 7–23.
5. See Kathryn Tanner, *Christ the Key* (Cambridge: Cambridge University Press, 2010), i.
6. Ernst Käsemann, *Jesus Means Freedom* (Philadelphia: Fortress, 1969), 67.
7. Eugene H. Peterson, *Practice Resurrection: A Conversation On Growing Up in Christ* (Grand Rapids: Eerdmans, 2010), 8.
8. A literal translation could be "receive what has been done in the body, whether good or evil."
9. Käsemann, *Jesus Means Freedom*, 68.
10. H. L. Sidney Lear, *The Hidden Life of the Soul* (New York: Longmans, Green and Co., 1935).

24

Listening to Paul's Letter to the Galatians

George Lyons

Introduction

Paul's letter to the Galatians often hides in the shadows of his longer letters. However, Galatians is noteworthy for several reasons. First, this was one of Paul's earliest letters and therefore reflects some of Paul's earlier thought. Second, this letter is more emotional in tone than some of Paul's other letters. Third, the letter is characterized by striking antitheses: divine versus human, before versus after, Spirit versus flesh, Christ versus law, faith versus works, and so on.

Ten Things to Keep in Mind When Reading Galatians

The interpretation of Galatians has been influenced significantly by the assumptions of its readers. Therefore, I wish to offer ten things to keep in mind when reading Galatians so that you may interpret this letter more carefully and responsibly.

I. Put your mirrors away and listen to the biblical text.

Until recently, most commentaries on Galatians claimed Paul wrote this letter to defend himself and his gospel against the charges of Judaizers. Jewish legalists allegedly accused him of being a second-rate apostle, dependent for his authority on the Jerusalem apostles. He was unfaithful to the true gospel and lowered the bar to accommodate Gentiles. So Paul wrote the letter to defend his independence from Jerusalem and his faithfulness to God's call to be an apostle and to preach the gospel to non-Jews.

I contend Galatians is *not* a defense letter. Paul is not responding to charges from Judaizers that he is an illegitimate apostle or that his gospel is deficient. So, *put your mirrors away and look at the text.* Paul is trying to persuade the Galatians they need not become Jews to be Spirit-filled Christians.

There is no reason to assume, as do "mirror-reading" interpreters, Paul was on the defensive. What evidence is there his Galatian detractors claimed his apostleship was of merely human origin? Only "mirror-reading!" Those who read Galatians as an apologetic letter *imagine* they can reconstruct what Paul's Galatian opponents said by reversing his denials and assertions. If Paul said, "I am apostle of God, not of people," they *assume* his supposed opponents said, "Paul is an apostle of men, not of God."

No interpreter consistently reverses all Paul's antithetical constructions in Galatians. To do so would result in implausible and contradictory claims by Paul's opponents. But no interpreter has shown how to decide which statements should be mirror-read and which not. This suggests the entire enterprise may be misguided.

There is a lesson here about the folly of most conspiracy theories: The theorists usually bring more to the table than the evidence can bear. So ... *put your mirror away and listen to the text.* A sympathetic reader gives a biblical author the benefit of the doubt.

2. Never forget you are reading another's mail.

As we read Paul's impassioned letter to the Galatians, we may squirm by how strongly he presses his case. But we can only guess what it was like to be among those first stunned, stung, and silenced as they heard it.

The opening lines of the letter give few clues to the turn in tone the apostle takes near the end of chapter 4. It begins as most ancient letters do. Those accustomed to reading Paul's letters as Scripture tend to skip these to get to "the real meat." If we take this tack, we miss the central point Paul wanted to impress upon his audience. Instead, take the prescripts and thanksgivings of Paul's letters seriously. They preview the letter. They introduce the central points of the correspondence.

Back in "the good old days," people actually wrote letters instead of dashing off an e-mail, updating their Facebook status, Twittering, or sending cryptic text-messages. Then, everyone understood the conventions of letter writing. When I was younger, I learned to address total strangers as "Dear." I also learned never to close a business letter with, "Love, George."

A good deal of the beginning of Galatians reflects cultural conventions of Paul's day. How seriously should we take what he wrote in these verses? After all, not everyone we call "Dear" really is! How do we sort out social expectations and serious practical implications?

Because we have other letters from Paul, we know that letters have similar openings. Convention dictated the basic three-part opening: sender, recipients, greetings. But the subtle differences matter. For example, Galatians, like most of Paul's community letters, mentions co-senders. But only in Philippians do Paul and his co-sender (Timothy) share the same title, "servants of Christ" (Phil 1:1). The Philippians letter especially emphasizes equality and servanthood. What should the unique features of Galatians lead us to expect?

The differences between Paul's letters and the letters of his contemporaries are also enlightening. Because we have read the rest of the New Testament, the greeting "grace and peace" does not surprise us. But the Galatian Christians did not have the New Testament. They would certainly have noticed unexpected variations from typical secular letters.

3. It is a miracle that Galatians is in the Bible.

It is remarkable that a church planter like Paul wrote letters offering pastoral care at a distance. It is even more remarkable that the Christian church saw fit to preserve and canonize them.

Among the literary genres in the Old Testament are books of law, narrative, poetry, wisdom, and prophecy. There are no letters. But within a century after Paul wrote to specific local churches, churches throughout the Roman empire were reading those letters as they gathered for worship. By this repeated practice, they came to recognize Galatians and his other letters as canonical Scripture alongside the ancient works of Moses, David, and Isaiah! And they read them, not as merely the letters of Paul, but as words from God.

That letters are part of the Christian Bible testifies to more than Paul's theological genius. Paul's readers across the centuries came to share with him the certainty that his message was not simply a clever human invention. Wesleyans have always agreed with Calvin on this: The inspiration of Scripture is twofold: God inspired writers and God inspires readers to recognize that divine inspiration.

4. It is no small thing to claim to speak for God.

Galatians is an apostolic letter. Paul spoke not for himself, but for God who called him. He spoke not to outsiders but to those who knew the cross (Gal 1:4) preceded the resurrection (1:1), although he reversed their order in the preface. He could use terms like "grace," "peace," "sins," "rescue," and "glory," because his readers knew what those words meant.

Paul assumed his converts would persevere as Christians. Thus, he wrote with shock and righteous indignation at what he learned was happening in Galatia. Circumstances prevented him from returning to address matters personally (see Gal 4:20). But the letter testifies to his conviction that their Christian future was seriously threatened (see 3:4; 4:11; 5:2–3, 7). He prayed that divine judgment might visit Galatian agitators.

Such calls for eternal damnation put off some Christians. "How could Paul be so confident he was right and the agitators wrong?" The intensity of Paul's alarm may trouble Christians who pride themselves on their tolerance of diversity and inclusivity. "Why do these petty theological differences bother him so much? Why can't we just get along? Why consign those who see things differently to hell?" Some dismiss the claim that there is just one gospel. Paul was intolerant of such tolerance. But Paul was especially intolerant of Christians, however well intentioned, who were so convinced theirs was the only way that they shook the faith of simple believers.

A variety of well-known Christians—from St. Augustine to John Wesley to P. F. Bresee—has advocated the principle, "In essentials, unity; in non-essentials, liberty; in all things, charity." How do we separate matters of indifference from the indispensable? What makes one version of the gospel true and another false? Paul holds up the Christological test. The gospel of Christ has the grace of Christ at its center.

But this begs the question: Which understanding of Christ? Even in Paul's day, there were competing Christologies. Still, Paul insisted that the gospel he preached and the Galatians first accepted was the true gospel. If his confident claim of divine inspiration persuades us, we will give diligent attention to grasping the gospel as presented in Galatians.

Doing so puts us in good company. The Christian church's canonization of Galatians reminds us that, for nearly two millennia, the Spirit has confirmed that this letter was not merely a timely response to Christian communities long ago. It is God's timeless gift of the gracious message of the cross of Christ.

5. Take apostolic authority seriously, but remember that you are not an apostle.

Since the second century, the church became increasingly institutionalized. Interpreters wrestled with the implications of Paul's claims to *unmediated* apostolic authority. Interest was piqued again as the Reformers appealed to the apostle in their struggle with the hierarchy of the Roman Catholic Church.[1] Even if we accept Paul's more generous (compared to Luke's) views of the qualifications necessary for an apostle, no apostles are alive today. A divine call to preach the gospel or to plant churches lacks one essential qualification: a personal encounter with the risen Lord (1 Cor 9:1). Paul considered his resurrection appearance the last (1 Cor 15:3–7).

Protestants generally assign to the Bible—particularly the New Testament, as the repository of the apostolic witness—the authority belonging to apostles in the era before the biblical canon was settled. Catholics vest that authority in the Magisterium, the consensus teaching of the church across the ages. Even Protestants who are reluctant to assign such authority to tradition concede that the ecumenical creeds and the early church fathers provide essential guidance on how to resolve the ambiguities of Scripture.

Some emphasize a "high view" of Scripture with words like inerrancy and infallibility. But the Bible never makes such claims for itself. *Those who take seriously Galatians as an apostolic letter will submit to its authority.* Wesleyans appropriately acknowledge the role of tradition, experience, and reason in the formulation and validation of Christian doctrine. But Scripture remains normative for Christian faith and practice. Whatever is not contained in Scripture is not to be an article of faith.

6. Every theory of biblical inspiration must confront the Bible we actually have, not speculate about the ideal Bible of pious imagination.

Biblical readers must take seriously the grammatical chaos

throughout Galatians 2:1–10 and its historical discrepancies when compared to Acts. In particular, one must deal with two issues. First, the manuscript tradition suggests that the scribes who preserved the sacred text were willing to revise it because the original autograph had grammatical errors. Second, whether interpreters consider Acts 11 or Acts 15 as the parallel events reported in Galatians 2:1–10, they must still acknowledge the differences between the two perspectives.

I am sympathetic with the opening words of Karl Barth's "Preface" to his epochal commentary on Romans: "The historical-critical method of Biblical investigation has its rightful place. . . . But, were I driven to choose between it and the venerable doctrine of Inspiration, I should without hesitation adopt the latter, which has a broader, deeper, more important justification. . . . Fortunately, I am not compelled to choose between the two."[2]

I have no more interest in pointing out errors in the Bible than I have in calling attention to my parents' shortcomings. I am indebted to them for their gift and nurture of life. Similarly, the Scriptures pointed me to Christ and continue to be "useful for teaching, for reproof, for correction, and for training in righteousness, so that everyone who belongs to God may be proficient, equipped for every good work" (2 Tim 3:16–17).

I am comfortable with my denomination's doctrine on "The Holy Scriptures," which traces it roots to Wesley's revision of the Thirty-Nine Articles of the Church of England. Nevertheless, a close reading of the Bible, here and elsewhere, makes it impossible to endorse extravagant claims of other Evangelical brothers and sisters. *Divine inspiration may be inerrant, but human reception never is.* Even if it were, theoretical inerrancy is inconsequential. After all, flawed and biased human beings must interpret the text.

7. Circumcision is the *big* issue in Galatians. Nobody cares about circumcision today. Why did it matter to Paul?

Circumcision was a traditional Jewish practice, a religious rite performed on all Jewish baby boys when they were a week old. The rite involved the surgical removal of the foreskin of the penis. Adult male converts to Judaism were required to be circumcised.[3] The Old Testament traces the practice of circumcision to the time of Abraham (see Gen 17). God required it of him when he moved from Mesopotamia to Canaan, where many Semitic groups practiced circumcision. When Philistines migrated from the Greek world into Palestine, they were considered odd because they were not circumcised.

Circumcision was not a significant boundary-marker separating Jews and Gentiles until the second century BC. Rather, circumcision allowed Israel to fit comfortably within their cultural context. The situation changed when Greeks, a non-Semitic group that did not practice the rite, invaded and dominated the region.[4] Greeks, like most other non-Jews in the western Mediterranean world, considered circumcision bodily mutilation and morally reprehensible. It left the *glans* exposed, suggesting that the male was perpetually aroused sexually.[5] By Paul's day, most full converts to Judaism were women. Gentile men, otherwise attracted to the worship of Israel's God and the ethic of Judaism, understandably declined conversion. They remain Jewish sympathizers—"God-fearers." The few who converted and were circumcised were considered morally indecent and shamed as sexual deviants by their pagan contemporaries.[6]

Paul's original audience fully understood about circumcision. The earliest Christians were all Jews, so male believers were already circumcised. As Christians began to evangelize non-Jews, the question of the necessity of circumcision arose (see Acts 10–11).

Today's readers of Galatians find the connection between Paul's report of his presentation of his gospel in Jerusalem and Titus' non-circumcision mystifying. In the United States, for instance, this bewilderment is partly due to the long and widespread practice of infant circumcision as a routine procedure performed for hygienic (not religious) reasons. We do not think about circumcision in the way early Christians did. We cannot imagine how anyone could consider such a surgical procedure a prerequisite for full Christian standing.

As we read Galatians with cultural awareness, we begin to realize the issue went beyond the surgery to what it symbolized. Early Jewish-Christian believers considered it necessary for Gentiles to convert to Judaism. They must receive this distinctive sign of the Abrahamic covenant to become part of the Christian church (see Gal 2:7–9, 12; 5:2–3, 6, 11; 6:12–13, 15).[7]

During the second century BC, the efforts of Antiochus IV to end the practice threatened the Jews' survival as God's holy people (see 1 Macc 1:60–61).[8] Defiantly, Jews made circumcision "an essential expression of the national religion" and one "worth dying for."[9] Following the Maccabean victory over the Hellenizers, "As a basic Jewish law, circumcision was in the Hell[enistic] Roman period one of the presuppositions without which intimate dealings with the Jews were not conceivable" (see Acts 10:28; 11:2–3).[10] Because the practice repulsed Greeks and Romans, they derided Jews as "the circumcision." In return, Jews maligned non-Jews as "the uncircumcision" (lit. "foreskins"; see Gal 2:7–9, 12; Acts 10:45; 11:2–3; Rom 3:30; 4:9, 12; 15:8; Eph 2:11; Col 3:11; 4:11; Titus 1:10).

The importance of circumcision as necessary for salvation grew among Jews during the first two centuries AD. When circumcision was made a capital crime during the second century AD, it merely reinforced its observance among Jews. This hastened trends promoting the parting of the ways of Judaism and increasingly Gentile Christianity.

Most devout Jewish Christians in Paul's day insisted circumcision was necessary for salvation (Acts 15:1). They argued, "Gentiles must be circumcised and required to keep the law of Moses" (15:5

NIV). But Paul resisted efforts to have Gentile converts circumcised (in Jerusalem or Antioch [see Gal 2:3–4] and in Galatia [see 5:2–3, 11; 6:12–13]). He insisted that "neither circumcision nor uncircumcision" really mattered (5:6; 6:15; see 1 Cor 7:19). But he apparently had no objection to Jewish-Christians remaining circumcised (1 Cor 7:18–19) or for them to have their sons circumcised (see Acts 21:21).

The presence of the Spirit in the lives of the Galatians was evidence enough that they were already children of Abraham, and so children of God. They did not need to be circumcised.[11]

8. Paul valued the truth of the gospel more than the unity of the church.

Most scholars assume that Galatians 2:1–10 and Acts 15 narrate the same event from different perspectives. At the so-called "Apostolic Council," leaders of the churches in Antioch and Jerusalem agreed that non-Jews need not become Jewish to be Christians. This agreement had the effect of marginalizing the rigorous defenders of circumcision whom Paul considered pseudo-Christians.

The decision of the Apostolic Council set the future course of the Christian movement. Had matters turned out differently, Christ's followers might have become little more than a Jewish sect. Apart from the Pharisees, they may have disappeared by the end of first century. Of course, the Pharisaic-rabbinic Judaism that emerged following the tragic events of AD 66–73 (especially the destruction of the temple) might have been quite different had it not been for "the parting of the ways" of Christianity and Judaism.[12]

The church must be a "big tent." Personal and cultural differences and political realities within the church call for accommodation and sanctified diplomacy. It is obviously not easy to live out the gospel in contentious situations. Some issues are so difficult or delicate as to require private discussions behind closed doors. But there are limits as to how far to stretch the tent poles from the center.

To preserve the truth of the gospel, apostles courageously resisted pressures of those calling for maintenance of the Jewish status quo. Paul stubbornly refused to compromise the new "freedom we have in Christ Jesus" (Gal 2:4) in the interests of unity. God called him to evangelize non-Jews—to bring them to faith in Christ, not to turn them into Jews. The evidence that God was working through his ministry convinced even a staunch conservative like James (2:9). Those unwilling to accept what God was doing earned the label "false brothers" (2:4).

Although our issues are different, the church must still make hard decisions. It remains difficult to separate personal and social biases from our commitment to the gospel. Will we heed those "concerned" voices calling us to return to the past or those "emerging" ones urging us to reach out to the future in culturally relevant ways? Tradition is not always wrong; the new is not always better. On some issues, we must hold onto what Christians have believed and practiced. On others, we must, out of Christian principle, change to serve the present age and preserve the truth for the next.

It is never entirely possible to distinguish sociological and theological considerations. To decide which takes priority—engagement or faithful resolve—in a given situation is no easier now than in the first century. There is always the possibility that our own certain convictions were only stubborn opinions, and that *we* were the false brothers and sisters.

We should not imagine that the Apostolic Council provides a timeless pattern for conflict management. Perhaps some issues do not lend themselves to a public (or private) Christian conference. Could the shrill voices on opposite extremes in the homosexuality debate sit around the same table and engage in civil discourse? The battle has already split some Christian communions. Are we ready for more casualties? Are some issues merely matters of partisan politics, such as abortion, immigration policy, health care, poverty, and environmental stewardship? Should we avoid dividing the church over such things? Or, by not discussing controversial contemporary issues, do we risk allowing confusion to erupt into chaos and anarchy?

If the Apostolic Council may be exemplary for resolving some contemporary dilemmas in the church, then we must:

- Have a clear sense of who we are as a community of Christians and what is central and thus non-negotiable to our Christian faith.
- Talk frankly with one another about the pressing issues, publicly and privately, as the situation demands. Like Paul, none of us wants our efforts on God's behalf to be "in vain" (Gal 2:2).
- See and recognize what God is doing in our world (Gal 2:7, 9) and follow God's lead. Unexpectedly and contrary to Peter's religious scruples (Acts 10:28), God used Peter to bring about the conversion of the Gentile Cornelius and his family (Acts 10–11). Afterwards, Peter asked, "Who was I to think that I could stand in God's way?" (Acts 11:17 NIV).
- Find a reasonable compromise, even if it means agreeing to disagree. We can affirm the different ministries of both Peter and Paul without requiring them to minister to the same audiences in the same ways (Gal 2:8).
- Be willing to sacrifice artificial unity "so that the truth of the gospel might remain" for future generations of Christians (2:5). Apparently, some principles are worth risking a church-split to defend.

9. Conversion begins a new life in Christ.

Before vs. After. Paul organizes his autobiographical narrative in Galatians 1:10–2:21 around the time contrast between "formerly" and "now" introduced in 1:10. At its conclusion in 2:20, "no longer" will contrast Paul's former egocentric existence under law and his present cruciform life of faith: "I died to the law . . . . I no longer live, but Christ lives in me. . . . [now (*nyn*)] I live by faith in the Son of God" (2:19–20 NIV).

Human vs. Divine. Crucial to the "formerly—now" contrast is Paul's emphasis on his earlier existence as dependence on humans and his present existence as depending on Christ/God alone. This contrast prepares for the critical antitheses that dominate the balance of the letter: flesh and Spirit, law and grace, slavery and freedom.

Whatever the Galatians had done and were contemplating doing—however close they were to falling from grace (Gal 5:2–3)—Paul refused simply to write them off. He cherished these converts as his "children" (4:19). He was confident the power of gospel persuasion could change their minds (5:10).

Interpreters reflecting on Galatians 1–2 have been preoccupied with Paul's relationship to Judaism and his conversion to Christianity.[13] The apostle's experience is certainly unique. Few Christians since Paul have been converted and called at the same time. But his appeal—"Become like me, for I became like you" (Gal 4:12)—suggests that he considered his conversion somewhat paradigmatic or typical.

But what did Paul want the Galatians to imitate from his experience? He emphasized that he allowed God to redirect his life. God's grace freed him from the chains of family tradition to become the person God intended. Paul insisted that only divine intervention could account for that dramatic change. The Galatians were to learn from Paul's example to reflect on their own conversions to determine the direction God set for them (see 3:1–5). Paul would urge them to reject the misguided human voice of the agitators, who were diverting them from the path God called them to pursue (see 5:2–12).

Paul's conversion did not empty him of his pre-Christian zeal. It merely redirected his misguided passion for the law toward preaching Christ. It is probably equally true that God does not waste the prior experiences and personal assets of ordinary converts. Like Paul, Christians should not expect conversion to transform them into anything other than the persons God already had in mind for them to become (see Gal 1:10–12; 4:12–20).

Paul apparently did not think being a persecutor of Christians was a prerequisite for conversion. We seem to delight in "hero sinners"—converts with night-and-day type conversions. The darker their pre-Christian story, the brighter the glow of their conversion! Sadly, this has communicated to those of us raised in church that our less-dramatic conversions are somehow deficient.

We should learn from Paul that mature believers generally give good advice. After all, Paul was offering just that to his troubled Galatian converts. But he did not consult with the Jerusalem apostles after his conversion because God urged him to begin fulfilling his long-delayed vocation immediately. Few converts are as uniquely equipped to begin fulfilling their callings as Paul was. Later, he was willing to submit his divinely revealed gospel to the scrutiny of Jerusalem "in response to a revelation" (Gal 2:2).

We don't need to travel to Arabia to fulfill our calling. Paul never said God sent him to Arabia. He went there in response to his calling to preach Christ among the Gentiles. Arabia was the nearest center of a non-Jewish population at the time. Those who profess a call to cross-cultural ministry might learn from Paul to begin fulfilling it where they are. Globalization has meant that it is seldom necessary today to cross an ocean to find opportunities for missionary service.

10. Conversion is only the beginning of the Spirit-filled life.

The nineteenth-century Holiness Movement's equation of the Spirit-filled life with the life of holiness is overly simplistic and has limited exegetical support. The Spirit is active at every stage in the Christian journey. The Spirit is the divine agent drawing sinners to faith in Christ. The Spirit effects our justification, sanctification, and glorification.

In Galatians, receiving the Spirit describes the experiential content of "becoming a Christian." The gift of the Spirit was irrefutable evidence that one had been justified (Gal 2:16), the distinguishing mark of Christian standing. A Christian without the Spirit was unthinkable for Paul.[14] But conversion and the accompanying gift of the Spirit are only the beginning (3:2) of the Christian life. We must continue to the goal (3:4).

In Jewish end-times expectation, Jews hoped for a future age distinguished not only by the coming of the Messiah but also the universal outpouring of the Spirit on all humanity (e.g., Isa 44:3; 59:21; Ezek 11:19; 37:1–14; 39:29; Joel 2:28–29). In Galatians, Paul explicitly identified the Spirit as the fulfillment of God's ancient promise given through Christ to all who believe (see Gal 3:14; 4:6). He emphasized that God's end-times generosity included Gentiles.

The law of Moses can diagnose the human problem, but it cannot cure it. The Spirit empowers believers to fulfill the law of Christ. Sometimes, the Spirit works through what we call "miracles." More often, the Spirit empowers believers to live courageously, obediently, and effectively in the quiet miracle of transformed lives.

Galatians also insists that only as we continue to "live by the Spirit" (Gal 5:16), to be "led by the Spirit" (5:18) and to "keep in step with the Spirit" (5:25), may we experience sanctification (see Rom 8:12–17). This is the essential basis for our hope of resurrection: the fullness of God's gift of salvation. Unlike Romans, Galatians never uses the explicit language of sanctification/holiness. Nevertheless, one can argue that, in substance, "Galatians is not about '*justification* by faith,' as Luther and his followers through the centuries have believed. It is about *sanctification* by faith. It is not about how one gets sins forgiven. It is about how one is to live when that initial forgiveness has been received."[15] Galatians is not about how to be saved or sanctified but about how to live the sanctified life.

In Galatians 5:18, the antithesis to being "under law" is being "led by the Spirit." One must not understand Christian freedom as personal autonomy or licentiousness (Gal 5:1, 6, 13–23). Rather, it is the divine empowerment to fulfill "the law of Christ" (6:2; cf. Rom 8:1—"the law of the Spirit of life")—to love our neighbor as ourselves.

In Galatians, both flesh and law are surrogates for the underlying issue of circumcision. Paul's recommendation to be led by the Spirit is the appropriate alternative to being circumcised. Circumcision concerned only with the matter of the flesh. Neither flesh nor law would enable the Galatians to achieve the spiritual ends they wished (Gal 5:17d). This achievement required the Spirit.

Paul was convinced believers should conduct their moral lives "by the Spirit" (Gal 5:16). The Spirit was to be not only the source of their new lives. They were to "keep in step with the Spirit" (5:25).

Conclusion

Paul's letter to the Galatians is a theologically significant work, not to mention its place with the Christian Scriptures. But we must *also* apply whatever we say about the truth and timeless authority of Galatians to the rest of the Christian canon. The *plenary* inspiration of Scripture emphasizes that biblical authority rests in the *wholeness* of the canonical witness, not only in our favorite books. The diversity of Scripture is not simply the result of the difficult political task of reaching ecumenical compromise. The canon defines the limits of Christian orthodoxy. Emphasis of a diverse strand within the canonical collection to the neglect of the rest risks moving to heretical extremes.

There are times when a church needs to breathe deep the fresh breeze of freedom blowing through Galatians. But there are also times when a morally complacent church needs to listen carefully and repentantly to James's reminder that faith without works is dead.[16] May the church, reading the Scriptures prayerfully and thoughtfully, have the discernment to sense the Spirit's guidance through the sacred text of Galatians.

---

1. John Kenneth Riches, *Galatians through the Centuries* (Blackwell Bible Commentaries; Malden, MA: Blackwell, 2008), 71–75.
2. Karl Barth, *The Epistle to the Romans* (trans. E. C. Hoskyns; London: Oxford, 1972), 1.
3. Rudolf Meyer, "*peritemnō ktl*," *Theological Dictionary of the New Testament* (ed. G. Kittel and G. Friedrich; trans. G. W. Bromiley; Grand Rapids: Eerdmans, 1968), 6:72–84.
4. Troy W. Martin, "Circumcision in Galatia and the Holiness of God's Ecclesiae," in *Holiness and Ecclesiology in the New Testament* (ed. K. E. Brower and A. Johnson; Grand Rapids: Eerdmans, 2007), 219–37.
5. Martin, "Circumcision in Galatia," 222–24.
6. Martin, "Circumcision in Galatia," 224–25.
7. See Meyer, "*peritemnō ktl*," 80.
8. Paul D Hanson, *The People Called: The Growth of Community in the Bible with a New Introduction* (Louisville: Westminster John Knox, 2001), 291–381.
9. Meyer, "*peritemnō ktl*," 77.
10. Meyer, "*peritemnō ktl*," 78.
11. Elinor MacDonald Rogers, *A Semantic Structure Analysis of Galatians* (ed. J. Callow; Dallas: Summer Institute of Linguistics, 1989), 117.
12. James D. G. Dunn, *The Parting of the Ways: Between Christianity and Judaism and Their Significance for the Character of Christianity* (2nd ed.; London: SCM, 2006).
13. Riches, *Galatians through the Centuries*, 87–95.
14. See Ben Witherington III, *Grace in Galatia: A Commentary on St Paul's Letter to the Galatians* (Grand Rapids: Eerdmans, 1998), 247.
15. William M. Ramsay, *The Westminster Guide to the Books of the Bible* (Louisville: Westminster John Knox, 1994), 425.
16. McKnight, *Galatians*, 34–46, 52–60.

25

Teaching Concepts and Themes from 1–2 Thessalonians

Terence P. Paige

C hristians may not think of 1–2 Thessalonians as "doctrinal" letters. They are often overlooked because of their brevity. But a
closer inspection shows that in these very early letters Paul already
has a sophisticated mission theology at work. It can be summarized
in the triad of faith, love, and hope, and it covers everything from
monotheism and salvation to eschatology.

What to Teach from 1–2 Thessalonians

1. Jesus

Paul calls Jesus "Lord" in these letters more than any other title.[1]
The Old Testament "day of the Lord," which was God's theophany
of judgment and deliverance, has become the day of the Lord Jesus
(1 Thess 5:2). He will act as cosmic judge, punishing the wicked (an
especial emphasis in 2 Thess 1:7–10; 2:8) and rescuing those who
believe the gospel from God's apocalyptic wrath on sinners (1 Thess
1:10; 5:9). Persons pray to him, together with God the Father (1
Thess 3:11; 2 Thess 1:1; 2:16) or alone (1 Thess 3:12–13; 2 Thess
3:16). A benediction is issued in his name (1 Thess 5:28). The church
is said to exist *in* God the Father and the Lord Jesus Christ (1 Thess

1:1; 3:8; 2 Thess 1:1). In summary, Jesus shares God's functions and honor.

Still, Paul has not totally merged Jesus with God. Jesus' story involves a historical person who was executed and buried, implicit in the mention of his resurrection (1 Thess 1:10; 2:15). He set an example that is known and imitated (1:6). The Lord Jesus, not the Father, appears at the end of the age to raise the righteous (4:16). The vivid hope of Christians is eternal life shared with Jesus, the heightened continuation of the mystical relationship already begun in this life (4:17; 5:10). Paul's words about Jesus clearly set the church on a theological trajectory that led to the formulation of the doctrine of the Trinity. He differentiates Jesus from the Father, yet treats him as divine. Jesus is the object of the church's faith, as well as its hope and love, in every century. Our redemption and future are centered in him.

2. Faith, love, and hope

The triad "faith, love, and hope" summarizes the gospel proclaimed and believed at Thessalonica (1 Thess 1:3; 5:8; faith and love, 2 Thess 1:3). This triad shows up in other letters and writers in the New Testament and early Christianity.[2] This may be an early instructional formula of the church. It helped a mostly pagan audience get a grip on Christianity. As a brief summary of what it means to be a Christian, it is still useful today—if the terms are defined carefully.

On the one hand, we cannot assume others hear these words as Paul used them, in a culture where the television show *Star Trek: Enterprise* had a theme song claiming, "I've got faith of the heart." On the other hand, in some Christian sub-cultures, "faith" is a code word for "God must give me whatever I wish for." This is the same idea as ancient magic: say the formula and the spirits *must* obey. And popular music speaks constantly of "love," but not often of the Christian variety. We must define our terms.

a. Faith Faith is trust in the one and only living God who calls through gospel and Spirit (1 Thess 1:5–6, 9–10; 2:12–13; 2 Thess 1:11). It has to do with accepting the gospel message about God's Son, Jesus Christ. Paul was concerned that persecution might endanger the Thessalonians' faith, and he rejoices when he hears they are sound (1 Thess 3:5–8). Faith is a relationship, not a thing. And all relationships, like gardens, must be tended so that they grow (2 Thess 1:3). Because faith is trust in God and the gospel (1 Thess 2:2, 8), it is intimately related to obedience, love, ethics, and hope in God's future for the saints.

b. Love Love is what God first demonstrated to humanity, and especially those who believe, who are called "beloved by God" (1 Thess 1:4). It is God's love that led to his giving hope in the gospel to us (2 Thess 2:16). This love is the church's strength and model: they are "taught by God to love," and Paul prays their minds will be directed to that love (2 Thess 3:5; 1 Thess 4:9–10). It reminds us of Jesus' call to be imitators of our heavenly Father (Matt 5:43–48; Luke 6:35–36). Love is one of the primary virtues for the community, the hallmark of their genuine faith and salvation (1 Thess 1:3; 2 Thess 1:3). The apostle encourages us to pray that love may increase, even when it is already present in healthy measure.

In 1 Thessalonians, the object of love most mentioned is other believers, with one mention of "all [people]" (1 Thess 3:12; see 3:6; 4:9, 10; 5:13). This continues in 2 Thessalonians (1:3), which adds the love of the truth (rejected by the wicked, 2:10) and may imply love for God (3:5). The latter is part of the Jewish *Shema* or creed recited daily and would normally be taken for granted in Christian teaching (Deut 6:4–5).

Interpretations of these letters often stress the apocalyptic aspects so much they overshadow nearly all other elements. It is important to notice how much Paul emphasizes the virtue of love in forging the church and strengthening its members when it is under pressure. This is still good advice. Paul does not use a common

Greek word for love here. There were other words in wide circulation for parental love, erotic-spousal love, and friendship love. Christians rejected these to choose a rare term, the noun *agapē* and the verb *agapaō*, so they could define what they meant by this "love." They wanted something different from what the culture offered to bind their community together. This holy love is like God's care for the world.

c. Hope Christian hope consists in a confidence that God will bring about the redemptive future he has promised. Paul shows a keen interest in eschatology in these letters. Roughly 23 percent of 1 Thessalonians and 39 percent of 2 Thessalonians deal directly with eschatological issues.[3] This is partly because there were external and internal problems that called forth an eschatological reminder.

The coming (or parousia) of Jesus Christ is a major theme in both letters. In the first letter, the church faces persecution and some sort of uncertainty about the fate of Christians who have died (they may have believed they would miss Christ's return).[4] Paul reminds them that expecting the Son's return was part of the basic gospel they received (1 Thess 1:10). He prays that they will be "blameless and holy in the presence of our God and Father when our Lord Jesus comes with all his holy ones" (3:13 NIV). His *parousia* is a comfort to believers; then the dead in Christ will be raised, and all the faithful will be with Christ (and one another) forever (4:17–18; 5:10–11). Paul appropriates the language of Old Testament theophany and military symbolism and attaches it to the *parousia*: Jesus will come as victorious, conquering lord at the head of an angelic army (3:13b; 4:16–17). It is a kind of "shock and awe" in which the Lord seizes the territory that rightfully belongs to him, rescues his people—including the dead!—and passes terrible judgment upon the rest. Paul implicitly presents Jesus as the counter to the reigning Roman emperor, who visited cities as "ruler of all" and whose empire claimed to bring "peace and security" to the world (4:15; 5:3).

The second letter addresses an error about the "day of the Lord" having already come (2 Thess 2:2). Paul informs them about what must precede the Lord's coming: the rise of the "man of lawlessness" and the age of apostasy in which satanic deceit reigns powerfully (2:3–12). He emphasizes that Jesus' coming entails the overthrow of evil. This also includes those who presently oppress the readers (1:6–10), those in the future who refuse the truth of the gospel and participate willingly in a system of deceit and idolatry (2:12), and those who will ultimately lead the world in its worst rebellion against God ever, demanding that Satan's man be worshiped as divine (2:4). Christ's mighty coming effortlessly sweeps away all satanic political powers and schemes "by the manifestation of his coming" and "with the breath of his mouth" (2:8 NRSV). As God reconciled the world in Christ, so God judges the world in Christ.[5]

Belief in the future resurrection of believers is rooted in the resurrection of Jesus himself (1 Thess 4:14; see 1 Cor 15; Rom 6:5). That historic event not only demonstrates God's ability to raise the dead. In some way, together with Christ's death, it achieved the saving relationship with the Father that enables this resurrection (1 Thess 5:9–10; cf. Rom 4:25). So the Christian's faith is not so much rooted in what God *will* do for *us* as in what God has *already done* in Christ. One can sum up the blessedness of future existence in the assertion that it involves eternal personal communion: "so that . . . we may live with him" (1 Thess 5:11 NRSV; cf. 4:17; 2 Thess 1:10; 2:14).

3. Christian ethics

The motivation for Christian ethics comes not only out of love for brothers and sisters, but also from the desire to "please God" (1 Thess 2:4; 4:1). It is to live in a manner worthy of God, who extended a gracious call into God's kingdom (1 Thess 2:12; cf. 2 Thess 1:5). Living "worthy" does not mean earning one's place in the kingdom. It means living in a way that befits the majestic, holy, loving God who called us. Most people invited to be part of a wedding party (bridesmaid, best man) would be glad to dress up for the occasion, even if they do not normally wear such clothes. They realize they are honoring their friend, and the clothing fits the solemnity and celebration of the occasion. This is like the sense of "living worthy" and "pleasing God." It fits with the shape of the coming kingdom.

4. Sanctification

The God-pleasing life involves sanctification (1 Thess 4:3, 7; 5:23), meaning that Christians wholly belong to God and that they are to reflect God's character as God's people (1 Thess 4:3).[6] It is possible because of the gift of the indwelling Holy Spirit given to believers, who marks believers as sacred to God (4:8; compare 1 Cor 6:19–20). It is not an option, but an obligation called forth by the character of the Spirit and God's will.

First Thessalonians urges us to consider that sanctification involves the body, the sexual and marital life. We are called to "avoid sexual immorality" (1 Thess 4:3 TNIV), meaning any sexual relationship outside heterosexual marriage (see Matt. 19:4–6; Gen 1:27; 2:24). Choosing a spouse should bring a person whom one respects into the orbit of a God-devoted life, rather than be a foolish choice of lust (1 Thess 4:4–6).

Christian views of the body and sexual ethics are as counter-cultural today as they were in Paul's day. It is probably no accident that immediately after discussing this Paul urges them to *love* one another with a pure love "more and more" (1 Thess 4:9–10). Sexual sin is not really "love," and it tends to destroy families and community life. As anyone who reads Paul knows, sanctification can be described both as a divine *gift* (1 Thess 5:23; 2 Thess 2:13; 1 Cor 1:2; 6:11) and as a *task*. But the "doing" of sanctification only refers to people who are called and gifted with the Spirit, as people under grace.

Christians are called to pursue peace with one another (1 Thess 5:13, 15, 23). This peace is an expression of their sanctification, for it expresses God's *shalom* and anticipates the "eschatological peace" of the age to come (5:23).[7] Paul's words forbidding retribution remind one of Jesus' teaching (Matt 5:43–48; Luke 6:27–36).

5. Working

Working to support oneself and one's family is a good thing, according to these letters. Supporting oneself prevents one from being in need (1 Thess 4:12; the Greek may mean needing "no one" or "nothing"). The unstated presupposition is the virtue of providing the necessities for oneself and one's immediate family. Although the church should be an interdependent community as Christ's body (1 Cor 12:12–27), that does not give permission to be a freeloader. Apparently, some capable of work had stopped. We do not know exactly why. It may be they claimed to be "Christian workers" like Paul and demanded the community support them.[8]

Paul stated that he refused support and worked as a model of right living (1 Thess 2:3–12). But in the next letter, the problem seems to have worsened. Paul orders the church community to stop supporting those capable of working and to "keep away" from them until they reform (2 Thess 3:6, 10). He reminds them of his example of working "so that we would not be a burden to any of you" (3:8 TNIV).

Another problem with the failure to work is its ultimate abuse of the body of Christ. Other believers are burdened with supporting those who do not work. Irresponsible freeloaders are taking money from the church's common fund that could care for those who *really* cannot work and have no one to support them. So Paul *orders* them to work (3:12)!

The failure to work is a bad witness to society. Paul is aware of how outsiders critically observe him and his companions. The same will go for his converts. It is no less the case in our day that our work-life and how we care for our families are part of our witness for Christ. In a society that can be skeptical of spiritual claims and spiritual people, one often must prove the genuineness of the gospel through the way we do business. If Christians become known for laziness or dishonesty with employers or customers, how will they convince people about the God they worship? If Christians do not take care of themselves and their families, who will take them seriously? Unsaved people may be spiritually lost, but they are not stupid. Paul urges us to win their respect so that the gospel may win their hearing (1 Thess 4:12). Overall, this theme of work, along with that of ethical modeling, suggests that doing evangelism in a hostile society involves absolute authenticity of lifestyle.

6. Imitation

The theme of imitation comes up repeatedly in 1 Thessalonians. Paul praises the Thessalonian Christians for imitating the Lord Jesus, the apostles, and the Judean churches because they endured persecution for believing God's word (1 Thess 1:6; 2:14). This implies the prior examples of faithfulness in persecution that the Lord and his disciples provided. In turn, Paul says the Thessalonians became a model for others to follow (1:7). Paul reminds them in emotional terms that he and his co-workers self-consciously modeled the holy love of the gospel they taught them (2:5–12). Their manual labor to support themselves reveals their genuine care by refusing to burden others. Paul appeals to this when he calls on the Thessalonians who have become disorderly to work and support themselves (1 Thess 2:9; 4:11–12; 2 Thess 3:8–13).

I often hear people say, perhaps in humility, "Don't look at me, look at Jesus." But I cannot imagine Paul as a pastor ever saying such a thing. He says just the opposite: "*Look at me* and learn about Jesus." This is how he expected shepherds to operate. Paul does not ask them to do anything he has not done. It is how Jesus taught and led his disciples.

7. Judgment

The theme of Jesus passing judgment on those "in darkness" at his *parousia* (1 Thess 5:3–6, 9) intensifies in 2 Thessalonians, apparently in response to increased persecution of the church (2 Thess 1:6–10; 2:8, 12). Paul uses apocalyptic language to emphasize Jesus' role as judge: he is "revealed from heaven in blazing fire with his powerful angels. [8] He will punish those who do not know God" (2 Thess 1:7–8 NIV). The language reflects Old Testament passages (particularly Isaiah and Daniel) and Jewish apocalyptic literature.[9] Where the Old Testament had the God of Israel coming as judge on the "day of the Lord" to punish the wicked, Paul places him with Jesus. Yet he is "revealed from heaven" not as a rival to God; he mysteriously shares his glory and his functions.

Despite the similarity to contemporary apocalyptic writings, significant differences also exist. Unlike those books, Paul gives no tour of heaven or hell, no extended description of the torments of the damned, no real guide to judgment day other than basic assertions about the awesome events involving humans' eternal fates. Some interpreters think this judgment language sounds too harsh and unlike Paul. However, we find the themes of God's final judgment of the wicked and Jesus' role as judge elsewhere (1 Thess 5:2–4, 9; Rom 2:3, 5–9; 1 Cor 4:4–5; 5:13; 2; 2 Cor 5:10; 2 Tim 4:1, 8).

Paul's main concern is to comfort the Thessalonians, who are currently powerless and persecuted by the powerful. Judgment day would see that overturned. God's people will find relief and bliss in the Savior's presence as they glorify their Lord, and they will be honored with him (2 Thess 1:7, 10, 12; 2:14). Their persecutors will become powerless and dishonored, and they will experience the destruction of everything they value (1:9–10). This is the choice the whole world must make: believe the truth of the gospel, or fall prey to a delusion about ultimate reality (2:2–4, 9–12).

Preached in the setting of a modern city, these apocalyptic scenarios may enthrall some. But they turn off others by their culturally outmoded ways of thinking. As foreign as these images may appear, however, we must let them stand. They are vital to the church's theological and mental health, if understood properly. The message of the *parousia* tells us that sinful powers have seized this world, but God stands in judgment over it. This age will come to an end, and all who have ever used and abused power will give account to the Lord of lords. It reminds God's people that God is attentive to their sufferings and evil. The day of wrath is postponed out of God's mercy, so that all may hear the gospel. Even in their suffering, Paul prays that God may bring about "every deed prompted by faith . . . so that the name of our Lord Jesus may be glorified in you" (2 Thess 1:11–12 TNIV).

Paul does not contemplate wrath in these letters because he delights in the thought of torturing enemies but because, in his world, evil has run rampant. Those who have unjustly mistreated or even killed believers have received no judgment. Neither does wrath seem to fall on the extortionate and violent Roman governors or their soldiers. And we too may look at the world around us and wonder, "Why doesn't wrath fall? Surely *this* is bad enough to merit God's judgment!" Even agnostics who recoil from the notion of divine judgment have an inner longing for justice in the world, wishing God would "do something" about Rwanda or Sudan or other evils. Second Thessalonians reminds God's people that a day of accounting will come.

8. Christians and suffering for the faith

Both letters deal with the issue of Christians suffering for their faith. In the first letter, suffering is a sign that their faith is genuine. They are imitating the faith living that endured suffering that Jesus and his first followers modeled (1 Thess 1:6–7; 2:14–15). The assumption is that persecution from a fallen world is normal, though it is nevertheless a danger to the soul (3:1–5). Paul is aware of the emotional toll that violence can take on a person and the temptation that would ensue to give up on the new religion. He himself had once used this tactic against Christians (Gal 1:13–14).

The second letter picks up the themes of enduring suffering as a mark of belonging to God (2 Thess 1:3–5). The world hated them for loving God's Christ. But as already noted, 2 Thessalonians is much more concerned with reassuring believers that God will execute judgment on their persecutors if they do not repent and believe in the truth of the gospel. This judgment will happen at the end of the age, when Christ returns (1:6–9; 2:8, 12; cf. 1 Thess 5:2–4). His return will mean an end of suffering and relief for believers who will enjoy resurrection bliss with Christ and one another (2 Thess 1:7, 10; 2:13–14).

One powerful lesson from these letters is the reminder that the church began as a minority and a stranger in its culture. A religiously pluralistic culture had no patience with Christianity's absolute claims or criticisms of its ancestral faiths. The church today also needs courage to stand as an alternative society, not with words alone but with its lifestyle. These letters call upon us to live as witnesses to the kingdom that is to come and to be undeterred by the criticism and social ostracism we may have to bear for that.

What *Not* to Teach from 1–2 Thessalonians:

1. The rapture

These letters are prime sources for the idea that believers will be raptured to heaven suddenly and secretly, "like a thief in the night," prior to the end of this age and Christ's second coming (see 1 Thess 4:17). Usually, this is thought to happen just before the "great tribulation,"[10] so that believers escape facing the Antichrist and all the evils of that time.

The secret rapture idea first began in Edward Irving's church, was then promoted by John Nelson Darby in the 1830s, and spread in America through prophecy conferences and the Scofield reference Bible.[11] In recent years, the *Left Behind*[12] series of books and movies has further popularized this scenario, which so many Christian media and pulpits repeat that many people assume this to be the only Christian view.

The problem with this view is that it seriously conflicts with 1–2 Thessalonians (let alone the other biblical texts). Paul hardly describes Jesus' return as "secret." War trumpets, angelic armies, and "clouds" (1 Thess 4:16–17) mark a stunning theophany on judgment day (see Dan 7:10; Joel 2:30–32; Isa 13:6–13). Paul does not picture any gap between Christ's raising dead saints and judging the wicked (1 Thess 5:2–3; cf. 2 Thess 1:6–10). These are all one event: the "day of the Lord."[13] And Paul specifically says that Jesus will *not* come for Christians "like a thief in the night" (1 Thess 5:2–4). The metaphor of the "thief" is not about secrecy; it implies violence and an unexpected attack, bringing the "sudden destruction" of the wicked (1 Thess 5:3–4). The contemporary equivalent might be to say Jesus will spring like a mugger in the dark. It is an image of *judgment*, not deliverance. The "wrath" Christians escape is not the great tribulation but God's ultimate judgment on those "in darkness" (1 Thess 5:9–10).

When Paul discusses an Antichrist figure in the second letter, the "man of lawlessness," he speaks as if Christians will be on earth to encounter him, to recognize this sign of the times, and to be prepared by the gospel not to be deceived by him (2 Thess 2:2–14). Paul teaches them that those who follow the call to God's kingdom should expect suffering from the world (1 Thess 2:14; 3:3–4; 2 Thess 1:4–5). The rapture theory encourages belief that God will enable Christians to escape suffering, a potentially dangerous thing to believe.

2. The Holy Spirit will leave the world

Some have taught that, when Antichrist comes, the Holy Spirit will leave the world (2 Thess 2:6–7). Supposedly, this is because Paul speaks in these two verses of a "restrainer" in both neuter and masculine genders who will be removed to allow the "man of lawlessness" to arise. And, it is said, only the Spirit can be both masculine (as a person) and neuter (the gender for the Greek noun *pneuma*, "spirit").

This has numerous theological problems associated with it. Will God the Spirit leave the world? How can people be converted during the tribulation without the Spirit, since Scripture declares that believers *must* have the Spirit if they belong to Christ (Rom 8:9–10)? The biggest problem is that it simply *assumes* the "restrainer" is the Spirit and then *assumes* the whole scenario of a pre-tribulation rapture of the church. That is a lot to squeeze out of a participle, because it appears twice having different genders. Nowhere else in the New Testament is there any hint God will remove the Spirit from the earth. Rather, the gospel promises the Spirit to *all* who call on the Lord, even during the tribulation (Acts 2:39; Gal 3:14; 1 Cor 12:3)![14]

3. Jews are especially under God's wrath

Some have taught that Jews are especially under God's wrath forever, according to 1 Thessalonians 2:16. Paul argues in Romans that *all* humanity is under wrath due to sin (1:18–3:20). Paul repeatedly sought to include the Jewish community in the gospel proclamation and the task of reaching Gentiles, but received a very mixed response (as Acts testifies). He is probably directing his extreme statements here against Jewish leaders in Judea, Thessalonica, and elsewhere who stirred up trouble against him.[15] They echo prophetic charges against Israel in the Old Testament, Jewish literature, and Jesus' teaching.[16]

Despite what Paul says here, the evidence suggests he continued to speak to the Jewish community about the gospel until he died (Rom 1:16; Acts 28:17–29). In Romans, Paul urged that the Gentile church not to give up on the Jewish people, but hope for their salvation (Rom 11:11–32).

402 THE BIBLE TELLS ME SO

The danger with an interpretation that makes one ethnic group eternally liable for the Messiah's death and under divine punishment is that it is one short step from that to the ill-treatment of Jews. The countless indignities and deaths Jews suffered in Europe from medieval times onward stand as evidence of such. As one example, the soldiers of the first Crusade (1096) on their way to the holy land paused in Germany to butcher Jews as enemies of Christ.[17]

Not many years ago, a teacher in a Christian school told one of my children that the holocaust was God's punishment on Israel for rejecting Messiah. Even if not intended to be spiteful, such nonsensical thinking can lead to tragic results. It would really be just as logical, if we believed this, to say that the Columbine massacre was God's punishment on schoolchildren. Let us make it perfectly clear: contemporary Jews are no more responsible for Messiah's death than you or I. *This text must be very carefully read in its historical context.*

4. Existentializing re-interpretations of Paul's eschatology

There is a temptation in some quarters to turn Paul's apocalyptic eschatology into code-language for the ever-present encounter with the eternal God. This may be a well-intentioned attempt to stress that God's eternity is outside our time, so the "kingdom" coming or Christ's coming happen whenever people hear and respond to the word of God.[18] Or it may come from an attempt to salvage some gospel core out of what is thought to be a mere cultural shell of language that moderns can no longer accept, as with Rudolf Bultmann's demythologization program.[19]

While this may seem to make apocalyptic more palatable, it comes at a high cost. The teaching of communal redemption is reduced to individual experience. The sense of God's control and judgment over time is lost. As God's kingdom "comes" at every moment, it is equally at no moment in any eschatological fashion. The world goes on as always, and this view acts as if world history is unimportant to God or the saints. But in the apocalyptic eschatology of Jesus and Paul, history matters. It is not only the soul that will be redeemed, but also the body; not only the church, but also the physical *cosmos*. That requires an actual moment when the Lord interrupts the history of this world and brings about its conclusion so that he may initiate its rebirth along with the resurrection of his saints (1 Thess 4:14–17; 5:8; Rom 8:18–23). The kingdoms of this world will be judged and the wicked will be displaced. It is only this concept of *coming* and *end* to history as we know it that can complete these promises.[20] Otherwise, we are in danger of transmuting the Christian doctrine of the resurrection into a Greek or Gnostic notion of the immortality of the soul. The latter loses the grand scale of salvation and restoration found already in Isaiah (Isa 2:2–4; 65:17) and expanded by Paul in light of Christ (Rom 8:18–23; 1 Cor 15:50–54; Col 1:20).

---

1. "Lord" for Jesus 24 times in 1 Thess; 22 times in 2 Thess.
2. See 1 Cor 13:13; Gal 5:5–6; Col 1:4–5; Heb 6:10–12; 10:22–24; 1 Pet 1:3–8, 21–22; *Barn.* 1.4; 9.8; Pol. *Phil.* 3.2–3; Ign. *Magn.* 7.2.
3. Using the Nestle-Aland version of the Greek text (27th edition).
4. Abraham J. Malherbe, *The Letters to the Thessalonians: A New Translation with Introduction and Commentary* (Anchor Bible 32B; New York: Doubleday, 2000), 261, 275, 284; Victor Paul Furnish, *1 Thessalonians, 2 Thessalonians* (Abingdon New Testament Commentaries; Nashville: Abingdon, 2007), 102.
5. James D. G. Dunn, *The Theology of Paul the Apostle* (Grand Rapids: Eerdmans, 1998), 295.
6. For a brief overview, see my essay, "Holiness in the New Testament," in *Be Holy: God's Invitation to Understand, Declare, and Experience Holiness* (ed. Joseph Coleson; Wesleyan Theological Perspectives; Indianapolis: Wesleyan Publishing House, 208), 43–55.
7. Jouette M. Bassler, "Peace in All Ways: Theology in the Thessalonian Letters," in *Pauline Theology. Vol 1: Thessalonians, Philippians, Galatians, Philemon* (ed. J. M. Bassler; Philadelphia: Fortress, 1994), 82–84.
8. Robert Jewett, *The Thessalonian Correspondence: Pauline Rhetoric and Millenarian Piety* (Philadelphia: Fortress 1986), 105; John M. G. Barclay, "Conflict in Thessalonica," *Catholic Biblical Quarterly* 55 (1993): 520–23, 528. Others propose the work stoppage was due to belief that the "day of the Lord" had arrived or was very near, or because some were involved in patronage relationships with wealthy citizens who supported them. I reject these alternatives in my forthcoming commentary on 1–2 Thessalonians in the New Beacon Bible Commentary series.
9. E.g., Ps 29:7; Isa 2:10–21; 4:5; 10:17; 66:15–16; Dan 7:9–14; 4 Macc 10:15; 12:11–12, 17–18; Sir 5:7; *Ps. Sol.* 2:31–35; 15:12–13; *1 En.* 62:1–11.
10. John Walvoord, *The Return of the Lord* (Findlay, OH: Dunham, 1955), 20–27. This standard dispensationalist scheme is repeated with variations in numerous publications and websites.

11. George E Ladd, *The Blessed Hope: A Biblical Study of the Second Advent and the Rapture* (Grand Rapids: Eerdmans, 1956), 39, 43–45; Dave MacPherson, *The Rapture Plot* (Simpsonville, SC: Millennium III Publishers, 1995), 3, 6, 9–10.

12. Jerry Jenkins, *Left Behind: A Novel of the Earth's Last Days* (Carol Stream, IL: Tyndale House, 1996). The same scenario is found in David Jeremiah, *The Prophecy Answer Book* (Nashville: Thomas Nelson, 2010), the number 10 bestseller among all Christian books combined according to the Christian Bookseller Association's January 2011 list.

13. Malherbe, *The Letters to the Thessalonians*, 291; Ben Witherington III, *1 and 2 Thessalonians: A Socio-Rhetorical Commentary* (Grand Rapids: Eerdmans, 2006), 144.

14. For discussion of interpretations of the "restrainer" see Gene L. Green, *The Letters to the Thessalonians* (Pillar New Testament Commentary; Grand Rapids: Eerdmans, 2002), 314–17; Colin R. Nicholl, *From Hope to Despair in Thessalonica: Situating 1 and 2 Thessalonians* (Cambridge: Cambridge University Press, 2004), 225–49; Witherington, *1 and 2 Thessalonians*, 209–12.

15. Karl P. Donfried and I. Howard Marshall, *The Theology of the Shorter Pauline Letters* (Cambridge: Cambridge University Press, 1993), 69–70.

16. 1 Kgs 19:10–14; 2 Chr 36:15–16; Neh 9:26; *Jub.* 1:12; *Exod. Rab.* 31:16; Mark 12:1–9; Matt 23:29–37; Luke 11:47–51; 13:34; and note Stephen's speech, Acts 7:51–52.

17. Abraham L. Sachar, *A History of the Jews* (5th ed. rev.; New York: Alfred Knopf, 1965), 188–89.

18. See discussion of positions, with criticism, in Jürgen Moltmann, *The Coming of God* (trans. M. Kohl; Philadelphia: Fortress, 1996), 14–22.

19. Rudolf Bultmann, "New Testament and Mythology," in *Kerygma and Myth: A Theological Debate* (rev. ed.; ed. H. W. Bartsch; trans. R. H. Fuller; New York: Harper & Row, 1961), 1–16.

20. Moltmann, *The Coming of God*, 20–21, 23–29.

26

"The Holy Spirit Says:"
Hearing and Preaching the Scriptures according to the Letter to the Hebrews

Kevin L. Anderson

W hat would it be like to go back in time to experience how an early Christian minister interpreted and preached from the Scriptures? To a great degree, this is possible when reading the earliest documents of the New Testament: Paul's letters.[1] Paul certainly engages in biblical exegesis as he responds to challenges within the churches. Because Paul wrote letters, however, he usually offers *ad hoc* treatments of burning issues. Perhaps with the exception of Galatians and Romans, he does not expound on Scripture to drive home an overarching point, as in a sermon.

Reading the Gospels brings us close to how early Christians—even Jesus—interpreted the Scriptures. The four Gospels view the life, death, and resurrection of Jesus through the lenses of the Scriptures. They give us many instances of Jesus' teachings and even glimpses of his deeper expositions of Scripture. However, if we are looking for a full-length sermon that displays an array of exegetical techniques and rhetorical skill, the Gospels will only whet our appetites.[2]

We do find examples of apostolic preaching in the book of Acts. Paul's speech at Pisidian Antioch may supply the best model of the sort of biblical exposition we seek (Acts 13:16–41). Nevertheless, even the longest speech in Acts takes only a few minutes to read. What we possess in Acts are not full-blown sermons but summaries. At best, these examples are only *representative* of early Christian scriptural exposition.

Then we come to the letter to the Hebrews. It turns out not to be a letter! Yes, it ends like a letter, with concluding exhortations, a request for prayers, a benediction, travel plans, and a closing greeting (Heb 13:1–25). But it does not begin or proceed like a letter at all. The author calls his composition a "word of exhortation" (13:22),[3] apparently a technical expression for a sermon that one would hear in an ancient Jewish synagogue (see Acts 13:15).[4] When we read Hebrews, we are reading some of the earliest Christian preaching!

Hebrews is not merely representative of early Christian preaching. It *is* a finely crafted sermon. It has an overarching purpose, related to a fundamental crisis in a particular Christian community: the threat of final apostasy. It has a sustained series of arguments, with relevant biblical exposition and exhortations, aimed at strengthening the audience's Christian confession. It is composed with cutting-edge Jewish-Christian exegetical principles and Greco-Roman rhetorical techniques of its day. We have no earlier or better specimen of what early Christian preaching looked like. Hebrews is an ideal resource for thinking about how we might approach and communicate the Scriptures like the early church.

This essay will focus on three sets of concerns as we look at Hebrews. First, we will be interested in how Hebrews uses the Scriptures as authoritative texts. How does Hebrews appropriate what we now call the Old Testament? Second, we will consider how Hebrews interprets the Scriptures. We will be concerned with the major interpretive principles employed. Third, we will attempt to glean insights from Hebrews concerning how to communicate Scripture to a contemporary audience. How does one not only interpret but also *preach* the Bible faithfully and effectively?

The Scriptures in Hebrews

1. Citing the Scriptures as divine speech

Hebrews is not alone in viewing the Scriptures as God inspired. Any New Testament author could have written, "All Scripture is God-breathed" (2 Tim 3:16). What is unique about Hebrews is the thoroughgoing way in which the writer views Scripture as divine speech. Remarkably, he never uses the common terms found elsewhere in the New Testament to denote "Scripture" (*graphē*) or "Scriptures" (*graphai*)—literally, "writing(s)." Instead, he refers to the Scriptures as "the oracles of God" (Heb 5:12 NRSV; "God's word" NIV) or perhaps "the word of God" (4:12; 13:7). Nor does he employ the standard New Testament formula to introduce quotations from the Old Testament, "it is written."[5] Overall, Hebrews avoids references to writing, with only one exception (13:22).

While Hebrews uses the word of God *written* (Scripture), the writer refers to it exclusively as the word of God *spoken*. The author expresses the pattern of revelation as divine speech in the sermon's first lines: "God spoke to our ancestors through the prophets," but "he has spoken to us by his Son" (Heb 1:1–2a). When introducing biblical quotations, Hebrews is negligibly interested in the human authors of the biblical texts (4:7; 9:19–20). Even in 4:7, the fact that God spoke "through David" is mentioned in order to demonstrate that the promise of divine rest still stands "a long time later" than when it was first announced at creation and denied to the wilderness generation of disobedient Israelites (see 4:1–6). In one instance, the writer vaguely introduces an Old Testament citation, "But someone has testified somewhere" (2:6 NRSV).

Otherwise, our author frequently introduces biblical citations as divine speech. Of the 35 quotations, twenty are ascribed to God,[6] four to the Son,[7] and five to the Holy Spirit.[8] He tends to introduce God as speaking, often in the present tense. While other New Testament writers use similar expressions to indicate that a prophet or Scripture speaks,[9] Hebrews introduces God as speaking directly. The great American evangelist, Billy Graham, would famously declare, "The Bible says." Hebrews would prefer to declare, "*God* says."

What do we make of this? Hebrews makes an implicit claim concerning the divine authority of the Bible. While the author is aware of the human authorship involved in the production of scriptural texts, he privileges God as the ultimate author. However, it is important to observe that he is not making explicit claims concerning any doctrine of Scripture. One might suppose that, like the prominent Jewish philosopher of that same era, Philo—as well as later ancient and medieval Christians—he held to an oracular view of the biblical text and viewed inspiration as mechanical (i.e., via divine dictation). But his actual use of Scripture does not support this.

On one hand, Hebrews can seize upon a single word or phrase in Scripture as bearing key significance for interpretation. See, for example, his isolation of the word "today" from Psalm 95:7 (Heb 3:13; 4:7), "new" from Jeremiah 31:31 (Heb 8:13), "will" from Psalm 40:8 (Heb 10:10), or the words "once more" from Haggai 2:6 (Heb 12:27). On the other hand, the author is capable of sculpting the biblical text to sharpen the message that he draws from it. For example, after quoting Psalm 40:6–8 in full (Heb 10:5–7), he repeats and condenses the quotation in 10:8–9. He pluralizes "sacrifice and offering" from Psalm 40:6a and then collapses them together with "burnt offerings and sin offerings" from Psalm 40:7b. He seems intent to represent the totality of many ineffective Levitical sacrifices in contrast to Christ's singular, effective sacrifice. In a condensed quotation from Jeremiah 31:31–34 in 10:17 (a full-length quotation is in 8:8–12), he then *adds* the phrase "their lawless acts" to Jeremiah.[10]

I am not suggesting that Hebrews plays fast and loose with the biblical text. On the whole, the writer is rather conservative in his transmission of Old Testament passages. He is no freer in quoting these than any other New Testament authors, and he certainly did not follow those at Qumran who routinely rewrote passages as a matter of interpretive practice.[11] He usually does not insert glosses that materially affect the message of the text. He aims to enhance or amplify the text's impact, not distort it. Nevertheless, his view of Scripture as divine speech does not lead him to reverence every word.

Hebrews' emphasis on God speaking presently and directly through the Scriptures is not borne strictly from a doctrine of biblical authority. It stems from a genuinely theological and pastoral framework of interpretation. Hebrews is not interested in Scripture merely as a static, exact record of what God said and did in the past. His lack of historical precision may frustrate the modern critic. Hebrews thinks the altar of incense stood within the Most Holy Place, rather than in the Holy Place (Heb 9:3). He anachronistically interprets an ancient "covenant" (diathēkē) also as a last will and testament (9:15–18). He assumes the patriarch Abraham believed in the resurrection of the dead (11:19), a belief that dawned in the second temple period. He telescopes events to take a panoramic view of them, rather than exploring an Old Testament scene with painstaking accuracy.[12]

Hebrews is interested in what the biblical text *means* "in these last days" when God has spoken definitively in the Son (Heb 1:2a), not in what it *meant*. The word of God is not a dead letter but "alive and active" (4:12). When one hears the divine voice in Scripture (see 12:25–27), God's warnings (8:5; see 3:15; 4:7), criticism (8:8), oath-taking (3:11; 4:3; 6:17; 7:20–22, 28), promises (6:13; 12:26), and solemn testimony (2:6; 7:17; 10:15) must be apprehended as having a direct bearing on present readers. Throughout Hebrews, there is a constant awareness that God not only spoke in the past in the biblical record but also speaks through it now.

2. Using a good translation of the Bible

A pet peeve of mine is when a preacher zeroes in on a particular word in an English translation of a passage, then rattles off definitions from Webster's dictionary—or worse, cherry-picks the definition that fits the theme of the sermon. At other times, a preacher might prefer the wording of a particular English translation for this same reason. This is a careless practice. It avoids the hard work of doing a proper study of the actual wording in the Hebrew or Greek text. It ignores the fact that English translations often cannot capture the precise nuance of the original text. Moreover, the network of definitions and synonyms for an English word will likely lead one down pathways even further away from the usage of the original word in its context.

To my surprise, the preacher to the Hebrews does something quite like this. His argument in Hebrews 9:15–28 turns on one specific word in Exodus 24:8 and Jeremiah 31:31 that refers to covenant. The author is aware that a covenant is an agreement or contract between two parties. It is sealed in blood and includes various covenantal obligations (9:19–20). However, in the Greek translation of the Hebrew Scriptures, the Septuagint, the Hebrew term for "covenant" (*berit*) is translated by the Greek word *diathēkē*, which can also refer to a last will and testament. Legally, a will cannot be executed until the one who made it dies. Thus, Hebrews argues instead for the necessity of Christ's death in order to provide our eternal inheritance, based on the legal understanding of the Greek term *diathēkē* (not the Hebrew word, *berit*).

In Hebrews' defense, the wordplay and the subtlety of his argumentation are far more creative than today's busy preacher who grabs an English dictionary or turns to the flashy paraphrase in *The Message*. Nevertheless, Hebrews' interpretations are not influenced by the Hebrew text of the Old Testament but by its Greek translation, the Septuagint. Apparently, our author did not know Hebrew and could not work directly with the Hebrew Scriptures. His distinctively Jewish methods of interpretation were probably transmitted to him through contact with the synagogue, yet within a predominantly Greek-language setting.[13]

"The Bible" for authors of the New Testament was the Greek

Septuagint. Unlike the apostle Paul, whose Pharisaic training kept him in touch with the Hebrew text of the Old Testament, the Septuagint profoundly influenced the thought, diction, and argument of Hebrews, to the exclusion of the Hebrew text.[14] There is no better illustration of this than the quotation from Psalm 40:6–8 in Hebrews 10:5–7. The somewhat opaque metaphor in the Hebrew text, "You have dug out two ears for me" (Ps 40:6), was rendered by the Septuagint, "a body you have prepared for me." Both express the notion of being prepared for ready obedience to God. But only the latter is susceptible to an incarnational reading. Crucial for Hebrews is that God prepared a "body" for Christ, so that the will of God could be accomplished "through the sacrifice of the body of Jesus Christ once for all" (Heb 10:10).

I am ambivalent about this textual basis for Hebrews' exposition. The Reformers were correct to insist that the standard for biblical scholarship is competent interaction with the original texts of the Bible in Hebrew and Greek. However, most preachers have never carried out this in practice. Most Christians have accessed the Bible chiefly through translations. The Eastern Orthodox churches still prefer the Septuagint as their authoritative text of the Old Testament.[15] Roman Catholics regarded Jerome's translation of the Bible, the Latin Vulgate, as their authoritative text for over a millennium. Even among Protestants, the impetus for faithful translations in the vernacular was most peoples' lack of facility in the biblical languages.

There are good reasons for Hebrews' use of the Septuagint as "the oracles of God." First, as already noted, the author was not educated to read the Hebrew Scriptures. For him, the *only* usable written source of the Scriptures would have been the Septuagint. Second, it is likely that he regarded manuscripts of the Septuagint as equally inspired by God as the manuscripts of the Hebrew Bible. Jewish (and later Christian) traditions attested to its equal status as inspired Scripture. The classic statement concerning the divine inspiration of the Scriptures in 2 Timothy 3:16 does not stipulate an application only to Hebrew manuscripts. Given the Greek-speaking addressee of the book (Timothy), it almost certainly assumes that the Septuagint is in view—not some pristine "original manuscript," but the many imperfect handwritten copies that were available. In the West, Augustine would eventually bring to full expression the Christian preference for the Septuagint over the Hebrew text.[16]

My intention in rehearsing these facts is not to overturn the Protestant position concerning the primacy of the Hebrew canon (over against the Alexandrian canon—the Septuagint). But Hebrews invites us to grapple with the nature of the word of God as it relates to Scripture. The word of God is not accessible only to the scholar who can probe the depths of the Hebrew and Greek texts of the Old and New Testaments. Scholarship is a gift to the church in order that she may drink from the purest fountains of divine truth for doctrine and practice. Yet scholarship is itself constantly being refined. Few would disagree that the venerable King James Version, for all its limitations, mediated God's word and grace to countless people in the English-speaking world for the past four centuries. But now we have translations that are far superior with respect to their textual basis and advances in scholarship.

I do not want to provide aid and comfort to preachers who have deficient ability—or none at all—to work with the Bible in its original languages. Today's preachers have abundant resources to "handle the word of truth correctly" (2 Tim 2:15). There are really no excuses for sloppy exegesis. Nevertheless, Hebrews compels us to believe that God chooses to speak even through imperfect translations and interpretation. Christians do not have the same attitude toward the Bible as adherents of Islam do toward their holy book: that God will only speak to those who read the Qur'an in Arabic. Although biblical scholars may not want to admit it, God can speak powerfully even through inappropriate interpretations of Scripture. God can communicate a word on target for our specific situation, even if it may not be regarded as normative for the church at large.

Major Principles for Interpreting Scripture in Hebrews

The interpretive principles and practices in Hebrews are so rich and varied that we cannot possibly survey them all. The task here is to point out the most significant or controlling principles of biblical interpretation in Hebrews.

1. Look to Jesus.

A repeated command in Hebrews is for readers to fix their attention on Jesus (Heb 3:1; 12:2–3; see 2:9). The author tells us that his sermon's main point is that Jesus is our great high priest who has been exalted to God's right hand and ministers in the true, heavenly sanctuary (8:1–2). Nothing is more critical to the readers' spiritual survival than holding fast to their confession of Christ (3:1; 4:14; 10:23). The realization that God has spoken in these last days through the Son (1:2a) is also the master key to unlocking the meaning of the Scriptures.

The author of Hebrews was an heir to an established tradition of the messianic interpretation of key Old Testament texts, such as Psalm 2:7, 2 Samuel 7:14, and Psalm 110:1 (see Heb 1:5, 13; 10:12–13). However, something more fundamental dominates the preacher's handling of the Old Testament. The unavoidable, nonnegotiable historical datum that controls the author's hermeneutic is the fact that Jesus was sent from God, suffered death on the cross, and was exalted to God's right hand. This train of events changes everything and fills in the author's broad vision of salvation history with high definition and color.

In the course of the preacher's sophisticated arguments for Christ as high priest in chapters 7–10, one fact stands out. The author speaks repeatedly of the monumental event of Christ's coming. The Levitical priesthood requires alteration—indeed, abolition—because another priest in the likeness of Melchizedek, Jesus, has appeared (Heb 7:11, 15). In chapter 9, we see that Jesus appears for us in God's presence (9:24). He has appeared "once for all at the culmination of the ages to do away with sin by the sacrifice of himself" (9:26). And he will appear a second time to bring salvation to those who await him (9:28).

2. That was then, and this is now.

Throughout his helpful little book on how to interpret the Bible, *The Blue Parakeet*, Scot McKnight often uses the shorthand statement—"That was then, and this is now"—to encapsulate the concept of progressive revelation.[17] This principle is nowhere more evident than in Hebrews. It is an outflow of the Christological principle of interpreting the Scriptures discussed above. Why are the sacrifices, priesthood, and law no longer valid ways of worshiping God? Why do we no longer approach Mt. Sinai with its fearful gloom, but Mt. Zion, the heavenly Jerusalem, in all its celebratory glory (Heb 12:18–29)? Why is the heart strengthened, not by eating ceremonial foods, but by God's grace (13:9)? The answer is Christ's coming to do away with sin decisively through the sacrifice of himself, making defunct the ministry under the old covenant.

There is still an organic unity between old and new revelation. Pointers to the new revelation are found in the old. The preacher sees, for example, that God's final rest was established at the creation of the world (Gen 2:2; in Heb 4:4) and rejected by the unbelieving wilderness generation (3:7–19). But later God spoke of another day, called "today" (Ps 95:7), in which God summons people to enter into divine rest (Heb 4:6–11). The preacher sees this same chronological sequence in Psalm 40:6–8. He sees, first, a time when many sacrifices were offered that were not pleasing to God (Heb 10:8). He sees, second, the coming of Christ to accomplish the divine will through his own death (10:9a). Christ's sacrifice effectively nullifies the preceding regulations and structures for worship (10:9b). A prominent text in Hebrews, Jeremiah 31:31–34, announces a coming new covenant (Heb 8:8–12). The establishment of the new covenant, according to Hebrews, clearly implies that the first one has been made obsolete (8:13).

3. We are living in the last days.

A corollary to the preceding two principles is the author's conviction that we are living in the last days (Heb 1:2a; 2:5; 3:13; 6:5; 9:26). This means believers in Jesus are living in the time of fulfillment (though complete possession of our promised inheritance still lies in the future; see 9:28; 12:25–29). The ramifications for biblical interpretation are manifold. Although the old covenant is passing away, God still speaks through the Old Testament as Scripture. God made promises and oaths in the Scriptures that are coming to realization in these last days. These include, primarily, the coming of a high priest in the order of Melchizedek (see 7:27–28) and our inheritance of the same heavenly homeland promised to the patriarchs (11:14, 16; 12:22–24, 28; 13:14). Both the faithful (such as Abraham [6:13–20] or Moses [11:24–28]) and the disobedient (such as the wilderness generation [3:7–4:13] or Esau [12:16–17]) still serve as examples, encouraging or cautionary, to believers under the new covenant. The old covenant with its sanctuary, priesthood, and sacrifices is passing away. But it still bears relationship to the ministry of the new covenant. The old is a sketch of the true picture that has come (10:1; see 8:5; 9:8–10).

Contemporary believers in Jesus stand at the climax of history. They are "God's house" or the people of God, which has its ancient origins in the people of Israel (see Heb 8:8–10). Jesus, the high priest, now presides over them (3:1–6; 10:21). They belong to the epoch in which salvation comes to the entire people of God. The faithful throughout all past biblical history looked forward to this momentous time when "only together with us would they be made perfect" (11:40)—through Jesus, "the pioneer and perfecter of faith" (12:2).

This means God's exhortations and admonitions to the people of God in the past also apply to members of God's house now. The warnings from Psalm 95:7 (Heb 3:7, 15; 4:7) and Habakkuk 2:4 (Heb 10:37–38) or the encouraging word from Deuteronomy 31:6 (Heb 13:5) may address readers directly. Scripture addressed to "sons" in Proverbs 3:11–12 now "addresses you as children" (Heb 12:5–6). We have come full circle in understanding how Hebrews can read the Scriptures as God's voice speaking to people today. It is easy for the author to contextualize the Scriptures for his readers, because he believes they belong to the same people of God to whom these words were originally addressed.

Exposition according to Hebrews

The author of Hebrews was a master preacher. His work presents a model of how to engage in effective and faithful exposition of Scripture. There are several important features of his work important to good preaching.

First, a rather accomplished individual composed Hebrews. Education is in fact an important concern for our author (Heb 5:11–14; 12:5–11). He received a consummate education, as is evident from his rhetorical prowess. He was educated in Jewish principles for interpreting Scripture. But the training mentioned in Hebrews is more than a "liberal arts" education. It is a curriculum of spiritual and moral training that will equip the student with wisdom: the ability to distinguish good from evil (5:13–14). The preparation of the preacher in spiritual maturity and holiness is the prerequisite for creating an effective "word of exhortation" (13:22).

Second, insofar as possible, the preacher to the Hebrews relates to his listeners with the right intensity and pastoral sensitivity. A striking feature of the sermon is its frequent use of the so-called hortatory subjunctive, translated "Let us..." (Heb 4:1, 11, 14, 16; 6:1; 10:22, 23, 24, 25; 12:1, 2, 28; 13:13, 15), as well as the first-person plural "we." The preacher does not talk down to or at his audience. He often includes himself in the exhortations and injunctions.

I wonder whether his sophisticated rhetorical argument was as challenging for his first listeners as it is for today's scholars. My wife has rightly observed that Hebrews was written for a sophisticated audience. If he missed some in his audience, this is a mistake in preaching that we should avoid. But I am convinced that many congregations do not grow because they are never challenged to think more deliberately and deeply about their faith. This is a mistake Hebrews does not make!

Third, Hebrews relates the questions and struggles of his audience to his exposition. We never successfully accomplish the task of preaching if we do not bring a divine message to real circumstances of real people in a particular time and place. Hebrews is devoted to shoring up the confidence and resolve of a congregation on the verge of giving up faith in Christ. At many points, the author connects his readers with the biblical text. Their hope in God's promise should be enduring like Abraham's (Heb 6:13–20). Their past experience of public shame, persecution, and loss of property—with the hope of "better and lasting possessions" (see 10:32–36)—clearly mirrors that of the Old Testament heroes of faith (ch. 11), especially Moses, who was "looking ahead to his reward" (11:24–26).

Fourth, Hebrews does not pull any punches in telling his audience the truth about their spiritual condition and its consequences. It has become fashionable today to avoid aspects of the gospel communicated in Scripture through forensic categories (e.g., forgiveness or cleansing from the guilt of sin and deliverance from God's wrath). Instead, we often favor a more therapeutic model (e.g., salvation from sin's effects on *us*, rather than the offense and defilement our sins create before a holy God).

By contrast, Hebrews has some terrifying warnings concerning God's fierce judgment on apostates (see Heb 6:4–8; 10:26–31). Some have accused Hebrews of an undue severity. However, it is important to see that such severity is part of a rhetorical strategy, based on what the author knows to be sober realities about God's nature. It is typical for the author to follow up his strong warnings with words of comfort and reassurance, emphasizing his confidence in his readers' final perseverance toward salvation (2:3–4; 6:9–12; 10:32–39; 12:28). Today's preachers should be no less honest and hopeful.

Finally, preaching in Hebrews has a grand purpose. This purpose goes beyond warnings against apostasy and calls to commitment. It should be the ultimate goal of all preaching, for it is the goal of all human life and of every believer's spiritual pilgrimage toward the city of the living God: worship. Flanking the central section of the sermon are calls to "draw near" to God in worship (Heb 4:16; 10:19–22)—calls that reach a rhetorical climax in 12:18–24. The crucial benefit of Christ's better sacrifice is its decisive cleansing of the conscience so that worshipers can approach the divine presence with confidence (10:19, 22; see 9:9, 14; 10:2). The conclusion to Hebrews shows readers how to receive God's unshakable kingdom thankfully and worshipfully (12:28): with the fruit of our lips in praise (13:15), our entire lifestyle and moral conduct (13:1–8, 16, 20–21), and in unflagging commitment to Christ—even to the extent of identifying with the disgrace of our crucified Lord (13:13; see 12:2).

---

1. See Richard B. Hays, *Echoes of Scripture in the Letters of Paul* (New Haven, CN: Yale University Press, 1989); and *Conversion of the Imagination: Paul as Interpreter of Israel's Scripture* (Grand Rapids: Eerdmans, 2005). For a treatment of biblical interpretation by New Testament authors, see Richard N. Longenecker, *Biblical Exegesis in the Apostolic Period* (2nd ed.; Grand Rapids: Eerdmans, 1999).

2. Even the famous Sermon on the Mount (Matt 5–7 // Luke 6:17–49) does not provide an actual sermon devoted to discerning God's voice in a particular scriptural text (or texts). It functions primarily as a collection of Jesus' teachings, though we find biblical interpretations throughout.

3. Unless otherwise noted, biblical quotations are from the NIV.

4. See William L. Lane, *Hebrews: A Call to Commitment* (Nashville: Thomas Nelson, 1985; repr. Vancouver: Regent College Publishing, 2004), esp. ch. 1; also Gabriella Gelardini, "Hebrews, an Ancient Synagogues Homily for *Tisha be-Av*: Its Function, Its Basis, Its Theological Interpretation," in *Hebrews: Contemporary Methods—New Insights* (Biblical Interpretation 75; ed. G. Gelardini; Atlanta: Society of Biblical Literature, 2005), 107–27.

5. His only use of the expression "it is written" occurs *within* a scriptural quotation (Heb 10:7).

6. Heb 1:5a, 5b, 6, 7, 8–9, 10–12, 13; 4:4; 5:5, 6; 6:14; 7:17, 21; 8:5, 8–12; 10:30a, 30b, 37–38; 12:26; 13:5.

7. Heb 2:12, 13a, 13b; 10:5–9.

8. See Heb 3:7b–11; 10:15; and evidently 4:3, 5, 7.

9. See Rom 4:3; 9:15, 17, 25; 10:16, 19, 20, 21; 11:9.

10. Another example relates to the changing and rearranging of Hab 2:3–4 in Heb 10:37–38.

11. See L. D. Hurst, *The Epistle to the Hebrews: Its Background of Thought* (SNTSMS 65; Cambridge: Cambridge University Press, 1990), 62.

12. In Heb 9:13, he combines elements from the Day of Atonement and red-heifer rituals; in 9:18–21, the elements of the inaugural covenant ceremony of Exod 24, the sacrifice of the red-heifer, and perhaps Passover. In 12:18–21, he conflates the scene of the Ten Commandments with God's wrathful response to the fashioning of the golden calf.

13. His Hebrew etymologies in Heb 7:2 are probably traditional, not based on personal knowledge of Hebrew.

14. See Radu Gheorghita, *The Role of the Septuagint in Hebrews* (WUNT 160; Tübingen: Mohr Siebeck, 2003).

15. *The Orthodox Study Bible* (Nashville: Thomas Nelson, 2008) has an Old Testament text consisting of the NKJV corrected by the Septuagint.

16. Augustine, *On Christian Doctrine*, 2.53–56.

17. Scot McKnight, *The Blue Parakeet: Rethinking How You Read the Bible* (Grand Rapids: Zondervan, 2008).

27

Practical Wisdom from James

C. Jeanne Orjala Serrão

M any have referred to the book of James as a New Testament wisdom book, because the author is specifically interested in how we live as Christians. It is an extremely practical book. The author does not seem to have much interest in explaining theological issues. In fact, the entire book only mentions Jesus twice! One should think twice about consulting this book to teach or preach about either the nature of Christ or the doctrine of the Trinity! James appears to take these foundational theological issues for granted. However, this book has much to offer regarding teachings and guidance for Christian living.

Before looking closely at the practical wisdom of this book, we must first consider some contextual matters. James appears to be a Jewish Christian writing primarily to Jewish Christians. Two of the most important contributions of Judaism to Christianity are profoundly apparent in James: ethics and monotheism (the belief in one God). The language of James is so monotheistic that it is sometimes difficult to know whether James is talking about God the Father or God the Son. My sense is that this distinction did not matter to James due to his strong monotheistic perspective.

I. The oneness of God

Christianity today is in need of a strong emphasis on the oneness of God. James is one of the best books that affirm this truth. Here we find that God is unique (Jas 2:19; 4:12). God is the Creator of human beings and all living creatures (1:18). God is the giver of all good gifts (1:17), including the perfect law (2:11). God is the "Judge . . . who is able to save and destroy" (4:12 NIV). God generously gives wisdom to all who ask (1:5). God tempts no one and is not tempted by evil (1:13). God is not fickle and undependable, nor is God's relationship with humanity unpredictable (1:17). The one who believes God and does what God says can be called "the friend of God" (2:23 NRSV). Conversely, the one who prefers the world is an enemy of God (4:4).

God defines righteousness (Jas 1:20). God chose the poor to be rich in faith and love, and to inherit his kingdom (2:5). God gives grace to the humble and comes near to those who come near to him (4:6–8). God is the powerful Lord of Hosts (heavenly armies), who hears the cries of the oppressed and administers justice (4:4). He is compassionate and pities those who endure suffering, even the righteous rich, like Job (5:11).

2. Obedient faith through love

The theme of James is salvation by obedient faith, which the author links to his definition of pure and undefiled religion. James is the only New Testament book to define "religion." For James, true religion is practical: "to visit orphans and widows in their affliction and to keep oneself unspotted by the world" (1:27).[1] A sermon or Bible study series on what a Christian's behavior should look like is a timely subject and James is a rich source for this.

Ethics as an important contribution of Judaism to Christianity is closely related to the idea of keeping the Jewish law. James first mentions the law as "perfect" and liberating from sin (Jas 1:25 NIV). This is no endorsement of legalism. James 2:12 reaffirms that God judges humanity according to this "law that gives freedom" (NIV).

James also describes the law as "the royal law" (Jas 2:8 NIV), citing the Old Testament command Leviticus 19:18 as its essence, "Love your neighbor as yourself" (NIV). This is the New Testament's most frequently quoted passage from the Pentateuch (Matt 5:43; 19:19; Mark 12:31, 33; Rom 13:9; Gal 5:14). James reminds his readers that one must keep *all* the law. If someone stumbles in one (i.e., the royal law), that person is guilty of breaking *the* law of God. James had in mind the entire law as a whole.[2]

Jesus said all the Law and the Prophets—the entire Jewish Scriptures—depended on two commandments: love God completely and love your neighbor as yourself (Matt 22:37–40). Paul claimed that the observance of Leviticus 19:18 "is the fulfillment of the law" (Rom 13:10 NIV), for the "entire law is summed up in keeping this one command" (Gal 5:14 NIV). James seems to be saying the same thing.

In James 4:11, the author mentions law without further elaboration. Because the context refers to slandering and judging one's brother or sister, it seems to point again to the royal law of loving relationships between human beings. By immediately identifying God as the "Lawgiver" (4:12 NIV), James seems to refer again to "the royal law" quoted earlier (2:8).

3. Maturity through trials

Another important issue in James is the nature and value of trials. The main importance of trials is that they develop character and bring maturity. James defines the mature as those who obey the law, treat everyone with respect, take action to correct wrong situations, and do the right thing. In a society where we try to avoid pain and look for the quickest and easiest way to get things done, James is an important corrective. Becoming mature is very difficult and takes time.

James uses the same Greek word (*peirasmos*) to refer to both trials and temptations. Thus, the distinction comes from the context rather than from the word. In the first chapter, James refers to trials in the sense of the ordinary troubles that come as part of human life (Jas 1:2, 12). These troubles build within believers an endurance that brings maturity and character. He urges his readers to be thankful for such troubles. Enduring these trials will eventually result in their Christian maturity.

In 1:13–14, however, James uses a verbal form of this same word to caution his readers not to attribute temptation as coming from God. In verse 13, James insists that "God cannot be tempted by evil" (NIV), nor will God tempt anyone. The addition of the word "evil" (kakōn) changes the meaning from just simply troubles to temptation.

Temptation for James comes from a person's own desires (Jas 1:14). God does not send them to test the strength of one's faith. Troubles and temptations are part of the normal human condition. But God sends neither, although God might use them to promote spiritual and personal maturity.

4. Sin

James approaches the topic of sin from a very helpful perspective. The term "sin" (singular or plural) appears six times in James (Jas 1:15; 2:9; 4:17; 5:15, 16, 20). The Greek word, hamartia, refers to missing the mark or goal of our lives in relation to God. It is an "offense in relation to God with emphasis on guilt."[3] Sin may refer to specific sins as well as the deviation in general from God's truth or law. For Paul in his letter to the Romans, it also refers to the state of being sinful (Rom 8:21, 24) and to a destructive evil power (Rom 5:12, 21).[4]

In 1:15, James uses the metaphors of reproduction and aging to refer to sin. A person desires to conceive and give birth to sin. But when sin is fully grown, it gives birth to death. James warns his audience not to blame God for temptation and sin. Sin comes from a person's own desires, not from God. The fault is completely that of the person who sins.

In James 2:9, the author calls favoritism "sin." It is sinful, because it violates the law of God. Here James calls sinners "transgressors," emphasizing his understanding of sin as the breaking of God's law (especially the royal law).

In 4:17, however, James moves beyond sins of commission, which defy God's law. Now he stresses that the failure to fulfill God's law—sins of omission are equally evil. For James, sin involves breaking God's law, whether that happens by an overt act of rebellion or by the simple neglect of full obedience.

In chapters 1–4, James refers to sin in the singular. There he defines it and explains its origins. In chapter 5, he explains the effect of sins on persons and communities. In his mind, sins and sickness are closely related (Jas 5:15–16). He urges his readers to "confess" their "sins to one another and pray" for mutual healing, physical and spiritual (5:16).

This holistic view of healing is consistent with the Jewish worldview of James's day. Jews viewed persons holistically, not compartmentalized into body and soul or body, soul, and spirit. It is also consistent with James's view that "works" or actions testify to who one is and what one believes at the deepest level. From this perspective, unconfessed sins might bring on illness.

James' closing sentence encourages the faithful to bring sinners back from their "wandering way" (Jas 5:20). The result will be salvation from death and the hiding of a multitude of sins. Here, the sin of the individual affects both the person and the community, so it is not just about an ultimate eternal death issue for each person.

5. Self-discipline and controlling our speech

James appropriately identifies the most difficult aspect of self-discipline and the one that shows the true extent of our maturity: controlling our speech. James says that no one can tame the tongue. It takes a change of nature only God can effect. When God changes persons on the inside, their behavior changes on the outside.

Speech or controlling one's tongue is a significant issue in James. He first addresses this issue in 1:26–27 in his discussion of true religion. Those who cannot control their tongues have a useless religion. James's discussion of speech in chapter 3 is in his discussion of teachers. The vehicle of the teacher's activity is speech. Therefore, the teacher's words will be judged more harshly than others will.

In 3:2–5, James notes how difficult it is to control the tongue. Even though it is so small, it has great impact—for good or ill. Verses 6–8 identify the fiery tongue as a world of evil in our bodies. Humans have tamed wild animals, but they seem unable to tame their own tongues. James notes the incongruity of the same mouth pronouncing both blessing and cursing (3:9–10). He implies that, if we *really* allow God to control our being—if we *really* have faith—blessing and helpful speech will naturally flow from our mouths (3:11–12). Only God can tame our tongues. What comes out of our mouths demonstrates our faith.

6. Faith that results in right actions

Many criticize James as a New Testament book that does not emphasize salvation by faith due of its emphasis on right action. But if one reads the book carefully, it is very apparent that James believes that faith is foundational to salvation—faith that results in right actions. So this subject addresses both a topic that one should *not* preach from James—salvation by works—and a topic that one *should* preach from it: saving faith will be visible in the believer's actions.

Faith and works are at the heart of most discussions of this letter. It is important to understand what James means by these words as related to salvation. He uses both words in 1:3–4. Here, the testing of faith develops endurance, which results in a mature work. This enables one to become mature and whole. Clearly, faith comes before works in this context.

In chapter 2, James addresses the relationship of faith and works in his exposition of the royal law: "Love your neighbor as yourself" (Jas 2:8 NIV). He deals first with the issue of faith. He points out that God chose the poor to be rich in faith. In 2:14, he asks about the value of a faith that does not produce works. An illustration immediately follows—of sending a hungry and naked brother or sister away with an empty blessing and no food or clothing. James concludes that faith without works is dead (2:17).

Conversely, James believes that one's faith is demonstrated by one's works (Jas 2:18). When one's faith does not produce actions that demonstrate one's beliefs, that faith is barren, sterile, and un-productive (2:20). He appeals to two Old Testament examples of active faith: Abraham and Rahab.

James concludes that "just as the body is dead without the spir-it, so also is faith without works dead" (Jas 2:26). James's position is that faith (demonstrated by works) brings salvation. However, pro-fessed faith that produces no works is not faith at all and does not result in salvation.

James ends his discussion of faith and works with faith. In 5:15, the prayer of faith brings physical and spiritual healing. The peti-tion of the righteous person (Jas 5:16) is strong and effective. The righteous person lives out one's faith in righteous action. Prayer without faith is as worthless as faith and wisdom without works (see 1:6–7).

The first time James employs the term "save" he says, "Receive the implanted word which is able to save your souls" (Jas 1:21). James emphasizes from the beginning that it is by receiving of the "implanted word" or the gospel (see 1:15) that one is saved.

In 2:14, James asks, "Can such faith save him?" not simply, "Can faith save him?" The grammar indicates that there is an impotent faith that does not lead to actions. Such professing believers have not truly received the gospel. Their so-called faith is unable to save them because it is not really faith, just empty profession. James insists that God is "able to save and destroy" (Jas 4:12 NIV). Once again, the focus is not on "salvation by works," but on God, who alone can save.

James 5:15 brings out the close relationship between physical healing and salvation from sin. The same verb used earlier referring to the salvation of one's soul (Jas 1:21) appears here to describe both bodily healing and forgiveness. James closes his letter by encouraging the community to pursue wandering sinners and restore them to the community. James 5:20 indicates that salvation from death refers to both physical and spiritual death.

James claims that the word (*logos*) regenerates and saves. James 1:18 refers to "the word of truth" (NIV) by which we are generated to be first fruits of God's creatures. This is in contrast to humanity's own desires that generate sin and lead to death. James further describes the gospel as "the implanted word that has the power to save your souls" (Jas 1:21 NRSV). This "implanted word" appears to parallel the embodied and enacted law of freedom or royal law. James challenges his readers to be doers of the word and not just hearers. Word and law in James are closely related. But James does not say that law saves or regenerates. That is the work of the implanted word or the gospel.

7. Wealth, poverty, and the Christian life

Because of James's Jewish context and the conditions of the Jewish Christians at the time, this book gives a typical Jewish prophetic warning against rich oppressors. They did not pay their workers justly, much less charitably. They may be living in luxury now, but misery awaits them in the future. James does not call these people "rich oppressors." He simply calls them "rich" and describes what he means.

We must be careful not to use James to preach against the rich or riches in an indiscriminant way or to preach that only the poor can be saved. In the first century AD, rich and poor had very specific connotations for the Jews, which are different for us today. Because of the actions of most the rich during the Syrian occupation that resulted in the Maccabean revolt, the rich were seen as betrayers of God and God's people. Furthermore, they participated in the systemic oppression of the rest of the Jewish people. They sided with the Syrians in order to maintain or increase their wealth and status.

The poor remained faithful to the law and the Jewish way of life. Jesus pronounced the poor as blessed in the Beatitudes. Peter commented that he had no silver and gold (Acts 3:6), and Paul identified himself and fellow Christians as poor (2 Cor 6:10). However, we do know that there were wealthy Christians from the beginning (Acts 2:45 and 4:32–37). The difference is that these wealthy Christians shared their wealth, took care of the poor, and did not take advantage of anyone. So again, the actions of the person reveal the inner nature, which is at the heart of James's teaching.

Wealth and poverty are significant issues for James's readers because of their social and religious context. He identifies with the poor. In 1:9–11 he contrasts the humble and the rich. He understands the world in a way that contradicts conventional wisdom. The humble enjoy a high status; the rich have low status.

Immediately following this paradoxical claim, James pronounces a blessing on those enduring trials. This is because they will receive "the crown of life" (Jas 1:12 NIV). He implies that the trials and troubles of the humble/poor bring about spiritual maturity. The apparently easy life of the rich does not allow them to develop spiritual and personal maturity or to receive the crown of life.

James uses an illustration of how differently the community treats rich and poor visitors to their synagogue (Jas 2:2–6). He reprimands the participants for favoring rich people. Their practice of showing favoritism caused the community to dishonor those God has chosen. James reminds them that God chose the poor of the world "to be rich in faith" and heirs of God's promised kingdom. The rich people to whom they offered deferential treatment were actually those oppressing the Jewish Christian community.

James includes a strong indictment of the rich (Jas 5:1–6). He considers the rich greedy people who got their wealth through corrupt and oppressive ways. He warns that God heard the cries of the oppressed and will bring the rich down. Their corrupt wealth will testify against them in the last days.

James's understanding of wealth and poverty arises from his understanding of the royal law. Humble/poor people share what they have with others. The greedy rich (whether or not in the community) hoard their belongings and send the hungry and naked out into the cold with an empty blessing instead of the necessities of life. James sees no distinction between the social gospel and the true gospel. He agrees with Jesus that "whatever you did for one of the least of these brothers and sisters of mine, you did for me" (Matt 25:40 NIV).

8. Prayer

At the end of his letter, James addresses the topic of prayer. He urges Christians to pray when they are in trouble and to request prayer when they are sick. We find the emphasis on prayer as asking God to meet specific needs. Jesus also encourages petition to be a part of prayer (see Matt 6:9–13). James says that prayer by mature Christians is extremely effective. This is appropriate at the end of his word of exhortation on what a mature Christians looks like.

James's view of prayer gives insight into his view of God. God wants God's children to be all they were created to be. In 1:5–6, James encourages his readers to ask God for wisdom and to believe wholeheartedly that God is generous and can give what they request. Those who doubt that God can or will give what they request will certainly receive nothing from the Lord (Jas 1:7).

James explains why one might not receive what one needs from God (Jas 4:2–3). First, one must come boldly to God and for what one needs. Second, one must request only what will bring one closer to God and promote spiritual maturity and goodness in one's life. When one asks for things to waste on pleasures, God will not answer that prayer.

Prayer is also a community activity (Jas 5:13–16). When members of the community suffer or are sick, they are to call the elders of the church to pray over them. James instructs his readers to confess their sins to one another and pray for one another.

James may have understood prayer as a time of communion with God. But his instructions on prayer are thoroughly practical in nature. When Christians need something—whether physical, emotional, or spiritual—they are to pray and ask God for what they need. Thus, James is not ashamed to petition God for anything. He encourages his readers to follow the example of Elijah, who was just like them. Elijah prayed for God to control the weather so unbelievers would come to understand who God was. God answered his prayer.

9. Anointing the sick

The Christian tradition of anointing the sick with oil originated with James 5:14. James understands healing to include not only recovery from physical illness but also divine forgiveness. James understands the inter-relatedness of sin and sickness, but this is probably not something that one could easily explain in a short sermon. However, this could be part of a series of Bible studies on the inter-relatedness of sin and sickness.

I would not suggest asking for divine forgiveness as a part of the healing prayer, except where it is properly understood. As we know from John 9:2, Jewish belief in the first century AD included the idea that someone's sin—either the parent's or that person's—caused sickness and other physical problems. We understand today that even the most mature Christian can become sick due to genetic predispositions, bacteria and viruses in the environment, and other conditions. But it is also true that sinful lifestyles can contribute to poor health.

10. Wholeness as persons

Wholeness is an important concept this letter. James under-stands humans as unified beings. Different parts may comprise us as humans, but those parts are so interrelated that each affects the other. In James's view, for salvation to be complete, it must affect the whole person. It brings wholeness to the personality.

James uses the term "whole" (*holon*) to refer to the law (Jas 2:10). For James, the law of God is consistent and summed up in the royal law: "Love your neighbor as yourself" (2:8 NIV). He uses that term again in his discussion of the necessity of controlling one's tongue (3:2–3). One who can do so can control or guide one's whole body. Nevertheless, this is merely a hypothetical possibility. Unaided humans cannot control their tongues. Only God has the power to do that. However, in 5:13–20, James does not use the term "whole." But he emphasizes that physical, emotional, mental, and spiritual wholeness are found only in communities that pray for one another, encourage one another, and constructively confront one another.

James paints a picture of a community in dynamic relationship with each other and with God. Sometimes, one is suffering, some-times cheerful, sometimes sick or weak, and sometimes wandering away. In all these situations, an appropriate communal response brings wholeness to the person and to the community.

11. Love and reconciliation

The final words of this sermon-letter deal with love and recon-ciliation. The community is to care for those who have wandered from the truth and gently bring them back. James concludes his letter with his central purpose in writing the letter. Although James goes into detail in describing the truth and how it works itself out in the lives of those who believe, it comes down to one thing. The purpose of the community of Christians is to keep everyone on the path towards God. This is what James tried to do through his letter. This is what Christians should do within their sphere of influence.

David Nystrom outlines three important theological ideas that James articulates in his concluding remarks to the letter (Jas 5:19–20).

1. "Christians have the opportunity and the responsibility to care for one another through the task of loving doctrinal and moral correction."[5] James's main concern is for the spiritual education and moral development of his readers' community. This does not mean that James does not value evangelism. However, that is not his priority in this letter.

2. "The penalty for sin is death; James will not equivocate on this."[6] James is not interested in sugarcoating the gospel. Whether one wanders into sin, or sins rebelliously, the penalty is death. So a Christian community should care for each one's spiritual condition with this solemn understanding that sin leads to everlasting death.

3. "In this process, the agent of reconciliation 'covers' a multitude of sins."[7] This work of reconciliation is very significant because those who lose their way will die spiritually and their evil works will be revealed on the day of judgment.

James charges the Christian community with turning the wanderer in the direction of God's truth. The result of this work can be life everlasting and the hiding of awful sins under the blood of Jesus. His book emphasizes the biblical idea that the spiritual condition of a fellow Christian is of concern to the whole community. James asks his readers to join him in this ministry of reconciliation—of bringing others to the knowledge and truth of God as revealed in Jesus Christ. This knowledge will result in and be validated by a lifestyle pleasing to God.

---

1. Unless indicated, quotations from James are the author's own translation.
2. Peter H. Davids, *The Epistle of James: A Commentary on the Greek Text* (New International

Greek Testament Commentary; Grand Rapids: Eerdmans, 1982), 117.

3. Spiros Zodhiates, ed. *The Complete Word Study Dictionary: New Testament* (Chattanooga, TN: AMG Publishers, 1992), 130.

4. William Bauer, *A Greek-English Lexicon of the New Testament and Other Early Christian Literature* (3rd ed.; trans. and ed. W. F. Arndt, F. W. Gingrich and F. W. Danker; Chicago: University of Chicago Press, 2000), 50–51.

5. David P. Nystrom, *James* (NIV Application Commentary; Grand Rapids: Zondervan, 1997), 318.

6. Nystrom, *James*, 318.

7. Nystrom, *James*, 318.

28

Theological Lessons
from the Letters of Peter and Jude
Daniel G. Powers

B elievers tend to gravitate to an exclusive selection of biblical writings. This tendency results in a "canon within the canon," which means that some parts of the Bible become more authoritative or useful than others. Few who focus on particular books more than others choose to focus primarily on the letters of 1–2 Peter and Jude. These writings, especially 2 Peter and Jude, are among the least popular New Testament books. Still, these overlooked letters incorporate many valuable and inspirational theological ideas and lessons. This essay highlights some of the theological and homiletical themes of these writings that deserve attention.

First Peter

First Peter is not a treatise of systematic theology, but it contains noteworthy theological ideas and lessons.

I. Proto-Trinitarian

One noticeable feature of 1 Peter is its proto-Trinitarian perspective of the divine Godhead. The letter recognizes the function of each person of the Godhead within the lives of believers.

Peter affirms God as the Creator of all things (1 Pet 4:19) and the Judge of the living and the dead (4:5). He recognizes God as the Father of Jesus Christ (1:3) and the Father of all believers (1:17). As the Holy One, God calls God's followers to be holy, even as God is holy (1:15–16). Significantly, he asserts that God is the Author and Initiator of salvation through God's foreknowledge (1:2). Not only does the author recognize God as the Father of Jesus in the proto-Trinitarian formula of 1:2. As the source of new birth (1:3), God is also the Father of Christians. First Peter makes it clear that the salvation of those who believe is the providential plan of God the Father.

The letter also displays a high Christology. Peter accepts the preexistence of Christ as the one "chosen before the creation of the world" (1 Pet 1:20).[1] Christ is Isaiah's servant of Yahweh (2:22–24) and the true paschal lamb (1:19). Through his resurrection, he is exalted to the right hand of God and exercises supremacy over all creation (3:22).

Peter connects salvation to believers' faith in and identity with Christ. He reiterates the centrality of Christ in the salvation of believers throughout the letter. Those who will be saved are obedient to Christ (1 Pet 1:2), reborn, and saved through his resurrection (1:3; 3:21). He describes believers as being rebuilt "into a spiritual house" and "a holy priesthood" as they come to Christ (2:5). Their calling is to follow Christ's example (2:21) and to "participate in the sufferings of Christ" (4:13; see 4:14–16). Finally, believers eagerly await Christ's imminent appearance when they will share in his glory and grace (1:7, 13; 5:4, 10). For Peter, the willingness to follow and obey Christ's call and commands identify true believers, rather than their philosophical declaration of trust and ultimate security based upon God's foreknowledge (1:2).

The Holy Spirit plays an essential role in the salvation of believers. The author portrays the Spirit as the "Spirit of Christ," who actively pointed the prophets to Christ's future suffering and glory (1 Pet 1:11). In the present age, the Holy Spirit sets apart believers to God (1:2) and energizes those who proclaim the gospel (1:12). The "Spirit of glory and of God" rests on those persecuted because of their faith in Christ (4:14).

Other New Testament passages similarly anticipate the later doctrine of the Trinity (e.g., Matt 28:19; 2 Cor 13:14; Eph 4:4–6; Jude 20–21). But 1 Peter is unique (see especially 1:2). Peter portrays the believers' salvation as intricately tied to the threefold work of God the Father, Jesus Christ, and the Holy Spirit. He recognizes each of the three persons of the Godhead as playing an important role in salvation. It would be premature to describe Peter's portrayal of the divine Godhead as a doctrinal Trinity. But he portrays the inter-related, distinct work of each personality in a way that foreshadows later Trinitarian understanding.

2. Suffering

Suffering is a central theme of 1 Peter. The occasion of this letter was the suffering of believers for the sake of Christ. Four sections of the letter deal specifically with suffering: suffering grief in various trials (1 Pet 1:6–7), unjust suffering of slaves (2:18–25), suffering due to the public confession of faith (3:13–18), and suffering "fiery trials" for the faith (4:12–19). Peter correlates the suffering of believers with the sufferings of Christ. He does this in a uniquely New Testament manner. Like Paul, Peter teaches that "the sufferings of Christ are ours" (2 Cor 1:5 NASB; see 2 Cor 4:7–12).

Peter never tries to explain how believers can avoid suffering. Rather, he calls them to endure it. The call to holiness and Christian discipleship is often a call to suffering. The New Testament does not promise a carefree life in this world. Instead, those who heed Christ's call often face hardship (John 14:18; Phil 1:29; Heb 13:13; Jas 1:2). Suffering is not presented as divine punishment or part of some divine plan. Rather, suffering comes from the believers' identity with Christ, who suffered and died. Suffering is not seen as punishment but an inherent feature of faith in Christ.

Although Peter suggests the devil causes suffering (1 Pet 5:8–9), he does not perceive it as something "strange" in believers' lives. Rather, suffering is a natural part of following Christ (4:12). Suffering for Christ's sake refines and purifies believers (1:7; 4:12–13). Moreover, just as God used Christ's sufferings to make salvation possible for believers (3:18), believers' exemplary suffering could have a redemptive effect (2:12; 3:1–2).

Suffering is not inevitable for believers (1 Pet 1:6), but every Christian must be ready to face it (1:7; 4:1). God does not assign every believer to the path of suffering. When suffering comes, it provides opportunity for believers to live according to God's will, in trust and doing good (4:14–19). Thus, the concern here is not *if* believers will face suffering but *how* they should respond. Like Christ, believers should respond to suffering in three ways. First, they should not respond with hate or retaliation (2:21–24; 3:9). Second, they should meet suffering with a spirit of submission (2:13–3:6; 5:6). Third, they should persist in doing good (1:15; 2:12–15, 20, 24; 3:6, 11, 13, 17; 4:2, 17, 19).

Peter provides a general principle as the guiding rule for believers' lives when they suffer (1 Pet 2:11–12). Christians must avoid sinful desires and maintain an exemplary lifestyle in an unbelieving and hostile world. When they do, unbelievers will be saved, and God will be glorified.

Peter offers encouragement to sufferers in several ways. First, suffering provides the test by which believers' faith and convictions are strengthened. It can serve as a refining fire to cleanse and beautify believers' lives and commitments (1 Pet 1:7; 4:17–18). Peter makes it clear that God does not cause the suffering believers face. But God can use that suffering to benefit and refine their lives and faith.

Believers may participate in Jesus' story through suffering. Peter's discussion of the endurance of unjust suffering leads to Christ's example. Ultimately, Jesus' life—including his death and resurrection—is the foundation for all New Testament ethics.

Although the context of his example pertains to slaves (1 Pet 2:21–25), it is relevant for every Christian who suffers injustice.

Believers share in Christ's passion and glory. This will be their permanent reward at the last day. This glory begins in the purified lives of those who participate fully in Jesus' death and resurrection. David L. Bartlett writes, "When Christ does return, those who have suffered for their faith will receive the reward of eternal glory, and the Spirit, which is the firstfruits of that glory, already is given to the faithful who suffer (1:7; 2:11; 4:13; 5:4, 10–11)."[2]

Faithful people are invited to suffer according to God's will (1 Pet 4:19). An inherent part of God's will is that believers continue to trust God and do good despite their suffering. Peter repeatedly emphasizes this exhortation to do what is good. The motivation for doing what is right is multifaceted. Believers are blessed when they do this (3:14; 4:14). God has called them to do this (1:15; 2:20–21). Christ suffered unjustly, and believers should follow his example (2:20–21; 3:17–18). Just as suffering came to Christ uninvited, it also comes to many believers in many uninvited forms: illness, persecution, abandonment, or pain. Such suffering should lead not to despair but to hope and comfort, as believers cast all their cares and anxiety on their Father who cares for them (5:7).

Suffering believers are encouraged because their good conduct under the stress of suffering may draw unbelievers to salvation (1 Pet 2:12; 3:1–2). Christians should live out their faith so clearly in threatening situations that their virtuous conduct may win observers over to the faith. Peter reminds his readers that faithfulness in suffering is a compelling witness.

3. Holiness

First Peter also emphasizes holiness. Holiness is not only spiritual but essentially ethical as well. Holiness of life is a natural byproduct of heart holiness. Peter envisages the importance of holiness in three areas of the believers' lives: personal, social, and communal.

Personal holiness is the foundational tenet of the letter. Note one of Peter's first imperatives: "But just as he who called you is holy, so be holy in all you do" (1 Pet 1:15). Through the Spirit's "sanctifying work" (1:2), the author describes the believers as "self-controlled" (1:13 NIV84), "holy" (1:15), "purified" (1:22), and free from "all malice and all deceit, hypocrisy, envy, and slander" (2:1).

Peter underscores the pervasive influence of holiness in the personal life of believers by calling his readers to be holy "in all you do" (1 Pet 1:15). This specific verb (anastrephō) is a favorite word in Peter's letter (1:15, 18; 2:12; 3:1, 2, 16; 2 Pet 2:7; 3:11). It means "to move about, to turn about." It refers to behavior or lifestyle. It covers "all actions, thoughts, words, and relationships."[3] Thus, Peter invites his readers to be holy in everything, including attitude and action. This call to holiness is extremely inclusive. No aspect of believers' lives falls outside the command to be holy.

Peter expected love for others to be the ultimate feature of holiness in believers' lives (1 Peter 1:22). Holiness affects the believers' relationship with God and with other people. Thus, Peter expected personal holiness to flow automatically into social holiness.

Whereas 1 Peter 1:13–2:10 deals with the believers' call and experience of personal holiness, 2:11–4:11 focuses on social holiness in terms of their relationship to non-Christians. For God's sake, believers were to obey the law of the government (2:13–14) and the king (2:13, 17). They were also to submit to their masters or husbands, even if they were unfair, cruel, or unbelieving (2:18–20; 3:1–2). Additionally, Peter was concerned that believers not offend unbelievers unnecessarily (2:11–12, 15; 3:15–16). Early Christians were often falsely accused on political grounds as enemies of the state, on religious grounds as atheists, and on ethical grounds as introducing unlawful customs.[4] Peter urges Christians to live in ways that refute such false accusations. The presupposition is that personal holiness will affect daily behavior and social relationships.

Personal holiness also leads to communal holiness. It affects the believers' relationships with one another. Peter stated that love, hospitality, service according to gifts, servant leadership, and humility should characterize relationships among believers (1 Pet 4:7–11; 5:1–7). These virtues were important because they led to unity within the church.

The purpose of communal holiness was twofold. First, the integrity and uprightness of believers' church relationships would make their lives easier, because they were innately good (1 Pet 4:8–10). Second, their exemplary relationships with each other would keep the community together during societal opposition and suffering (5:1–5). Holiness was the keystone of the believers' defense and response to the constant threat of suffering in a hostile society.

Second Peter

Second Peter is arguably the most neglected book in the New Testament. Despite the fact its opening verse claims the apostle Simon Peter as its author, people express more doubts about the authenticity of 2 Peter than any other New Testament book. Its argumentative and negative outlook intensifies its unpopularity. The immoral lifestyle and errant doctrine of false teachers threatened the letter's original readers. The author attacks and rebukes these opponents mercilessly. The aggressive onslaught of 2 Peter's criticism of false doctrine and its teachers puts off many readers.

Nonetheless, 2 Peter offers a message today's believers should not be so quick to ignore. This letter reminds Christians that the Scriptures and the apostolic tradition provide the only solid foundation for truth. It warns believers of the risk of being carried away by lofty-sounding arguments or a lifestyle of selfish convenience. Sometimes believers need the reminder of the dangers of false teaching as well as the truth of God's plan of salvation through Jesus Christ. Second Peter is the passionate broadcast of these important reminders.

1. Day of judgment

The letter strongly affirms Christ's return accompanied by a day of judgment. As in Peter's time, today's society flaunts sexual promiscuity and blatantly disregards a virtuous and moral lifestyle. Many people scoff at personal accountability or a day of judgment for their conduct. Their hollow excuse is that God would not deny the fulfillment of their pleasure. Peter reminded believers that people could not do this and get away with it in God's world. God's judgment of sin and sinners is certain.

The final judgment will resemble God's acts of judgment recorded in the Old Testament. Peter reminds his readers of God's judgment on fallen angels (2 Pet 2:4) and the wicked people of Noah and Lot's days (2:5–6). Scripture establishes the pattern of God's destructive judgment on wickedness and sin. The certainty of judgment there is like a dark cloud that hovers incessantly (sometimes imperceptibly) above every human who ever lived. The justice of God may be delayed, but it cannot be avoided.

Alongside this dark pattern of judgment is a promising pattern of divine deliverance of the righteous. The silver lining of that dark cloud is the promise of God's grace. As with Noah and Lot, God will rescue those who seek and follow God. Indeed, God can be trusted to save the righteous on the last day (2 Pet 2:5–9).

Second Peter is the only New Testament writing that explicitly describes God's judgment as accompanied by the world's destruction by fire (2 Pet 3:7, 12). This image is probably derived from Old Testament portrayals of the "day of the Lord" (Ps 97:3; Isa 66:15–16; Dan 7:9–10; Mic 1:4; Mal 4:1). In such apocalyptic texts, the image of fire is often not intended literally; rather, "it means purification and the destruction of evil when God comes to judge the world."[5]

Peter explicitly connects fire with judgment by clarifying that the world is reserved for fire on the day of judgment (2 Pet 3:7). The association of fire with the destruction of the ungodly implies that fire relates more to the judgment of sinners than to the destruction of the world. Peter's anticipation of "a new heaven and a new earth" (3:13) probably foresees a time when the created order will no longer be subject to the effects of ungodliness and sin (see Rom 8:18–22; 1 Cor 15:24–28).

The creation of the world took place by the power of God's word. Likewise, the power of God's word destroyed the world with water during the days of Noah. In the same way, God's word will effect divine judgment and destruction on the world by fire at the last day (2 Pet 3:5–7). This divine word will also create the anticipated new heaven and earth (3:13). Peter connects the second coming with the day of judgment. God is the Judge of the last day (3:5–10), but this day corresponds with the day of Christ's return (3:4).

Second Peter reminds its readers that divine perspective on time is different from the human perspective. While Christ's return may appear tardy and overdue from a human viewpoint, it is not so for God (2 Pet 3:8). The apparent delay in Christ's return is due to God's patience. This allows more time for believers to pursue holiness (3:15). It also provides more opportunity for the ungodly to repent (3:9). But Christ will return at an unexpected time, and the world will be subjected to judgment (3:9–10). Then, the ungodly will be condemned and destroyed (2:1, 3b, 9–10a, 12; 3:7, 16). But believers will be warmly welcomed into the eternal kingdom (1:11), where they will dwell in a new heaven and earth (3:13).

2. Scripture and apostolic tradition

Second Peter strongly asserts that orthodox Christian doctrine is based on the dual foundation of Scripture and apostolic tradition (2 Pet 1:16–21; 3:2). Peter asserts that the Holy Spirit enabled apostles and prophets to bear witness to "the power and coming of our Lord Jesus Christ" (1:16). The false teachers denied that Christ was powerful (2:1–22) and was coming again (3:1–13). The false teaching is based on empty, lofty-sounding arguments that appeal to the lustful desires of sinful humanity (2:18). In contrast, Peter urges his readers to recall the words of the holy prophets (Scripture) and the teachings of Jesus (tradition) and the apostles who pass it on (3:2). In the midst of conflicting claims and conclusions, Peter appeals to a dual foundation for Christian authority to determine right doctrine and behavior:

1. the words of the holy prophets, and
2. the teaching of the Lord and Savior transmitted through the apostles.

In affirming this foundation for "wholesome thinking" (3:1), Peter "stresses the link between the prophets who foreshadowed Christian truth, Christ who exemplified it, and the apostles who gave an authoritative interpretation of it."[6]

Peter's letter reminds Christians of their responsibility as faithful stewards of Christian tradition and teaching. Peter denigrated the grandiose-sounding doctrine of the false teachers because it was empty. Believers must establish their teaching on the solid rock of Scripture. One cannot substitute fine-sounding arguments or lofty words for the rich substance of the faith as taught in Scripture. Peter establishes Scripture and apostolic tradition as the litmus test for orthodox Christian teaching.

3. Divine inspiration

We find one of the New Testament's greatest statements about divine inspiration in 2 Peter. Popular understanding of the inspiration of Scripture moves toward two extremes. One extreme emphasizes the divine origin of inspiration (*God* inspired the Bible) to the point that human involvement is virtually eliminated. The other emphasizes the human origin of inspiration (*humans* wrote the Bible) to the point that divine involvement is practically eliminated.

Peter articulates a mediating position: "men spoke from God" (2 Peter 1:21 NIV84) Prophets chose their words according to their own vocabulary, style, and social situation. But the words they chose were the words that God wanted them to use to communicate God's message to humankind. He does not explain exactly how they could speak their own words as the words of God. Peter simply asserts that this happened "as they are carried along by the Holy Spirit" (1:21). We will never fully understand divine inspiration. But no doctrine of Scripture can neglect *either* the human participation *or* the divine inspiration in the origin of Scripture.

With the phrase, "men spoke from God as they were carried along by the Holy Spirit" (2 Pet 1:21), Peter establishes the paradoxical truth of the divine-human interplay in inspiration. The false teachers claimed that prophecy was only human in origin. Peter confirms human participation in the writing of Scripture. But he insists that these human words were from God, who inspired the writers through the Holy Spirit. The verb translated "carried along" (*pherō*) was used to describe a ship driven by the wind (Acts 27:15, 17). "The prophets raised their sails, so to speak … and the Holy Spirit filled them and carried their craft along in the direction he wished."[7] It remains a mystery precisely how this happens. But Peter affirms that, as the prophets spoke, God spoke.

Likewise, the apostles' testimony is inspired inasmuch as they were eyewitnesses of Christ's majesty (2 Pet 1:16) and heard God's voice concerning Christ (1:17–18). Surprisingly, Peter considers an unspecified collection of Paul's letters as inspired Scripture (3:16). Just as the Holy Spirit moved the Old Testament prophets, Paul wrote his letters "with the wisdom that God gave him" (3:15). This precedent later facilitated the church's establishment of a Christian canon that was deemed both authoritative and inspired along with the Old Testament Scriptures.

4. Evidence of a holy lifestyle

A fourth theme in 2 Peter is the emphasis on the believers' holy lifestyle as an inherent reflection of their faith in Christ. Peter urges believers "to live holy and godly lives" (2 Pet 3:11). Holiness is not a special hobby for a few extremely devout believers. Rather, Peter calls *all believers* to a lifestyle of holiness as the only appropriate way for Christians to prepare for the Lord's coming. Believers anticipate a new heaven and earth where righteousness will dwell (3:13). Consequently, they must make a concerted effort to live holy lives that are fit to dwell in this new world (1:5).

Peter's list of virtues (2 Pet 1:5–7) describes what holy and godly lives look like and illustrates how Christian faith is to be worked out in personal and social behavior. He urges believers to pursue and possess the virtues "in increasing measure" so that they remain effective and productive (1:8). Peter also urges believers to continue to "grow in the grace and knowledge of our Lord and Savior Jesus Christ" (3:18). There is never an appropriate time for believers to stop in their growth or to fall back on imagined laurels of their secure position of salvation (3:17). If believers want to live in the glorious home of righteousness, their faith must demonstrate itself in a holy lifestyle. This is foundational to the call to holiness of heart and life.

The false teachers' denial of Christ's return and judgment led them into immoral sensuality and greed. According to 2 Peter, bad teaching results in bad behavior. Likewise, incorrect behavior reflects an incorrect faith. "Immoral behavior is an affront to Christ's status as Lord and Savior. It amounts to denying his authority and maligning the way of truth (2:1–2)."[8] Thus, a pervasive theme of 2 Peter is that true saving knowledge of Jesus Christ as Lord and Savior will motivate believers to make every effort to live virtuous and holy lives. Christians must continue to grow in their relationship (*epignōsis*) with the Lord and in their knowledge (*gnōsis*) of the Lord until the very end.

Peter calls his readers to live holy and godly lives as they anticipate Christ's return. When he comes, believers should be at peace with Christ. This is possible only as they imitate Christ in their daily behavior (2 Pet 3:14). Believers should live holy lives. The word translated "holy" (*hagios*) means "pure, blameless" as well as "set apart" for God. Believers should reflect God's character of holiness. They should live godly lives (3:11), reflecting the God they come to know in Christ. The language is similar to that of 1 Peter, where believers are urged to live lives of holiness and righteousness (1 Pet 1:15–16, 22; 2:1–2, 12, 15; 3:1–2, 16). In both letters, Peter asserts that a standard of holiness must permeate every area of believers' lives. Anything less than holy and godly conduct marks a deficiency in the believers' preparation for the Lord's coming. Peter's language ensures that holiness of heart and life is both possible and expected of true believers.

Jude

Although Jude is one of the shortest and least familiar writings in the New Testament, it contains several key teachings that believers would benefit learning.

1. Christian faith and practice

One important theme of Jude is his emphasis upon the content of the Christian faith. The majority of the letter is a polemic against false teaching. But Jude never specifies what constitutes correct teaching. Rather, he "assumes that there is a 'faith' committed to the Church, a truth by which it stands or falls and which is not to be tampered with."[9]

Thus, one major theme focuses on the Christian faith. Jude calls his readers to adhere to the proclamation of the gospel— "the Faith"—as received from the apostles (Jude 3, 5, 17). Paul and other early believers spoke of faith in a subjective sense ("I believe in . . ."). However, Jude speaks of faith in an objective sense ("I believe that . . ."). He emphasizes the *content* of faith, not the *act* of believing.

Despite Jude's emphasis on the Christian faith, his concern is not doctrinal issues, but the moral implications of errant doctrine. Just because someone claims to be spiritual does not make it so (Jude 14–19). One's upright and holy behavior must demonstrate true spirituality. His opponents' rejection of moral constraints led to blatant and shameless immorality. The false teaching of the intruders had become a "license for immorality" (4). For Jude, correct beliefs lead to correct behavior. Likewise, false beliefs lead to improper behavior. Although Jude does not identify the content of his opponents' heresy, their immoral and improper behavior proved their false doctrine and teaching. Although it might not be immediately apparent, the fruit of bad faith often turns out to be rotten and deplorable.

2. Living in the end times

Jude says believers are already living in the last days. The presence of scoffing opponents indicated that the end time was imminent (Jude 17–19). Just as God acted in the past to condemn sinners, God will judge sinners at the last day (5–13). Conversely, faithful Christians will receive mercy. And God will reward them with eternal life (2, 21, 24).

Heightened eschatological expectation assigned believers a double duty. First, they must remain faithful themselves as they "contend for the faith" (Jude 3, 20–21). This calls for more than self-defensive measures. Jude calls for the church to take the offensive against those who pervert the Christian faith. He appeals to Christians to contend for the faith, both positively and aggressively. Believers should articulate their doctrinal convictions. They should also commit themselves to a lifestyle corresponding to that faith. Jude expects believers to pursue the Christian life with the same dedication and passion as an athlete in training. Since the verb translated "contend" is in the present tense, the expectation is that believers will continue this work.

Second, they must try to save others from the fire of judgment by extracting them from the false teachers (Jude 22–23). Believers must examine the passion and determination they exhibit in their evangelistic and outreach efforts. Jude urges his readers to aggressive action—to "snatch others from the fire" (23).

Jude's words do not give permission for rude and insensitive methods of reaching out to the lost. But many will be eternally lost unless some caring Christians are willing to risk misunderstanding or rejection to "snatch" them from the fire. The words "snatch others" mean that not *all* evangelistic efforts should be aggressive and confrontational in their approach. But these words imply that at least *some* evangelistic efforts must be aggressive and forceful. Otherwise, an entire group of people run the risk of being eternally lost.

3. Christology

Jude affirms the lordship of Jesus Christ repeatedly and powerfully (Jude 4, 14, 17, 21, 25). Christ not only preserves believers in their salvation (1), but salvation is possible only through him (25). As "Sovereign" (4) and "Lord" (4, 14, 17, 21, 25), Christ demands obedience. Ultimate salvation requires the lifelong obedience of Christians to him (21).

Those who live immoral lives deny the lordship of Jesus Christ (Jude 4). These people will be judged and condemned (5–13). Throughout the letter, salvation is inextricably linked to Christ the Savior. Salvation is only possible through the keeping power of God and God's Son, Jesus Christ (1, 24). The moral behavior and obedience to Christ of true believers provides the evidence of salvation.

Despite his strong Christology, Jude underscores the interconnected work of God the Father, Jesus Christ the Son, and the Holy Spirit in the salvation of believers. Accordingly, God's love provides the foundation for believers' salvation (Jude 21). The "mercy of our Lord Jesus Christ" is both the means and agency of that salvation (21). And the Holy Spirit guides and empowers the prayers of believers as they pursue this salvation (20). Thus, although salvation occurs through the enabling mercy of Jesus Christ, Christians are granted assurance of this salvation as they build themselves up in the faith, pray in the Holy Spirit, and keep themselves in God's love (20–21).

_____

1. Unless indicated, biblical quotations are from the NIV translation.
2. David L. Bartlett, "The First Letter of Peter," in *The New Interpreter's Bible* (12 vols., ed. L. E. Keck; Nashville: Abingdon, 1998), 12:252.
3. Frederic R. Howe, "The Christian Life in Peter's Theology," *Bibliotheca Sacra* 157 (2000): 306–7.
4. Charles S. Ball, "First and Second Peter," in *The Wesleyan Bible Commentary* (6 vols., ed. C. W. Carter; Grand Rapids: Eerdmans, 1966), 6:260.
5. Michael Green, *The Second Epistle of Peter and the General Epistle of Jude: An Introduction and Commentary* (Tyndale New Testament Commentaries 18; Grand Rapids: Eerdmans, 1987), 144.
6. Ibid, 135.
7. Ibid, 102.
8. Watson, "The Second Letter of Peter," 331.
9. G.R. Beasley-Murray, *The General Epistles: James, 1 Peter, Jude, 2 Peter* (Bible Guides 21; New York: Abingdon, 1965), 74.

29

This We Proclaim:
Preaching from the Johannine Letters

Rick L. Williamson

A Context for the Texts

When we open our Bibles seeking to understand 1, 2, and 3 John, several challenges appear. First, we are doing something our parents told us *not* to do. We are reading someone else's mail! These letters were not written *to* us, but they are important *for* us. After all, Paul's teaching applies to these books as well: "Scripture is God-breathed and is useful for teaching, rebuking, correcting and training in righteousness" (2 Tim 3:16).[1]

A second challenge is that we only have one side of the conversation. When we listen to someone talking on the phone, we can only piece together the contents of that exchange. Sometimes, the New Testament writers give us some of the other "voice." For instance, Paul writes, "Now for the matters you wrote about" (1 Cor 7:1), and then addresses issues the Corinthian Christians mentioned in an earlier letter. Even then, details are missing or sketchy.

A third challenge is that the sender and the recipients of these letters lived long ago and far away. They were very different from us. Issues of time, geography, and culture increase the challenge for us to read with good understanding.

Responsible interpreters do not read the Bible in a "daily vitamin" sort of way: shaking out a random verse while paying no attention to its original context. We ask the basic questions of the journalist: "Who?" "What?" "Why?" "When?" "Where?" "How?" and eventually "So what?" Only when we identify with the characters, understand the historical setting (time and place), and come to grips with the cultural context—all of this to a limited extent— can we better understand what these letters may have originally *meant*.

At that point, we can begin to understand what they now *mean*. Meaning arises in part from the context (history, literature, and culture) of the written text—that is, what stands *behind* the text and shapes it. Key words and themes *in* the text also convey meaning. Finally, these letters offer meaning for us as we engage the text in serious study. Life lessons flow *from* the text.

1. Who Are the People in This Scripture Story—Author?

These writings were early identified with John, Jesus' disciple (Irenaeus, *Against Heresies* 3.16.5; Tertullian, *Against Marcion* 5.16).[2] Some think the closing lines of the Gospel of John point to a "Fourth Evangelist," a redactor (editor) who preserved and formalized the traditions received from the Apostle John. Others consider the letters' author to be part of a Johannine "school," a faith community that shared a theological worldview derived from John.[3] The Gospel of John and 1 John may have come from the same hand.[4]

The letters of 2 and 3 John came from "the elder" (2 John 1; 3 John 1), probably a title of honor indicating a position of responsibility in the churches (see Acts 14:23; 15:22; 16:4; 1 Tim 4:14; 5:17). The title may also suggest advanced age. To keep things simple, this essay will refer to the author of 1 John as "John," and the author of 2 and 3 John as "the elder."

2. Who Are the People—Those who Remained—in This Story?

These letters were addressed to Christians, whom the author calls "brothers" (1 John 3:13, 14, 16; 3 John 3, 5, 10) and "children of God" (1 John 3:1, 2, 10; 5:2, 19). They are "dear children" (9 times in 1 John) or "children" (3 times in 2 John; once in 3 John). Family-like relationships mark their faith. They know what love is because Christ died on their behalf, and they are expected to love one another accordingly (1 John 3:16). John reminds them that they are forgiven, know God, have conquered the evil one, and have God's word living in them (2:12–14). Knowing and living in such essential truths will keep them from sin (2:1). He also warns them about any who would deceive them (2:26) and lead them out of the Johannine fellowship.

3. Who Are the People—Those who Left—in This Story?

A key part of the story appears in 1 John 2:18–19, 26. A group once identified with the Johannine churches had left (2:19). John is distressed that anyone would leave the church and might persuade others to follow suit. There is an adversarial element also in 3 John. Diotrephes refused to acknowledge the elder's authority (3 John 9), spread false rumors, and refused fellowship to some of the elder's traveling ministers.

4. When Did This Happen?

Most New Testament scholars think that these letters were written in the last decade of the first century AD. If they followed the Gospel of John chronologically, as most believe, then a date in the 90's makes most sense.[5]

5. Where in the World Did This Happen?

The letters contain no references to any cities or regions. However, early tradition identified the letters with Ephesus. This western part of modern Turkey was a center of Christian activity. Paul spent time there during his second and third missionary journeys. According to Acts, Paul ministered longer in Ephesus than any other location (Acts 19). Ephesus was one of the seven churches addressed by Revelation (Rev 2:1–3:22). Western Turkey continues to claim strong traditional links to the Apostle John. Contemporary tour guides of that part of the world are eager to take tourists to locations traditionally associated with John the Apostle. Countless icons of John's face adorn the churches (and gift shops!) of that area.

6. What Is the Big Deal Anyway?

These letters focus importantly on Christology. Some had left the Johannine churches (1 John 2:19). The rift was between the orthodoxy identified with John and a "super-sized" Christology that overemphasized Jesus' divinity in the Gospel of John. These secessionists had such a lofty view of Christ that they denied his true humanity. John insisted that Jesus came "in the flesh" (4:2; 2 John 7). He vigorously began 1 John depicting Christ as having been "heard . . . seen with our eyes . . . looked at and our hands have touched" (1 John 1:1).

John understood that the denial of Jesus' humanity resulted in damaging errors. Some separated the Christ (only a heavenly being) from Jesus (the earthly man). They taught that Christ only *seemed* to be human. Some believed that the Christ spirit came upon Jesus of Nazareth at baptism and accompanied him during his earthly ministry, but that this heavenly spirit separated from Jesus prior to his death on the cross. Thus, so they believed, Jesus died on the cross but "the Christ spirit" did not. Then, since the Christ had already been whisked to heaven (for he cannot die), no resurrection was needed.

Enjoy the "Sweet Spots"—
Attractive Texts in These Letters

Our study now turns to ten powerful passages in these letters. I call these "sweet spots," because they are choice Scripture portions that "beg" us to study, teach, and preach them.

1. 1 John 1:1–4 — Christ's humanity as key to our holiness

Most believers in Jesus today are quick to defend his divinity. Unbelievers often embrace his humanity and affirm him as a great teacher or inspirational leader. But in the letters of John, the dangerous challenge arose from some who overemphasized Christ's divinity, even to the point of the denial of his true humanity.

The prologue of 1 John (1:1–4) distinctly emphasizes the humanity of Jesus Christ. Three times, John asserts that they had "seen" the Lord (1:1, 2, 3) and that this vision continued to affect them (the Greek perfect tense refers to past action with continuing effect). Twice, John affirms that they "heard" the Lord (1:1, 3) and his message continued to "move" them (again, perfect tense). That is, they could not get away from what they had seen and heard. We must understand the context for 1 John to appreciate the Christological threat in that time. Having done that, our challenge is to hold to a view of Christ that affirms and balances both his divinity and humanity. When we allow the pendulum to swing too far in either direction, the result is theological error.

John's emphasis of Jesus' full humanity demonstrates that humans can live a holy life (4:2; 2 John 7), since Jesus was "tempted in every way, just as we are—yet he did not sin" (Heb 4:15). Being "in the flesh" did not keep Christ from living in ways that were pleasing before God. Likewise, we humans can live a holy life.

2. 1 John 1:8–9 — Confession of sin leading to pardon and purity

John argues against people who were claiming either they had never sinned or sin did not affect them as "spiritual" beings (1 John 1:8). But John insists that denying we have "sin" (*hamartia*, the singular form here may refer to sinfulness as *condition*) is self-deception. This denial of this truth blocks the pardon and purity that follows upon genuine confession of "our sins" (1:9). How many people sit in churches each week, desperately needing to abandon denial and admit their sinfulness, so they might receive forgiveness and purification?

Many people flippantly acknowledge they sin, but then they quickly excuse themselves by saying, "I'm only human." They affirm the biblical reality of sin (see Rom 3:23), but then they promptly dismiss responsibility for change. The view that all are sinners but that sin is of no consequence robs people of the rich promises in this passage. When we dare to "confess our sins," we tap into God's awesome grace that brings pardon and cleansing. This promise comes from God who is "faithful and just" (1 John 1:9), so we need not wonder whether God will do as God said. Although the promise is conditional, the outcome is not after we meet the conditions.

3. I John 2:1–2 — Atoning sacrifice and prevenient grace

In warm, endearing language, John writes, "My dear children." Just verses before, John argued that all experienced sin (1 John 1:8, 10). Now he makes a surprising (at first glance) and lofty call. He writes, "so that you will not sin" (2:1). John had surely not forgotten what he had just written, that we all have sins on our record and sinfulness with which to deal (1:8–10).

John would agree with Paul that "all have sinned" (Rom 3:23). But John would also agree with Paul that an ongoing practice of sin is not a necessity (see Rom 6:1). Although sin is universally experienced, it need not define us into our future. If we do sin, we have "one who speaks to the Father in our defense—Jesus Christ the Righteous One" (1 John 2:2 NIV84). The Apostle Paul aptly stated, "Christ Jesus came into the world to save sinners—of whom I am the worst" (1 Tim 1:15).

John Newton, former slave ship captain turned Christian and author of the timeless hymn "Amazing Grace," late in life observed, "My memory is nearly gone, but I remember two things: That I am a great sinner and that Christ is a great Savior."[6]

This great Savior is always in pursuit of his wayward children, seeking to redeem "the whole world" (1 John 2:2). God follows after us, seeking to win our heart. Before we have even a first faint turning toward God, we are the objects of divine grace. This grace precedes our coming to faith and is appropriately called "prevenient," from two Latin words meaning "to come before." God's prevenient grace comes to us before we come to God, and it enables our coming to God.

4. I John 3:1–3 — The lavish love of God

God loves us more than words can say. As John conveys the exceeding greatness of divine love, he uses vivid language. His statement, "How great [potapēn] is the love" (1 John 3:1), uses the language of magnificence (see, e.g., Mark 13:1). When Jesus' disciples marveled at his great power, they used similar language: "What kind [potapos] of man is this?" (Matt 8:27). So John's exclamation really sounds like this: "What massive and magnificent love! What kind of love is this?" The refrain of the gospel song "My Savior's Love" by Charles H. Gabriel suggests this:

> "O how marvelous! O how wonderful! And my song shall ever be:
> O how marvelous! O how wonderful! Is my Savior's love for me!"

This lavish love enables us to be called "children of God" (1 John 3:1). We not only receive a particular designation—"children"—but also become expressions of *God's character*. The relationship reshapes us. Although we are children "now," there is more to our redemption than we experience here and now (3:2). However, this not-yet-known future identity is clearly Christ-likeness: "we shall be like him" (3:2). Christian holiness takes its identity from the character and attitude of Jesus.

John calls the readers to "purify themselves" (1 John 3:3 NRSV). It is important to note that the verb translated "purify" is in the present tense, which suggests an ongoing, dynamic translation: "be continually purifying" (author's translation). This does not mean that persons do the purifying work. Rather, we must invite God into our lives so God's purifying presence may accomplish that work. In that sense, we are purifying ourselves.[7]

Attention to our spiritual condition prepares us for entry into the divine presence.[8] In John's day, pilgrims for Passover would present themselves "for their ceremonial cleansing" (literally, "so that they might sanctify [hagnisōsin] themselves"; John 11:55).[9] Similar to John's call to purify self is the majestic line in Jesus' prayer in John 17:19, "I sanctify [hagiazō] myself." 1 John 3:3 does not present purity as future reward but that which qualifies one to see God (see Matt 5:8).

5. 1 John 3:16–18 — Love that takes action

In the movie *Wind Talkers*, a Marine, Joe Enders, carries a Navajo soldier out of the heat of battle back to safety. Although he saves the soldier, Enders is fatally shot. The Navajo soldier offers his dying friend the reassurance, "We saved a lot of Marines today, Joe." The kind of heroism that gives up one's life to save others happens countless times in war, catastrophic events, and quieter, less dramatic moments of life. The supreme example of Jesus, who "laid down his life for us" (1 John 3:16) becomes a defining image of the other-centered living that should characterize Christians.

One might present this theme during a memorial service dedicated to those who fell in battle or a natural disaster, who gave up their own lives so others might live. Thankfully, we may not have to make these kinds of difficult choices. But when John says "we ought to lay down our lives for our brothers and sisters" (1 John 3:16), he presses the challenge onto all readers in every age. He speaks of laying down one's life through providing "material possessions" (3:17). In language reminiscent of James, John calls for a Christian love that leads us to live generously toward others with actions, not simply with a few empty words (3:18; cf. Jas 2:14–17).

6. I John 4:4 — God who has overcome the world

God, who lives within us, is greater than the one in the world. Indeed, "the prince of this world now stands condemned" (John 16:11). There is a clear and present spiritual victory for all who have the living Christ within. While spiritual darkness is a reality (1 John 2:18; 3:12; 2 John 7), we are not to fear Satan or give Satan too much credit!

John declares that his original readers had already overcome those of "the spirit of the antichrist" (1 John 4:3–4). The verb translated "have overcome" (perfect tense) indicates a past victory with continuing effect. They had defeated the enemies of truth who preferred darkness, and the victory still holds! While *God* has overcome the world, John states that the divine victory over those who "speak from the viewpoint of the world" (4:5) was achieved *through John's readers* who obediently responded to God. God does not hurl lightning bolts to erase spiritual enemies. Rather, God shares divine life with us (we are "dear children . . . from God" and have God's presence "in you") so that we become partners in the battle against evil.

Many people in the pews live as though the outcome of the spiritual battle of the ages is still too close to call. But there is no doubt about that outcome in Scripture. Satan is a defeated foe whose days are numbered (John 16:11). "The darkness is passing and the true light is already shining" (1 John 2:8). Although Satan still prowls around the world "like a roaring lion looking for someone to devour" (1 Peter 5:8), Christians need not be oppressed and defeated by evil.

7. I John 4:7–12 — God's love to us, God's love through us

John presents a wonderfully preachable message. God showed immeasurable love to us through Jesus' sacrifice, so we should love each other. Love comes from God (1 John 4:7) and appears wherever people live in love. Living in love is the evidence that we are children of God.

John asserts that love is not an emotion to be felt so much as action to be taken. God's "love . . . sent his Son as an atoning sacrifice" (1 John 4:10). Love acts. Love moves toward others in redeeming ways. True God-like love cannot remain on the sidelines. When we have received God's love, we become part of a "relay team."

When my wife and I were married in a little North Dakota town, my family members parked their camper at the home of a friend of my wife's family (there was no campground to be found). This friend, a devoted Christian, provided water, electricity, and access to his house for days while my family attended the various activities around our wedding. When I said I did not know how I could repay him, he replied, "Just pass it on." As part of God's love relay team, we are called to "pass it on." As John reminded his readers, "since God so loved us, we also ought to love one another" (4:11).

8. I John 4:12, 17–18 — Love made perfect

When God lives in us, God's love can be "made complete in us" (1 John 4:12). This completion of divine love is relational: "Whoever lives in love lives in God, and God in him" (4:16). God's love does not achieve its intended purpose separate from others. Rather, God's redemptive love finds its completion in being "made perfect in love" (4:18) among believers (4:17). The community of faith provides the context for the fulfillment of God's purposes.

We may sometimes wonder how to live out God's calling when living among sometimes fickle, even contrary and carnal people! But there is no other way. When Moses led the people of God from Egypt, he expressed exasperation about the people, whom he called "rebellious and stiff-necked" (Deut 31:27). At other times, he interceded on behalf of these same people and almost begged for God's forgiveness (e.g., Exod 32:32). God's holiness finds validation through people and among people. If it is not evident in human relationships, it is counterfeit.

Here John seems to echo Jesus' words, "Be perfect as I am perfect" (Matt 5:48). This is not perfection of performance but of God's love doing its transformative work in lives. Such love "drives out fear" (1 John 4:18). The persons in whom God's love is genuinely and deeply at work will no longer fear God's judgment, the fear that "has to do with punishment" (4:18). We can live in peace and assurance before God now.

9. I John 5:13–15 — Assurance of eternal life

John pronounces a deeply comforting claim: we can *know* that we have eternal life. John was eager that his followers have assurance of their relationship with God. The Gospel of John ends by saying that it was written so that the readers might know that Jesus is the Christ (John 20:31). Here John ends by saying that he wrote this letter so that his readers would know that they have eternal life. This salvation—which John describes in terms of knowing Christ and having eternal life (1 John 5:13; cf. John 3:15)—is not something for which John believes we can only hope. Rather, we can have and experience this eternal life now.

10. 2 John 5–6; 3 John 3–4 — Walking with God and one another

Walking is a rich metaphor for living in relationship with God. To walk with God is to obey God, to "keep in step with the Spirit"

(Gal 5:25). Walking is an ongoing activity, not a static experience. Walking with the Lord will deepen our love for others making the same journey. The idea of spiritual development as relational will keep us from the error of thinking we can be "lone ranger" Christians who can live separated from others.

Watch Out for These Mine Fields— Tough Texts in the Letters

In addition to the promise of the ten powerful passages in the three Johannine letters, there are six "mine fields" that we must also briefly consider that hold some peril for the teacher/preacher if they are used without careful and prayerful study.

1. 1 John 1:8–2:2 — Atonement

How do we communicate the amazing benefit of Christ's death for us, yet not become too involved with technical language and speculation? The text calls us to celebrate the personal transformation that Isaac Watts so powerfully described: "At the cross, at the cross where I first saw the light, and the burden of my heart rolled away." In whatever way we might interpret the cross, one thing is certain: it declares the absolute sufficiency of Christ's death. His death achieved its intended purpose or goal. In this sense, we should hear Jesus' cry from the cross, "It is finished" (John 19:30).

2. 1 John 2:18–19; 2 John 7 — "Antichrist" and "antichrists"

Many are surprised that John employs both the singular form "antichrist" and the plural "antichrists." After all, doesn't everyone know that *the* Antichrist is a grand, personified, evil individual? One person, certainly not several? And doesn't everyone know that *the* Antichrist is an end-times character, not a first-century figure?

John's concern was not some anti-God activity two thousand years into his future. John wrote, "Children, it is the last hour" (1 John 2:18) in the *first* century. What might John tell us about first-century individuals that were so dangerous as to be labeled "antichrists"? A responsible reading of these verses does not hit the fast-forward button and zoom to the twenty-first century (or whenever "the last hour" might be). John had in view people operating in divisive ways among churches in his area of influence in the first century. He wrote to combat false teaching *then*. Specifically, he confronted a docetic-type Christology and the personalities agitating his churches. These antichrist references in 1 John and 2 John should not be used to build a scenario of end-times, twenty-first century speculation.

3. I John 2:26–27 — Anointing

For John, anointing refers to action by the Spirit of God that enables Christians to understand God's truth better. Anointing assists us in comprehending and embracing correct doctrine, not in finding "new" truth. John may be using the term as a counterpoint to his opponents (see 1 John 2:19), who apparently claimed special knowledge. John's word choices here function as a clever word-play—"You have an anointing [*chrisma*] that permits you to distinguish the true Anointed One [*Christos*] and his teaching from the antichrists [*antichristoi*] and their false claims."

4. I John 3:4–6, 9–10 — Sin

One might misunderstand this passage to teach that we *cannot* sin once we become Christians. But sin is not *impossible*. Rather, willful sin is *unnecessary* for those who walk "in the light" and continually experience purifying by "the blood of Jesus" (1 John 1:7). John's repeated use of present tense verbs suggests that those born of God do not habitually practice sin. Sin as rebellion (3:4) has been conquered. As Charles Wesley so appropriately stated, Christ "breaks the power of canceled sin" ("O for a Thousand Tongues to Sing").

5. I John 3:21–22 — Prayer

A careless reading of the passage that we "receive from him anything we ask" (1 John 3:22) leads to error in our understanding of prayer. A belief that making prayerful requests with the correct formula (e.g., "in Jesus' name") obligates God to honor our requests turns prayer into magic and makes it selfish. The context in 1 John 3 suggests we are in a better position to hear from God when we are generous with our material possessions and live out God's love (3:17–18). How can we *always* get what we ask from God? By aligning ourselves so closely with God's purposes that we want what God wants. When our heart beats in rhythm with God's heart, then our asking will be on target. When "we keep his commands and do what pleases him" (3:22), we can pray with success.

6. 3 John 9–10 — Confrontation

This sharp word from "the elder" might be used as justification for using the pulpit, Sunday School lectern, or a time of public "testimony" to blast someone in the church—to "call attention to what he is doing" (3 John 10). But should we? We are wise to remember that the Bible does not necessarily *prescribe* everything that it *describes*. The Christian leader who confronts another must rely heavily on the Holy Spirit to convict the divisive individual (lest *we* become the divisive one). When we confront someone, it must be a truly important issue and not just over our wounded pride, or worse, as a power grab.

Closing Thoughts

These small letters offer rich lessons. Their value far exceeds their length. The God of love and light shines from these pages and seeks to transform all who will hear and "walk in the light" (1 John 1:7).

1. Unless noted, biblical quotations are from the NIV translation.
2. F. F. Bruce, *The Epistles of John: Introduction, Exposition, and Notes* (Grand Rapids: Eerdmans, 1970), 18.
3. R. Alan Culpepper, *The Johannine School: An Evaluation of the Johannine-School Hypothesis Based on an Investigation of the Nature of Ancient Schools* (Society of Biblical Literature Dissertation Series 26; Missoula, MT: Scholars, 1975), 261–90.
4. Alan England Brooke, *A Critical and Exegetical Commentary on the Johannine Epistles* (International Critical Commentary 45; Edinburgh: T.&T. Clark, 1912), xviii.
5. John Christopher Thomas, *The Pentecostal Commentary on 1 John, 2 John, 3 John* (Cleveland: Pilgrim, 2004), 10; Raymond E. Brown, *The Community of the Beloved Disciple* (New York: Paulist, 1979), 97; Bruce, *The Epistles of John*, 31.
6. Jonathan Aitken, *John Newton: From Disgrace to Amazing Grace* (Wheaton: Crossway, 2007), 347.
7. Rick Williamson, *1, 2, & 3 John* (New Beacon Bible Commentary; Kansas City, MO: Beacon Hill Press of Kansas City, 2010), 113.
8. Raymond E. Brown, *The Epistles of John: Translated, with Introduction, Notes, and Commentary* (Anchor Bible 30; Garden City, NY: Doubleday, 1982), 397–98.
9. Georg Strecker, *The Johannine Letters: A Commentary on 1, 2, and 3 John* (trans. Linda M. Maloney; Hermeneia 57; Minneapolis: Fortress, 1996), 91.

30

Come, Lord Jesus:
Thoughts on Interpreting Revelation
Carol J. Rotz

Many heaved a collective sigh of relief when the twenty-first century dawned without the predicted cataclysmic events ending the world. For Americans, the September 11 tragedy brought the possibility of an apocalyptic end of the world into focus. Some in religious and secular communities focused on another date. Based on a Mayan calendar, the year 2012 became the new end-of-the-world cipher.

This and all other end-of-the-world dates depend more on legend and fanciful thinking than on biblical prophecy. Secular doomsayers point to the worldwide economic crisis, global warming, and natural disasters as indicators of the end of the world. Those who seek biblical signs of the end in contemporary events typically receive the scorn of a skeptical world.

In this time when apocalyptic events seem to be a part of life, the church must take seriously the final book in the Christian canon. Offered here are thoughts to consider as we read and interpret the book of Revelation in times like these.

1. The book of Revelation is for the church.
Even in the midst of apocalyptic angst, the book of Revelation

has too often been misinterpreted, neglected, or caricatured. As a result, Christians have lost its message of hope and encouragement, which is balanced by warning and responsibility.

There are good reasons that many do not mine the riches of this book. Revelation is complex. Its relationship to wisdom literature ensures that readers use discernment to understand it. On the one hand, the Apocalypse (its Greek name) reflects its namesake genre. On the other hand, it transcends it[1] with a worldview that protests oppression and presents an alternate, hopeful reality.

Revelation's symbolic universe reflects contemporary apocalyptic writings and interacts with its socio-political and religious world. It is prophecy (Rev 1:3; 22:7, 10, 18, 19) that lays out future consequences based on present choices. God's message for the church demands response with eternal implications. The book's letter framework strengthens its rhetoric with a pastoral concern for the recipients. John reflected upon the visions and wrote them down in a complex literary work designed for oral presentation in and for the church. As such, it is a book of worship.

The narrative operates at several levels. Its Greek is very irregular,[2] with many Semitisms reflecting its Old Testament roots (over 500 references). The reader must understand the various characters and larger-than-life action sequences on their own terms without literal or allegorical manipulation. The evocative force rather than the details of a vision often carries the message.

The context is also complex. The first-century Roman Empire's political, economic, religious, and cultural imperialism is well documented, but sometimes specific references are illusive. The images' theological significance stands out, but the reader can only understand them in connection to these other contextual matters. Translating the vivid, often disturbing pictures into abstract language always loses something. The symbolism demands wisdom to unwrap its substance in light of its contemporary political, social, economic, and religious background as well as its place within

Israel's faith and history. Even images that John explains (e.g., the seven stars in Rev 1:16, 20) require insight. Some things that needed no explanation for the first recipients (e.g., the beast's number; 13:18) are no longer recoverable after nearly two millennia.

The narrative and rhetorical (pastoral) logic moves the story of God's plan for humankind through a progression of visions that alternate opportunities for the recipients to respond to God's grace with warnings of punishment. The visions relate more to this theological trajectory than any linear or chronological sequence. Revelation is not as concerned with the last things as with the One who is "the first and the last" (Rev 1:17; 2:8; 22:13).

After the reader recognizes and overcomes these complexities, the message from God is both encouraging and convicting. The church and the world need to hear its good news. But with so many misconceptions about the Apocalypse, what should we say? What issues should we leave out and what truths should we proclaim? We may need to unlearn some things. Here are some suggestions.

2. Don't focus on dates.

A difficult thing about interpreting Revelation is the baggage of popular speculative eschatology. Historically, there have been many interpretations about what Christ meant when he spoke of his coming at "the end of the age" (Matt 13:39, 40, 49; 24:3; 28:20). Many first-century believers looked for Jesus' return in their lifetime (Mark 13:30; Luke 21:32). Each generation since then has believed they would witness his second coming.

Current American evangelicals are especially influenced by dispensationalism that emerged around 1830. John Nelson Darby developed the idea, based on a vision by Margaret MacDonald, a 15-year-old Scottish girl. D. L. Moody and the Scofield Reference Bible popularized it in America. It was established academically at Dallas Theological Seminary.

The system's eschatology includes a secret pre-tribulation rapture, Christ's post-tribulation return, and a millennium in which Christians living through the tribulation repopulate the earth while the resurrected saints rule. Unfortunately, this system has so dominated the American evangelical view of eschatology that many cannot read Revelation any other way. Others avoid the book completely and prefer fictional accounts or systems that neatly chart the future. We should avoid these elements in Bible studies and sermons.

3. Don't argue over millennial theories.

Only once does Scripture mention the millennium (Rev 20:2–7), and that one passage is the basis of three "millennial" scenarios. In it, the devil is bound, and Christ and his church reign for a thousand years. The early church adopted a view that the Lord would return and reign for a thousand years before the final judgment. In the fourth century, Augustine rejected that view. He contended that the kingdom of God was already evident in the church. He understood the millennium as the age between Pentecost and Christ's return, during which the church would increasingly overcome evil. This became the dominant view for the next 1,500 years.

The disillusionment of the two world wars of the twentieth century caused a resurgence of pre-millennialism.[3] In this modern view, the social order will deteriorate before Christ's return, as evil expands through an end-time government. After the second coming, Satan has no influence for a thousand years, and the martyrs or all resurrected saints will reign with Christ.

At the other end of the spectrum is modern post-millennialism, which holds that Christ will return after the church ushers in a thousand years of peace and Christian dominance. Some believe this will occur through evangelism and expansion. Others expect the establishment of a theocratic kingdom.

A-millenialism understands the thousand years as symbolic for all history since Christ's resurrection victory over Satan. The church is a light to the nations. Satan is limited in his ability to deceive since his punishment has already begun. of the three options, a-millennialism is the most helpful. However, no option fully satisfies the attempt to move from Revelation's visionary world to historical reality. Therefore, some have adopted a kind of "eschatological ag-nosticism." Pan-millennialism says with tongue-in-cheek optimism that all will "pan out" in the end. Even this approach is better than focusing on chronology instead of God's redemptive plan.

4. Don't wait for the rapture.

Rapture is another widespread misunderstanding that takes on a life of its own with a variety of timelines. The primary passage is 1 Thessalonians 4:17 (the Latin verb for "caught up" is *rapio*). The idea is that Christians will be snatched from the earth to meet Christ in the air, either at his return or up to seven years before it. Taking Daniel 9:25–27 as inspiration, advocates select and string togeth-er Bible verses to fit various timelines. Proponents claim support in Revelation as well (Rev 3:10; 4:1–2; 5:9–10; 7:9–17; 11:11–19; 11:15; 12:5; 14:14–20; 19:11–20:6; and the church not being men-tioned in chapters 4–18).[4]

Many discredit the idea of rapture, but others support the idea just as vigorously.[5] Unfortunately, the whole discussion focuses on the wrong question. The message of Revelation is not that Christians will escape God's good creation. The book offers insights on how to live in the tension between present realities and future hope.

5. Don't look for the Antichrist.

A popular, unbiblical idea understands "the Antichrist" as a thoroughly evil world leader who will appear near the end of time. The view assumes that the false prophets in Matthew 24, the an-tichrists of 1–2 John, the man of sin of 2 Thessalonians 2, and the beast of Revelation 13 are the same entity. This incarnation of evil will use his political power to persecute the church in the years just preceding Christ's second coming.

"Antichrist" is made up of two Greek words that literally mean "against" or "instead of" (*anti*) "the anointed one" (*Christos*). The Johannine letters (1 John 2:18, 22; 4:3; 2 John 7) correct the misunderstanding of only one antichrist who will come in the future. In those letters, many antichrists were already deceiving people and dividing the church. According to 1 and 2 John, an antichrist is anyone who denies the messiahship and/or humanity of Jesus.

The beast of Revelation is certainly against Christ, but the imagery is more complex. Satan, the beast, and the false prophet form an anti-Trinity. The dragon who is Satan (Rev 12:9) seeks the allegiance that belongs only to God. The beast with a healed fatal wound (13:3) shares the dragon's throne (13:2) and mimics the Lamb of God who alone is worthy (5:12). The two-horned beast (13:11) who is called the false prophet (16:13) is the spirit of evil. These animal representations of evil powerfully embody the fearsome nature of evil and certainly fulfill the Johannine definition of antichrist. In Revelation's visionary narrative, they are defeated enemies (12:10) who are thrown into a lake of fire (19:20; 20:10).

6. Don't obsess over the "666 riddle."

Hexakosioihexekontahexaphobia (fear of the number 666) is a part of Western society. The source is Revelation 13:18, but the number has taken on a life of its own. It occurs in other biblical contexts. Solomon received 666 talents of gold each year (1 Kgs 10:14; 2 Chr 9:13), and 666 descendants of Adonikam return from the Babylonian exile (Ezra 2:13). But the riddle of the beast's identification has fascinated Christians for centuries.

Although Irenaeus (*Against Heresies* 5.30) cautioned in the second century against rash conclusions using gematria, it has always been a popular method for solving the puzzle. In this system, each letter of the alphabet represents a number, and names are derived from the sum of its letters. Many names may equal 666 if they are manipulated,[6] but the exercise has little to do with the invitation for those with insight to "calculate the number of the beast" (Rev 13:18 NIV).

The first recipients already knew *who* the beast was, although that historical reference has been lost.[7] The challenge was to recognize that this well-known beast was Satan's representative. The number six (one less than the perfect number seven) symbolizes lack or incompleteness.[8] Its triplication emphasizes the beast's deficiency. As "man's number" (Rev 13:18), it may refer to humanity's foolish attempts at self-sufficiency. In Revelation's visionary logic, the number constitutes a demonic parody on the perfection of the number seven. It is blasphemous to worship this beast who deceives some by pathetically mimicking God.

The energy spent on this riddle is better spent listening to Revelation theologically. As a letter to the church, it comforts those facing persecution. It challenges those tempted to compromise with an unchristian culture. And it urges all to worship God and be a part of the *missio Dei*. These and other great truths are what we should proclaim with joy and authority. The following are but a few illustrations of the rich pastoral theology of the Apocalypse.

7. The Creator is our Father.

God does not directly take part in the action of Revelation. However, the book is thoroughly theocentric. The One who sits on the throne in the center of heaven is surrounded by creatures, elders, and angels (Rev 5:11; 7:11). The four creatures representing the created order praise God for bringing all things into existence (4:6–11). All creation glorifies God and the Lamb (5:13). The plagues that fall on the earth (8:6–9:21; 16:1–11) are not judgment on the created order but on those who reject God and align themselves with evil. They press the ungodly to repent (9:20–21; 16:9, 11). Ultimately, God makes creation new (21:1–5).

This God who is worthy of all praise and adoration is the Father

(Rev 1:6; 2:27; 3:5, 21; 14:1) of Jesus Christ, the Lamb. Through this relationship, the Father extends inheritance and paternity to all who wish to respond in love and obedience (1:6; 14:1; 21:7). God promises blessings on the repentant (1:3; 14:13; 16:15; 19:9; 20:6; 22:7, 14), including fellowship so intimate that it is hard to conceive (7:17; 21:3, 4). In the New Jerusalem, the martyrs will emerge from under the altar and take their place with the Lamb on the very throne of God (3:21). The saints become the bride adorned for her husband in purity and love (19:7; 21:2, 9). The water of life flows freely (22:1, 2), and God's children receive their inheritance (21:7).

8. The Lamb is our shepherd.

In the rich Christology of Revelation, the Lamb is the major image (28 times) for the one who shares God's throne (Rev 3:21; 5:6; 7:17; 22:1). As "Alpha and Omega" (1:8), God (1:8; 21:6) and Christ (1:17; 22:13) are the first and the last (1:17; 22:13), "the beginning and the end" (21:6; 22:13). Both exhibit wrath against evil (6:16) and provide salvation (7:10).

Jesus shed his blood (Rev 5:9; 7:14; 12:11) and triumphs as the slain Lamb (5:6, 9, 12; 13:8). He is also the conquering ram (5:6; 17:14), "the Lion of the tribe of Judah" (5:5), and "the root of David" (5:5). This shepherd-messiah (7:17) will welcome and care for his followers in heaven (7:9–10; 14:1; 21:22–23; 22:1, 3) as his bride (19:7, 9; 21:9). The Lamb's sacrifice initiates the ultimate defeat of Satan. It is the basis of the saints' victory (12:11) and status as citizens and priests of the kingdom of God (1:6; 5:9–10).

9. The Spirit guides and directs.

John says four times that he is "in the Spirit" (Rev 1:10; 4:2; 17:3; 21:10). This means that the Spirit provided visions and auditions that overshadowed John's normal sensory experience (see Matt 22:43; Luke 1:7; 2:27; Acts 19:21; 2 Cor 12:18). The Spirit speaks the words of Christ in rebuke, encouragement, promise, and/or threat to draw the church to faithful witness as they live in anticipation of Christ's triumphant return. It is this testimony of Jesus that is the "Spirit of prophecy" (19:10). The church is given the power to prophesy (11:3). The Spirit affirms the blessing of those who fulfill that vocation and who will find rest from their labors (14:13). The Spirit joins the church (the bride) in calling for Christ's return and for all to receive the gift of life (22:17).

Like many images in Revelation, the depiction of the Spirit is challenging. The seven spirits (Rev 1:4; 3:1; 4:5; 5:6) symbolize the Holy Spirit (see Isa 11:12; Zech 4:2, 10). Like the seven-branched lampstand in the earthly temple (Exod 40:25), they burn before God's throne in heaven (1:4; 4:5). The Lamb's seven eyes recall the eyes of the Lord that range throughout the world (Zech 4:10). The Lamb's seven horns may (5:6) also represent the Spirit.[9]

10. Satan is a loser.

In Revelation, an unholy anti-Trinity that opposes God and the church represents evil. The dragon, beast, and false prophet claim worldwide authority (Rev 13:1–10), but they are not dominant. The decisive battle in heaven (12:10–12) signals Satan's defeat by Jesus' sacrifice on the cross (5:6, 12). A vanquished enemy wages all other battles (including the cosmic attack on the woman who is a great sign; 12:1). An opponent whose evil power is limited and whose time is short wages the ongoing attack (12:12).

Satan and his subordinates oppress and ensnare the world through deceit. The beast's mark (Rev 13:16–17) mimics God's sealing of the saints (7:3). The healed head wound (16:13) imitates Jesus' death and resurrection (5:6). The dragon gives the beast his power, throne, and "great" authority (13:2) in an attempt to copy the relationship of God and Christ. The false prophet's demand for worship (13:8, 14–15) is a poor imitation of the spontaneous worship of God and Christ that punctuates the entire narrative.

11. The church participates in God's mission.

The story of God's redemptive purposes is directed to the church, as indicated in the seven letters (Rev 2:1–3:22) and Revelation's general epistolary framework (1:4ff; 22:21). The first-century church was insignificant in the Mediterranean world where the Roman Empire dominated every aspect of life. But Revelation provides another perspective. The church is not only the company of the redeemed (3:5; 15:2–4). It is the channel through which God will both save (11:1–14) and rule (2:26ff; 3:21; 20:4–6) the world. The two witnesses (11:3–12) represent the church as examples of the church's mission and hope of salvation. They have power like Moses, Elijah, and Jeremiah to bring plagues (Exod 7:19; 1 Kgs 17:1) and preach with fire (Jer 5:14). Like Zerubbabel and Joshua, they are lampstands and olive trees (Zech 4:3, 11). Their faithful testimony in the midst of affliction calls the church to her ministry of warning and promise. They are killed and mocked (Rev 11:7–10) but, like Christ, they are resurrected and ascend to heaven (11:11–12).

John shares the believers' "suffering and kingdom and patient endurance" (Rev 1:9 NIV) in a ministry of active resistance to the powers of evil. Like Antipas (2:13), the church is called to faithful witness that includes sacrifice and suffering as they follow Jesus, *the* faithful witness (1:5; 3:14; 14:4). The churches in Ephesus, Thyatira, and Philadelphia serve as examples of the perseverance required of the saints (2:2, 3, 19; 3:8). Those who overcome will be abundantly rewarded (2:7, 11, 17, 26; 3:5, 12, 21).

12. Worship God alone.

Revelation is designed for sharing in the context of the worship of Christian communities (Rev 1:3). It includes spontaneous praise throughout the book. The hymns form part of the saints' resistance that celebrates and anticipates God's victory. They declare that suffering saints will be vindicated and reign with God (5:10). They create an interpretive framework for the surrounding narratives.

Worship (*proskyneō*) occurs in heavenly scenes (4:10; 5:14; 7:11; 11:16; 15:4; 19:4; 20:4) as well as earthly ones where evil powers are worshiped (9:20; 13:4, 8, 12, 15; 14:9, 11; 16:2; 19:20). We are invited to worship God through the heavenly hymns.

The hymns in chapters 4 and 5 exhibit two primary forms of the awareness of God. An awed perception of divine holiness (Rev 4:8; cf. Isa 6:3) is coupled with a deep consciousness of utter dependence on God (Rev 4:11). These hymns declare that, because of divine holiness and sovereignty over history (4:8), God alone is worthy of worship. God is the creator and sustainer of all things (4:11). The Lamb is also worthy of worship (4:11; 5:12, 13). He is already victorious (5:5) through his sacrificial death (5:6, 9, 12). The Lamb has purchased the people of God from among the nations (5:9).

In addition, the saints sing "a new song" (Rev 14:1–5; see 5:9). They celebrate both the defeat of the dragon (12:10) and salvation (7:9–17). At the seventh trumpet, heavenly voices celebrate the arrival of God's kingdom (11:15–19). An angel celebrates divine justice (16:5–6), and there is a unified response from the altar (16:7). The hallelujah choruses (19:1–10) celebrate God's just judgments (19:1–5) and the return of Christ (19:6–10).

13. True power is Lamb power.

True power is victory through sacrifice, as demonstrated by the Lamb who was slain (Rev 5:12; 13:8) to provide salvation (7:10, 14). The Lamb conquers the beast, false prophet, and the earth's armies with a double-edged sword (1:16; 2:12, 16; 19:15, 21). But in contrast to those that the enemy wielded, this sword protrudes from his mouth and represents the word of the one who is the Word (19:13).

Those who follow the Lamb overcome because of his sacrifice and "the word of their testimony" (Rev 12:11 NIV), even when it means physical death (6:9; 20:4). In the passages where nikaō ("conquer" or "overcome") is used, Satan and the evil powers conquer by killing (11:7; 13:7). But Christ and his followers para-doxically overcome by dying (2:7, 11, 17, 26; 3:5, 12, 21; 5:5; 12:11; 15:2). This radical picture undermines conventional understandings of success and power. Following the Lamb means demonstrating this kind of power.

14. Life choices have consequences.

The calls for the church to repent (Rev 2:5, 16, 21, 22; 3:3, 19). The plagues highlight the possibility of repentance and show God's mercy. God's judgment is righteous and true (16:7; 19:2). Divine wrath is a very real part of the divine response to evil (11:18; 14:10, 19; 15:1, 7; 16:1, 9, 16; 19:15). The consequences of following the beast and accepting its mark contrast with the promises to those who receive the seal of God (7:3). God's seal represents protec-tion, guidance, and salvation (7:10). It identifies the followers of the Lamb. The mark of the beast stands for God's rejection in favor of an anti-Christ lifestyle.

In chapter 14, three angels proclaim the logic of the gospel. The first angel proclaims the eternal gospel and calls all people to wor-ship God in light of judgment (Rev 14:6–7). Another angel announces the destruction of evil through the symbol of Babylon's fall (14:8). A third angel describes the punishment of those who reject God's mer-cy (14:9–11). An almost word-for-word description of their choice frames the message: they "worship the beast and its image and re-ceive its mark" (14:9, 11 NIV). There is no middle ground. A person either identifies with God and bears the mark of divine allegiance or wears the insignia of the beast and worships an idol.

Those who choose the beast drink the maddening wine of Babylon's adulterous (idolatrous) lifestyle (Rev 14:8). As an inevi-table consequence, they will drink the "wine of God's fury" (14:10 NIV). The wine is not the diluted mixture of wine and water of the Roman world. There is no easy out, no softening of the conse-quences. The burning sulfur of Sodom's punishment (Gen 19:28) is a particularly nasty picture of torment because it sticks to the body. The word itself (*theion*) may be derived from *theos* (God) and understood as "divine incense" used to "purify and prevent contagion."[10] It hints at the continuing possibility of salvation that the Lamb provided (14:10).

Even in the midst of judgment, the "eternal gospel" (Rev 14:6) holds out the possibility for reconciliation. One may refuse it, but God's mercy does not waver. God's heart must ache as people continue to reject salvation and suffer the consequences. Judgment is not simply sorting people into one destiny or another. It exposes truth that can result in reconciliation and healing. Many do turn, give glory to God (11:13), and share in the rewards for those whose names are written in the book of life (3:5; 20:12; 21:27). An innumerable multitude will stand before the throne and the Lamb triumphantly (7:9), worshiping God (15:4), bringing glory in to New Jerusalem (21:26), and walking in its light (21:24).

15. Revelation is a never-ending story.

Like all good narratives, Revelation has a beginning, middle, and end. Theological trajectories build throughout the narrative and conclude without any doubt that God's plans for fellowship with humanity will be fulfilled. The kingdom of God has come through Christ (Rev 12:10). The evil trio is thrown into a lake of burning sulphur (20:10), all are judged (20:11–15; 21:8), and the saints receive their reward (21:6–7). The end of the cosmos occurs, there is a new heaven and earth (21:1), and the New Jerusalem comes to earth (21:2). But what seems to be the definitive ending concludes with an invitation. In chapter 1, Christ is pictured as coming with the clouds (1:17). In the final chapter, Christ announces that he is coming soon (22:12). In between, the end is anticipated in the many visions, but it never arrives. What has already been accomplished is continually held in tension with what is not yet fulfilled.

The Creator God who is our Father has not ceased being

creative. The Lamb who is our shepherd has provided everything necessary for our salvation and introduced the kingdom of God. The Spirit who guides and directs calls everyone to reject evil, repent, and choose allegiance to the One who alone is worthy of worship. That choice will result in a lifestyle of sacrifice, obedience, and faithful testimony that calls others to enter the kingdom as citizens, servants, and priests. The bride who longs for the coming of the bridegroom also yearns for all to enter the New Jerusalem. "Amen. Come, Lord Jesus" (Rev 22:20).

---

1. A traditional list of characteristics of apocalyptic literature includes symbolism, pessimism, dualism, determinism, and a narrative framework. See John J. Collins, "Apocalyptic Literature," in *Dictionary of New Testament Backgrounds* (ed. C. A. Evans and S. Porter; Downers Grove, IL: InterVarsity, 2000), 41.

2. See G. Mussies, *The Morphology of Koine Greek as Used in the Apocalypse: A Study in Bilingualism.* (Leiden: Brill, 1971).

3. The scenario is, of course, much more complicated than this brief overview can indicate. For a good summary see Richard Connors and Andrew C. Gow, eds., *Anglo-American Millennialism, from Milton to the Millerites.* (Leiden: Brill, 2004).

4. See Michael J. Svigel, "The Apocalypse of John and the Rapture of the Church," *Trinity Journal* 22 (Spring 2001): 23–74, who critiques each passage but maintains that the child snatched to heaven in Rev 12 represents the church.

5. See, e.g., Barbara Rossing, *The Rapture Exposed: The Message of Hope in the Book of Revelation* (Boulder, CO: Westview, 2004); and Gleason Archer, Three Views on the Rapture: Pre; Mid; or Post-Tribulational? (Counterpoints: Exploring Theology; Grand Rapids: Zondervan, 2008).

6. Some manuscripts open a different range of possibilities, where the number is 616 (see Bruce Manning Metzger and United Bible Societies, *A Textual Commentary on the Greek New Testament: A Companion Volume to the United Bible Societies' Greek New Testament* (4th rev. ed.; New York: United Bible Societies, 1994), 750.

7. The early church first identified Nero and then Caligula as the Antichrist. For a historical summary, see Bernard McGinn, *Antichrist: Two Thousand Years of the Human Fascination with Evil* (San Francisco: Harper, 1994). For an American history, see Robert Fuller, *Naming the Antichrist: The History of an American Obsession* (New York: Oxford University Press, 1995).

8. Paul S. Minear, *I Saw a New Earth: An Introduction to the Visions of the Apocalypse* (Washington: Corpus, 1968), 258.

9. See Richard Bauckham, "The Role of the Spirit in the Apocalypse," *Evangelical Quarterly* 52/2 (1980): 66–83.

10. Timothy Friberg, Barbara Friberg, and Neva F. Miller, *Analytical Lexicon of the Greek New Testament* (Baker's Greek New Testament Library; Grand Rapids: Baker, 2000), 195.

CONTRIBUTORS:

KEVIN L. ANDERSON, Ph.D.
Associate Professor of New Testament
Department of Bible, Theology, and Philosophy
Asbury University
Wilmore, Kentucky

STEPHEN J. BENNETT, Ph.D.
Associate Professor of Bible
College of Bible and Christian Ministry
Nyack College
Nyack, New York

A. WENDELL BOWES, Ph.D.
Professor of Old Testament Emeritus
School of Theology and Christian Ministries
Northwest Nazarene University
Nampa, Idaho

LAURIE J. BRAATEN, Ph.D.
Professor of Biblical Studies
Department of Biblical and Theological Studies
Judson University
Elgin, Illinois

ROBERT D. BRANSON, Ph.D.
Professor of Biblical Literature Emeritus
School of Theology and Christian Ministry
Olivet Nazarene University
Bourbonnais, Illinois

DENNIS R. BRATCHER, Ph.D.
Executive Director
Christian Resource Institute
Oklahoma City, Oklahoma

W. RANDOLPH BYNUM, Ph.D.
Adjunct Professor of Bible
School of Theology and Christian Ministries
Northwest Nazarene University
Nampa, Idaho

FRANK G. CARVER, Ph.D.
Professor Emeritus of Religion
Point Loma Nazarene University
San Diego, California

JOSEPH E. COLESON, Ph.D.
Professor of Old Testament
Nazarene Theological Seminary
Kansas City, Missouri

C. S. COWLES, D.Min.
Professor of Religion Emeritus
Northwest Nazarene University
Nampa, Idaho

SARAH B. C. DERCK, M.A., Ph.D. cand.
Visiting Professor of Religion
School of Theology and Ministry
Indiana Wesleyan University
Marion, Indiana

JIM EDLIN, Ph.D.
Professor of Biblical Literature and Languages
School of Christian Ministry and Formation
MidAmerica Nazarene University
Olathe, Kansas

TERENCE E. FRETHEIM, Ph.D.
Elva B. Lovell Professor of Old Testament
Luther Seminary
St. Paul, Minnesota

THOMAS J. KING, Ph.D.
Professor of Old Testament
Nazarene Bible College
Colorado Springs, Colorado

MICHAEL E. LODAHL, Ph.D.
Professor of Theology and World Religions
School of Theology and Christian Ministry
Point Loma University
San Diego, California

GEORGE LYONS, Ph.D.
Professor of New Testament
School of Theology and Christian Ministries
Northwest Nazarene University
Nampa, Idaho

KARA J. LYONS-PARDUE, M.Div., Ph.D. cand.
Assistant Professor of New Testament
School of Theology and Christian Ministry
Point Loma Nazarene University
San Diego, California

MARK A. MADDIX, Ph.D.
Professor of Christian Education
Dean, School of Theology and Christian Ministries
Northwest Nazarene University
Nampa, Idaho

RANDY MADDOX, Ph.D.
William Kellon Quick Professor of Theology and Methodist Studies
Duke Divinity School
Duke University
Durham, North Carolina

MITCHEL MODINE, Ph.D.
Associate Professor of Old Testament
Asia-Pacific Nazarene Theological Seminary
Taytay, Rizal, Philippines

THOMAS JAY OORD, Ph.D.
Professor of Theology and Philosophy
School of Theology and Christian Ministries
Northwest Nazarene University
Nampa, Idaho

TERENCE P. PAIGE, Ph.D.
Professor of New Testament
Houghton College
Houghton, New York

DANIEL G. POWERS, Ph.D.
Professor of New Testament
Nazarene Bible College
Colorado Springs, Colorado

CAROL J. ROTZ, D.Litt. *et* Phil.
Professor of New Testament (Retired)
School of Theology and Christian Ministries
Northwest Nazarene University
Nampa, Idaho

C. JEANNE ORJALA SERRÃO, Ph.D.
Professor of Biblical Literature
Dean, School of Theology and Philosophy
Mount Vernon Nazarene University
Mount Vernon, Ohio

DANIEL B. SPROSS, Ph.D.
Professor of Biblical Theology and Literature
School of Religion
Trevecca Nazarene University
Nashville, Tennessee

BRENT A. STRAWN, Ph.D.
Associate Professor of Old Testament
Candler School of Theology
Emory University
Atlanta, Georgia

JASON STURDEVANT, M.Div., Ph.D. cand.
Ph.D. Candidate in New Testament Studies
Princeton Theological Seminary
Princeton, New Jersey

RICHARD P. THOMPSON, Ph.D.
Professor of New Testament
School of Theology and Christian Ministries
Northwest Nazarene University
Nampa, Idaho

RICK L. WILLIAMSON, Ph.D.
Professor of Biblical Literature
School of Theology and Philosophy
Mount Vernon Nazarene University
Mount Vernon, Ohio

KAREN STRAND WINSLOW, Ph.D.
Professor of Biblical Studies
Graduate School of Theology
Azusa Pacific University
Azusa, California

JOHN W. WRIGHT, Ph.D.
Professor of Theology and Christian Scripture
School of Theology and Christian Ministry
Point Loma Nazarene University
San Diego, California

CPSIA information can be obtained at www.ICGtesting.com
Printed in the USA
BVOW062112200212

283374BV00001B/1/P